W9-BSX-230

BANFF, JASPER & GLACIER
& GLACIER
NATIONAL PARKS

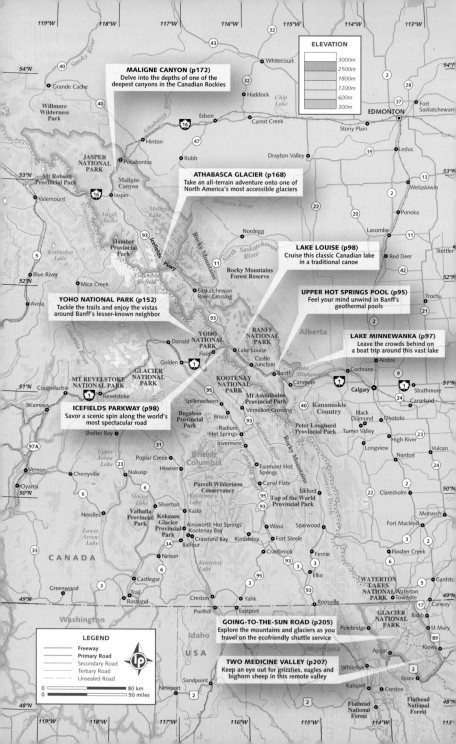

ELEVATION

	3000m
	2500m
	1800m
	1200m
	600m
	300m

MALIGNE CANYON (p172)
Delve into the depths of one of the
deepest canyons in the Canadian Rockies

ATHABASCA GLACIER (p168)
Take an all-terrain adventure onto one of
North America's most accessible glaciers

LAKE LOUISE (p98)
Cruise this classic Canadian lake
in a traditional canoe

UPPER HOT SPRINGS POOL (p95)
Feel your mind unwind in Banff's
geothermal pools

YOHO NATIONAL PARK (p152)
Tackle the trails and enjoy the vistas
around Banff's lesser-known neighbor

LAKE MINNEWANKA (p97)
Leave the crowds behind on
a boat trip around this vast lake

ICEFIELDS PARKWAY (p98)
Savor a scenic spin along the world's
most spectacular road

GOING-TO-THE-SUN ROAD (p205)
Explore the mountains and glaciers as you
travel on the ecofriendly shuttle service

TWO MEDICINE VALLEY (p207)
Keep an eye out for grizzlies, eagles and
bighorn sheep in this remote valley

LEGEND

Freeway
Primary Road
Secondary Road
Tertiary Road
Unsealed Road

0 _____ 80 km
0 _____ 50 miles

BANFF, JASPER & GLACIER NATIONAL PARKS

Spanning the Continental Divide along Canada's western edge, the three national parks of Banff, Jasper and Glacier are the heart and soul of the Canadian Rockies. This is a place where you're forced to rethink your sense of scale and readjust to a world viewed through wide-angle goggles: an untrammeled landscape of snow-flecked mountains, panoramic horizons and sky-stretching views where you're never quite able to take in the whole picture. In the high mountains you can almost feel the earth's machinery at work, shaping, molding and sculpting the surrounding landscape, and every year thousands of people arrive to explore the trails, wonder at the views and cherish nature's handiwork for themselves. Ditch the cell phone, pack up the tent and strap on those boots; the wilderness is calling, and it's about time you answered.

2

Glaciers

Glaciers are an essential part of the
Canadian Rockies experience. Few natural
features can take your breath away with
such effortless ease, but make the most of
them while you can – in a world grappling
with climate change, no one's sure what
the future holds for these icy giants.

1

Author Tip

Most of the famous glaciers are visible from viewpoints dotted along major roads, but while these scenic pullouts make seeing the glaciers much easier, it also guarantees that they're usually crammed with sightseers and plagued with the buzz of passing traffic. Thankfully, you'll often find a hiking trail nearby where you can wallow in the views without any unwelcome distractions.

❶ Athabasca Glacier

The most-visited glacier (p168) in North America is part of the huge Columbia Icefield, the largest expanse of ice this side of the Arctic. You can even travel right onto the ice aboard an all-terrain Snocoach.

❷ Grinnell Glacier

Named for the 19th-century conservationist George Grinnell, this beautiful glacier (p210) lies in Glacier's Many Glacier Valley. It's an 18.7km (11.6-mile) hike there and back, but the views more than make up for the effort you'll expend in getting there.

❸ Jackson Glacier

The fifth-largest glacier (p206) in Glacier National Park was originally joined to the nearby Blackfoot Glacier but by 1939 melting ice had separated them into two glaciers. The classic viewpoint is on Going-to-the-Sun Rd.

❹ Crowfoot Glacier

This distinctive glacier (p125) along the Icefields Parkway was named in the early 1900s for its resemblance to a bird's foot, but over the last century one of its three toes has melted away.

❺ Saskatchewan Glacier

Lurking at the end of a deep glacial valley overlooked by nearby Mt Andromeda and Mt Athabasca, the Saskatchewan Glacier (p117) is best seen from the crest of Parker Ridge, beside the Icefields Parkway.

❻ Victoria Glacier

One of the six glaciers after which the Plain of Six Glaciers is named, the Victoria Glacier (p109) is famous for the rumbling avalanches that crash down from its upper slopes as morning sun melts the ice.

Backcountry Hikes

For a true taste of freedom, nothing beats an adventure into the untamed backcountry, where the outside world is still (just about) kept at bay. With a pack on your back and a tent in tow, you'll be able to venture deep into the areas of the national parks most visitors never get the chance to see. Hidden meadows, distant glaciers and secret lakes await, and we all know a marshmallow tastes best browned over an open fire. What are you waiting for?

Author Tip
The backcountry areas unsurprisingly contain some of the most popular trails in the parks, and with limits on hiker numbers and mandatory reservations on backcountry campgrounds, you might find your chosen route is booked out if you leave things till the last minute. So plan ahead; reservations at backcountry campgrounds are accepted up to three months in advance, and by booking ahead you'll be able to steal a march on rival hikers.

1 Tonquin Valley
Classic hiking territory (p182) with colossal mountain scenery, plenty of trails and no roads. Kip out under the stars or get your beauty sleep in a rustic backcountry lodge.

2 Skyline Trail
Many seasoned pros rate this (p180) as one of the best hikes in Canada, and with good reason. You'll feel like heaven is close enough to touch on this sky-scraping adventure.

3 Egypt Lake
Lakes, lakes and more lakes – all idyllic and isolated – are the main draw for backcountry enthusiasts tackling this area (p118).

4 Skoki Valley
In winter Skoki (p118) is a skiers' haven, but in summer the melting snow reveals a network of backcountry trails crisscrossing their way across the desolately beautiful landscape of the high mountains.

5 Lake O'Hara
Shuttle tickets into Lake O'Hara (p153) are like gold dust in summer, as it's well known among trail baggers as one of Yoho's best backcountry hikes.

6 Mt Assiniboine
Assiniboine's pointy peak (p119) is an unmistakable Banff landmark, as well as many hikers' backcountry destination of choice. It's only accessible on foot (or by helicopter), so you'll need determination to get here.

Scenic Lookouts

You only have to browse a postcard rack to get an idea of the stunning vistas that lie in store for you in the three mountain parks, and while you'll be able to sample the jaw-dropping scenery just by driving along the mountain roads, for the truly explosive vistas you'll have to expend a bit more effort.

6

Author Tip
Since many lookouts are at high altitudes, the weather is particularly prone to misbehaving. Hiking to a viewpoint only to discover that the scenery's cloaked in cloud is a frustrating experience, so it pays to be prepared. Check the weather forecast the day before your hike, and double-check it the following morning – if it's still set fair, break out the boots and hit the trail. Take along warm, windproof layers and a waterproof, too – it can be pretty chilly at the top.

4

❶ Bow Summit Lookout
Perched high above the cerulean-blue bowl of Peyto Lake, this abandoned fire lookout (p116) now affords one of the best views along the southern Icefields Parkway.

❷ Standish Ridge
Accessed from Sunshine Meadows, on the border between British Columbia and Alberta, this wooden-decked viewpoint (p114) overlooks the historic Simpson Valley and Monarch Range.

❸ Sulphur Mountain
You can reach this amazing panorama (p95) either on foot or via the Banff Gondola, but the scenery's equally unforgettable either way – sweeping views of the Bow Valley, Mt Rundle and Banff town far, far below.

❹ Jasper Tramway
The eastern Rockies and Jasper town spread out beneath you from this classic viewpoint (p170) at the top of Whistlers Mountain, reached by tram and best at sunset.

❺ Old Fort Point
Tick off the peaks from the viewpoint (p178) at the end of the Old Fort Trail – the Colin Range, Mt Edith Cavell and the aptly named Pyramid Mountain are all on show.

❻ Swiftcurrent Lookout
Sky-topping scenery greets you after a stiff uphill slog through Swiftcurrent Pass in Glacier National Park to this lookout (p213).

6

Wildlife

For many people, the parks' abundant wildlife is a highlight of their trip. Whether it's a playful pika, a whistling marmot or a bugling elk, you're bound to cross path with some of the parks' wilder inhabitants – although you'll need a bit more luck i you're looking for rarer creatures such as moose, eagles and the mighty bruins.

3

Author Tip
You'll often stumble across wildlife mooching around the roadsides in all three parks, especially in the early morning and at dusk. The quieter roads away from the main highway are especially good spots to try. However, if you do see wild creatures, don't be tempted to stop and take photographs. It places extra stress on animals and encourages them to lose their natural fear of humans. Bring a good telephoto lens if you want to take pictures, and keep your distance.

⑤ Elk & Moose
The mighty moose (p66) was once widespread but its numbers have taken a dramatic tumble over the last century. Elk (p65) are still a fairly common sight.

⑥ Hoary marmots
Sometimes known as whistle pigs, due to their distinctive warning call, these furry mammals (p66) can often be seen along high mountain trails.

① Wolves
Long persecuted by settlers, the wolf (p65) was hunted almost to the point of extinction in the Canadian Rockies. North Fork Valley in Glacier is home to one of the last surviving wild packs in the mountain parks.

② Birds
Several birds of prey (p67) make their home in the Rocky Mountains, including ospreys, great horned owls and golden eagles.

③ Bears
Glimpsing a bruin (of either the grizzly or black variety) in the wild is an unforgettable experience, especially if the bear (p64) happens to have cubs in tow. Just remember to keep your distance!

④ Bighorn Sheep
Resident in all three parks, these nimble-footed creatures (p65) can often be seen grazing around lake shores and mountain pastures in summer.

MALIGNE TOURS
BOAT HOUSE

4

Lakes &
Waterfalls

The lakes and waterfalls of the Canadian
Rockies often held a special spiritual
significance for First Nations people, and
gazing at a thundering cascade or paddling
out to the center of a peacock-blue lake,
it's impossible not to share their sense of
awe and wonder.

3 4
5
2 1
6

3

Author Tip

Don't let bad weather put you off visiting these watery wonders. Heavy rain often brings out the best in waterfalls, as the extra water adds to the force of the cascade and makes for a more spectacular show. The same goes for the lakes – while sunlight inevitably brings out the strongest colors and reflections, mist and rain can also reveal an entirely different side of the lakeside scenery.

① Johnston Canyon

The twin falls of Johnston Canyon (p106) often freeze in winter, transforming the rushing cascade into an elegant column of ice.

② Takakkaw Falls

The Cree dubbed this cascade (p152) 'magnificent' with good reason: it's the biggest waterfall in Yoho National Park and also one of the largest in Canada.

③ Athabasca Falls

Meltwater from the Athabasca Glacier feeds one of Jasper's tallest falls (p169).

④ Maligne Lake

Discovered by the groundbreaking explorer and adventurer Mary Schäffer in 1908, Maligne Lake (p172) is best seen at dawn, when the waters blaze with the rainbow colors of the rising sun.

⑤ Lake Louise

This glacial gem (p98) boasts perhaps the most famous view in the Canadian Rockies, bordered by mountains and the avalanche-prone Victoria Glacier.

⑥ Moraine Lake

Once featured on the Canadian $20 bill, this lake (p100) sits at the end of the famous Valley of the Ten Peaks, surrounded by the snow-covered Wenkchemna Peaks.

Adventure Sports

If it's outdoor pursuits you're after, then you're in luck – Banff, Jasper and Glacier are a dream come true for adrenaline junkies. There are hundreds of ways to get active in the great outdoors, ranging from the relatively sedate pastimes of canoeing and horseback riding to full-blown extreme sports such as mountaineering, downhill mountain biking and ice climbing.

Author Tip
Many outdoor sports require a considerable investment just to get started, especially those requiring loads of expensive gear, such as skiing and snowboarding. But if you're not sure which sport to try, get in touch with one of the parks' many multi-activity providers and take a few introductory lessons, which nearly always include the use of equipment in the fee.

❶ Heli-Hiking
If you've got time to spare and money to burn, heli-hiking (p146) allows access to the kind of trails most walkers only dream about.

❷ White-Water Rafting
Whether it's on the Kicking Horse or the Kananaskis, you'll find rafters (p47) braving the rapids armed with nothing but a flimsy paddle and an inflatable raft. Insane or inspired?

❸ Rock & Ice Climbing
If the idea of dangling from a sheer rock face or a wall of ice sounds appealing, then rock (p49) and ice climbing (p53) offer the ultimate ways to get acquainted with the mountains.

❹ Skiing & Snowboarding
Banff, Jasper and Golden are all carving out a name for themselves on the snow circuit (p50), with a choice of resorts, hundreds of off-piste adventures and groomed runs and, of course, tons of reliable snow.

❺ Dogsledding
Mush, mush – if you've always harbored a secret soft spot for *White Fang*, now's your chance to try the real thing (p46).

❻ Snowshoeing
Just because there's snow outside doesn't mean the hiking has to stop. Strap on your snowshoes (p51) and get stomping – just make sure you know how to follow the trail under all that snow.

Descending a spur in Banff National Park

Contents

Regional Map Contents

Jasper National Park p164

Banff National Park p85

Glacier National Park p200

The Authors

OLIVER BERRY

Having grown up around the cliffs of Cornwall, wandering around in high places has become something of a habit for Oliver. He's since explored the trails of countries all over the globe, including the United States, New Zealand, France, Corsica, Scotland, Austria and the South Pacific, but he's never found anywhere that can measure up to the Canadian Rockies. Obviously he jumped at the chance to write the 2nd edition of this book, and seems to have come through relatively unscathed despite the obstacles posed by high-altitude thunderstorms, a recalcitrant compass and a potentially nasty episode with an enraged marmot. He's currently back in the UK working on other projects, but hopes to get back to Canada as soon as the snows thaw.

My Banff National Park

When I'm in the mountains, I like to be up at the crack of dawn, sling my gear in the pack and shoot out the door just in time to see the sun peep over the peaks. Then it's up to Lake Louise for a trip up one of my favorite trails, the Plain of Six Glaciers (p109): first along the lakeshore, then along the valley wall and out at last for a restorative brew and some homemade cake at the teahouse (p109). Back down via the glorious lookout of the Big Beehive and the Lake Agnes teahouse (p110) before checking in to one of my favorite cabins at the Storm Mountain Lodge (p159), just over the border into Kootenay. The next day I'll take another hike – my favorites include Parker Ridge (p117), the Garden Path Trail (p113) and Paradise Valley (p112) – or, if I've brought along my bike, I might just head back to Banff for

a gentle spin along the Sundance Trail (p121) and aim to reach the Marsh Loop (p102) late in the day. You couldn't ask for a more tranquil place to watch the sun go down. If I'm feeling really flush, I might even treat myself to a meal at the Bison Mountain Bistro (p141).

LONELY PLANET AUTHORS

Why is our travel information the best in the world? It's simple: our authors are independent, dedicated travelers. They don't research using just the internet or phone, and they don't take freebies in exchange for positive coverage. They travel widely, to all the popular spots and off the beaten track. They personally visit thousands of hotels, restaurants, cafés, bars, galleries, palaces, museums and more – and they take pride in getting all the details right, and telling it how it is. For more, see the authors section on www.lonelyplanet.com.

THE AUTHORS

BRENDAN SAINSBURY

A veteran of hiking and biking excursions in over 60 different countries, Brendan first discovered the Canadian Rockies in 2003 during a brief visit to Banff. As a native of the spatially challenged UK, he was mightily impressed by the region's gargantuan peaks and dramatic sense of scale, and resolved one day to return. The opportunity arose far quicker than he imagined. Brendan tied the knot with a Vancouver-based doctor in 2004 and happily agreed to swap smoky London for pine-scented British Columbia. He now lives less than a day's drive from the 'Crown of the Continent' and makes hastily planned hiking sorties east whenever his writing schedule allows.

My Glacier & Waterton Lakes National Parks

Rising early, I get the 8am Tamarack Shuttle to Cameron Lake in Waterton and tackle the hiking roller coaster that is the Carthew-Alderson Trail (p232) before lunch. Trying to avoid looking like a stereotypical Englishman, I order 'high tea' (love those scones!) in the Prince of Wales Hotel (p238) before catching another bus down to the Many Glacier Hotel (p225) for a night of rare luxury in one of America's best rustic lodges. The next day is a hiking extravaganza involving a strenuous climb up to Swiftcurrent Pass (p212) followed by a vista-studded stroll along the Highline Trail (p210) – two of the most spectacular high-country hikes anywhere. Crawling exhausted into the Logan Pass Visitor Center (p203), I requisition a Going-to-the-Sun Rd shuttle down to St Mary and grab a life-saving dinner in the homey Park Cafe (p240).

Waterton Lakes
National Park

Cameron Lake ○○ Carthew-Alderson
Trail

Many
Glacier
Swiftcurrent Pass ○ ○ St Mary
Highline Trail ○ Logan Pass

Glacier National Park

Destination Banff, Jasper & Glacier National Parks

If it's a taste of the wilds you're looking for, then you're in luck – the three national parks of Banff, Jasper and Glacier make up one of the last great areas of wilderness in North America. While the cities swell, the skyscrapers stack up and the interstates sprawl, the mountains stand as a pillar of permanence against an increasingly motorized, globalized, pressurized world, where time is always at a premium and there never seem to be enough hours in the day. For over a century travelers, explorers, artists and adventurers have been hightailing it to Canada's high mountains in search of solitude and sanctuary, and the tradition of escape continues through to the present day; every year millions of visitors descend on the national parks to drink in the views, dine out on the scenery and experience a slice of the great outdoors for themselves.

While today's Rocky Mountains aren't quite the same untouched landscape experienced by trailblazing pioneers such as Tom Wilson, Mary Schäffer and Jimmy Simpson at the end of the 19th century, they're still a fantastic place to experience Mother Nature in her rawest, rudest state. Clearwater falls cascade down wooded valleys; bighorn sheep, whistling marmots and antlered elk graze on the high mountain pastures; glaciers glower, rivers rush and snow-crested mountains stretch to the far horizons. It's a place of stunning and sometimes savage beauty, and despite the modern veneer of signposts, access roads and maintained trails, there's still a whiff of wildness on the mountain breeze.

With such a wealth of natural wonders to discover, it's hardly surprising that the Rockies have become one of Canada's busiest outdoor playgrounds. Every year the parks welcome over five million visitors through their gates, from hikers in search of backcountry trails to snowboarders in search of ungroomed powder. There's an outdoor pursuit to suit every temperament: canoeists cruise the waters of the mountain lakes, rock climbers clamber up cliffs and mountaineers set out to conquer the peaks, while horseback trips mosey old-style along the historic passes and backcountry tracks. But even the most sedentary sightseers find that visiting the mountains has a curious way of broadening their horizons; whether it's gazing at the mountains, contemplating an age-old glacier or plummeting down a pristine slope, few visitors leave the national parks without gaining a new, and rather more panoramic, perspective on the world.

'It's a place of stunning and sometimes savage beauty'

The skyrocketing visitor numbers, increased revenue and continuing popularity of the parks are all good news for cash-strapped park authorities and local tourism officials, but success inevitably comes at a price. Tourism is by far the biggest money-spinner for the three national parks these days, but not everyone's happy about the increasingly commercial and tourism-driven direction the national parks seem to be taking. The extra visitors have inevitably placed an ever-increasing burden on the Rockies' fragile environment, and though government statutes place strict limits on the amount of development that can take place within the parks' boundaries, many of the gateway towns around the edges of the parks, such as Golden and Canmore, continue to grow at an exponential rate. Glaciers across all three parks are in high-speed retreat, almost certainly as a direct result of global warming, so the wisdom of adding more traffic to the parks by expanding the Trans-Canada Hwy between Banff and Lake Louise has been seriously called into question. The gloomiest estimates have even suggested that most (if not all) of the parks' glaciers could disappear within the next century. And even the most skeptical naysayer has to concede that the accumulated effect of thousands more feet tramping the trails and thousands more wheels on the parks' roads inevitably has to have some kind of effect on the mountain environment, and the chances are it isn't going to be good.

Nothing symbolizes the struggle between the commercial and environmental pressures facing park authorities than the plight of that shaggy symbol of the Canadian Rockies, the great grizzly bear. Despite the introduction of dedicated bear management programs, grizzlies are still suffering as a direct consequence of the expansion of human activity in and around the mountain parks. According to park estimates, grizzly numbers in Banff are down to around 60, with around twice that in Jasper and just a handful in Glacier, Kootenay and Yoho – in total between 500 and 700 bears are thought to still live in the Alberta area. Compare this figure to British Columbia, which still boasts a fairly healthy grizzly population of around 17,000, and you'll have some idea of the astonishing decline in grizzly numbers in the eastern Rockies over recent decades. While diminishing bear habitat and the painfully slow reproduction rate of adult grizzlies has inevitably had some bearing on the decline, 'human-caused mortality' is still the number-one cause of bear death in this part of Canada. Regardless of whether a bear is knocked down by a train, killed on the highway, or shot as a result of becoming habituated to eating human garbage, the end result is still the same: one less bear.

But it's not all doom and gloom. Recent programs, including area closures and hiking restrictions in key areas during the crucial berry season, have helped to reduce human-bear encounters in Banff. Protection measures such as radio tagging, backcountry cameras and wildlife corridors have helped give park authorities a better understanding of grizzly movement and migration. And following careful management, some of the parks – notably Jasper and Glacier – have even reported a slight rise in the number of grizzly sightings in comparison to previous years. And on the wider environmental front, Glacier is leading the way with a fleet of biodiesel fuelled buses to tackle its growing traffic problem, while initiatives to promote everything from bike use to wind turbines and recycling have pushed sustainability issues well up the parks' agenda. Everyone knows the world has to get greener, and in the precious natural environment of the Canadian Rockies, the stakes are higher than anywhere.

'between 500 and 700 bears are thought to still live in the Alberta area'

Planning Your Trip

Whether you're a meticulous pre-planner or a freewheeling nomad, it pays to do some research before you set out for the parks. Banff, Jasper and Glacier cover a vast expanse of ground and pack in a formidable range of sights – far too many to see in a single trip, so it's worth pinpointing what you want to see before you leave to get the most out of your visit. If you only have limited time, it's more sensible to explore one particular park rather than trying to zip around all three at lightning speed – you'll spend less time behind the wheel, have more time to explore, and be able to get to the more remote sights and hikes. But one of the real joys of the Rockies is the sense of freedom you'll discover in the mountains, so it's important to be a little flexible with your plans – whether that means stopping for a sudden riverside picnic, veering down an unexplored trail, or just sitting still to catch the sunset over a snow-topped mountain peak.

WHEN TO GO

Choosing when to visit the parks depends on what you want to get up to once you're there – there's not much point pitching up in July if you're a dedicated downhill skier. Though the parks are in theory open year-round, in practice many visitor services and facilities in remote areas (especially in Glacier and along the Icefields Parkway) shut up shop for the winter season between November and May. The busiest season of all is July and August, when prices are at a premium and roads and attractions are most crowded. The shoulder seasons make a good compromise; there are fewer visitors, rates are lower and trails are quieter, and if you're lucky, you might even be rewarded with a spell of brilliant sunshine in among the spring and autumn showers.

See p249 for more information.

Reservations are also a really good idea, especially for backcountry hikes (where visitor numbers are limited) and for popular hotels, activities and tours; in July and August, when the parks are at their busiest, booking ahead is pretty much essential.

Spring

Spring comes late to the parks – the snows often don't even begin to thaw until late May, and you'll usually find stacks of snow at higher elevations way into June. It's one of the most unpredictable seasons, but it can be a fantastic time to visit; the wildlife emerges to welcome in warming temperatures, flowers and grasses spring up from beneath the snowmelt and the first hardy hikers begin to visit the reopening trails. But seasonal rains, muddy tracks and strong spring winds can make it a frustrating season too, especially if you're planning on doing any outdoor pursuits; though most activities (such as biking, rafting and climbing) start up again around mid-May, the actual dates can vary considerably according to the caprices of Mother Nature.

Summer

Summer's the season, if you want to explore the parks in depth. By July and August, nearly all trails are open and the vast majority of activities, including fishing, horseback riding, high-level hiking and backcountry camping, are in full swing. Temperatures creep steadily upwards toward the midsummer highs in late July and early August, and dusk usually

PLANNING YOUR TRIP

COPING WITH CROWDS

Since most people come to the parks to escape the city's hustle and thrum, it can be disheartening to discover that even the mountain parks are far from tailback-free. With a combined annual visitor quota of over five million people, it's not really surprising that Banff and Jasper sometimes suffer from overcrowding, especially around key sights and scenic viewpoints. The worst spots tend (obviously) to be the places which everyone wants to see: Lake Louise, the Banff Gondola and Sulphur Mountain, Banff town, Moraine Lake, Johnston Canyon and Peyto Lake on the Icefields Parkway are particularly prone to the summer squash, as are Maligne Lake, the Miette Hot Springs and the Athabasca Falls in Jasper. But don't fret – here are our top tips for giving the crowds the slip.

First, set out early for the big sights. Get there before 8am or 9am and you may well have the place to yourself while other sightseers slumber; you'll have a much better chance of seeing wildlife in the early morning, too. Alternatively, try late evening, when many visitors value the rumble in their stomachs more than the sunset views. Second, don't stick to the roadside viewpoints – you'll have a much better shot at solitude (and often much better views) by taking one of the nearby trails, especially after an hour or so's worth of walking. The longer and tougher trails are also much less popular; if it's steep and twisty, chances are it'll be much quieter than the trails on the flat. Third, take minor roads wherever you can – they might be slower going, but they're usually more scenic and generally a lot less busy than the main highways. Fourth, ask around for local tips on some lesser-known sights – we've left some secret places in the parks for you to discover for yourself. And lastly, avoid the peak season in July and August; the light and the weather are usually just as good in late September and October, but the trails are far, far, quieter and the prices are much, much cheaper.

doesn't arrive till between 9pm and 10pm, so you'll have plenty of time to pack in the sights. It's also a fantastic season for wildflowers and nature-watching, with most animals out and about in search of food after the long winter.

But summer's not without its drawbacks. As always in the mountains, the weather has a mind of its own and clear days can see sudden downpours or even a snow shower at high elevations, so be prepared. Exceptionally dry summers also bring the threat of forest fires, so fire restrictions are often enforced in campgrounds and areas are closed in the event of a wildfire breaking out. It's also the priciest season to visit: hotels ramp up the rates to make the most of swelling visitor numbers, and you'll often find yourself paying a hefty surcharge simply for arriving a couple of weeks later into the summer season.

All the major sights and campgrounds around the parks are at their busiest during the summer season, and by midday popular spots are usually crammed to capacity, especially around Banff and Lake Louise. Check out the boxed text above for tips on avoiding the summertime crush.

The Rocky Mountain World Heritage Site is made up of four national parks (Banff, Jasper, Yoho and Kootenay) and three provincial parks in British Columbia (Mt Robson, Hamber and Mt Assiniboine).

Autumn

Autumn is (literally) a golden time to visit the parks. As the summer temperatures fade, the mountain forests turn into a riot of reds, golds and fiery oranges and you'll feel the crisp chill of winter on the evening air. September is the best month to visit: hotel prices drop, the evenings still have plenty of light to hike by and most facilities (such as campgrounds and attractions) remain open. By mid-October the temperatures drop dramatically and many campgrounds shut down; by November you'll see the first flurries of snow blocking the higher trails and making many backcountry hikes inaccessible.

Winter

Winter in the parks has its own special magic, but you'll have to be prepared to deal with the bone-chilling temperatures. Snow and ice blanket the landscape and many high trails are out of bounds to everyone except dogsledders, snowshoers and cross-country skiers, while snowboarders and downhill skiers hit the slopes around Banff, Lake Louise, Golden and Marmot Basin. Banff town and Jasper town are almost as busy in mid-winter as mid-summer; many of the hotels are booked solid with winter-sports fans, and the restaurants and bars are buzzing with all sorts of après-ski attractions. The other parks and more remote areas of Banff and Jasper are much quieter, with many services and minor roads closed. Some places (such as Glacier and the Icefields Parkway) shut down almost completely. Prices in winter are usually lower than in mid-summer, although they take another spike upwards during busy holiday periods, especially over Christmas and New Year. January is also the coldest month; the average maximum temperature is a bitter -9°C (16°F).

COSTS & MONEY

There are all kinds of ways to visit the Rockies. While some visitors are keen to cut costs and camp on the cheap, others are happy to splash out on a once-in-a-lifetime cross-continent railway adventure. How much you spend really depends on the kind of holiday you're looking for. We've provided sleeping and eating ideas to suit all budgets throughout this book.

If you're happy to sleep under canvas, cater for yourself and provide your own entertainment, camping is the cheapest (and some say best) way to experience the parks. In Banff and Jasper, camping at major campgrounds costs between C$20 and C$30 for a tent and two people, dropping to around C$15 at the more basic rural sites. In Glacier, campgrounds inside the park cost between US$15 and US$20. Hostels are another popular budget option; a night in a HI dorm will set you back around C$20 to C$35, although some independent hostels have lower rates. Cheap food is easily available from local supermarkets, shops and delis, and most hostels have kitchens where you can prepare your own meals. All told, budget travelers can squeeze by for around C$50 to C$60 per day.

Midrange travelers have the broadest range of choice. You can find private doubles in B&Bs or motels for between C$50 and C$100, while more luxurious hotel rooms or lodge cabins go for between C$125 and C$250 per night. Factor in the cost of a full meal in a midrange restaurant (C$30 to C$40 per head), admission costs (C$10 to C$20) and car hire (C$30 to C$40 per day), and you should find a budget of C$400 to C$450 per day will comfortably cover the cost for two people traveling around the parks in high summer.

At the top end, you can easily splash out in excess of C$1000 per day by staying in the top hotels and eating in the most lavish restaurants; throw in a few deluxe options such as helicopter trips and private tours and you might even be able to tip your budget to over C$1500 per day.

Activities are bound to be one of your major spends, especially if you're interested in things like horseback riding and white-water rafting. Costs for these vary a lot, depending on what you want to do, but you should expect to spend between C$75 and C$150 on an organized trip and substantially more for multiday adventures and expensive guided activities such as rock climbing, fishing and mountaineering.

PLANNING YOUR TRIP

'Activities are bound to be one of your major spends'

Entrance Fees & Passes

Day passes to Banff and Jasper cost C$8.90/7.65/4.45 per adult/senior/child; family and group passes are also available for C$17.80. Daily fees to Waterton are C$6.95/3.45 per adult/child. Passes should be displayed on your vehicle's windshield or rear-view mirror, and can be purchased at park information centers or tollbooths along major roads.

If you're visiting for more than a week, or you're stopping in other national parks (such as Kootenay and Yoho), it's worth buying an annual **Park Pass** (adult/child/senior/family C$62.40/31.70/53.50/123.80), which covers entry to all of Canada's 27 national parks. Discovery Passes also include entry to 78 national historic sites in Canada – ask at one of the entry tollbooths for details. Visa, MasterCard, American Express, traveler's checks and good old-fashioned cash are all accepted as payment.

Seven-day entry passes to Glacier cost US$25/15 per vehicle in summer/winter, or US$12/10 if arriving on foot or bike. An annual pass costs US$35 per vehicle. Entry to Waterton is not included.

BOOKS

The classic trail manual is the venerable *Canadian Rockies Trail Guide* by Patton and Robinson. Practically every walk in the Canadian mountain parks is covered, with detailed trail descriptions and lists of key junction points. It's a little dry, and the photos are B&W, but it still makes the best trail-side companion.

For a more opinionated take, try *Don't Waste Your Time in the Canadian Rockies* by Kathy and Craig Copeland. The trails are divided into various categories (from Premier to Don't Do), and the text is written in a lively, impassioned style that gives you a vivid sense of the relative merits of each route. The color photos are lovely, too.

Epic Wanderer by D'Arcy Jenkin documents the life of one of the continent's great mappers and explorers, David Thompson. It's an engaging and action-packed read, and provides some fascinating background on the blood, sweat and toil that lies behind the present-day national parks. You'll never look at a map in quite the same way again.

There are plenty of bear books around, but *Grizzly Country* by the naturalist and photographer Andy Russell is arguably the best. Concentrating on solid facts and fascinating stories gleaned from a lifetime spent living and working with bears, it's the finest all-round book for getting inside the mind of the grizzly.

For a take-anywhere guide to the mountain scenery, you can't top *Handbook of the Canadian Rockies,* a lively, readable and encyclopedic overview of the Rocky Mountain environment. There are sections on flora, fauna, geology and history, as well as tips on everything from pitching your tent to lighting your campfire.

Forgotten Highways by Nicky Brink and Stephen Brown explores the stories behind many of the classic trails and highways across the Rockies, ranging from old Indian roads to pioneering fur-trading routes.

A Hunter of Peace: Old Indian Trails of the Canadian Rockies is Mary Schäffer's account of exploring the Bow Valley, surrounding mountains and her 1907 discovery of Maligne Lake. Originally printed in 1911, this more recent edition is illustrated with her drawings and colored lantern slides.

The *Sibley Field Guides* are a wonderful series of natural history guides, covering birds, animals, trees and plants you'll come across in North America, with informative text and photos, and illustrations to help you identify the different species. The waterproof covers come in handy during a rain shower, too.

Despite being set in Montana, the spectacular backdrops in Ang Lee's movie *Brokeback Mountain* were actually filmed in Kananaskis Country, just southwest of Banff.

If you've ever battled with a recalcitrant flysheet or toiled with your tent pegs, then *The Happy Camper* by Kevin Callan is for you. It's a fun and informative compendium of camping information, packed with useful anecdotes, recipes and handy tips on how to make the outdoors experience more enjoyable and, ultimately, more rewarding.

MAPS

The best topographical maps are produced by **Gem Trek Publishing** (☎ 403-932-4208; www.gemtrek.com), which has several excellent 1:100,000 maps covering Banff, Jasper and Waterton Lakes, as well as Lake Louise and Yoho, Bow Lake and The Crossing, Columbia Icefield, Canmore, Kananaskis and several other areas. All major trails and points of interest are clearly marked on the maps, which are supposedly waterproof and tearproof (although in practice they'll only take so much punishment). They're available everywhere, including from retail stores, bookstores, grocery stores and many gas stations.

National Geographic's *Trails Illustrated* series offers topographical, waterproof, tearproof maps of Glacier and Waterton Lakes, while the United States Geological Survey (USGS) publishes a 1:100,000 topographical map for Glacier National Park.

Map Art Publishing (☎ 403-278-6674; www.mapart.com) produces a range of road maps covering the Canadian Rockies.

INTERNET RESOURCES

The internet is a great resource when it comes to trip planning, but finding the information you need can be a challenge. Your first port of call for general info should be the websites for **Parks Canada** (www.parkscanada.gc.ca) and the **National Park Service** (www.nps.gov), where you'll find details of everything from visitor fees and park regulations to up-to-date trail information and weather forecasts.

American Park Network (www.americanparknetwork.com) A good online resource with plenty of background information on US parks, including Glacier.

Atlas (www.atlas.gc.ca) Huge repository of maps of Canada, with downloadable maps covering everything from climate change to population migration.

Banff Tourism Bureau (www.banfflakelouise.com) The main portal for tourist information in Banff, with advice on hotels, restaurants and activities.

Blackfeet Nation (www.blackfeetnation.com) History, culture and news of the Blackfeet Indians.

Discover Jasper (www.discoverjasper.com) Advertising driven, but has loads of suggestions on hotels, activity companies and tours.

Glacier National Park (www.glacier.national-park.com) Online guide to visiting Glacier with lots of useful practical advice.

Hike Alberta (www.hikealberta.com) Great hiking blog with a big database of possible trails.

Jasper Tourism & Commerce (www.jaspercanadianrockies.com) Jasper's main tourism site, with sections on transport, hotels, dining and even weddings.

One Day Hikes (www.onedayhikes.com) Excellent online trail guide with hundreds of classic routes in the Rockies.

Travel Alberta (www.travelalberta.com) Alberta-wide tourism site.

Waterton Park Visitors Association (www.watertonchamber.com) Comprehensive visitors guide covering all the essentials, including lodging, transport, hiking and even places of worship.

USEFUL ORGANIZATIONS

Alpine Club of Canada (☎ 403-678-3200; www.alpineclubofcanada.ca; Indian Flats Rd, Canmore) The main organization for Canada's mountaineers, rock climbers and alpine guides runs backcountry huts, training programs and courses.

'Your first port of call for general info should be the websites for Parks Canada and the National Park Service'

PLANNING YOUR TRIP

FESTIVALS & EVENTS

Spring

Heat Up the Rockies (www.heatuptherockies.com) This mountainside festival, held in March/April, is a relative newcomer, with highlights including gigs, live events and a street-hockey tournament.

Jasper Festival of Music & Wine Famous musicians play their hearts out around the concert halls and mountainsides of Jasper (in April), with wine tastings to accompany the music.

Canmore Children's Festival (www.canmorechildrensfestival.com) Pageantry, puppet shows, workshops and magic displays keep the little ones entertained at this yearly children's knees-up in Canmore (May).

Summer

Banff Day In celebration of the history of Banff, the Whyte Museum swings its door ajar for an annual open house in June.

Banff TV Festival The great and the good of the TV world descend on Banff in June for special screenings, talks and TV-themed events.

Banff Rod Run Souped-up, shiny hot rods and classic cars spin round the streets of Banff for this three-day festival (in June) of all things automotive.

Canada Day Food booths, fireworks and outdoor concerts in celebration of the nation. Events take place in Banff, Jasper and Glacier on July 1.

North American Indian Days The largest of several celebrations held on the Blackfeet Reservation throughout the year, this July event has displays of traditional drumming and dancing and the crowning of this year's Miss Blackfeet.

Banff Summer Arts Festival (www.banffcentre.ca/bsaf) In July/August culture takes centre stage for this month-long showcase of artistic activity at the Banff Centre, hosting everything from opera, theater and street performance to art exhibitions.

Jasper Heritage Folk Festival (www.jasperfolkfestival.com) Every second year, Canadian folk musicians join forces with strummers, drummers and singers from across the globe for concerts and gigs in Centennial Park in August.

Jasper Heritage Rodeo (www.jasperheritagerodeo.com) Since 1926 bull-riders, steer-wrestlers and calf-ropers have been congregating in Jasper for this annual hoe-down and rodeo, held in mid-August.

Autumn

Banff International String Quartet Competition (www.banffcentre.ca/bisqc) A world-famous contest for the cream of the world's classical string quartets, held at the Banff Centre in September.

Wordfest Famous authors, creative writing workshops and literary talks come to Banff during this three-day celebration of the written word, held in October.

Banff Mountain Film Festival Since the mid-1970s, the three-day film festival has celebrated the spirit of mountain adventure through films, videos and lectures. Big-name explorers and mountaineers usually attend; held in November.

Winter

Winterstart This hip Banff street party, held in November, is aimed at the snowboarding and winter-sports crowd, and includes the Ski Big 3 Rail Jam and Santa's Parade of Lights.

Jasper Welcomes Winter In November/December craft fairs, fun runs and outdoor skating herald the arrival of winter in Jasper.

Jasper in January Winter festival in Jasper National Park with plenty of family-friendly events, including cross-country skiing, sleigh rides, skating and a chili cook-off.

Ice Magic During this annual competition, held in January at the Fairmont Lake Louise, teams of ice carvers from across the globe battle it out to create elaborate sculptures fashioned from 136kg (300lb) blocks of ice

Banff/Lake Louise Winter Festival This winter-themed knees-up has been an institution in Banff since 1916, and it's still going strong almost a century later. Events such as spelling bees, street parades, sled competitions and even a 'chili challenge' hit the streets of Banff town in January/February, and there's always a big wrap-up party that finishes off the celebrations in style.

Root Beer Classic Sled Dog Races Mushers and husky teams compete over a 24km (15-mile) dogsled course in Polebridge, Montana in March.

Big Mountain Ski Annual Furniture Races Settees with skis and beds on sleds take to the slopes in this zany downhill furniture race in Whitefish in April.

Friends of Banff (☎ 403-762-8918; www.friendsofbanff.com; Banff Information Centre, 224 Banff Ave, Banff) Nonprofit organization that helps protect the park and provide services like ranger talks, educational programs and guided walks. Also at Bear & Butterfly (214 Banff Ave, Banff).

Friends of Jasper (☎ 780-852-4767; www.friendsofjasper.com; Jasper Information Centre, 500 Connaught Dr) As above but for Jasper.

Glacier Institute (☎ 406-756-1211; www.glacierinstitute.org; 137 Main St, Kalispell) Provides educational courses, youth camps and field research programs in Glacier.

Glacier Natural History Association (☎ 406-888-5756; www.glacierassociation.org) Works with park authorities to protect Glacier's natural environment and publishes information booklets.

Mountain Parks Heritage Interpretation Association (www.mphia.org) Accreditation body for official hiking guides in the Canadian Rockies.

Waterton Natural History Association (☎ 403-859-2624) Education and natural history organization in Waterton, which also runs a small museum.

Itineraries

ROCKIES ROADTRIP

Two Weeks

This wonderful tour packs in the essential sights in the three main parks, from massive glaciers to wild valleys and misty mountaintops.

- Start with a spin around **Jasper town** (p169) before whizzing north via **Maligne Canyon** (p172) and **Maligne Lake** (p172).
- Head south along Trans-Canada Hwy 1, stopping at the **Athabasca Glacier** (p168) and the huge **Columbia Icefield** (p169).
- Cross into Banff and explore the glaciers, lakes and sky-topping mountains of the southern **Icefields Parkway** (p125).
- Indulge in a teahouse hike starting at **Lake Louise** (p110) and a canoe ride on **Moraine Lake** (p100).
- Detour along the **Bow Valley Parkway** (p123) and gawk at the views aboard the **Banff Gondola** (p95).
- Veer south to Glacier National Park and drive along the stunning **Going-to-the-Sun Road** (p206).
- Straddle the Continental Divide at **Logan Pass** (p206).

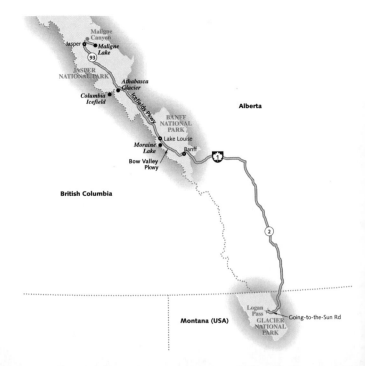

BANFF BASICS   **One Week**

- Kick off with some culture at the **Whyte Museum** (p92) and the **Buffalo Nations Luxton Museum** (p96).
- Explore Banff's hot-water history at the **Cave and Basin** (p96) before taking a dip at the **Upper Hot Springs Pool** (p95).
- Take a scenic boat trip around **Lake Minnewanka** (p97), Banff's largest lake.
- Splash out on some top-class Canadian cuisine at the **Maple Leaf** (p140).
- Watch out for wildlife on the **Marsh Loop Trail** (p102) or while you cycle the **Sundance Trail** (p121).
- Stroll along the catwalk trail to the twin waterfalls in **Johnston Canyon** (p106).
- Sleep pioneer-style in the scenic log cabins at **Baker Creek** (p136).
- Follow the lakeside path along **Lake Louise** (p98) up to the **Plain of Six Glaciers** (p109).
- Enjoy an upper-crust supper in a converted train carriage at the **Station Restaurant** (p143).
- Clamber to the top of the rock pile on **Moraine Lake** (p100) and stare down the Valley of the Ten Peaks.
- Head for the flower-filled **Sunshine Meadows** (p113), with incredible views along Simpson Pass.

In a week you'll have enough time to delve deep into Banff. This whistle-stop route takes in some classic attractions, with scope for side trips if you've got more time to spare.

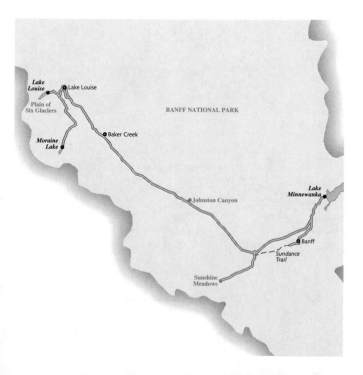

ITINERARIES

JASPER'S NORTHERN ROUTE   **Two Days**

It's not all inhospitable wilderness. For a glimpse of some of Jasper's less foreboding secrets, take in this relaxing but picturesque jaunt along the park's northern arteries.

- Start this tour in the east, at Pocahontas, before heading south for a soothing soak at **Miette Hot Springs** (p173).
- Meander along the twisting path to **Sulphur Pass** (p180) on the Fiddle River Trail.
- Stop off at **Maligne Canyon** (p172) for close-up views of plunging waterfalls and gaping chasms.
- Head south on the **Maligne Lake Road** (p185) scanning the roadside for bears and elk.
- Hike around the **Moose Lake Loop** (p174) and book a ticket on a boat tour to serendipitous **Spirit Island** (p172).
- Drive to Jasper and reserve an overnight room in the exquisite **Pyramid Lake Resort** (p194).
- Go for an early morning hike around the **Mina & Riley Lakes Loop** (p177).
- Join the queue for coffee and pastries at the buzzing **Bear's Paw Bakery** (p195).
- Ride the tramway, or tackle the 8km (5-mile) hike, to the top of **Whistlers Mountain** (p170).
- Visit **Jasper Pizza** (p195) and fortify yourself with a 10-inch special from the wood-fired oven.
- Head west on Hwy 16 for sunset views of awe-inspiring **Mt Robson** (p196).

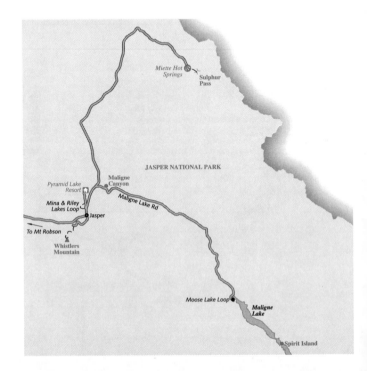

GLORIOUS GLACIER   **One Day**

- Kick off in 'rustic' luxury at the blissful **Glacier Park Lodge** (p241) in East Glacier.
- Grab a cinnamon bun 'to go' at **Brownie's Grocery & Deli** (p241).
- Soak up the sublime scenery around **Two Medicine Lake** (p207).
- Pick up news, views, information and inspiration at the **St Mary Visitor Center** (p203).
- Stop off at **Sun Point** (p206) and stretch your legs on the trails around **St Mary Lake** (p206).
- Press on to Logan Pass and hike the short trail up to the **Hidden Lake Overlook** (p209).
- Descend the steep but scenic Going-to-the-Sun Rd and have lunch at **Jammer Joe's** (p225), beside the Lake McDonald Lodge.
- Take a canoe out onto the clear glacial waters of **Lake McDonald** (p220)
- Linger in Apgar village and grab an ice cream from the side window at **Eddie's Cafe** (p225).
- Drop by for dinner and a beer at the **West Glacier Restaurant & Lounge** (p242).
- Head back along the Theodore Roosevelt Hwy (US 2) stopping off for a sunset vista at the **Goat Lick Overlook** (p219).

Cross the Continental Divide twice in one day in this rugged ramble through the Rockies, along some of the wildest and most visually stunning roads in North America.

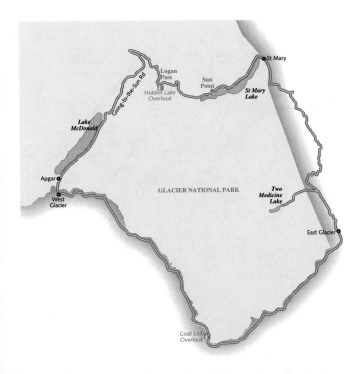

ITINERARIES

YOHO & KOOTENAY   **Five to Seven Days**

With so many natural attractions in Banff itself, it's easy to forget about the other nearby national parks. This route takes in the glorious country around Yoho and Kootenay.

- Begin with some high-octane thrills in **Golden** (p160), the adrenaline capital of the Canadian Rockies.
- Travel east into Yoho and overnight in the quaint railway town of **Field** (p154).
- Take a guided hike up to the **Burgess Shale** (p152), a prehistoric fossil bed perched high in the mountains.
- Take in the thundering plunge of **Takakkaw Falls** (p152).
- Step up to the challenge on the fantastic hike along the **Iceline Trail** (p154) or remote **Lake O'Hara** (p153).
- Chill out with some leisurely canoeing around **Emerald Lake** (p152).
- Detour into Kootenay and trek up to the dramatic **Stanley Glacier** (p157).
- Explore the limestone gorge of **Marble Canyon** (p157) and the natural ochre beds known as the **Paint Pots** (p157).
- Rest those weary bones with a relaxing plunge in the **Radium Hot Springs** (p158).

CRUISIN' K-COUNTRY   **Four Days**

- Base yourself in the booming little town of **Canmore** (p144).
- Enjoy a pooch-powered ride at a **dog-sledding kennel** (p145) in Canmore.
- Descend into the depths of the **Rat's Nest** (p145) cave system.
- Indulge in some fine dining at **Quarry** (p148), Canmore's top restaurant.
- Test your nerves on the bike tracks at **Canmore Nordic Centre** (p145)
- Explore traditional First Nations culture on a guided hike with **Mahikan** (p101).
- Swing by the **Grizzly Paw** (p147) for home-brewed beer and gourmet burgers.
- Head into the mountains along the dirt-track **Smith-Dorrien Hwy** (p148), stopping off to explore picnic spots and scenic areas en route.
- Sleep under canvas at one of the campsites around **Kananaskis Lakes** (p150).
- Take a horseback trip into the hills from **Boundary Ranch** (p150).
- Follow one of the quiet trails in **Peter Lougheed Provincial Park** (p148).

Ditch the crowded trails and pricey hotels in Banff by following this tour around the lesser-known highlights of Canmore and Kananaskis National Park.

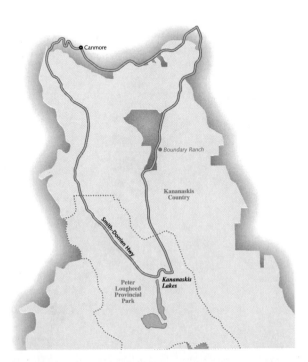

ITINERARIES

HIKING HEAVEN   Two Weeks

For many people hiking goes hand-in-hand with any worthwhile trip to Canada's mountain parks. This round-about route takes in a handful of classic hikes in Jasper and Banff.

- Power past the Angel Glacier on the **Path of the Glacier & Cavell Meadows Trail** (p175).
- Gaze out across the Columbia Icefield along **Wilcox Pass** (p176).
- Follow your nose on the smelly path to **Sulphur Pass** (p180).
- Look out for Bullwinkle on the **Moose Lake Loop** (p174).
- Tackle the leg-stretching climb up **Parker Ridge** (p117) for unmatched views of the Athabasca Glacier.
- Stroll among subalpine forest and wild mountain scenery in **Larch Valley** (p111).
- Clamber up to a panoramic viewpoint of the Icefields Parkway from **Bow Summit Lookout** (p116).
- Savor the silence while looking out across the **Consolation Lakes** (p105).
- Admire the alpine flowers on the ascent over **Healy Pass** (p114).
- Throw your voice (and listen for the echo) in the **C-Level Cirque** (p107).
- Hike up to the high-mountain **Mt Assiniboine Lodge** (p119) and head out for side trips to Wonder Pass, Gog Lake and the Nublet.

Activities

Whatever your reason for visiting the Rockies, chances are it has something to do with the great outdoors. While many visitors seem content to view the national parks from behind the steering wheel, this is a region that's crying out for closer inspection, whether that means plummeting down the mountains on a bone-shaking bike ride, scrambling up a sheer cliff face or tackling some of the famous hiking trails that crisscross their way through the mountain ranges. There are endless ways to expend your energy, regardless of whether you visit in the height of summer or the depths of winter, for as soon as the throngs of hikers and bikers depart with the arrival of the year's first snows, they're almost immediately replaced by a steady stream of snowboarders, ice climbers, heli-skiers and telemarkers, all desperate to experience the pristine powder and quiet solitude of the wintry mountain parks. And for those of a more sedentary persuasion, there are still plenty of outdoor pursuits to keep your interest piqued, from wildlife safaris to horseback rides and fishing trips. So what are you waiting for? Dig out those boots, break out the skates or strap on those snowshoes – it's a great big world out there…

SUMMER ACTIVITIES

Most summer activities in the national parks take place between May and September, although the exact periods vary according to seasonal conditions. You're usually guaranteed the best weather in July and August, so unsurprisingly these are also the busiest periods for outdoor-activity companies; book ahead to make sure of securing your place.

Banff National Park has in excess of 1600km (1000 miles) of hiking trails, while Jasper isn't far behind with more than 1200km (745 miles).

Hiking & Backpacking

If there's one activity that sums up the spirit of the Rockies, it's hiking. Banff, Jasper and the surrounding parks are a mecca for mile-eaters, and no matter where you travel in the parks, chances are there's a scenic trail nearby that'll whisk you up spectacular mountains, into picturesque forest or down a dramatic gorge. It's a destination *par excellence*

GOING SOLO

For many people it's the chance for some much-needed solitude that makes the idea of hiking in the mountains so irresistible, but it's worth thinking carefully if you're planning on going solo. Walking alone (especially in the backcountry) is obviously more risky – your chance of encountering aggressive wildlife is greater, there's no one to go for help if you get into trouble or sprain an ankle, and you'll have to rely on your own map-reading and navigational skills, so there's no one else to blame if you get lost! Several trails in Banff National Park are also covered by group access restrictions (p108) for much of the summer, which means hikers are required to hike in groups of four or more to minimize the risks of bear encounters.

On the other trails, it's worth taking a few extra precautions if you're on your own. Be particularly wary about wildlife around noisy streams or dense forest. Sing loudly on the trail, shout and clap your hands to warn animals of your approach, especially if you're downwind (which means animals won't smell you before they see you). Pack a compass and a good trail map, check trail warnings and take along some bear spray (and know how to use it), just in case. But don't fret too much. Most animals want to avoid you even more than you want to avoid them, and in summer there will almost certainly be other hikers on the trail anyway. As long as you're sensible, hiking solo is quite feasible – but as the scouts always say, it pays to be prepared.

HIKING IN BANFF NATIONAL PARK

Name	Hike type	Start location	Round-trip distance	Duration	Difficulty	Elevation change
Bow Glacier Falls	day	Num-Ti-Jah Lodge	7.2km (4.4 miles)	3hr	easy-moderate	95m (310ft)
Bow River Falls & the Hoodoos	easy	Banff	10.2km (6.4 miles)	4hr	easy	60m (197ft)
Cascade Amphitheatre	day	Mt Norquay parking lot	13.2km (8.2 miles)	5hr	demanding	650m (2099ft)
C-Level Cirque	day	Upper Bankhead picnic area	8.8km (5.4 miles)	4hr	moderate-demanding	510m (1640ft)
Consolation Lakes Trail	easy	Moraine Lake	6km (3.8 miles)	2hr	easy-moderate	70m (213ft)
Fenland Trail & Vermilion Lakes	easy	Banff	2.1km (1.3 miles)	30min	easy	nil
Garden Path Trail & Twin Cairns Meadow	day	Sunshine Village	8.3km (5.1 miles)	3½hr	easy-moderate	185m (607ft)
Healy Pass	day	Sunshine parking lot	18.4km (11.4 miles)	6hr	moderate-demanding	665m (2148ft)
Helen Lake	day	Helen Lake parking lot	12km (7.4 miles)	4hr	moderate-demanding	560m (1804ft)
Johnston Canyon & the Inkpots	easy	Johnston Canyon parking lot	11.6km (7.2 miles)	5hr	moderate	215m (705ft)
Lake Agnes & the Big Beehive	day	Fairmont Lake Louise	10.2km (6.4 miles)	3hr	demanding	390m (1263ft)
Larch Valley & Sentinel Pass	day	Moraine Lake	11.6km (7.2 miles)	4-5hr	moderate	740m (2381ft)
Marsh Loop	easy	Banff	2.5km (1.6 miles)	1hr	easy	nil
Mt Assiniboine & Lake Magog	back-country	Sunshine Village	57.6km (35.8 miles)	4-5 days	moderate-demanding	45m (144ft)
Paradise Valley & the Giant's Steps	day	Paradise Valley parking area	20.3km (12.6 miles)	6-7hr	moderate-demanding	400m (1310ft)
Parker Ridge	day	Parker Ridge parking lot	4km (2.5 miles)	2hr	moderate	275m (892ft)
Peyto Lake & Bow Summit Lookout	day	Peyto Lake parking lot	6.2km (3.8 miles)	2hr	moderate-demanding	230m (760ft)
Plain of Six Glaciers	day	Fairmont Lake Louise	13.5km (8.4 miles)	4-5hr	moderate	340m (1115ft)
Stewart Canyon	easy	Lake Minnewanka parking lot	5.6km (3.5 miles)	1½-2hr	easy	nil
Sulphur Mountain	day	Banff Gondola terminal	11km (6.8 miles)	4hr	demanding	670m (2150ft)
Sundance Canyon	easy	Banff	2km (1.2 miles)	1hr	easy	145m (476ft)

Wildlife Watching • View • Great for Families • Waterfall • Bicycles • Restrooms • Public Transportation to trailhead

for experienced hikers, but it's got plenty to offer the novice walker too, with loads of easy trails and interpretive paths that are ideal for families. Some paths also feature paved sections specially designed for wheelchair users. The views on practically any hike are infinitely more rewarding than those you'll get from inside an automobile, so it pays

Features	Facilities	Description	Page
		Flat trail skirting the Bow Lake shoreline and crossing rubbly moraines to a crashing glacial waterfall	116
		Scenic, partly paved riverside walk leading to a forest trail and rock features	101
		Tough uphill hike through high mountain scenery into a hidden natural amphitheater	108
		From an abandoned mining town, ascend through forest for lofty views of the Minnewanka area	107
		Escape the Moraine Lake crowds into wild mountains and glassy lakes	105
		A quiet ramble through forested fen that's often frequented by birds, small mammals and elk	102
		Wonderful walk through high mountain meadows, lakes and stunning lookouts	113
		Rewarding walk that affords fantastic glimpses over wildflower meadows and the Continental Divide	114
		Little-visited route up to a remote mountain tarn, with unparalleled vistas along the Icefields Parkway	117
		Paved boardwalk trail through a classic river canyon, with an optional hike on to colorful alpine ponds	106
		A lung-busting hike straight up the mountainside to one of Lake Louise's famous teahouses, with an extra challenge up switchbacks to the Big Beehive viewpoint	110
		This popular trail starts out steep and then meanders through beautiful native larch forest on its way to a skyscraping alpine pass	111
		An unusual loop around a rich, marshy wetland near Banff townsite, visited by all kinds of birds, butterflies and dragonflies	102
		An unforgettable journey into the wild backcountry and the shining spire of Mt Assiniboine	119
		One of Banff's classic trails, circling a jaw-dropping valley encircled by the parking area towering Ten Peaks	112
		A tough switchbacking climb leads to a stunning knife-edge ridge overlooking the Saskatchewan Glacier	117
		A busy trail through forests to the lookout above Peyto Lake, which leads onto a much quieter climb to the crest of Bow Summit	116
		Glorious walk up the edge of a dramatic valley to a glorious viewpoint over two major glaciers	109
		Start on the paved Lake Minnewanka shoreline trail and then head over rougher ground along the side of a picturesque canyon	104
		While most people cheat and zip up via the gondola, you'll have the satisfaction of following in Norman Sanson's shoes to the tip of Sulphur Mountain and amazing views over the Banff townsite	107
		Combine a paved riverside trail, navigable by bikes and wheelchairs, with a short, pedestrian-only canyon loop	103

Wheelchair Accessible   Ranger Station   Backcountry Campsite   Picnic Sites   Restaurant Nearby

to put in some effort; once you're out on the trail, you're guaranteed a grandstand view of some of the most awe-inspiring natural scenery in North America.

We've detailed many of our favorite hiking routes in this book, but it's worth picking up a dedicated trail guidebook detailing distances, elevations,

HIKING IN GLACIER NATIONAL PARK

Name	Hike type	Start location	Round-trip distance	Duration	Difficulty	Elevation change
Avalanche Lake Trail	easy	Avalanche Creek shuttle stop	6.4km (4 miles)	2½hr	easy-moderate	145m (475ft)
Dawson-Pitamakin Loop	day	North Shore trailhead	30km (18.8 miles)	8hr	demanding	910m (2935ft)
Gunsight Pass	back-country	Jackson Glacier Overlook	32km one way (20 miles)	2 days	moderate-demanding	930m (3000ft)
Hidden Lake Overlook Trail	easy	Logan Pass visitor center	5km (3.2 miles)	2hr	easy-moderate	150m (494ft)
Highline Trail	day	Logan Pass visitor center	12km (7.6 miles)	5½hr	moderate	255m (830ft)
Iceberg Lake Trail	day	Swiftcurrent Motor Inn	14.5km (9 miles)	5½hr	easy-moderate	370m (1190ft)
Quartz Lakes Loop	day	Bowman Lake campground	20.5km (12.8 miles)	7hr	moderate	765m (2470ft)
Red Eagle Lake Trail	day	1913 Historic Ranger Station	24.5km (15.2 miles)	8hr	moderate	90m (300ft)
Siyeh Pass Trail	day	Siyeh Bend shuttle stop	16.6km (10.3 miles)	6hr	moderate-demanding	1040m (3345ft)
Sun Point to Virginia Falls	easy	Sun Point shuttle stop	11.5km (7 miles)	4hr	easy	90m (300ft)
Swiftcurrent Pass	day	Swiftcurrent Motor Inn	12km (7.6 miles)	6hr	moderate-demanding	650m (2100ft)
Trail of the Cedars	easy	Avalanche Creek shuttle stop	1.3km (0.8 miles)	30min	easy	16m (54ft)

Waterton Lakes National Park

Name	Hike type	Start location	Round-trip distance	Duration	Difficulty	Elevation change
Carthew-Alderson Trail	day	Cameron Lake	19km (11.8 miles)	6hr	moderate	610m (1968ft)
Crypt Lake Trail	day	Crypt Landing	17.2km (10.3 miles)	6hr	moderate-demanding	710m (2296ft)
Lower Bertha Falls Trail	easy	Waterton townsite campground	6km (3.7 miles)	1½hr	easy-moderate	150m (490ft)
Tamarack Trail	back-country	Rowe Lakes trailhead	31.6km one way (19.6 miles)	2 days	moderate-demanding	1460m (4700ft)

Wildlife Watching | View | Great for Families | Fishing | Waterfall | Restrooms | Drinking Water

maps and compass bearings for specific routes (*The Canadian Rockies Trail Guide* is the standard textbook for most self-respecting hikers). A good-quality topographical map of the area you're hiking is also essential – the Gem Trek maps (see p27) are the best for the Canadian parks.

There are scores of excellent trails around Banff town, with the Bow Valley Parkway, Sunshine Meadows (p113) and Cascade Mountains (p108) all within easy reach, but for many people the finest walks are around the high mountains and lofty lookouts surrounding Lake Louise (p98). The trails around the Icefields Parkway, Jasper and Glacier are generally quieter than those in Banff, so you'll have a better chance of spotting wildlife and you'll find it easier to indulge in some solitary hiking. It's also worth considering exploring outside the main park borders: Yoho National Park (p152) is crammed with wonderful walks, especially around Yoho Valley and Lake O'Hara, while Kootenay National Park (p157) and Kananaskis

Features	Facilities	Description	Page
		Very popular forested walk to a stunning lake	208
		A lengthy but rewarding hike around the true 'Crown of the Continent'	214
		See snowfields, glaciers, lakes and more over two riveting days	215
		Quick scamper to a spectacular lookout	209
		Phenomenal scenery for miles as you head to Granite Park Chalet	210
		Leads to one of the most impressive glacial lakes in the Rockies	212
		Shimmering lakes in Glacier's most remote valley	214
		Long but gentle hike to a renowned fishing lake	211
		Diverse views on the way to a dramatic, windy pass	211
		Sun-dappled valley trail to a trio of beautiful waterfalls	209
		Pleasant valley ramble followed by a sharp climb to the Continental Divide	212
		A short route through mature forest	208
		Memorable hike offers beautiful scenery and sweeping views	232
		Involves tunnel crawling and a cable-assisted walk along sheer cliffs	233
		An easy, early evening ramble to a secluded waterfall	232
		Waterton's big backcountry adventure through glacial moraines and vibrant wildflower displays	234

Public Transportation to Trailhead   Wheelchair Accessible   Ranger Station   Backcountry Campsite   Picnic Sites   Boat Shuttle

Country (p148) are where the locals hike while the tourists clog the trails inside Banff National Park.

WHEN TO HIKE

The peak hiking season is mid-May to September. Outside these months, snow covers many trails, with some passes remaining blocked until late July. Generally June to September offers the most reliable hiking conditions, although it's often worth waiting until the warmer weather arrives in July and August if you're planning on overnighting. These are also the busiest hiking times, and if you're after quieter walking the shoulder months are probably a better bet. September's a particularly lovely month to hike, as fall brings a sea of autumnal colors. Hardy hikers will also find a few trails that stay open deep into winter, especially around Banff and Jasper towns; if you're exploring other areas you'll need snowshoes (p51).

ACTIVITIES

HIKING IN JASPER NATIONAL PARK

Name	Hike type	Start location	Round-trip distance	Duration	Difficulty	Elevation change
Lake Annette Loop	easy	Annette Lake parking lot	2.4km (1.5 miles)	40min	easy	nil
Maligne Canyon	day	Maligne Canyon parking lot	4.2km (2.6 miles)	1½hr	moderate	100m (328ft)
Mary Schäffer Loop	easy	Maligne Lake parking lot	3.2km (2.2 miles)	45min	easy	negligible
Mina & Riley Lakes Loop	day	Jasper-Yellowhead Museum	9km (5.6 miles)	3hr	easy-moderate	160m (525ft)
Moose Lake Loop	easy	Maligne Lake parking lot	2.6km (1.6 miles)	45min	easy	negligible
Old Fort Point Loop	day	Jasper	3.5km (2.2 miles)	1½hr	moderate	140m (443ft)
Path of the Glacier & Cavell Meadows Trail	day	Cavell Meadows parking lot	9.1km (5.6 miles)	3hr	moderate-demanding	400m (1300ft)
Skyline Trail	back-country	Maligne Lake	45.8km one way (28.7 miles)	2 days	moderate-demanding	1400m (4526ft)
Sulphur Pass via Fiddle River Trail	day	Miette Hot Springs parking lot	5.2km (3.2 miles)	2hr	easy-moderate	170m (558ft)
Tonquin Valley	back-country	Marmot Basin Rd	53.2km (33 miles)	2-3 days	demanding	710m (2296ft)
Whistlers Summit	day	Whistlers Rd	7.9km (4.9 miles)	3½hr	demanding	1280m (4125ft)
Wilcox Pass	day	Wilcox Creek campground	11.2km (6.9 miles)	3½hr	moderate	340m (1100ft)

🦌 Wildlife Watching 👁 View 👪 Great for Families 〰 Waterfall ♨ Thermal Features 🚲 Bicycles 🚻 Restrooms 🚰 Drinking Water

DIFFICULTY LEVEL

The highest mountain in the province of Alberta is Mt Columbia in Jasper, which tops out at an impressive 3747m (12,294ft).

Throughout the book we've graded all hikes according to three different difficulty levels:

Easy Mostly flat, simple walking on clearly defined trails, suitable for families and inexperienced hikers.

Moderate Usually featuring some elevation gain, steep sections and ungroomed trail (such as rubble, stones or moraines). Suitable for any hiker with an average level of fitness.

Demanding Expect very steep climbs, sections of exposed and unmaintained trail, difficult terrain and occasional tricky route-finding. Ideal for fit, well-equipped people and experienced hikers.

DAY HIKES

Most walks in this book are classed as 'day hikes,' a term that covers everything from an hour-long woodland stroll to an eight-hour haul to a mountain pass. Generally, any route that takes less than eight hours to complete, or covers a round-trip of less than 24km (15 miles), is just about practical for a day hike. While you might not quite reach the edge of the true wilderness in a single day, you can still experience an astonishing variety of terrain and reach plenty of wonderful views.

BACKCOUNTRY HIKES

While most people concentrate on day hikes, for a true wilderness experience you have to spend a few nights out in the wild. There are hundreds of backcountry routes scattered around the parks. Some string together a

Features	Facilities	Description	Page
		Surrounded by views of well-known peaks, this loop can be finished with a plunge in the lake	173
		One of the Rockies' deepest canyons, providing dramatic views of waterfalls and sunken gardens	179
		Holds the famous view first seen by Mary Schäffer	174
		Takes you into the woods to remote lakes	177
		Offers a peaceful, verdant forest and the chance to spot a moose	174
		Panoramic views of the mountaintops around Jasper town	178
		See Angel Glacier resting atop a sapphire lake afloat with icebergs, while the meadows offer amazing views	175
		The Rockies' premier backcountry trail, offering infinite views across the mountains	180
		A stroll for the senses – follow your nose to the original sulfur springs	180
		Wildlife, lush meadows and sparkling lakes, all in the shadow of the Ramparts	182
		A long walk up a steep hill through three different life zones	178
		Look out over the Columbia Icefield to some of the Canadian Rockies' highest peaks	176

Public Transportation to Trailhead   *Wheelchair Accessible*   *Ranger Station*   *Backcountry Campsite*   *Picnic Sites*   *Snack Shop*

pair of day hikes with a night in a backcountry campground, while others are multi-day epics that venture into distant and little-visited corners of the national parks. Trips can last anywhere from a couple of days to a couple of weeks, and vary widely in difficulty; the majority are within the capabilities of most hikers as long as you're properly equipped and reasonably fit. The Skoki Valley (p118), Egypt Lake (p118), Bryant Creek and Mystic Pass areas, plus the glorious trails around Mt Assiniboine (p155), are all classic backcountry destinations in and around Banff. Up in Jasper, you could try the Tonquin Valley (p182) or the Skyline Trail (p180). Glacier has the Gunsight Pass Trail (p215) and the northern end of the Continental Divide Trail (p216); while Lake O'Hara (p153) and the Iceline Trail (p154) are the best backcountry areas in Yoho National Park.

Conditions in the backcountry can change quickly, so take all the necessary equipment and check with parks staff for weather forecasts and trail reports before you set out. See the Clothing & Equipment chapter (p271) for advice on the recommended gear.

RESPONSIBLE BACKCOUNTRY CAMPING
The general rule in the backcountry is to leave everything as you find it – the **Leave No Trace** (www.leavenotrace.ca) website has some excellent advice on ways to reduce your impact on the backcountry environment. In most areas, you'll be camping in designated campgrounds; stick to the

ACTIVITIES

KNOW YOUR LIMITS

With such a scenic smorgasbord around the national parks, it's easy to get carried away with enthusiasm when you're planning your first trip. But it's important to remember that most of the trails around the Rockies are definitely not (if you'll pardon the phrase) a simple walk in the park. Many traverse difficult terrain, often passing over sections of rockfall, boulders, scree and even ice; trails can be muddy and slippery in wet weather; and many routes have significant elevation drops and gains that make the going much more difficult than the basic out-and-back distance might initially suggest.

Having said that, very few trails are beyond reasonably fit hikers with a modicum of experience, but it pays to be realistic about your limits. There's no point busting a gut to cover 10 miles on the first day, as you'll only increase the chance of spraining an ankle or taking a fall. Start out with an easy, short day hike and slowly tackle longer and more challenging routes as your fitness and awareness improve. Most importantly, carry the necessary equipment – T-shirts and sneakers are for the tennis court, not for the trail. Sturdy boots, rain gear, warm layers, a hat, sunscreen, bug repellent and plenty of water (2L per person) are all essential items, even on day hikes. A cell phone and basic first-aid kit aren't a bad idea either. See the Health & Safety chapter (p264) for more details.

---

tent pads or pitch on sites previously used by other campers to avoid unnecessary damage to the landscape. Keep your campsite clear of clutter to avoid attracting unwanted visitors, and store food, toiletries and cooking equipment in bear-proof lockers, or suspend them between two trees at least 4m above the ground and 1.3m from each tree trunk. In remote areas without any designated campgrounds, pitch your tent at least 50m (165ft) from the trail and 70m (230ft) from any water source. Try to use biodegradable soap and wash dishes well away from rivers and streams. Most importantly, you're required by law to pack out all garbage – the rule of thumb is that if you pack it in, you have to pack it out too.

Campfires are usually allowed but a portable stove is more ecofriendly, as it prevents unnecessary scorching of the ground. If you do have a campfire, try to minimize the amount of wood you use, and don't cut *anything* down to burn as fuel – dead wood is okay, green wood certainly isn't. Keep a close eye on the fire at all times, and make sure it's completely out before you leave. Fire restrictions often come into effect for campsites during periods of elevated fire risk, so heed the warnings.

At designated sites you'll find pit toilets, but in the event of an emergency out on the trail, move well away from the path and 70m (230ft) from any water source, dig a hole, do the deed and then cover it with dirt. Pack out toilet paper in a sealed plastic bag.

> Philip Abbot has the grim honor of being the first recorded climbing fatality in North America. He died in 1896 during an attempted ascent on Mt Lefroy, near Lake Louise.

HIKING RULES & PERMITS

No matter where you're hiking, you'll need a valid park pass (see p26 for an overview of current park fees) and, if you're exploring the backcountry, you'll also need a wilderness permit for each night of your stay – see the individual park chapters for details. You'll also need to book your chosen campgrounds with parks staff and it's often a good idea to leave a trip itinerary if you're traveling in remote country or doing any hazardous activities (such as mountaineering or rock climbing).

Out on the trail, it's important to exercise the usual precautions to keep the country safe and unspoilt. Stay on the trails and don't cut across switchbacks, avoid stepping on fragile plants and grasses, heed any trail closures and pack out all your garbage.

ACTIVITIES

GUIDES

For most day and backcountry hikes, employing the services of a guide isn't really necessary, although it can be a great way to become familiar with the natural history and heritage of an area, especially if you have limited time or kids in tow. There are many trained hiking guides in the area – contact the park visitor centers for details, and make sure the guide you choose is accredited by the Mountain Parks Heritage Interpretation Association (MPHIA).

Cycling

Despite what you might hear from some disgruntled mountain bikers (especially around Banff), cycling is still a great way to explore the parks. While it's true that parks authorities have cracked down on the number of unauthorized and bike-accessible trails in recent years, there are still plenty of routes open to mountain bikers around Banff town, Lake Louise, Kananaskis and Jasper. There are also dedicated bike parks at the Canmore Nordic Centre (p120) and the Kicking Horse Resort (p160) in Golden, which has its own cyclist-friendly gondola and a huge network of mountain trails. Waterton Lakes also has a small selection of bike routes, but Glacier is currently off-limits to all off-road riders. Road riding is also popular along the Bow Valley Parkway, Minnewanka Loop and the Icefields Parkway, but let's be honest – you won't get away without tackling a few hills.

Backcountry Biking in the Canadian Rockies is the classic textbook for off-road bikers, with detailed descriptions of lots of classic routes around the mountain parks.

Trail conditions vary widely – some are flat, easy, paved trails, while others are technical singletracks stuffed with hazards such as downed branches, rocks and knotted roots. Wear a helmet, take a puncture repair kit and remember that cyclists are particularly prone to surprise bear encounters as they travel much faster and more quietly than hikers. Make plenty of noise and slow down in thick forests, near rivers and on windy days.

Bikes and equipment can be rented in Banff, Jasper, Waterton, Kananaskis, Canmore and Golden. Road bikes, full-suspension bikes and front-suspension hardtails, as well as car racks, kids' bikes and children's chariots are all available, and many rental companies also offer shuttle services to trailheads or guided trips along classic routes in the parks.

Canmore-based **Canadian Rockies Trail Tours** (☎ 403-760-9521; www.cdnrockies .com) runs mountain biking trips right across the Rockies, including Banff, Jasper, Kananaskis and Golden.

Wildlife-Watching

With a rich and varied animal population ranging from bighorn sheep to wolverines, elk and grizzly bears, you should have plenty of opportunity to glimpse the parks' wilder residents. As always, the best times for wildlife-watching are dawn and dusk away from major roads, especially around the more remote areas of Jasper and Glacier, but even in Banff you're bound to cross paths with various fuzzy and furry creatures. In general, animals tend to go wherever humans don't, so the quieter

---

ZIP-LINING

Hiking too humdrum? Mountain biking too mundane? Then make a beeline for **Banff Zipline Tours** (☎ 403-760-3394; Beaverfoot Rd), near the Yoho–Kootenay border, where you can plunge down three sets of death-defying zip-lines at hair-raising speeds while the tree tops and forests whip past far below. Kids and closet paratroopers will feel right at home, but vertigo sufferers should probably look elsewhere for their kicks…

ACTIVITIES

MUSH, MUSH!

If you're looking to release your inner Inuit, head to Canmore (p145) or the Jasper Adventure Centre (p189), where you'll find several professional dog-hound companies offering guided trips out into the wilderness behind your very own team of yapping huskies. There are short taster trips and one-day expeditions with a professional dog musher, but for the ultimate thrill you can also head out on a multi-day expedition in charge of your very own team. Eat your heart out, *White Fang*.

---

areas of Kananaskis and Kootenay are also excellent places for wildlife seekers; Kananaskis is also famous for the annual migration of around 6000 golden eagles, which takes place through the valley every fall. The Vermilion Lakes and the Bow Valley Parkway are both common hangouts for elk, caribou, birds and even the occasional black bear; you'll also sometimes spot grizzlies on the avalanche slopes and more remote trails around Lake Louise. And even if you don't manage to spot any of the bigger animals on your travels, you're absolutely guaranteed to see lots of the smaller ones – hoary marmots, pikas and ground squirrels are all constant companions on the high mountain trails.

If you're really desperate to see some larger mountain wildlife, you can take guided wildlife tours in Banff (p91) and Jasper (p188), which visit popular wildlife spots around the respective parks, or visit a grizzly bear refuge at the Kicking Horse Resort (p160) or the Northern Lights Wolf Centre (p160), both near Golden. Getting out on the water is another great way to view wildlife, and you'll have a pretty good chance of spotting creatures aboard a boat trip on lakes such as Minnewanka (p97) or Maligne (p187), or on a wildlife float trip along the Columbia River (p161).

Fishing

There's nothing quite like casting a line into a clear mountain stream and reeling in something fishy for supper, and with hundreds of waterways and lakes open for angling, the mountain parks are unsurprisingly a paradise for aspiring anglers. Arctic grayling, rainbow trout, brown trout, brook trout, lake trout, northern pike, mountain whitefish and lake whitefish are all abundant, although most of the parks have a catch limit on the majority of rivers and some operate on a catch-and-release policy. You'll also need to be up on your fish identification as some species, including bull trout and kokanee salmon, are endangered and you will be heavily fined if you're caught in possession of one of these species by park authorities.

Fly-fishing is the most common form of angling in Banff, Jasper and Glacier, although you'll also find a few coarse fishing devotees around. The Bow River and Lake Minnewanka are both popular spots near Banff, while Maligne Lake, Pyramid Lake and Princess Lakes are among the top areas in Jasper. Lake McDonald and St Mary Lake are the most accessible fishing lakes in Glacier. The season in Canada generally runs from June to September, with a slightly extended season in Glacier. Unless you're an experienced angler, you might find it worthwhile to employ the services of a local guide, who can provide all the gear and tackle and lead you to the choicest waters. For details of local operators, see p127 (Banff), p188 (Jasper) and p220 (Glacier).

FISHING PERMITS

In the Canadian parks you'll need a national park fishing permit valid for the stretch of water in which you're planning to fish. The daily catch limit on most rivers and lakes is two fish; you'll be given a list of catch-and-possession limits when you purchase your fishing permit, as well as details of catch-and-release rivers and protected species. It is illegal to fish with natural bait, chemical attractants or lead tackle, so stick to the likes of tinsel, silk and feathers. You cannot have more than one line in the water at a time and may not fish from two hours after sunset to one hour before sunrise.

No fishing permit is required across the border in Glacier. Five fish is the general possession limit, although this depends on the size and species of what you've caught. Some waters are catch-and-release zones only. Casting on the park's boundaries may require a Montana state fishing license, and waters on Blackfoot reservation land (such as part of Lower Two Medicine Lake) require permits from the reservation.

Horseback Riding

If you're after a really authentic mountain experience, you can't beat seeing the parks from the saddle. People have been taking pack trips around these parts since the days of the earliest settlers, and the horseback tradition remains strong to this day. Many trails in Banff and Jasper are open to horseback riders as well as hikers, and horses are also welcome at many backcountry campgrounds and lodges, so there's plenty of opportunity for day trips as well as more adventurous backcountry expeditions. Most people choose to saddle up with a local guiding company, but it's possible to bring along your own steed. See p59 for information on horse trails and equestrian facilities, or consult the individual parks chapters for more detailed advice on guiding companies. If you're trotting off into the Canadian backcountry, you'll need a grazing permit in addition to your wilderness pass.

Alberta Outfitters Association (☎ 800-742-5548; www.albertaoutfitters.com) and **Montana Outfitters & Guides Association** (☎ 406-449-3578; www.montanaoutfitters .org/) both have comprehensive listings of pack-trip companies and outfitters.

White-Water Rafting & Float Trips

If you're the kind of person for whom the idea of hurtling down a raging torrent of river aboard an inflatable raft sounds appealing, then you're in luck – the Rockies have some of the best white water in Canada. Trips are

---

THE SOUND OF SILENCE

If you're tired of the throngs, seek out these oases of peace and quiet and bask in the sounds of – well, not very much at all, actually.

The Inkpots, Banff (p106) You'll have to hike up from Johnston Canyon, but you're guaranteed to give the crowds the slip.

Stewart Canyon, Banff (p104) Most people mill around the edge of Lake Minnewanka and never make it to this gorgeous canyon.

Bow Glacier Falls, Banff (p116) Stroll along the shore of Bow Lake to a practically deserted glacial valley.

Grizzly & Larix Lakes, Banff (p113) Beautiful, bewitchingly quiet lakes at the end of the easy Garden Path Trail.

Horseshoe Lake, Jasper (p169) An idyllic blue-green lake often missed by visitors traveling the Icefields Parkway.

Cavell Meadows, Jasper (p175) This side route off the popular Path of the Glacier trail is nearly always less packed.

Two Medicine Valley, Glacier (p207) Peaceful valley off the well-beaten Going-to-the-Sun Rd.

HOT SPRINGS HEAVEN

Thanks to their unique position straddling a deep geological fault line, Banff and Jasper sit directly atop a network of geothermal hot springs where the water gushes out from deep underground at a superheated temperature, laced with all kinds of rock salts and minerals that bestow supposedly therapeutic properties. People have been soothing their weary bones in the hot springs of the Rockies for centuries, and Canadians still like nothing better than a hot dip in an outdoor tub. You can take the plunge at various locations, including Miette Hot Springs (p173), Banff's Upper Hot Springs Pool (p95) and Radium Hot Springs (p158), although the original springs at the Cave and Basin National Historic Site (p96) are now off-limits to protect the endangered Banff Springs snail.

---

available for everyone from novice paddlers to experienced rafters, and to make choosing your trip easier, the rapids systems are graded into six degrees of difficulty, ranging from I (easy) to VI (near-impossible). Equipment, safety gear and trained river guides are all supplied by the activity company, and though it can be pretty white-knuckle at times, in general white-water rafting is remarkably safe – although you'll need to be prepared to get soaked to the skin. Most operators also offer sedate float trips on rivers, which are ideal for families and often provide a good way of spotting water birds and wildlife. The rafting season is May through September, with highest river levels (and, therefore, the most rapids) in spring.

The most renowned areas for rafting are along the Kicking Horse and Kananaskis Rivers (see p127); Canmore and Golden both have plenty of operators who run trips. Jasper also has its own network of white-water rivers; see p187 for details.

'First Nations people have been using traditional canoes in Canada for thousands of years'

Canoeing, Kayaking & Boating

Rafting's not the only way to explore the Rockies' rivers. First Nations people have been using traditional canoes in Canada for thousands of years (an example followed by the early European settlers and 'voyageurs'), and canoeing and kayaking are still among the best ways to get out and about on the water. Nonmotorized boats (including canoes, dinghies and kayaks) are allowed on nearly all waterways in the Canadian parks, but motorboats are banned on the majority of lakes and rivers, with Lake Minnewanka being one exception. The rules are less strict in Glacier, with most waterways open to boats, but check specific regulations and access rules with park authorities in advance if you're bringing your own vessel.

In Banff the best places for canoeing are Lake Louise, Moraine Lake, Bow River and Vermilion Lakes. You can also paddle on Emerald Lake in Yoho and Pyramid and Maligne Lakes in Jasper. Canoes and kayaks are available for hire at all these locations; expect to pay around C$25 to C$35 per hour, including life jackets, paddles and boat hire.

Glacier has perhaps the best range of locations for canoeing and boating, with all sorts of vessels available at Apgar, Lake McDonald, Two Medicine and Many Glacier, and boat launching ramps at McDonald, Bowman, Swiftcurrent, Two Medicine and St Mary Lakes for those with their own sailboat. In Waterton, Cameron Lake is probably the best lake for sailing, with rowboats, kayaks and canoes for rent.

If paddling sounds a bit too much like hard work, lazy landlubbers can also enjoy leisurely boat cruises on several lakes, including Lake Minnewanka in Banff, Maligne Lake in Jasper and lots of lakes (such as McDonald, St Mary, Swiftcurrent and Josephine) in Glacier.

ACTIVITIES

Rock Climbing & Mountaineering

With so many gigantic peaks and sheer rock faces, Banff and Jasper are both well-known destinations for rock climbers, but the mountainous terrain is generally challenging and technical and mostly more suited to experienced alpinists than rock-climbing rookies. With many mountains that top out above 3050m (10,000ft), frequent rockslides and landslips and notoriously changeable weather conditions, it's not a place to be taken lightly – novice climbers should definitely take an organized tour and even experienced climbers should consider employing the services of a local mountain guide. The **Alpine Club of Canada** (☎ 403-678-3200; www.alpineclubofcanada.ca) and the **Association of Canadian Mountain Guides** (☎ 403-678-2885; www.acmg.ca), both based in Canmore, provide general advice on climbing in the Rockies and can help put you in touch with mountain guides.

CMH Mountaineering (☎ 800-661-0252; www.cmhmountaineering.com) and **Yamnuska Mountain Adventures** (☎ 403-678-4164; www.yamnuska.com) both offer introductory sessions and guided trips to some of the easier local peaks, and can also organize much more challenging expeditions for dedicated peak baggers. Half-day trips cost around C$65 to C$95, and two-day beginner courses start at around C$150.

> If you don't fancy trying full-blown mountaineering, *Scrambles in the Canadian Rockies*, by Alan Kane, brings together over 150 straightforward ascents designed for hikers with a head for heights.

Hang-Gliding

For real daredevils, soaring through the air on a glorified kite is the ultimate adrenaline rush. Hang-gliding is banned in Banff, Jasper and Waterton (along with parachuting, paragliding, snowmobiling, hunting and various other niche activities that conflict with fundamental park goals), but you can still take to the air in Golden, especially around the renowned Mount 7 area, which hosts many international hang-gliding competitions. Contact the **Hang Gliding and Paragliding Association of Canada** (HPAC; ☎ 416-243-0469; www.hpac.ca) for details of qualified instructors based

---

MARC KLASSEN, MOUNTAIN GUIDE

My oldest brother, Karl, is an adventurous soul who tried climbing and skiing when he was a teenager and he moved to Banff soon after finishing school to pursue these interests. I was introduced to the sport by him and eventually we both took the Association of Canadian Mountain Guides certification exams so we would be able to spend as much time as possible in the mountains.

I've climbed, skied and guided in many areas around the world but, to be honest, there's nowhere quite like the Rockies – they have the best combination of accessible wilderness, variety and high-quality climbing of any place I have visited. 'Accessible wilderness' may seem a contradiction in terms, but in many places in the Rocky Mountain parks you can have a solitary mountain experience a few minutes' walk from your vehicle.

It's tough to pick a favorite climb in Banff, but I would probably have to choose the South Ridge of Mt Victoria from Abbot Pass, with a descent down the Huber Ledges. This is a classic mountaineering day, starting from the historic Abbot Hut, climbing a beautiful, narrow snow and rock ridge with incredible views of Lake Louise and Lake O'Hara. The descent takes you down a glacier and a series of rock ledges, and it looks kind of unlikely from above but everything links together. Overall a grand day out in the mountains – never too difficult but challenging all your climbing skills.

I definitely feel I am part of a long tradition of climbing, especially as a guide. Guides led many of the early climbs in the area, and continue to be instrumental in ensuring the safety of many climbers in the Rockies. I think it is important for people to keep climbing as it fosters an appreciation of the special place we have here, and that appreciation translates into people wanting to preserve our environment and the parks system.

ACTIVITIES

nearby, all offering tandem flights and covered by the appropriate HPAC insurance.

Golf

Forget Augusta and St Andrews – if it's an unforgettable 18 holes you're after, then you've definitely found the place. The Banff Springs Golf Course and Jasper Lodge Golf Course are among the most scenic places to swing a club on the planet. Both were designed in the 1920s by the renowned Canadian course designer Stanley Thompson, and boast stunning mountain scenery and unspoiled forest (as well as the occasional wandering elk or caribou). As always, golf in the Rockies is neither cheap nor casual – a round in summer will set you back at least C$150, and you'll be expected to dress smartly and act sensibly – but you certainly won't forget the back nine in a hurry. Cheaper rates and friendlier fairways are also on offer in East and West Glacier, Waterton Lakes, Radium Hot Springs and Kananaskis Country.

WINTER ACTIVITIES

Just because the winter snows have set in, don't think you'll be snuggled up in front of the hearth with your feet up. The explosion of interest in winter sports over recent years has brought a whole new wave of visitors to the park during the colder months, and there's no shortage of activities to keep you occupied – from husky-powered dogsledding in Canmore to snowboarding and snowshoeing around Lake Louise, Banff and Jasper.

> Out There publishes useful online activity guides to Banff and Jasper – check them out at www.out-there.com/bnf.htm and www.out-there.com/jasper.htm.

Skiing & Snowboarding

While they might not be quite as well known as more established Canadian resorts, the mountain parks have a rapidly growing reputation among skiers and snowboarders. With more than five months of solid snow every year, several resorts and, of course, plenty of mountains to slide down, it's hardly surprising that snow junkies have started to flock en masse to Banff and Jasper. And while there are enough groomed runs and après-ski activities to satisfy the most discerning winter-sports fan, for many people the real attraction in this part of Canada is the chance to explore the off-piste areas and untouched powder: heli-skiing is seriously expensive but guarantees you access to crowd-free slopes and stunning alpine scenery. Around Golden you can even try out the booming sport of cat-skiing, where you'll travel to pristine slopes on the back of an all-terrain snowcat. Certainly beats a boring old gondola…

The three main resorts in Banff are Mt Norquay, Lake Louise and Sunshine Village, all of which are covered under the **Ski Big 3** (www.skibig3.com) banner. Lift passes covering all three resorts are available, or you can buy individual resort passes if you only have a limited time in the mountains. In Jasper, the main skiing center is Marmot Basin, along the Icefields Parkway. The slopes and facilities are generally a little quieter than in Banff, so Marmot makes a good destination if this is your first time on the snow. The facilities at all the resorts are excellent, with ski and snowboarding schools, child-care facilities, terrain parks and half-pipes for snowboarders, public transportation to the slopes and lots of groomed and powder runs. The bars and restaurants in the towns of Banff and Jasper are also within easy reach, so you'll have plenty to keep you busy once your day on the snow is over. See p129 for more details on the Banff resorts, and p189 for the lowdown on Marmot Basin.

There are also two resorts in Kananaskis at Nakiska (p150) and Fortress Mountain (p150), while the Kicking Horse Resort (p161) in Golden

---

EXTREME PURSUITS

Looking for that extra edge of adrenaline? No problem – the mountain parks have plenty of sports to get your blood pumping.

- Plumb the inky depths of the **Rat's Nest** (p145) cave system near Canmore
- Soar through the skies en route to pristine trails on a **heli-hiking** (p146) expedition
- Pedal down the mountains at the high-octane **Kicking Horse Resort** (p160)
- Clamber aboard a snowcat for a spot of **cat-skiing** (p161)
- Scramble around the peaks around **Mt Edith Cavell** (p187) or **Lake Louise** (p127)
- Scuba dive to sunken wrecks in **Upper Waterton Lake** (p237) or a drowned town in **Lake Minnewanka** (p97)
- Scale a frozen waterfall in **Waterton Lakes** (p237) or **Jasper** (p189)
- Challenge the rapids on **Kicking Horse River** (p160) and **Kananaskis River** (p145)

---

is perhaps the destination of choice for snow fans in the know. As it sits just outside the boundaries of the national parks, restrictions on activities are much less severe, and you'll find more than 162 hectares (405 acres) of skiable terrain on offer, as well as esoteric activities such as tubing, snowmobiling and heli-skiing. Even better, the resort offers a daily 'First Track' program, where you can shell out for the privilege of being the first to experience the day's snow at 7:30am sharp.

Whitefish Mountain Resort at Big Mountain (p244), 11.2km (7 miles) south of Whitefish, is another prime winter-sports destination, with the excellent Fishbowl terrain park, a vertical drop of 717m (2353ft) and 93 marked trails spread over a massive 1215 hectares (3000 acres). You can even try a spot of night-riding, and look out for the annual Furniture Race (p28) down the Big Mountain slopes – it has to be seen to be believed.

Alberta's six fantastic ski resorts are covered by a comprehensive information site at www.skicanadianrockies.com.

Cross-Country Skiing

While most skiers choose to bomb down the mountainside in search of their winter thrills and spills, an increasing number of people are taking to the more sedate form of cross-country skiing as a way of experiencing the parks in all their wintry glory. Cross-country skiers have the chance to explore the empty backcountry deep into midwinter; many trails around Banff, Lake Louise and Jasper are specifically kept open for use by telemarkers from December through March, with a more limited range of trails also open in Glacier, Waterton, Kananaskis and Yoho. Park authorities supply trail maps of all the open routes, and you'll find lessons and equipment rental from most outdoor activity operators and some ski schools.

Cross-country skiers need to be particularly alert to the dangers of avalanches, especially in remote areas. Park staff recommend that you carry emergency supplies, an avalanche beacon, a full repair kit, a compass and a detailed topographical map on any cross-country skiing trip, as trails aren't always signposted and can be difficult to make out under all the snow cover. Remember also to check trail conditions before you set out.

Snowshoeing

Trudging through the snow in hiking boots is more purgatory than pleasure, but strap on a pair of snowshoes and you'll have access to a whole new world of winter walking. Snowshoeing has been practiced

Tests have shown that you burn 45% more calories using snowshoes than walking or jogging at the same speed.

by Aboriginal people in the Rockies for hundreds of years, and it's one of the easiest and most enjoyable ways to explore the winter wilderness (although walking around with two oversized tennis rackets strapped to your feet certainly takes a little bit of getting used to). Many of the trails kept open for cross-country skiers also have parallel tracks for snowshoers, and there are plenty of routes to explore around Jasper, Banff and Glacier – avoid trudging on the ski trails themselves, as this damages the groomed track and makes life much harder for the telemarkers. As always, parks staff can help with route maps and condition reports for current trails.

There are a few useful tips if you're new to snowshoeing: stick to level trails wherever possible, as walking uphill is quite a challenge in snowshoes; take along walking poles for balance; and make U-turns to turn around rather than trying to backtrack, as you'll inevitably end up tangling up the tails of your shoes with a faceful of powder for your troubles. Snowshoes can be hired from most outdoor operators and ski stores in Banff and Jasper.

Ice Skating

Ice skating in the frozen Rockies has more than a hint of fairy-tale magic around it, but you need to choose your location carefully as lake ice can be treacherous. Areas of Lake Louise in Banff, Lac Beauvert and Pyramid Lakes in Jasper, and Emerald Lake in Yoho are properly maintained from around November to January, so you'll be able to rent skates as well as glide on reassuringly solid ice.

HOW TO BE GOOD

The work of protecting the parks for future generations doesn't just fall to the rangers. Many dedicated park lovers choose to volunteer their free time to work for good causes ranging from nature surveys to trail maintenance.

If you're an aspiring volunteer, your first port of call should be the **Banff Volunteer Centre** (www.volunteerbanff.ab.ca), which maintains lists of hundreds of volunteering opportunities around the park. The Friends organizations in **Jasper** (www.friendsofjasper.com), **Banff** (www.friendsofbanff.com), **Yoho** (www.friendsofyoho.ca) and **Kananaskis** (www.kananaskis.org) also have lots of opportunities every year – you could find yourself doing anything from banding birds, monitoring wildlife, working on park radio or leading a full-moon hike.

The parks themselves often have vacancies. Banff offers several volunteer programs, including park ambassadors to help visitors learn and respect the mountain environment, citizen scientists to participate in research and monitoring programs and helping hands to participate in trail maintenance, litter blitzes and rehabilitation work. Check out www.pc.gc.ca/pn-np/ab/banff/edu /edu5v_e.asp for more information.

Jasper and Waterton sometimes accept volunteers, including campground hosts who greet campers and provide information in exchange for a year's park pass. You'll need to apply early for any available positions – contact the park authorities directly or the **Parks Canada National Volunteer Program** (volunteer.coordinator@pc.gc.ca; 4th fl, 25 Eddy St, Hull, Quebec, Canada K1A 0M5). The deadline for applications is December 1 for the next year's summer and autumn positions, or June 30 for winter and spring placements.

Glacier National Park usually has plenty of summer volunteering opportunities, covering everything from conservation programs to campground hosts. Visit www.nps.gov/volunteer for the latest programs. You could also contact the **US Forest Service** (www.fs.fed.us/r4/volunteer).

The **Glacier Institute** (www.glacierinstitute.org) accepts applications for its teacher naturalist programs at Big Creek Outdoor Education Centre and Glacier Park Field Camp, helping with educational activities between March and September. Most positions include a small monthly stipend.

ACTIVITIES

Ice Climbing

Once the winter snows set in, many climbers break out the crampons and ice axes for a spot of ice climbing – frozen waterfalls in Banff, Jasper and Glacier make ideal spots for this challenging but exhilarating sport. Parks Canada produces a free leaflet, *Waterfall Ice Climbing and Avalanches in Canada's Mountain Parks*, which details the most popular locations and also provides useful advice on the serious threat of avalanches. You'll need an experienced guide – try **Yamnuska Mountain Adventures** (☎ 403-678-4164; www.yamnuska.com) or **On Top Mountaineering** (☎ 403-678-2717; www.ontopmountaineering.com), and expect to pay around C$450 to C$500 per person for a full day's climbing. Prices become more affordable for larger group sizes.

An annual Mountain Festival is held in Banff every autumn, bringing together the year's best films, books and mountain adventurers from across the globe. Check out www.banffcentre .ca/mountainculture /festivals.

ACTIVITIES

Kids & Pets

Greenhorn actors are often warned by seasoned old thesps never to work with kids or animals, and you'll find many parents who would say the same adage applies to the great outdoors. While many moms and dads turn pale and clammy at the merest thought of traveling with the kids far from the comforting fallbacks of Nintendo and cable TV, the national parks are actually fantastic places to explore *en famille*. It'll certainly take some extra planning, but with a bit of research you'll find hundreds of family-friendly destinations and activities scattered around the parks – from ranger programs and nature walks to trailside cookouts around an open fire. And if you just can't bear to leave home without Fido in tow, you'll also find that the three parks have a pretty tolerant attitude toward bringing pets.

Canadian Rockies with Kids by Scott Regehr and Philip Smith provides a good all-round overview of the various challenges you'll face traveling as a family in the Rockies, and has lots of useful ideas on activities and must-see sights, as well as useful itineraries.

BRINGING THE KIDS

First things first. There are some basic practical considerations if you're bringing the kids. Firstly, accommodations. The vast majority of hotels will happily accept kids, and many places allow children under a certain age to stay in their parents' room for no extra charge (the exact age varies according to the hotel, but it's usually under 12, 15 or 16). Extra pull-out beds are often available; otherwise ask for a triple-bed or family room. As always, it's worth thinking about staying in a hotel that has good facilities (games rooms, saunas and swimming pools are always popular) to fend off the boredom once the day's activities are done.

Despite the rather basic accommodations, hostels can actually be really good for families – booking out a whole dorm is usually far cheaper than an equivalent hotel room, although you'll sometimes have to be prepared to deal with hostel-specific issues such as late-night noise and the odd inebriated backpacker stumbling around the foyer. The large, efficient HI hostel in Banff has brilliant facilities (such as its own climbing wall) as well as private self-catering cabins that are ideal for families. The HI Lake Louise also has dedicated family rooms.

The situation for younger kids is a bit less straightforward. Few of the parks' hotels have on-site day-care facilities (the Banff Springs Hotel is one of the few exceptions), but the larger and more efficient hotels can usually rustle up baby cots/cribs and many have also started to offer baby-sitting services in conjunction with local providers. **Childcare Connections** (☎ 403-760-4443; childcarebanff@yahoo.ca) offers baby-sitting services in Banff, and the **YWCA** (☎ 403-760-3200; crc@ywcabanff.ab.ca) maintains a list of registered child-care providers. In Jasper, contact the **Jasper Activity Center** (Map p170; ☎ 780-852-4666; Pyramid Lake Rd).

Most kids love the idea of camping, but they might not be so keen after three days of dealing with no showers, ice-cold running water and pit toilets. It might be worth considering one of the larger campgrounds that are more geared-up for kids, such as Tunnel Mountain, Johnston Canyon and Lake Louise in Banff, or Whistlers or Wapiti in Jasper, where you'll also find regular park interpretive programs as well as 'roving rangers' from one of the Friends organizations. You'll also be well placed for the handy distractions dotted around Banff and Jasper towns (such as ice cream and playgrounds), a worthwhile consideration once the initial enthusiasm for toasted marshmallows and fire-crisped wieners has inevitably worn off.

Most restaurants in the parks are kid-friendly, with the exception of some of the more upmarket and top-end establishments. Kids' menus are fairly widespread, especially in hotels and the main town restaurants, and staff are usually pretty understanding about kids sharing their parents' main meals (though it's always worth buying extra drinks or side dishes to keep them sweet). A few restaurants even have small play areas kitted out with toys, coloring books and activities where the kids can entertain themselves until the meals turn up.

In Alberta and Montana, as in much of the rest of Canada and the US, it's a legal requirement that children under the age of six and weighing less than 40lb (18kg) – 60lb in the US – are secured in a properly fitted child safety seat. Drivers are responsible for ensuring that other passengers are safely secured and wearing seat belts; it'll be you who has to pay the fine if you're stopped and the kids aren't belted up. If you're renting a car, safety seats for toddlers and children are available from all the major companies, but you'll incur an extra charge (usually around C$6 to C$10 per day). You'll need to reserve them at the time of booking – if you're booking online, they're often quoted as an add-on once you've gone through the main reservation process.

Lastly, remember that driving distances from the airports (and in the parks themselves) can be quite long. While there's lots of scenery to view out the window, even mountains can get a little tiresome for little 'uns after a few hours. Try to break up the journey with regular stops and combine driving trips with other activities such as short hikes and sightseeing excursions.

Author Linda White and illustrator Fran Lee have collaborated on a series of great kids' books, including *Cooking on a Stick*, *Sleeping in a Sack* and *Trekking on a Trail*. They take a lighthearted approach to the outdoors life, with nature charts, activity tips and recipe ideas plus plenty of bright, bold pictures.

Fun Stuff for Families
ACTIVITIES

There's a huge range of things you can get up to in the parks – the only limit is your imagination (or, more likely, your kids'). Inevitably it's the outdoor pursuits that are the real attraction and you'll be glad to hear that practically all the activities on offer are open to families. Wildlife walks, white-water rafting, canoeing and horseback riding are all popular family pastimes, and all activity providers are well set up for dealing with undersized clients.

Top of the list in terms of all-round family fun has to be hiking. Many of the trails around the parks are flat, well maintained and easily within the scope of active kids. Trails that combine the sights are usually more

---

TOP 10 KIDS' ACTIVITIES

- Take a dip at the **Upper Hot Springs Pool** (p95) or **Radium Hot Springs** (p158)
- Hit the trail on an easy hike in **Banff** (p101), **Jasper** (p173) or **Glacier** (p208)
- Ride the sky on the gondolas in **Banff** (p95) or **Lake Louise** (p100)
- Saddle up for a **horse-riding trip** (p47)
- Paddle the waters of **Lake Louise** (p100) or the **Bow River** (p127)
- Take a nature trip on the **Vermilion Lakes** (p102)
- Jump aboard a boat cruise on **Lake Minnewanka** (p97) or **Maligne Lake** (p187)
- Pedal the hills at the **Canmore Nordic Centre** (p120)
- Explore the ice aboard the Athabasca Glacier's all-terrain **Snocoaches** (p168)
- Plummet down the mountain attached to a high-speed **zip-line** (p45)

fun for inquiring young minds, so try to find walks that take in a mix of forest, mountain, river and canyon, or wind their way through well-known wildlife habitats. Several trails have interpretive panels to help you get to grips with the features at which you're looking.

Ideal family walks include Johnston Canyon (p106), Sundance Canyon (p103), Fenland Trail and Vermilion Lakes (p102), the Marsh Loop (p102), Consolation Lakes (p105) and the Garden Path Trail (p113) in Banff; the Mary Schäffer Loop (p174) and Moose Lake Loop (p174) in Jasper; and for very energetic kids, you could try the challenging Crypt Lake Trail (p233) in Waterton. Take extra care around canyons, river crossings and trails with any kind of drop-off. You'll find many more ideas in the individual park chapters.

Nature walks are especially good for kids. **Discover Banff Tours** (☎ 403-760-5007; www.banfftours.com) offers a morning and evening wildlife tour and visits to a grizzly bear refuge occupied by an orphaned bear called Boo. Also consider tagging along on an organized hike; many local guides are accredited by the Mountain Parks Heritage Interpretation Association (MPHIA) and are specifically trained to help visitors understand and learn about the park. Most guides have plenty of experience dealing with children and despite the cost it can be a good way of keeping your kids engaged with the world they're walking through.

Cycling is another excellent activity, with plenty of easy trails dotted around the parks that are specially designed for families. Most bike-rental companies offer kids' bikes, child helmets and protective pads, as well as child chariots for younger children. See p120 and p182 for suggestions on good family trails in Banff and Jasper respectively.

All canoeing and rafting companies provide suitable boats for kids, or spaces in adult boats, along with children's life vests. If you don't feel like traveling under your own steam, there are also boat cruises on Lake Minnewanka (p97) and Maligne Lake (p187), plus several lakes around Glacier provided by the **Glacier Park Boat Company** (☎ 406-257-2426; www.glacierparkboats.com).

Seeing the park from horseback is another exhilarating way for kids to explore the trails. Most horse-trip companies provide small ponies and child-friendly saddles, and cater for complete novices as well as experienced riders. **Holiday on Horseback** (☎ 403-762-4551; www.horseback.com) has lots of easy rides in Banff and also offers an evening trail cookout (complete with BBQ steak and homemade baked beans) that's guaranteed to get young cowboys and cowgirls excited. You can usually visit the horses at Spray River Corral and the Warner Stables, near the Cave and Basin in Banff; phone ahead to check the stables are open for visitors.

Dogsledding is another great kids' activity but, rather obviously, there needs to be some snow on the ground to do much mushing. Some operators open their kennels for tours in summer, including **Snowy Owl**

Kids Can Press publishes a series of lively, colorful wildlife guides for younger readers, with titles on owls, beavers, eagles and other North American beasties. Find out more at www.kidscanpress.com.

TOP FIVE FAMILY HIKES

- Johnston Canyon (p106), Banff National Park
- Garden Path Trail (p113), Banff National Park
- Consolation Lakes (p105), Banff National Park
- Moose Lake Loop (p174), Jasper National Park
- Crypt Lake Trail(p233), Waterton Lakes National Park

Tours (☎ 403-678-9588; www.snowyowltours.com) in Canmore; you'll get to meet the dogs, see how they're trained and maybe even take a summer-style sled trip.

For a really memorable day trip, all-terrain Snocoaches operated by **Brewster** (☎ 1-877-423-7433; www.columbiaicefield.com) chug right up onto the Athabasca Glacier for views of the Columbia Icefield and the surrounding mountains; clambering aboard one of these massive machines feels rather like stepping into a science-fiction movie, and it's guaranteed to be an adventure to remember for the whole family. Nearby, the **Icefields Center** (☎ 1-877-423-7433; Icefields Parkway) has lots of displays explaining the science behind the glacier. If you can stretch to the sky-high price tag, heli-hiking is another amazing once-in-a-lifetime excursion that'll really stick in their memories. Choppers sweep across stunning mountain scenery and access remote areas most visitors will never be lucky enough to see, and hikes with experienced guides can be specifically tailored for families. Contact **Icefield Helicopter Tours** (☎ 403-721-2100; www .icefieldheli.com).

Everyone knows you have to shout 'mush' to get a dog team going, but there are lots of other commands too, including 'gee' for left, 'haw' for right, and 'whoa' to stop.

The gondolas at Lake Louise (p100) and Banff (p95) also make a good outing, zipping up the mountainsides for absolutely unforgettable views across the parks; you might even catch sight of a grizzly or black bear around Lake Louise in summer, so bring binoculars. For more vertigo-inducing thrills, **Banff Zipline Tours** (☎ 403-760-3394; Beaverfoot Rd), near the Yoho–Kootenay border, has three white-knuckle zip-lines where you can hurtle down the mountainside above the Kicking Horse River at speeds of up to 30mph (50km/h); once you've regained your composure, guides intersperse the descents with nature talks.

For more ordinary activities, or to fill the inevitable rainy day, you'll find swimming pools at the **Jasper Aquatic Center** (☎ 780-852-3663; 401 Pyramid Lake Rd) and the **Banff Center** (☎ 403-762-6100; 107 Tunnel Mtn Dr), which also has a gymnasium, squash court and climbing gym. There are bowls, rails and ramps to grind at the **Banff Skatepark** (☎ 403-762-1147), next door to the twin ice rinks at the **Banff Recreation Center** (☎ 403-762-1235; Norquay Rd).

In the winter season, skiing and snowboarding take over as the main outdoor pastimes. All of the ski resorts in Banff, Jasper and Kananaskis have facilities and runs that are specially tailored for younger users, and child-size skis, snowboards, goggles and gear are all easily available for hire. Ski lessons and snowboard schools, as well as day-care and baby-sitting services, are also available at most resorts, allowing mom and dad to enjoy the tougher slopes (and the après-ski) with a clear conscience. For more info, the website for Banff's three big ski resorts (www.skibig3 .com) will give you some idea of what's on offer.

CAMPS & EDUCATIONAL PROGRAMS

For something more structured, kids can sign up for nature programs in all of the parks. Glacier operates the National Parks Service's excellent **Junior Ranger Program** (www.nps.gov/learn/juniorranger.htm), in which kids pick up a free ranger booklet from park visitor centers. The booklet contains activities, questionnaires, quizzes and games to complete during their stay; they'll earn a Junior Ranger badge and a certificate when the book's completed. There's no age limit for the program – it's not entirely unknown for parents to get carried away and complete a book of their own in pursuit of that all-important ranger's badge. Before you even set out for the national park, kids can sign up to become a 'webranger' at www.nps.gov/webrangers, where there's lots of online games, puzzles and activities to pique their interest.

In Banff and Jasper, Junior Naturalist programs are run in summer by the Friends organizations. These short events usually last for a couple of hours and combine games and outdoor activities with nature talks and short trails. They're designed to be fun, informal and educational, and parents are welcome to tag along. Friends of Banff also conducts a regular nature walk around Vermilion Lakes, and offers 'edukit' rentals containing lots of educational materials (including slides, books, puppets and even fur, antlers and skulls) about bears, elk and wolves; these are really designed for large groups and school programs. You can also pick up a free 'hiking kit' (including guidebooks and binoculars) from Friends of Jasper, or join its regular Jasper history tours. Contact **Friends of Banff** (☎ 403-762-8918; www.friends ofbanff.com) and **Friends of Jasper** (www.friendsofjasper.com) for more information. You can join several other interpretive walks around the parks, including hourly walks and talks at the top of the Banff and Lake Louise Gondolas and a Banff Culture walk provided by the Whyte Museum (p92).

Parks Canada also provides regular educational programs at main campgrounds in Banff, Jasper, Waterton and Kootenay, with slide shows, talks, films and activities exploring many aspects of the park, including wildlife, natural history and geology.

There are also organized summer camps that your kids can join, either as single-day stints or as part of a multi-day program. Banff has the best selection. There's a range of week-long **day camps** (per day/week C$35/125; ⏱ 9am-4pm Mon-Fri) for six to 12 year olds, exploring topics such as nature, outdoor skills, science, sports and the wild west. Kids between eight and 12 can join week-long **specialty camps** (C$188) exploring a specific activity (eg mountain biking), while 12 to 14 year olds can join one of the **Go! Camps** (per week C$114-168), which take in everything from canoeing to photography. Fourteen to 17 year olds can participate in the **Summit LIT** (C$141-168) program, which runs for four or five days, and concentrates on guiding and leadership skills. Bookings can be made for all the camps by calling ☎ 403-762-1251.

The **Glacier Institute** (☎ 406-756-1211; www.glacierinstitute.org) runs organized camps, outdoor education courses and youth camps, covering everything from wolf pups and fly fishing to backcountry skills. Week-long courses cost between US$285 to US$350, although shorter programs are often available. Many of the programs are run as family days, allowing parents and kids to follow the courses together.

Several museums have specially tailored facilities for kids, including the Whyte Museum (p92) in Banff, where you can rent out kids' 'museo-packs,' and the Jasper-Yellowhead Museum (p171), where there's a fun kids' activity room. Children will probably also love the stuffed beasties on display at the Banff Park Museum (p93) and the Luxton Museum (p96).

Pick up the free *Bear Guardian Adventure Manual* from Banff park visitor centers. It contains games, puzzles, quizzes and color-in pictures exploring many of the issues about traveling through bear country. Remember, it's for the kids, not you.

You'll find some more good ideas for things to do and places to see with kids in Banff and Jasper at www.travelforkids .com/Funtodo/Alberta /alberta.htm

BRINGING THE PETS

For many people, visiting the national parks is very much a family affair and often that doesn't just mean mom, pop and the kids. Plenty of people also decide to bring their pets along on their park adventure, and while it's certainly not outside the bounds of possibility, you definitely need to be prepared for the added complications that come with having your beloved little companion in tow.

For most people, bringing pets to the parks generally means packing the pooch, so here are the basic rules for canines as they currently stand. In Banff and Jasper, dogs are allowed on most trails and at most campgrounds (both front and backcountry), but you're required to keep

KIDS & PETS

DOGGIE DOS & DON'TS

It's worth noting that service and guide dogs are also welcome in the parks, although they should wear reflective vests to indicate their working status to park authorities and other trail users.

- do keep dogs leashed at all times
- do clean up after them on the trail
- do keep them quiet and under control in campgrounds
- do check them regularly for ticks and other parasites
- do bring along extra water, food and supplies if you're camping in the backcountry
- don't let them run off into the undergrowth, especially in grassy meadows or wooded areas
- don't leave them locked in hot cars or RVs
- don't assume everyone likes dogs

---

them securely leashed at all times (the rules are the same whether they're a dachshund or a Doberman). In Glacier, dogs are allowed in drive-in campgrounds, along park roads open to motor vehicles and in most picnic areas, and are banned from *all* park trails. You are required by law to clean up after your dog, so remember to bring along a couple of plastic bags or a pooper-scooper.

If you're camping, it's worth remembering that not everyone will think Fido is as loveable as you do, so it's important that you keep dogs under control at all times and stop them from running off into the undergrowth (where they might pick up ticks, fleas and other parasites) or generally bothering other campers. It's also good manners to try to keep the old dawg quiet – after a hard day's trekking, weary hikers tend not to take very kindly to a yap-happy hound, and it certainly won't win you any friends in the campground. Keep them leashed, keep them quiet and check their fur regularly for ticks they may have picked up during the day. It's also worth bringing along an extra blanket or two in case of unseasonally cold conditions; needless to say, you'll also have to bring along all the necessary supplies, including food, brushes, flea spray and any other medication. It's also worth noting that few hotels in Banff, Jasper or Glacier accept pets, and those that do will likely slap on a surcharge of at least C$10 per pet.

In addition to the official rules, it's also worth remembering that to many wild animals – including elk, caribou, coyotes and wolves – dogs are perceived as a threat, while to other beasties (such as cougar and bears) they resemble prey. Either way, bringing your dog along the trail puts you at increased risk in the event of an animal encounter – previously placid bears have been known to become enraged due to the noise of a barking dog. Equally, leaving your dog leashed up for hours on end in a campground or locked up in the ovenlike conditions of an RV isn't really much of a holiday for them, so it's worth thinking really hard about exactly what they're going to gain from being brought along on the trip. All things considered, they might well be happier being left in the relative comfort of a kennel back home – you might miss them while you're away, but you'll be guaranteed a warm welcome once you're back home.

Horse Trails & Equestrian Facilities

If you're a horse owner, it's also feasible to think about bringing along your trusty steed to the park. Most of the trails in Banff, Jasper and Glacier are open to horses with a few notable exceptions – see p89 for details on Banff trails, or contact park authorities for detailed advice on which routes aren't open to horses. This isn't an option for novice horse trekkers – you'll be traveling through wild, remote country and traversing difficult terrain, so it's only worth consideration for experienced, well-equipped equestrians. If you just fancy a quick day ride, or you don't want the hassle of transporting your own horse to the park, contact one of the commercial horse guiding companies (see p47), some of which will let you bring your own animal on organized trips and provide stabling facilities.

If you're traveling into the Canadian backcountry, you'll need to purchase a Wilderness Pass (C$9.90) as well as a grazing permit (C$1.70) for every night you're planning to spend out (in Glacier, backcountry permits are free but advance reservations incur a levy of US$20). It's always worth checking with parks staff about trail conditions before setting out, as some paths can be muddy and slippery, making them unsafe for horses; look out also for swollen rivers and snow cover at high elevations at certain times of year. You'll need to submit a detailed trip itinerary to parks staff when you purchase your pass, and depending on factors such as grazing quotas, campground usage and trail popularity, you might find yourself unable to follow a particular route – reservations for backcountry campsites are accepted up to three months ahead, and booking is highly recommended. Most backcountry campgrounds in Canada accept stock, but some in Glacier are closed to horse use.

If you need to hold your horse in the park overnight, either at the start or end of the trip, there are public corrals in Jasper at the trailheads at Portal Creek, Poboktan, Beaver Creek, Maligne Pass, Whirlpool River, Nigel Creek, Dorothy Lake, Miette Lake and Miette Hot Springs, and in Banff at Pipestone River, Mosquito Creek and 2km (1.2 miles) east of Saskatchewan crossing along Hwy 11. Depending on the corral, maximum stays are usually between 48 and 72 hours.

For more information, consult the following websites:

Banff (www.pc.gc.ca/pn-np/ab/banff/activ/activ6a_e.asp)
Glacier (www.nps.gov/glac/planyourvisit/privatestockuse.htm)
Jasper (www.pc.gc.ca/pn-np/ab/jasper/activ/activ4_E.asp)

Environment

Majestic, indomitable and bursting with life, the Canadian Rockies are environmentally unique. Formed over 170 million years ago when a massive collision in the earth's crust caused a giant lateral displacement known as the Lewis Overthrust, the mountains today are the product of several millions of years of glaciation and are endowed with one of the richest and most biologically intact ecosystems in North America.

Anointed rather regally with the title 'Crown of the Continent,' national parks from Glacier up to Jasper support diverse and sizable populations of bears, cougars, bighorn sheep and moose – as well as myriad trees, shrubs, wildflowers and lichens. The region also exhibits a plethora of powerful glaciers, relics of a colder and mightier age, although their numbers are rapidly dwindling.

THE LAND

Geologically speaking, the Canadian Rockies are a rock-lover's paradise, a caustic mix of towering mountain chains and multicolored terrain that is considered to be one of the most important fossil localities in the world. Everywhere you look you'll see graphic evidence of 1.5 billion years of the earth's history laid out like hieroglyphics in well-preserved sedimentary strata. Even more dramatic are the region's crenellated peaks and U-shaped valleys, a lasting testimony to the awesome power of ancient glaciers and ice fields.

The First Supercontinent

In the beginning there was nothing much at all. And then, approximately 1.5 billion years ago, sediments began to be laid down in an inland sea within a supercontinent known as Rodinia (a combination of landmasses that later broke apart into the continents we recognize today). Consisting of sands, silts and cobbles, these ancient sedimentary layers are now so deeply buried that they appear on the earth's surface in only a few places, two of which are Waterton and Glacier National Parks. On the west side of the parks, the oldest layer is known as the Pritchard Formation and preserves evidence of a deep sea that can be seen in thin layers of fine green rock along MacDonald Creek. Other strata such as the Altyn, Appekunny and Snowslip formations are also evident in places such as St Mary Lake and Logan Pass. Perhaps the most eye-catching and easy-to-recognize layer of rock is the brick-red coloration of the Grinnell Formation that is spectacularly exposed in Red Rock Canyon, in Waterton Lakes National Park.

The Big Breakup

About 750 million years ago, the supercontinent Rodinia began to break up along a giant rift, creating a new shoreline where North America split off from the future continents of Australia and Antarctica. Various sediments accumulated in an ancient sea during this epoch and, over time, these deposits hardened to form limestone, mudstone and sandstone.

A significant transition occurred around 570 million years ago, with the onset of the Cambiran period, a transitional era that sparked an incredible proliferation of complex new fauna in what became known as the 'Cambrian explosion.' Embedded in the region's rock, many well-preserved fossils of multicellular organisms remain from this period,

The US Geological Survey (www.usgs.gov) runs a highly regarded climate change research program based out of West Glacier, Montana. Studies inside Glacier National Park include retreating glaciers, forest modeling and fire ecology.

and have taught scientists much about evolution and the development of species diversity worldwide. Some of the planet's best Cambrian fossils were uncovered at the Burgess Shale site in Yoho National Park in 1909.

The Cambrian era was followed by a long period of relative stability as desert landmasses eroded and sedimentary layers accumulated along the continental coastline. For a period of over 350 million years the dozens of different rock layers that comprise the bulk of the peaks in today's Canadian Rockies were laid down in contrasting bands, documenting an encyclopedia of geological history, a record that shows how seas advanced and retreated numerous times across the region.

Collision Course

This period of stability came to a close around 200 million years ago when the continental plate began a steady march westward, pushing against the part of the earth's crust that lies under the Pacific Ocean. Like a slow-motion collision, the leading edge of the continental plate buckled against the impact. At first, the buckled edge may have simply created folds in the earth's crust, but over time these folds became steeper and started to fracture under the stress. Extending progressively eastward, the fractures reached the region of the Canadian Rockies about 100 million years ago where dynamic tectonic movement pushed up a huge wedge of rock and displaced it over 80km (50 miles) to the east, forming the basis of the mountains we see today.

The main period of compression reached its apex 60 to 80 million years ago, then subsided slowly, leaving behind layers of deep old Paleozoic rock wedged up on top of younger Mesozoic rock. This compressing process is known as thrust faulting and it geologically sets the northern Rockies apart from their smoother southern cousins, which were formed by broader tectonic uplifting.

Glaciers

For the past 60 million years, the primary force in the Canadian Rockies has been erosion, not deposition. The most dramatic erosive process has been that of glaciation, precipitated by the great glaciers and ice fields of the Ice Age that have sculpted rugged peaks and gouged out deep valleys from Pocahontas to Marias Pass. Two million years ago, huge sheets of ice covered much of the Canadian Rockies. These giant sheets produced incredible amounts of weight and pressure, and as tongues of ice crept across the landscape they tore apart rocks and transformed narrow V-shaped ravines into broad open valleys. Trillions of tons of debris were left behind when the ice finally retreated 10,000 years ago, much of it forming distinctive ridges called moraines, such as the one that the chateau at Lake Louise is perched on.

'Nearly every feature seen in the Canadian Rockies today is a legacy of the Ice Age'

Nearly every feature seen in the Canadian Rockies today is a legacy of the Ice Age. Peaks that were simultaneously carved on multiple sides left behind sharp spires called horns, as can be seen at Mt Assiniboine. Mountains that had glaciers cutting along two sides ended up as sharp ridges known as arêtes. Side streams flowing into valleys that were deepened by glaciers were often left hanging in midair, creating hanging valleys, with the streams pouring out as waterfalls down sheer cliffs.

Glaciers Today

Even though the Ice Age ended 10,000 years ago when the great ice fields gradually retreated, the story of ice and glaciers in the Canadian Rockies

ROCKY MOUNTAIN LIFE ZONES

Three distinct zones of life can be found in the Canadian Rockies, each with its own local environment and species.

At the lowest elevations, a great variety of plants and animals find their homes in the montane zone, a band of cool, damp, mostly continuous forest. This zone occupies major valley bottoms and the sunny lower slopes of mountains. Despite its ecological significance, this zone covers only about 5% of the parks' total area, and much of that area has been significantly impacted by the construction of roads, buildings and towns, as well as the passage of millions of visitors each year.

The montane zone occurs below 1525m (5000ft) and is characterized by forests of Douglas fir, white spruce, lodgepole pine and quaking aspen. Streams along valley bottoms are lined with two types of cottonwoods. These valley bottoms are critical winter habitat for elk, deer, bighorn sheep and their predators – wolves, coyotes and mountain lions – as well as other mammals that are pushed downslope by deep winter snows.

By one definition, the subalpine zone extends from the highest-growing aspen to the treeline, or about 1525m (5000ft) to 2285m (7500ft). This is also the zone where the greatest accumulations of snow occur, and accordingly, these so-called 'snow forests' are damp, cold and mossy. At the upper limits, where summer temperatures are barely adequate for trees to replace winter-killed needles, trees of the subalpine zone become stunted and barely grow above knee height. At lower elevations in the subalpine zone, taller trees such as subalpine fir and Engelmann spruce grow in dense stands.

Subalpine habitats cover roughly 50% of the Canadian Rockies, making them a dominant feature of these parks. This is the zone of mountain goats, grizzly bears, golden eagles, broad-tailed hummingbirds and Clark's nutcrackers. During the summer, deer, elk, and moose are frequently in this zone, though they leave for lower elevations with the onset of winter.

The highest and most austere zone is the land above the trees, the alpine zone, where few plants and very few animals are hardy enough to survive the extreme cold and wind. Surprisingly, in many areas it's even too cold and windy for snow to accumulate. In this region of rock and ice, the main animals are pikas and marmots, although grizzly bears, elk, deer and bighorn sheep can be common in alpine meadows during the late-summer growing season. Numerous alpine plants have bright, dramatic flowers, making this a favorite destination for wildflower enthusiasts.

is far from over. Mini ice ages have regularly altered the climate in the years since, the most recent of which peaked in the 1840s when the frozen tip of the Athabasca Glacier reached as far as the present day Icefields Center – it has retreated 1.6km (1 mile) since 1844. Even today, along the spine of the Continental Divide, smaller ice fields continue to craft and shape the landscape, although recent concerns about climate change suggest that the glaciers in Glacier National Park (which now number only 26) will be all but extinct by the year 2030. Waterton Lakes National Park is already a glacier-free zone.

WILDLIFE

Rising like snow-coated sentinels above the plains and prairies of Alberta and Montana, the Canadian Rockies protect a narrow, wildlife-rich corridor that stretches across the continent from northern Canada to Mexico. With the adjacent lowlands taken over by roads, farms and cities, the mountains have provided a final refuge for wolves, mountain lions, bears, elk, deer and many other large mammals. While populations of these animals are only a fraction of their former numbers, they are still impressive enough to lure wildlife enthusiasts to the region by the truckload.

Animals
LARGE MAMMALS
While the prospect of seeing 'charismatic megafauna' is one the region's biggest draws, the Canadian Rockies support nearly 70 species of mammals, including eight species of ungulate (hoofed mammal). In the fall and winter, many large mammals move down into valleys for protection against the weather; high concentrations can be seen along the Icefields Parkway during these seasons.

BEARS
The black bear roams montane and subalpine forests throughout the Canadian Rockies in search of its favorite food: grasses, roots, berries and the occasional meal of carrion. Frequently, they can be seen along roadsides feeding on dandelions. While most black bears are black in color, they can also be light reddish brown (cinnamon). Black bears are somewhat smaller than grizzlies and have more tapered muzzles, larger ears and smaller claws. Small claws help them climb trees and avoid their main predator, grizzly bears, which are known to drag black bears out of their dens to kill them. Although they are generally more tolerant of humans and less aggressive than grizzlies, black bears should always be treated as dangerous.

The endangered grizzly bear once roamed widely in North America, but most were killed by European settlers, who feared this mighty carnivore. Today 100 or so may inhabit the parks covered in this book, but with males roaming 3885 sq km (1500 sq miles) in their lifetimes, they aren't particularly easy to see or count. Male grizzlies reach up to 2.4m (8ft) in length (from nose to tail) and 1.05m (3.5ft) high at the shoulder (when on all fours) and can weigh more than 315kg (700lb) at maturity. Although some grizzlies are almost black, their coats are typically pale brown to cinnamon, with 'grizzled,' white-tipped guard hairs (the long, coarse hairs that protect the shorter, fine underfur). They can be distinguished from black bears by their concave (dish-shaped) facial profile, smaller and more rounded ears, prominent shoulder hump and long, nonretractable claws.

Both bears are omnivorous opportunists and notorious berry eaters with an amazing sense of smell that's acute enough to detect food miles away. Their choice of food varies seasonally, ranging from roots and winter-killed carrion in early spring to berries and salmon in the fall. Before hibernation, bears become voracious. Black bears will eat for 20 hours straight and gain an incredible 1.8kg (4lb) each day before retiring to their dens, and grizzly bears are known to eat 200,000 buffalo berries a day.

Some time in October, bears wander upslope to where snows will be deep and provide a thick insulating layer over their winter dens. There the bears scrape out a simple shelter among shrubs, against a bank or under a log and sink into deep sleep (not true hibernation, since their body temperatures remain high and they are easily roused). Winters are particularly hard, since bears live entirely off their fat and lose up to 40% of their body weight. Females who have been able to gain enough weight give birth to several cubs during the depths of winter, rearing the cubs on milk while she sleeps.

Recent figures for grizzly bear numbers in Alberta Province, Canada (Jasper, Banff and Waterton National Parks) are cited as approximately 850, suggesting an upward trend from 10 years ago.

DOGS
The cagey coyote is actually a small opportunistic wolf that devours anything from carrion to berries and insects. Its slender, reddish-gray form

is frequently seen in open meadows, along roads and around towns and campgrounds. Coyotes form small packs to hunt larger prey such as elk calves or adults mired in deep snow. Frequently mistaken for a wolf, the coyote is much smaller – 11.3kg to 15.8kg (25lb to 35lb), versus 20.3kg to 65.3kg (45 to 145lb) for a wolf – and runs with its tail carried down (a wolf carries its tail straight out).

The gray wolf, once the Rocky Mountains' main predator, was nearly exterminated in the 1930s, then again in the 1950s. It took until the mid-1980s for them to reestablish themselves in Banff, and today they are common only from Jasper National Park north; in Glacier National Park, wolves can be found in North Fork Valley. Wolves look rather like large, blackish German shepherds. Colors range from white to black, with gray-brown being the most common color. They roam in close-knit packs of five to eight animals ruled by a dominant (alpha) pair. The alpha pair are the only members of a pack to breed, though the entire pack cares for the pups. Four to six pups are born in April or May, and they remain around the den until August. Packs of wolves are a formidable presence, and they aren't afraid of using their group strength to harass grizzly bears or kill coyotes, but more often they keep themselves busy chasing down deer, elk or moose for supper.

HOOFED ANIMALS

Living on high slopes near rocky ridges and cliffs, bighorn sheep are generally shy creatures of remote areas. Unlike other parts of their range, however, bighorn sheep in the Canadian Rockies come down to roadsides in search of salts, invariably causing traffic jams of excited visitors. Males, with their flamboyant curled horns, spend summer in bachelor flocks waiting for the fall rut, when they face off and duel by ramming into each other at 96km/h (60 mph). Their horns and foreheads are specially modified for this brutal but necessary task. When not hanging around roadsides looking for salt and handouts (strictly forbidden), bighorn sheep use their extraordinary vision and smell to detect humans up to 300m (1000ft) away and keep their distance, making them extremely difficult to approach.

Occupying even steeper cliffs and hillsides, pure white mountain goats are a favorite with visitors. Finding one is another matter altogether, because goats live high on remote cliffs and are seldom observed close up. These cliffs provide excellent protection from predators, and both adults and kids are amazingly nimble on impossibly sheer faces. Occasionally they descend to salt licks near roads. In Jasper they occur in high densities on Mt Kerkeslin; around Banff try scanning the slopes of Cascade Mountain; and in Glacier National Park you might see goats at Logan Pass.

Two species of deer are common in valleys and around human dwellings throughout the region. More common by far are the mule deer of dry, open areas. Smaller, and with a large, prominent white tail, are the white-tailed deer of heavily forested valley bottoms. Both species graze extensively on grasses in summer and on twigs in winter. Delicate, white-spotted fawns are born in June and are soon observed following their mothers. Adult males develop magnificent racks of antlers in time for their mating season in early December.

Weighing up to 450kg (1000lb) and bearing gigantic racks of antlers, male elk are the largest mammals that most visitors will encounter in these parks. Come September, valleys resound with the hoarse bugling of battle-ready elk, a sound that is both exciting for its wildness and terrifying,

The Glacier Institute (www.glacierinstitute .org), based in Glacier National Park, is a private nonprofit organization that offers outdoor education courses and youth camps to lovers of the great outdoors.

ENVIRONMENT

because hormone-crazed elk are one of the area's most dangerous animals. Battles between males, harem gathering and mating are best observed from a safe distance or from your car. While numbers increase dramatically in winter, quite a few elk now spend their entire year around towns like Banff and Jasper, where they can be dependably observed grazing on yards and golf courses.

At 495kg (1100lb), the ungainly moose is the largest North American deer. Visitors eagerly seek this odd-looking animal with lanky legs and periscope ears, but they are uncommon and not easily found. Moose spend their summers foraging on aquatic vegetation in marshy meadows and shallow lakes, where they readily swim and dive up to 6m (20ft). Visitors can look for moose in the Miette Valley of Jasper, around Upper Waterfowl Lake of Banff, in the McDonald Valley of Glacier and in similar areas. The male's broadly tined antlers and flappy throat dewlap are unique, but like their close relative the elk, moose can be extremely dangerous when provoked. Moose are no longer as common as they were in the days when they freely wandered the streets of Banff; numbers have been reduced due to vehicle traffic (roadkills), a liver parasite and the suppression of the wildfires that rejuvenate their favorite foods.

Small Mammals

Hardly noticed among their giant brethren are dozens of smaller mammals roaming mountain forests and meadows. Common around picnic areas and roadside viewpoints are golden-mantled ground squirrels. Striped on their bodies like a chipmunk, these bulging beggars are fearless in their pursuit of handouts, climbing onto visitors' shoes and legs, doing everything possible to look cute and hungry. Because they hibernate and need to put on a lot of fat, ground squirrels become extremely focused on gaining weight in late summer and start looking like butterballs by September.

Hikers into the realm of rock and open meadow will quickly become familiar with two abundant mammals. When you encounter a pika, you are likely to hear its loud bleating call long before you spot the tiny, guinea pig–like creature staring back at you with dark beady eyes. Pikas live among jumbles of rocks and boulders, where they are safe from predators, but they still have to dart out into nearby meadows to harvest grasses that they dry in the sun to make hay for their winter food supply.

Another rock dweller is even more of a tempting morsel for predators. Hoary marmots are plump and tasty, but they have a system for protecting themselves. First, they stay near their burrows and dart in quickly when alarmed. Second, all the marmots on a hillside cooperate in watching out for predators and giving shrill cries whenever danger approaches. Marmots may shriek fiercely when humans come near, warning everyone in the neighborhood about the approach of two-legged primates. The Whistlers, a mountain outside Jasper, is named after these common rodents.

The aquatic beaver has a long history of relations with humans. Reviled for its relentless efforts to block creeks and praised for its valuable fur, the Canadian Rockies' largest rodent is now widely recognized as a 'keystone species,' an animal whose activities have a tremendous influence on the lives of many other species. Dozens of animals, like ducks, frogs, fish, moose and mink, depend on beavers for their livelihood. Although their numbers have declined as much as 90% in recent decades, beavers are still fairly common around marshes and ponds in valley bottoms. Here, each beaver cuts down as many as 200 aspens and willows per year, feeding on the sweet inner bark and using the trunks and branches to construct dams.

The Canadian Rockies is home to 69 naturally occurring species of mammals, including elk, coyote, wolves and grizzly and black bears, and the only fully protected caribou herd in North America.

Birds

Although more than 300 species have been found in the Canadian Rockies, birds are readily overshadowed by the presence of so many charismatic large mammals. It takes a real bird nut to turn their attention to a diminutive mountain chickadee when they could be watching male elk battle over harems of females or bighorn sheep scale rocky cliffs. However, casual observers will notice some of the more conspicuous species without even trying.

You'd be hard pressed to find a campsite or picnic table where you aren't quickly approached by gray jays hoping for a handout. These grayish little tricksters glide in silently and sidle up confidently next to your food. After a few moments they may help themselves to as much as they can carry – there are good reasons why they've been nicknamed 'camp robbers.' They stash most of their food away in small caches for winter.

The stash master, however, is the larger Clark's nutcracker. Each nutcracker buries up to 98,000 seeds in thousands of small caches across miles of landscape then returns to dig them up over the course of several years – an unbelievable test of memory. Seeds that are left behind, either accidentally or intentionally, sprout into future forests. Scientists estimate that most of the subalpine forests in the northern hemisphere have been planted by nutcrackers, making these birds the architects of mountain forests.

Two large raptors (birds of prey) are worth mentioning because they are so frequently encountered. Working their way along rivers and lakes are white and brown fish hawks, better known as ospreys. Fairly common from May to September, when the ice is melted, ospreys specialize in diving into water to catch fish. Ospreys are most often seen soaring over lakes, scanning the water for fish. Plunging feet first into the water, ospreys grab fish up to 90cm (3ft) deep then fly off to eat their scaly meal on a high perch. Osprey nests are enormous mounds of sticks piled on top of dead trees or towers.

In recent years the Canadian Rockies has gained some fame for its spectacular golden eagle migration. Each year 6000 to 8000 golden eagles migrate both north and south along a narrow corridor on the east side of the main mountain divide (the official count site is near Mt Lorette, in Kananaskis Country, just east of Banff). Spring migration peaks at the end of March, and fall migration peaks in October. Over 1000 golden eagles have been counted in a single day, so bring your binoculars. While migrating, golden eagles do little feeding, though some pairs stay for the summer and nest on high, remote cliffs. These massive birds are impressive predators, feeding mainly on rabbits and ground squirrels but also taking down adult deer, swans and cranes on occasion.

Of the region's eight species of owl, only the great horned owl is familiar to most visitors. Fearless around humans, highly vocal and sometimes active in the daytime, these large birds are a perennial sight around towns and campgrounds at lower elevations.

Amphibians

Very few amphibians and even fewer reptiles do well in the relative cold of these northern latitudes.

The definitive Canadian frog (found as far north as the Arctic Circle) is the wood frog, which occurs from low elevations up into the alpine zone. At the highest elevations, their season of activity is shortened to mere months – not much time to wake from hibernation, breed, fatten up and prepare for the next winter. Easily recognized by its dark mask,

TV survival experts Bear Grylls (Man versus Wild) and Les Stroud (Survivorman) have both been dropped unceremoniously into the Rocky Mountains to demonstrate their deft survival skills to millions of armchair viewers.

the wood frog wanders far and wide and is often found far from the nearest water.

More attached to water are the tiny boreal chorus frogs, which fill the night with their trilling songs in late April. Active at night around marshes and ponds, chorus frogs are identified by long dark stripes running down their brownish bodies.

Fish

According to some people, parks and mountains are a place where you go to camp and fish. Since high mountain lakes have no native fish, wildlife agencies, parks and concerned citizens have for decades added countless millions of fish to lakes in order to 'improve' the visitors' experience. For instance, at least 119 lakes in Banff have been stocked with non-native fish, even though a mere 26 lakes contained fish historically. As a consequence, native fish populations and aquatic ecosystems (in these lower lakes) have suffered, and several species of non-native fish are now doing quite well. As an official policy, fish stocking in these parks was phased out only recently – in 1971 in Glacier and 1988 in Banff and Jasper.

Native fish include the threatened bull trout, whose dwindling populations are protected by law. Once the most widespread native fish in the Canadian Rockies, bull trout are now seen reliably at only a few sites. Your best bet is Peter Lougheed Provincial Park, south of Canmore, where they migrate up creeks out of Lower Kananaskis Lake from late August to mid-October. They are distinguished from other trout by their lack of black lines or spots, so fishermen use the motto 'no black, put it back' as a reminder to return bull trout to the water if one is accidentally caught.

Representative of the nine non-native fish that have become common, brook trout are now found in most low-elevation streams and lakes. Prized for fishing, brook trout can be recognized by their olive-green color, reddish belly and yellow squiggly lines along their back.

Aquatic habitats in the Canadian Rockies support many more kinds of fish than just trout – 40 species in all. Healthy populations of mountain whitefish make this one of the more readily seen native species. These bottom-feeders prey on small invertebrates in the major watercourses and lakes. Uniformly gray and growing to 25.4cm (10 inches), whitefish are best seen while spawning in mid-October at Banff's Fenland picnic site.

'Come in the right season and you'd be hard pressed to avoid buzzing hordes of mosquitoes'

Insects

Except for mosquitoes and a handful of conspicuous butterflies, most of the Canadian Rockies' 20,000 or so insect species go unnoticed. Very little is known about the distribution and life history of most species, even though these organisms are extremely sensitive to environmental change and serve as key indicators of ecosystem health.

Come in the right season, however, and you'd be hard pressed to avoid buzzing hordes of mosquitoes. Fortunately, the mosquito season in most areas peaks for only a few weeks, in late June to early July. This season is shifted into July and August at higher elevations, but around marshy areas it can persist all summer. Mosquitoes are specialized flies that use long, piercing mouth parts to feed on plant juices. After mating, males die, while females seek a meal of blood to get enough proteins to produce their eggs. Adult mosquitoes are an extremely important food for many birds and bats (which eat hundreds per hour), and countless aquatic animals live on mosquito larvae in ponds and marshes. Mosquitoes transmit a variety of diseases, so it's best to avoid being bitten whenever possible.

Although butterflies are a showy and widespread feature of nearly every habitat, nothing compares to the spectacle of hilltopping. Many flying insects, including butterflies, congregate on sunny peaks to court and mate, and on a good day you may witness thousands of fervent insects.

Plants

The Canadian Rockies are home to over 1000 species of plants, comprising a fairly diverse mix for such a relatively cold, northern climate. One of the main reasons for this mix is that the Continental Divide not only creates a strong elevational gradient but also splits the region into west-side and east-side habitats. With a wet, ocean-influenced climate on the west side and a dry, interior climate on the east side, this geographic split is a very significant division. Adding to the region's botanical diversity are alpine plants from the arctic, grassland plants of the eastern prairies and forest plants from the Pacific Northwest.

Because the parks cover such a span of habitats and elevations, it's possible to find flowers from March until the end of August, and taking time out to smell the flowers will definitely enrich your park visit.

TREES

Except for areas of rock, ice or water, landscapes of the Canadian Rockies are mostly covered with coniferous forest. Only a handful of species are present, and these are easy to identify – learning to recognize these species is a lot of fun, plus it makes it easier to understand the layout of life zones and to predict where you might find specific animals.

Montane and subalpine forests are dominated by two spruces, white spruce and Engelmann spruce. Both have sharp-tipped needles that prick your hand if you grasp a branch. White spruce occurs mainly on valley bottoms, and Engelmann spruce takes over on higher slopes, but the two frequently overlap and hybridize. Cones on white spruces have smooth, rounded tips on their scales, but Engelmann spruces have narrow, jagged tips on theirs. Many animals feed on spruce seeds or rely on spruce forests for their livelihood in some way.

Sharing the higher slopes with the Engelmann spruce is the abundant subalpine fir, the namesake tree of the subalpine zone in the Canadian Rockies. Recognized by their flattened, blunt-tipped needles, subalpine firs have characteristically narrow, conical profiles. This shape allows the trees to shed heavy winter snows so their branches don't break off under the weight.

At the uppermost edges of the subalpine forest, mainly growing by themselves on high, windswept slopes, are whitebark pines. Intense wind and cold at these elevations can cause these trees to grow in low, stunted mats. Their squat, egg-shaped cones produce highly nutritious seeds favored by Clark's nutcrackers and grizzly bears, but an introduced disease is threatening this important tree and the animals that depend on it.

One of the oddest trees of the Canadian Rockies is the subalpine larch, a rare tree found most easily in Larch Valley, just south of Lake Louise. Although it's a conifer, this remarkable tree has needles that turn golden in September then drop off for the winter in October. This makes places like Larch Valley a photographers' paradise during the peak display.

After fires or other disturbances, lodgepole pines quickly spring up and form dense 'doghair' thickets. In some areas, lodgepoles cover many square kilometers so thickly that the forests are nearly impossible to walk through. These conditions eventually promote hot fires that create seedbeds for more lodgepoles; in fact, lodgepole cones are sealed in resin that only melts and releases seeds after a fire.

Synonymous with the expansive evergreen forests of Alberta and British Columbia, the Douglas fir tree is named after Scottish botanist David Douglas (1799–1834), who first visited Jasper in 1827, when he wrongly declared Mt Brown and Mt Hooker to be the highest peaks in North America.

ENVIRONMENT

A beautiful tree of dry, open areas, the quaking aspen has radiant, silver-white bark and rounded leaves that quiver in mountain breezes. Aspen foliage turns a striking orange-gold for just a few weeks in fall (call parks before visiting, because each year the display peaks on different dates). Aspens consist of genetically identical trunks arising from a single root system that may grow to be more than 40.5 hectares (100 acres) in size and include up to 47,000 stems. By sprouting repeatedly from this root system, aspens have what has been called 'theoretical immortality,' and some aspens are thought to be over a million years old.

SHRUBS

The term 'shrub' is a somewhat arbitrary label for small woody plants with multiple stems, but it can be hard to decide whether a plant is a shrub, since some trees can have many stems as well. These small woody plants may grow as low alpine mats, dense thickets or single plants on slopes or meadows.

Shrubby relatives of their tree cousins are common juniper and creeping juniper. Very common in montane and subalpine zones, both have the same bluish berry-like cones found on all junipers (originally used to flavor gin). Common junipers grow up to 90cm (3ft) high and have stout, prickly needles, and creeping juniper forms a prostrate trailing mat with scaly leaves. Squirrels and grouse snack on the bitter berries.

With blue berries that are delicious and sweet instead of bitter, blueberries provide an immensely popular treat for humans and bears alike. Half a dozen species occur in the Canadian Rockies, with common names like huckleberry, grouseberry, bilberry and cranberry. Often these plants grow in patches large enough that berries for a batch of pancakes or muffins can be harvested within minutes.

Closely related and similar in appearance to blueberry plants is the kinnikinnik, also known as bearberry. This ground-hugging shrub has thick glossy leaves and reddish woody stems. Its leaves were once mixed with tobacco to make a smoking mixture, and the berries have been a staple food for many First Nations peoples.

It's something of a surprise to encounter wild roses growing deep in these woods, but at least five types grow here. All look like slender, somewhat scraggly versions of what you'd see in a garden, but otherwise, there's no mistaking them. Their fruits are pear-shaped and turn red-orange during fall; popularly known as rose hips, these fruits are rich in vitamins A, B, C and E and are used to make tasty jams or teas.

WILDFLOWERS

The flowering season in the Canadian Rockies begins as soon as the snows start to melt. Though delicate in structure, the early rising glacier lily pushes up so eagerly that the stems often unfurl right through the snow crust. Abundant in montane and subalpine forests or meadows, each lily produces several yellow flowers, with six upward-curled petals. Wherever lilies occur in great numbers, grizzlies paw eagerly through the soil in search of the edible bulbs.

Within days of snowmelt, pretty purple pasqueflowers (aka prairie crocuses) cover montane slopes. Growing close to the ground on short, fuzzy stems, these brilliant flowers stand out because of their yellow centers. Later in the summer, 'shaggy mane' seed heads replace the flowers. All parts of this plant are poisonous and may raise blisters if handled.

One of the most photographed flowers of Glacier National Park is the striking beargrass. From tufts of grass-like leaves, the plant sends up

'The flowering season in the Canadian Rockies begins as soon as the snows start to melt'

1.5m-high (5ft) stalks of white, star-shaped flowers that may fill entire subalpine meadows. Grizzlies favor the tender spring leaves, hence the plant's common name.

Hike almost anywhere in these mountains and you're bound to encounter the easy-to-recognize bluebell, with its large, bell-like flowers held up on a long, skinny stem. This plant's other common name, harebell, comes from Scotland, but its meaning is not certain. After flowering, seeds are produced in capsules that close in wet weather then open in dry winds to scatter the seeds far and wide.

Many visitors know the familiar Indian paintbrush for its tightly packed red flowers, but fewer know that the plant is a semiparasite that taps into neighbors' roots for nourishment. By stealing some energy from other plants, paintbrushes are able to grow luxuriantly in desolate places like roadsides or dry meadows, where they are often the most conspicuous wildflower. Of the dozen species in the Canadian Rockies, a great number attract hummingbirds, making paintbrush patches one of the best sites for finding the beautiful birds.

Another very common roadside flower, gaillardia (aka brown-eyed Susan) looks like it belongs in a garden somewhere and is in fact a source of some favorite garden varieties. Like small, brown-centered sunflowers, these plants present a bright sunny face that makes them a welcome addition to the landscape in July and August. A closer look reveals a characteristic feature; each petal ends in three deep lobes that give the flower a frilly edged look.

The big, showy cow parsnip, with its huge, celery-like stalks and umbrella-shaped flower clusters, is a familiar sight along streams and in moist aspen groves throughout the region. This plant can grow over 1.8m (6ft) high, and walking among them can make you feel small. The stems are eaten by many animals and favored by grizzlies, so caution is urged when approaching a large cow parsnip patch. Humans are advised against eating these plants because of their similarity to several deadly species.

More localized in its distribution, but sometimes confused with cow parsnip because it has the same large leaves, is the aptly named devil's club. This stout, 2.7m-high (9ft) plant practically bristles with armor. Completely covered in long, poisonous spikes (even the leaves are ribbed with rows of spines) that break off in the skin when contacted and cause infections, this plant further announces itself with its strong odor and large clusters of brilliant red berries. Despite these features, devil's club has a rich and important history of medicinal use among First Nations tribes of the area.

LICHENS, FUNGI & MOSSES

Out of several groups of lesser-known and mostly unappreciated species (mosses, fungi, liverworts etc), lichens are worthy of pause.

Obvious in subalpine conifer forests are the neon-yellow strands of wolf lichen growing on tree trunks everywhere. Look closely and notice how the lichens stop abruptly at a line that's several feet off the ground. This is the height of the winter snowpack. This is the only species of lichen that's known to be poisonous, and it was formerly mixed into bait set out to poison wolves, hence its name.

Of the many species that grow on rocks, none are as common or easy to identify as the map lichens. This familiar group of species covers rocks with yellow-green crusts that have black mottling, creating a map-like look in older specimens. These lichens live a very long time (at least 10,000 years) and grow at a rate that's measured in fractions of a millimeter per

ENVIRONMENT

'Hike almost anywhere in these mountains and you're bound to encounter the easy-to-recognize' bluebell' century. Scientists have been able to measure lichen colonies and use this data to calculate the advance and retreat of Ice Age glaciers, a technique that's described on the Path of the Glacier interpretive trail at Mt Edith Cavell (p169).

ENVIRONMENTAL ISSUES

Despite their remoteness and relatively late colonization, the Rocky Mountain parks have long been pioneers in the field of wilderness protection. Banff was Canada's first – and the world's third – national park when it was inaugurated in 1885, while Jasper, Waterton and Glacier (all given protective status by 1910) were three more early beneficiaries of the nascent North American conservation movement. But, with conflicting commercial interests and an inordinate influence wielded by the all-powerful cross-continental railway companies, early park rules were sketchy and haphazard. Waterton once boasted an oil well, and Jasper flirted briefly with coal mining, while Banff developed – and still retains – a large and relatively prosperous town site.

But as the public perception of wilderness areas changed, so did the parks. In 1911 the Canadian government formed the Dominion Parks Branch (an early incarnation of Parks Canada) as the world's first national park coordinating body, and in 1930 the National Parks Act laid down the first firm set of ground rules for conservation and preservation. While the parks today still promote recreation and education as an inte-

FIRE MANAGEMENT

Whether viewed on TV news reports or witnessed first hand by people in the front line, the sight of wildfires raging uncontrollably through vast tracts of pristine North American wilderness is both frightening and disturbing. But the reality of this seemingly destructive process is a little more complicated.

Unhindered by man-made forces, wildfires are perfectly natural events that have occurred regularly in Rocky Mountain forests for thousands of years. From an ecological standpoint, they are highly beneficial, opening up new habitats, prompting the growth of fresh seedlings and replenishing soil nutrients with decomposed organic matter that is rich in nitrogen. Indeed, some species such as lodgepole and jack pines don't just benefit from periodic fires, they are entirely dependent on them to survive and germinate.

The problem – as always – comes with human interference. From the early 1900s to the late 1960s conventional wisdom in North American national parks dictated that all forest fires were suppressed no matter what their cause, strength or damage potential. Such meddling with the ecosystem quickly led to an unnatural build-up of combustible material on forest floors, meaning that when a natural fire did ignite it generally burned hotter, wilder and for far longer than was preferable. Examples of such devastating blazes are particularly vivid in Glacier National Park where the scars of the 2003 Robert Fire, which destroyed 15,800 hectares (39,000 acres) of forest on the north shore of Lake McDonald, are still clearly visible from the Going-to-the-Sun Rd.

In recent years park authorities, recognizing the environmental benefits of sensible fire management, have carefully monitored annual blazes and let them run their natural course. In some cases trained firefighters have even started small, carefully monitored fires in order to flush out bushy shrubs and accumulated deadwood. Fires that are either started by humans and/or threaten human life and property are still actively suppressed.

Glacier National Park, where the influence of natural fire has colored almost every aspect of the park's embattled ecosystem, provides an interesting outdoor laboratory for travelers keen to observe the landscape-altering effects that fires have wrought. A visit to the North Fork Valley, scene of the 1988 Red Bench Fire, the 2001 Moose Fire and the 2003 Robert Fire will uncover a kaleidoscope of thriving forest, all in varying stages of recuperation.

gral part of the overall wilderness experience, the concept of ecological integrity has now taken center stage.

Tourism and the ongoing impact of millions of visitors trampling through important wildlife corridors is still one of the parks' most ticklish issues in modern times and nowhere is this problem more apparent than in Banff. Boasting an incorporated town with a permanent population of over 8000 people, along with main roads, a ski resort and nearly five million annual visitors, Banff's environmental credentials have long been a subject for hot debate. Comparisons with Glacier (governed by the US parks system) further south are particularly telling. Long lauded as one of the continent's most pristine parks, Banff's smaller American cousin is a veritable wilderness with no population center, no fast-food franchises and no water-sapping golf courses. Furthermore, Glacier bans bikes from all park trails, runs an environmentally friendly free shuttle service to minimize car pollution, and has barred its historic lodges from installing supposed modern 'luxuries' such as TVs and room phones. Not surprisingly, the park's unique ecosystem is frequently acclaimed for its rich biodiversity and its grizzly bear population is said to be one of the healthiest in North America.

But it's not all weighty cross-border comparisons. In 1996, a two-year investigation by the Banff–Bow Valley study group provided a crucial turning point in Banff's modern evolution. Putting forward 500 urgent recommendations – a list that included everything from population capping to quotas on hiking trails – the study prompted the implementation of a 15-year development plan designed to redress the park's ecological balance and save its priceless wilderness from almost-certain long-term damage. More than 10 years on and progress has certainly been made, though recent concerns about climate change have given the issue fresh urgency. The future is still anyone's guess.

SUSTAINABILITY

The behavior of individual visitors in the parks can play a vital part in ensuring their long-term health and sustainability. Here are a few basic guidelines:

- Don't litter – use bear-proof containers and recycling bins, and pack out everything you pack in.
- Stay on the trail – wandering 'off-piste' or bushwhacking your own path damages flora and causes erosion.
- Don't feed the animals – interfering with the ecosystem can have dire consequences for both animals and humans.
- Use public transport whenever possible – Glacier has a free, environmentally friendly shuttle bus designed to dissuade drivers from using the increasingly traffic-choked Going-to-the-Sun Rd, while the Canadian parks have a number of less comprehensive paying options.
- Support local volunteer organizations – many people work tirelessly to protect fragile park wildernesses from degradation and neglect, and you can join them; see p52.
- Refrain from removing any objects, however small, from the wilderness – if each one of the parks' five million visitors picked a single flower and removed a solitary stone, the cumulative effect for the fragile ecosystem could be disastrous.
- Use resources responsibly: if you're staying in a hotel take shorter showers; if you're driving around, consider car-pooling; if you're eating out, go local.
- Gain knowledge and then share it – talk to rangers, read the local literature and swap ideas with other hikers on the trail.

ENVIRONMENT

'Banff's environmental credentials have long been a subject for hot debate'

History

For a comprehensive history of the Rocky Mountain parks go to the website of Parks Canada (www.pc.gc.ca) or the US National Park Service (www.nps.gov).

Due to the absence of any written testimony, the Rockies' early historical jigsaw is full of missing pieces. The region's oldest remains – uncovered at Vermilion Lakes near Banff in the 1980s – date back nearly 11,000 years and are thought to belong to descendents of primitive Stone Age people who ventured over a frozen land bridge across the Bering Strait during the last ice age. By the arrival of the first Europeans in the mid-18th century, First Nations people – such as the Blackfeet, Kootenay, Cree, Peigan and Stoney – were living in scattered nomadic tribes who subsisted by stalking bison, bighorn sheep and elk through the region's lush river valleys.

By the late 18th century, European exploration had edged unstoppably west, stoked by the thriving fur trade and sponsored by powerful commercial corporations such as the Hudson Bay Company and its bitter rival, the Northwest Company. In a bid to establish new trading routes nearer the Pacific, Scotsman Alexander Mackenzie became the first European to cross the Rockies in 1793, when he navigated along the course of the Peace River to the headwaters of the Fraser and, with the help of Aboriginals, bushwhacked his way through to Bella Coola in British Columbia. Other explorers soon followed, most notably Lewis and Clark, who passed within 80km (50 miles) of Marias Pass near Glacier in 1805–06.

BANFF NATIONAL PARK

Long a home to Peigan, Stoney and Kootenay Aboriginals, the area now occupied by Banff National Park was first explored by Europeans in the early 1800s. One early prospector was Northwest Company surveyor David Thompson (p79), who battled his way across Howse Pass to the Columbia River in 1807. Over the ensuing half-century many other visitors followed, including stalwart Hudson Bay Company governor George Simpson, whose well-documented travels in the 1840s sparked another surge of rampant exploration. In 1857 the Royal Geographic Society commissioned the Palliser Expedition to determine settlement potential and the possibility for future railway routes in western Canada. Geologist James Hector led the party through the Banff area, where they traversed six mountain passes, including Howse Pass and Kicking Horse Pass.

The area's future was effectively sealed in 1875 when Kicking Horse Pass, just west of Banff, was chosen, over the more northerly Yellowhead Pass (in present-day Jasper), as the route for the nascent Canadian Pacific

TIMELINE Banff National Park

10,000 BC	1750	1800s	1882	1885
First Nations tribes begin to settle and hunt throughout the Rockies	European explorers and traders arrive in the area	Europeans begin exploring the area in search of a railway pass to the west coast	William McCardell and Frank McCabe discover the Cave and Basin hot springs	The Trans-Canada Railway is completed, and a federal reserve is established around Cave and Basin hot springs

Railway (CPR). It was during the building of this railway in 1882 that two laborers (William McCardell and Frank McCabe) stumbled upon the Cave and Basin hot springs at the base of Sulphur Mountain and the establishment of Banff National Park was set in motion.

The Birth of a Park

While Stoney Aboriginals had known about the springs and their supposed healing powers for centuries, it took the entrepreneurship of McCardell and McCabe to bring the waters to national attention. But, halted before they were even out of the starting blocks, the workers' tentative proposal to develop the springs as a lucrative tourist destination was ruthlessly quashed by a Canadian government that had already, surreptitiously, made similar plans of its own.

In 1885, as the last spike was driven into the transcontinental railway at Craigellachie in British Columbia, a 26-sq-km (10-sq-mile) federal reserve was established around Banff Springs by the Conservative government of John A MacDonald. Sensing a tourist bonanza, the fledgling Canadian Pacific Railway (CPR) was quick to jump on the bandwagon. 'If we can't export the scenery, we'll import the tourists,' announced CPR president William Van Horne portentously in 1886. His idea was to build a luxurious chain of grand hotels across the railway network that would lure in wealthy tourists and repay the railway's outstanding loans. The plan clearly worked. Opened in 1888 as the grandest and most expansive hotel in the chain, the chateau-style Banff Springs Hotel was a runaway success and quickly established itself as an icon of Canadian architecture.

By 1888, over 5000 tourists had been ferried into the embryonic park to be rejuvenated in the magic spring water, and Banff town boasted 300 permanent residents, as well as churches, hotels, saloons and shops. The national park, which had been Canada's first – and the world's third – when it was created in 1885, was expanded in 1892 to include the area surrounding Lake Louise and, before long, Banff boasted another of Van Horne's fairy-tale hotels, the beguiling Chateau Lake Louise.

Welcoming the Masses

A coach road was opened to Banff in 1911, and the following year public traffic was allowed into the park. Suddenly the wilderness was accessible to all kinds of visitors, rather than just wealthy Victorians, and the opportunities for outdoor recreation multiplied. Campsites were set up on Tunnel Mountain and at Two Jacks Lake, and affordable lodging began to appear in the Bow Valley. Pursuits diversified; skiing, the arts and short-

1888	1892	1911	1914–18	1930
Banff Springs Hotel opens	The reserve is enlarged to include Lake Louise as mountaineers begin scaling the area's peaks	A road from the east is opened to Banff, increasing the number of visitors	Prisoners of war are detained in camps within the park; their labor is used to improve the park's infrastructure	The National Parks Act is passed, establishing Banff's present-day boundaries

In 1885 Banff became the world's third national park, after Yellowstone in the US, inaugurated in 1872, and Royal National Park in Australia, founded in 1879.

lived sports like ice boating all drew participants and spectators. A road was built to Norquay ski slopes, and Lake Louise soon began to welcome skiers as well. The year 1917 saw the initiation of the Banff Winter Carnival, a week of everything from dances to dogsled races.

Throughout WWI, immigrants from enemy countries were detained in camps below Castle Mountain and near Cave and Basin hot springs. Forced to labor, they established much of the infrastructure throughout the park, including making horse trails car-friendly. In the 1930s similar work was taken up by relief workers during the Depression, when the Icefields Parkway was first initiated. Relief workers also built gardens in Banff town and an airfield for private planes.

The National Parks Act, passed in 1930, established the boundaries of the park much as they are today, along with many of the conservation laws that are still in place. While the number of tourists to the park diminished during WWII, Banff became a popular honeymoon destination in the 1940s and 1950s, attracting returning war veterans and their brides. By 1962, when the Trans-Canada Hwy officially opened, the park had begun to market itself as an international holiday destination.

Balancing Act

Banff gained further global recognition as a summer and winter resort with the 1988 Winter Olympics in nearby Calgary. Although events were actually held at Nakiska ski resort in Kananaskis Country and the Nordic Centre in neighboring Canmore, the Olympics drew tourists and publicity to the park. Banff town's economy boomed, further strengthening the tourism infrastructure. In 1990, after more than a century of being governed federally, Banff town was granted the right to become a self-governing community. That year, the CPR train service, which had played such an important role in the town's late-19th-century take-off, was discontinued, as trains carried on through Banff town to the west coast.

These days, an estimated five million people pass through Banff annually. Due to the environmental pressure caused by such large numbers, many feel that the town has been stretched to its limits and the wilderness is being compromised. In 1996 the Banff–Bow Valley study compiled a 75-page document, *At the Crossroads*, relating to these and other issues. Stoking the fears of many, the report stressed that if Banff's development plans and burgeoning visitor numbers were allowed to continue unchecked, the park's ecological integrity would be caused irrevocable harm.

But, while the penny may have dropped for some, the debate still rages. In 1997 the government backed the Banff National Park Management Plan, a

1940	1984	1990	1996	2002
Icefields Parkway opens	Banff, along with Jasper, Yoho and Kootenay, is declared a Unesco World Heritage Site	Banff town becomes self-governing, and the Canadian Pacific Railway service is discontinued	The Banff National Park Management Plan is implemented	Banff National Park receives 4.7 million annual visitors

15-year strategy to redirect the park toward a more sustainable future. With five years left to run, the plan's final results are bound to serve as an important litmus test, not just for Banff, but for national parks everywhere.

JASPER NATIONAL PARK

First Nations peoples traditionally used the land that is now Jasper National Park as seasonal hunting and gathering grounds. It wasn't until the 1800s, when fur traders began to push west across the continent, dislocating various indigenous groups, that some First Nations tribes began utilizing the Athabasca Valley as a more permanent base.

Soon after, a dispute with Peigan people, over access to Howse Pass near present-day Banff, led British-Canadian explorer David Thompson (p79) to look for a new route across the Rockies to link up with lucrative trading centers on the west coast. Veering north during the winter of 1810 he trudged with his party through deep snow to the top of Athabasca Pass, crossing the Continental Divide in January 1811.

Before departing for Athabasca Pass, Thompson left fellow explorer William Henry in the Athabasca Valley, where he established Henry House, the region's first staging post, situated close to Old Fort Point, near present-day Jasper town. In 1813 the Northwest Company established a more permanent post, 40km (25 miles) to the east, at Jasper House on Brulé Lake, which remained in operation until 1884.

In an effort to build good trade relations, the traders were encouraged to take Aboriginal wives. In doing so, a distinct Métis (French for 'mixed blood') culture was formed, and the unique language of Michif arose. Descendents of the Métis continued to farm in the Athabasca Valley well into the 20th century, greatly influencing the area's development. In 1910 they were given compensation payments and forced to leave their land, which by then had become a federal reserve.

Adventurers & Mountaineers

In the early 1860s, around 200 pioneers set out from Ontario with their sights on the gold rush in British Columbia. The Overlanders, as they would come to be known, passed through Jasper and struggled over Yellowhead Pass, the park's present-day boundary with Mt Robson Provincial Park. The planned two-month journey turned into six months of near starvation. Poorly equipped and inexperienced, a number of men died en route, either swept away by turbulent rivers or from hypothermia. The only woman to accompany the group managed to survive, giving birth upon reaching Kamloops.

Jasper National Park

10,000 BC	1750	1793	1800s	1811
First Nations tribes begin to settle and hunt throughout the Rockies	European explorers and traders arrive in the area	Alexander Mackenzie becomes the first European to cross the Rocky Mountains via the Peace and Fraser River systems	Dislocated First Nations tribes begin to settle in their hunting grounds along the Athabasca Valley	David Thompson is the first European to cross the Athabasca Pass and establishes a post near present-day Jasper town

HISTORY

With the fur trade in decline and a new national park in Banff prospering to the south, mountaineers and adventurers began heading into Jasper's rugged wilderness in search of unnamed peaks and fabled glacial lakes. In 1906 Irish-born mountaineer and surveyor AO Wheeler founded the Alpine Club of Canada and began organizing periodic assaults on Mt Robson. Three years later he was instrumental in helping two colorful local characters, Reverend Kinney and Donald 'Curly' Philips, in their brave but ultimately abortive attempt on the summit. The mountain was eventually conquered by Austrian Conrad Kain in 1913.

Another unlikely park pioneer – and perhaps the area's first real tourist – was Mary Schäffer, a spirited Philadelphia widow who ventured to Jasper in the early 20th century to – in her own words – 'turn the unthumbed pages of an unread book.' Her quest was an elusive mountain lake known to the Stoney Indians as Chaba Imne. Guided by a map sketched from memory by Stoney Aboriginal Sampson Beaver 14 years earlier, she became the first non-Aboriginal to set eyes on Maligne Lake in July 1908.

> It would be hard to find scenery beautiful enough to provide a backdrop for Hollywood screen legend Marilyn Monroe, but both Banff and Jasper did a good job when they were chosen as film locations for her 1954 classic *River of No Return*.

The Emergence of a Park

Jasper's founding, rather like Banff's, is closely entwined with the development of the railway. Passed over in the 1880s by the Canadian Pacific Railway in favor of Kicking Horse Pass in Banff, Jasper got its revenge in 1903 when Wilfred Laurier's government gave the go-ahead for the Grand Trunk Pacific Company to build a line from the west coast through Yellowhead Pass. All too aware of how the railway had significantly boosted the fortunes of Banff, the Ministry of the Interior opportunistically created Jasper Forest Park in 1907, the Rocky Mountains' fifth – and Canada's sixth – national park.

Built between 1910 and 1913, construction of the railway reached the tiny settlement of Fitzhugh at mile marker 113 in 1911, bringing an immediate influx of adventurers, mountaineers and railway workers. Almost overnight the burgeoning town jumped from a population of 125 to around 800 and was promptly renamed Jasper after Jasper Hawse, a fur trading manager who had been based at the Jasper House trading post in the 1820s.

Before the passage of the National Parks Act in 1930, the park faced far fewer limitations on its industrial and commercial development. Consequently, in the 1910s, local outfitters and guides, eyeing a potential business bonanza, sprang up all over the Athabasca Valley intent on bringing the wilderness to the masses. Plans for an enlarged town were laid out, a school was built and clearing began for roads and climbing

1850s	1907	1908	1910–21	1911
Adventurers and mountaineers explore the region	Jasper Forest Park is established	Mary Schäffer discovers Maligne Lake	Jasper supports a small but short-lived coal mining operation at Pocahontas, which grows to accommodate 2000 miners	Grand Trunk Pacific's railway reaches the shantytown of Fitzhugh, which is renamed Jasper two years later

DAVID THOMPSON: STARGAZER

The history of Jasper National Park will always be synonymous with David Thompson, an indefatigable British-born explorer who was nicknamed the 'Stargazer' by the First Nations people but who is better remembered as the 'greatest mapmaker who ever lived' by those who had the good fortune to follow in his footsteps.

Born in London in 1770 to Welsh parents, Thompson migrated permanently to Canada in 1784, and began working for the Hudson Bay Company in Churchill, Manitoba, as an office clerk (at the age of 14). Showing an aptitude for surveying and astronomy, the young Thompson quickly developed sufficient navigational skills to become a fur trader and in 1792 he undertook his first official mapping expedition to the lake-speckled forests that litter present-day Saskatchewan and Alberta.

Nurturing an insatiable thirst for exploration and adventure, Thompson defected to the rival Northwest Company in 1797 and was immediately mandated with the task of surveying the hotly disputed fur-trading posts that studded the new US–Canadian border. In 1806, in response to the American-sponsored Lewis and Clark expedition, Thompson was sent west in order to establish new Northwest Company posts closer to the Pacific. His mission was given fresh urgency four years later when New York trader John Astor sailed a ship around Cape Horn in a bid to set up a rival American trading post at the mouth of the Columbia River in present-day Oregon. Racing to beat him via a precipitous overland route, Thompson was initially blocked by hostile Peigan people at Howse Pass in the Rocky Mountains. Undaunted, he audaciously changed tack, pushing north through uncharted territory into the area now occupied by Jasper National Park.

In January 1811 Thompson was led, exhausted but defiant, to the top of Jasper's snow-covered Athabasca Pass by Aboriginal Thomas the Iroquois. Surveying his beleaguered party during the historic crossing, he wrote, 'my men were the most hardy that could be picked out of a hundred brave hardy men, but the sense of desolation before us was dreadful, and I knew it.' Against all odds, Thompson made it across the Rocky Mountains and down the Columbia River to the sea, arriving just two weeks after Astor. In the process he pioneered what would become one of the most important east–west transportation links in the Canadian fur trade.

Thompson, who had married a half-white, half-Aboriginal Cree woman in 1799, went on to father 13 children before retiring to live in relative obscurity in Montreal. He died almost penniless at the age of 87 after a 58-year marriage. During his lifetime Thompson meticulously mapped nearly four million sq km of North American wilderness. His maps were deemed so accurate that they were still being used over 150 years later.

trails. The first grocery store opened in 1914, meaning that residents no longer had to wait for a month's supply by train from Edmonton. The following year, 10 crudely constructed tents were set up for visitors on the shores of Lac Beauvert; an encampment that would soon metamorphose into the Jasper Park Lodge.

1928	1930	1940	1950s	1984
The road to Edmonton opens	The National Parks Act is passed, establishing Jasper's present-day boundaries	Icefields Parkway opens	Jasper is well established as a tourist destination	Jasper, along with Banff, Yoho and Kootenay, is declared a Unesco World Heritage Site

In 1910 a coal mine was established at Pocahontas, near the eastern boundary of the park. A small mining town grew up in the vicinity, but was short-lived. The coal that was mined from the area burned at a high heat and was virtually smokeless, making it useful for warships during WWI. But, with the war over by 1918, and competition heating up with larger operations in the industrial east, the mine was shut down and the town dismantled by 1921.

The haunting opening shot of a car ascending a long, narrow, winding road in Stanley Kubrick's seminal horror movie *The Shining* was filmed on the Going-to-the-Sun Rd in Glacier National Park in 1980.

Sharing the Limelight

The road from Jasper to Edmonton was opened in 1928 and by the onset of WWII, legions of Depression-era workers had completed the legendary Icefields Parkway linking Jasper to Lake Louise. In 1930 the National Parks Act was passed, fully protecting Jasper as the largest park in the nation and tourists began visiting in their droves; famous guests included King George VI, Marilyn Monroe and Bing Crosby. By 1948 the Athabasca Glacier had become a major sight, and the Banff-based Brewster brothers manufactured a ski-equipped Model A Ford truck to cart tourists out over the ice.

Since the 1950s, Jasper's tourism infrastructure has been gradually strengthened. Major highways into the park have been paved and roads to sights like Maligne Lake and Miette Hot Springs have been cleared or upgraded. In 1961 the Marmot Basin ski area got its first rope tow while, three years later, the Jasper Tramway took its first trip to the top of Whistlers Mountain.

As tourism to the park has steadily increased – pushing the two million mark in 2005 – Jasper town has had to battle with questions of sustainability and conservation. With the boundaries of the town pretty much set since the 1980s, the focus has instead shifted toward a 'quality visitor experience' and the preservation of the park for future generations.

GLACIER NATIONAL PARK

The ancestors of Montana's present-day Native Americans have inhabited the Glacier region for over 10,000 years. At the time of the first European contact, two main indigenous groups occupied the Rocky Mountains region. The prairies in the east were controlled by the Blackfeet, a fiercely independent warrior tribe whose territory straddled the border with Canada, while the valleys in the west were the hunting grounds of the Salish and Kootenay.

In the mid-18th century, when trappers and explorers began to arrive out west, the Blackfeet controlled most of the northern plains and adjacent mountain passes. Although they resisted the European invaders at

Glacier National Park

10,000 BC	1750	1806	1885	1891
Native Americans begin to settle and hunt throughout the Rockies	European explorers and traders arrive in the area	The Lewis and Clark expedition passes to within 80km (50 miles) of the Glacier area, but misses Marias Pass	Park pioneer George Bird Grinnell visits the area and discovers the Grinnell Glacier in the Many Glacier Valley	James J Hill's Great Northern Railroad arrives in the region, crossing Marias Pass and establishing stations in East and West Glacier

first, a catastrophic smallpox epidemic in 1837 dealt them a deadly blow, wiping out 6000 of their 30,000 population. Linked spiritually to the land, the Blackfeet knew Glacier as the 'Backbone of the World' and within the area of the park, many sites – such as oddly shaped Chief Mountain – were considered sacred to the people.

A romantic wanderer, James Willard Shultz spent many years living among the Blackfeet people, whom he considered his relatives and closest friends. As a result, he became one of the first European American men to lay eyes on much of Glacier's interior. In the 1880s he introduced the area to Dr George Bird Grinnell, a leading conservationist and editor of the influential *Forest & Stream* magazine. So overawed was Grinnell by the sight of Glacier's mountains, rivers and lakes that he dubbed the area the 'Crown of the Continent' and lobbied Congress for 10 years until, in 1910, President Taft signed the bill that created Glacier National Park.

Visitors began coming regularly to the park around 1912, when James J Hill of the Great Northern Railroad instigated an intense building program to promote his newly inaugurated line. Railway employees built grand hotels and a network of tent camps and mountain chalets, each a day's horseback ride from the next. Visitors would come for several weeks at a time, touring by horse or foot, and stay in these elegant but rustic accommodations.

But the halcyon days of trains and horse travel weren't to last. In response to the growing popularity of motorized transportation, federal funds were appropriated in 1921 to connect the east and west sides of Glacier National Park by a new road. Over a decade in the making, the legendary Going-to-the-Sun Rd was finally opened in 1932, crossing the Continental Divide at 2025m (6646ft) Logan Pass and opening up the park to millions.

That same year, thanks to efforts from Rotary International members in Alberta and Montana, Glacier joined with Waterton Lakes in the world's first International Peace Park, a lasting symbol of peace and friendship between the USA and Canada.

WWII forced the closure of almost all hotel services in the park, and many of Glacier's rustic chalets fell into disrepair and had to be demolished. Fortunately, nine of the original 13 'parkitecture' structures survived and – complemented by two wood-paneled motor inns that were added in the 1940s – they form the basis of the park's accommodations today.

Over the years, the 80km (50-mile) Going-to-the-Sun Rd has been the primary travel artery in the national park and, for many, its scenic highlight. Still sporting its original stone guardrail and embellished with myriad tunnels, bridges and arches, the road has been designated

HISTORY

1896	1900	1910	1912	1932
The Blackfeet reluctantly accept the US government's offer to purchase what is now known as Glacier National Park, for US$1.5 million	After lobbying by the Great Northern Railway, the US Congress declares the Glacier area a forest preserve	US President Taft signs a bill creating Glacier National Park	Great Northern Railroad begins building grand hotels and chalets within Glacier National Park (and later, Waterton Lakes) to promote its railway line	The scenic Going-to-the-Sun Rd is completed, connecting the east and west sides of the park

Waterton Lakes was originally known as the Kootenay Lakes Forest Reserve, Banff was once called Rocky Mountains Park, and Jasper formerly went under the name of Jasper Forest Park.

a national historic landmark and a historic civil engineering landmark. In the 1930s a fleet of bright red 'jammer' buses was introduced onto the road to enable tourists to gain easy access to the park's jaw-dropping scenery; the same buses still operate today, though they were refitted in 2001 and now run on propane.

To counter the demands of increased traffic, park officials introduced a free shuttle-bus service in 2007, to help ease congestion on the Going-to-the-Sun Rd. During its first season, the service was successful in persuading a significant percentage of Glacier's drivers to leave their cars at freshly built transit centers, a move that has helped substantially in alleviating human encroachment and preserving the park's wilderness for future generations.

Glacier has always faced an annual battle with summer fires; indeed the park's first superintendent, William R Logan, fought over 20,234 hectares (50,000 acres) of burn in his first year. The summer of 2003 – the hottest on record – was another devastating burn-fest with lightning-started fires blazing over 55,240 hectares (136,500 acres), or 10% of the park's total tree cover. Unfortunately, the fires also burned a large hole in the area's tourist-dependent economy. The heat was turned up again in 2006 when over 12,950 hectares (32,000 acres) was razed in the Red Eagle Fire on the south side of St Mary Lake. Faced with an ever-warmer climate; fires, stressed ecosystems and melting glaciers are just three of the stiff environmental challenges facing Glacier in the future.

WATERTON LAKES NATIONAL PARK

The Kootenay and Blackfeet people roamed the mountains and plains of southern Alberta for thousands of years, shifting location by season. Bison, which First Nations people followed to the eastern prairies, were central to the tribes' survival and hunters used the animals' meat, hide, bone and horns for supplies and materials. South Kootenay Pass was a nexus for Kootenay people heading east to the area around Chief Mountain to hunt bison. A classic hunting method was to stampede bison over cliffs like the famous Head-Smashed-In Buffalo Jump, about 18km (11 miles) northwest of Fort Macleod, which is now a Unesco World Heritage Site. This site was used for hunting bison until the early 19th century.

Horses brought to the region in the early 1700s provided efficiency in hunting, but also warring between tribes. Ever the warriors, the proud Blackfeet expanded their territory west, eventually edging out the Kootenay but, over the next century and a half, European-born diseases inflicted many deaths among the tribes. The bison were also becom-

1995	1997	2003	2006	2007
Glacier and Waterton Lakes National Parks are designated a Unesco World Heritage Site	Going-to-the-Sun Rd is designated a national historic landmark	Larger-than-normal fires tear through Glacier National Park, resulting in over 55,240 hectares (136,500 acres) of burned forests and many closures	The Red Eagle Fire destroys 12,950 hectares (32,000 acres) around St Mary Lake	The park introduces a fleet of free, environmentally friendly shuttle buses on the Going-to-the-Sun Rd and opens a new transit center in Apgar village

ing increasingly endangered and by the mid-1880s their numbers had dwindled to zero.

Englishman Peter Fidler, of the Hudson Bay Company, is thought to be the first European to have explored this southern portion of the Canadian Rockies, setting out in 1792. Explorer Thomas Blakiston first came upon Waterton Lakes in 1858, naming them after famous British naturalist Charles Waterton.

The seed to designate the area a reserve was sown by Fredrick William Godsal, a rancher and conservationist in southern Alberta who had the prescience to see that, if the beautiful lakes region was not hastily set aside as protected land, private interests would soon take hold. In 1893 Godsal wrote a letter to William Pearce, the superintendent of mines, another longtime advocate for preserving the region. Pearce urged government officials in Ottawa to consider the issue and, in 1895, what is now known as Waterton Lakes, was given protective status by the Canadian federal government as a forest park.

In the days before the 1930 National Parks Act, Cameron Valley had a brief stint as an 'Oil City', beginning in 1902, when copious barrels of the liquid gold poured out from western Canada's first oil well. The oil discovery also led to the foundation of a townsite whose first structures included a cookhouse, stable and blacksmith's shop. In 1910, 150 town lots were offered for leasehold at C$15 per annum and the settlement opened up its first hotel but, when the oil dried up prematurely a few years later, local businesses quickly turned their attention to tourism.

Fortunately, the changes occurred just as Louis W Hill, son of Great Northern Railroad magnate and 'Empire Builder' James J Hill, was formulating a plan to link Waterton to his great chain of railway-inspired hotels as a means of circumventing prohibition in the United States. Occupying a prime perch overlooking windy Upper Waterton Lake, the Swiss-style hotel, which opened in 1927, was named for the then Prince of Wales (later Edward VIII) in a futile attempt to lure the soon-to-be-sovereign to the establishment (although the prince visited Waterton in 1927, he stayed at a nearby lodge instead).

Linked with Glacier in the world's first International Peace Park in 1932, Waterton had the distinction of becoming the first Canadian national park to be designated a Unesco Biosphere Reserve in 1979. In 1995 it gained an additional honor when, along with Glacier, it was declared a Unesco World Heritage Site. Now, with decreasing native fish populations and the increasing fragility of the ecosystem, the goal is to find out how to keep a park like Waterton sustainable as well as enjoyable.

Founded in 1906 by Irish-born surveyor and mountaineer AO Wheeler, the Alpine Club of Canada still stands at the sharp end of mountaineering in the Canadian Rockies. Check out its excellent website, www.alpineclubofcanada.ca.

HISTORY

Waterton Lakes National Park

10,000 BC	1895	1927	1932	1979
First Nations tribes begin to settle and hunt throughout the Rockies	The Canadian government grants protective status to the land around Waterton Lakes, paving the way to national park status	The Great Northern Railway opens the emblematic Prince of Wales Hotel on a grassy promontory overlooking Upper Waterton Lake	Canada and the USA declare Glacier and Waterton Lakes an International Peace Park – the world's first	Waterton Lakes National Park is designated a biosphere reserve

Banff National Park

'No scene has ever given me an equal impression of inspiring solitude and rugged grandeur.' So said the explorer Walter Wilcox when he first clapped eyes on the Valley of the Ten Peaks, near Lake Louise, in 1899, and it's a maxim that could happily apply to the whole of Banff National Park. Few places in the world can match Banff for sheer, unadulterated natural splendor. It's an outdoor arcadia, wildlife haven and alpine wonderland all rolled into one awe-inspiring bundle, where stately rock spires pierce the clouds, great glaciers trundle down the mountainsides and sawtooth crags stand in sharp relief against a wide-open sky. In summer, wildflowers fill the meadows and hikers and horseback riders take to the mountain trails; in winter, snow cloaks the land while the boarders cruise and the bruins snooze.

With such an amazing array of natural attractions, it's hardly surprising that Banff has always ranked as one of the busiest national parks in North America. Ever since three rail workers discovered the natural hot springs at the foot of Sulphur Mountain in 1883, people have been flocking to Banff to admire the scenery for themselves, assisted by the tracks laid across the Rocky Mountain passes by the Canadian Pacific Railway. These days the motorcar has taken over from the iron horse as the main means of transport, and the park throws open its gates to an astonishing annual roll call of more than three million visitors; as a result that all-important sense of 'inspiring solitude' can be hard to come by in high summer, but with a little bit of planning (and some backcountry hiking) you'll find there's still plenty of wilderness left to discover on the doorstep of Canada's most popular national park. Whether you're paddling the still waters of Moraine Lake, clambering to the crest of Standish Ridge or staring up at the icy pinnacle of Mt Assiniboine, one thing's for sure – Banff is a place that will be with you long after you've left for home.

HIGHLIGHTS

- Zipping up the mountainside aboard the gondolas in **Banff** (p95) and **Lake Louise** (p100)
- Savoring hot tea and homemade cakes at the **Plain of Six Glaciers Teahouse** (p109)
- Paddling out into the heart of **Moraine Lake** (p100), encircled by the snowy sentinels of the Wenkchemna Peaks
- Venturing into the wilderness on a backcountry trip to **Mt Assiniboine Provincial Park** (p155)
- Staring along the Continental Divide from atop **Standish Ridge** (p114)

▪ Total Area: 6641 sq km (2564 sq miles)	▪ Elevation Banff town: 1383m (4537ft)	▪ Average high/low temperature in July: 70/45°F

Banff National Park

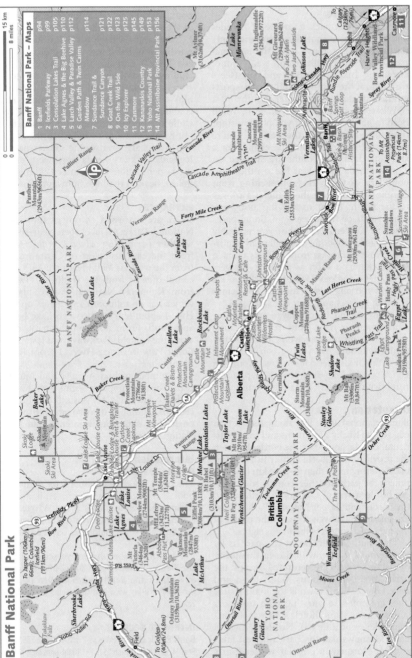

When You Arrive

Wind the clock back a couple of decades and Banff was essentially a summer-only destination, but these days the national park is bustling with people year-round, attracting hikers, cyclists and sightseers throughout the summer, and winter-sports enthusiasts during the colder months.

Whatever time of year you visit, you'll need to purchase a pass if you plan on stopping anywhere inside the park; if you're caught without one, you'll be eligible for a stiff fine. Entry tollbooths are situated in Trans-Canada Hwy 1 at the southeastern boundary of the park (approaching from Canmore) and along the Icefields Parkway to the north. If you're arriving along any other roads or from nearby national parks (such as Kootenay or Yoho) you probably won't pass a tollbooth, so you'll need to purchase your park pass from a Parks Canada visitor center as soon as possible. Rangers often make random roadside checks, so it's not worth trying to skip the fees. For details about the passes and their costs, see p26.

Passes should be displayed inside your windscreen or from your rear-view mirror, which means you won't have to stop at the tollbooth every time you enter the park. You'll also receive the free *Mountain Guide,* a useful newspaper with maps and a rundown of the park's main attractions.

Orientation

Banff National Park lies along the eastern edge of the Rocky Mountains and the Continental Divide, nestled on the border between the provinces of Alberta and British Columbia. Covering more than 6641 sq km (2564 sq miles), the park stretches from its southeastern border (west of Canmore) northwest to the border with Jasper National Park. Trans-Canada Hwy 1 travels through the center of the park and connects the major sights.

The southern section of the park is by far the busiest area, with the vast majority of visitor services concentrated around the park's two conurbations, Banff town and Lake Louise. Banff town is the main visitor hub, crammed to bursting with outdoors stores, shops, bars, hotels and restaurants (plus plenty of tourists). North of town is Lake Minnewanka, the park's largest lake, and Mt Norquay, a popular winter-sports destination. Sunshine Meadows, another popular skiing area, is to the west, just south of the scenic Bow Valley Parkway.

Lake Louise village lies 58km (36 miles) northwest of Banff town along Trans-Canada Hwy 1 and has limited services, including gas stations, a post office, a grocery store, a bookstore and outdoors supplier, plus several large hotels. Lake Louise itself is about 8km (5 miles) west of the village, while the beautiful mountain-backed Moraine Lake is 13km (8 miles) to the south. North of Lake Louise, the glacier-packed Icefields Parkway heads northwest, entering Jasper National Park after 122km (75.6 miles), beyond the high Sunwapta Pass.

ENTRANCES

There are five road entrances into Banff National Park. All are open year-round, weather permitting. Hwy 1 enters Banff from the east just west of Canmore and from the west via Yoho National Park. You can also enter from the south on Hwy 93 from Kootenay National Park. This entrance has no tollbooth and meets up with Hwy 1 about halfway between Lake Louise and Banff. From north of the park, enter along the Icefields Parkway from Jasper National Park or along Hwy 11 from Rocky Mountain House.

A number of hiking trails lead into the park. The most popular begins from Kananaskis Country (via Mt Assiniboine Provincial Park), although it is also possible to enter on foot or skis from Kootenay and Yoho National Parks.

Information
BOOKSTORES

There's a good selection of local-interest books, topographical maps, trail guides, nature and wildlife titles at the Whyte Museum, the Bear & Butterfly and the Friends of Banff gift store inside the Banff Information Centre.

For a more comprehensive selection, try the **Viewpoint** (Map p94; ☎ 403-762-0405; 201 Caribou St, Banff) or the **Banff Book & Art Den** (Map p94; ☎ 403-762-3919; www.banffbooks.com; 94 Banff Ave, Banff).

INTERNET ACCESS

Banff Public Library (Map p94; ☎ 403-762-2661; 101 Bear St, Banff; per 30min C$1; ⊙ 10am-8pm Mon-Thu, to 6pm Fri & Sat, 1-5pm Sun)

Cyberweb Internet Café (Map p94; ☎ 403-762-9226; basement, Sundance Mall, 215 Banff Ave, Banff; per 10min C$1; ☉ 9am-midnight)

Underground Studio (Map p94; ☎ 403-760-8776; basement, Park Ave Mall, 211 Banff Ave, Banff; per hr C$6; ☉ 9am-1am)

LAUNDRY
Cascade Coin Laundry (Map p94; ☎ 403-762-3444; ground fl, Cascade Plaza, Banff; ☉ 8am-10pm Mon-Sat, to 8pm Sun)

MONEY
Alberta Treasury Branch (Map p94; ☎ 403-762-8505; 317 Banff Ave, Banff)

Bank of Montreal (Map p94; ☎ 403-762-2275; 107 Banff Ave, Banff)

CIBC (Map p94; ☎ 403-762-3317; 98 Banff Ave, Banff)

Custom House Currency Exchange (Map p94; ☎ 403-660-6630; Park Ave Mall, 211 Banff Ave, Banff)

Foreign Currency Exchange (Map p94; ☎ 403-762-4698; Clock Tower Mall, 110 Banff Ave, Banff)

POST
Banff Post Office (Map p94; ☎ 403-762-2586; 204 Buffalo St, Banff)

TOURIST INFORMATION
Banff Information Centre (Map p94; ☎ 403-762-1550; banff.vrc@pc.gc.ca; 224 Banff Ave, Banff; ☉ 9am-5pm spring & autumn, 8am-8pm summer, 9am-4pm winter) The main park visitor center can answer practically any question about exploring the park. You can also pick up leaflets, trail maps and guides on everything from angling to mountain biking. You can also purchase wilderness passes and get advice on hiking trips from the backcountry trails desk, plus check on the latest bear sightings, trail reports and weather forecasts. Hiking guidebooks are available for consultation at the back of the office, where there are also computers for helping you plan backcountry trips. A cinema and lecture room often hosts talks, screenings and educational programs during the summer.

Banff Tourism Bureau (Map p94; ☎ 403-762-8421; www.banfflakelouise.com; 224 Banff Ave, Banff; ☉ 9am-5pm spring & autumn, 8am-8pm summer, 9am-4pm winter) Opposite the Parks desks in the information center, this helpful tourism information desk provides advice on accommodations, attractions and activities in Banff, as well as a free phone for making hotel and restaurant reservations.

Friends of Banff (Map p94; ☎ 403-762-8911; www.friendsofbanff.com; Bear & Butterfly, 214 Banff Ave, Banff) A nonprofit organization that supplements the work of park authorities by providing educational programs, guided walks and general information on the park. Look out for its 'roving interpreters' around campgrounds and scenic spots. It also runs a guided walk to the Vermilion Lakes (adult C$10, children under 12 free) and operates Banff Park Radio (101.1FM/103.3FM in English/French). Its latest venture is an in-car GPS tour guide detailing over 1500 locations around the Canadian Rockies (including Banff, Yoho and Kootenay). Units can be rented from the Bear & Butterfly for C$40 per day.

Friends of Banff Gift Store (Map p94; ☎ 403-762-5232; 224 Banff Ave, Banff) In the information center, next to the tourism bureau desk, this gift shop and information center has a great selection of books, maps and Banff-themed souvenirs, from cuddly grizzlies to First Nation crafts. More souvenirs are on sale at the Bear & Butterfly (p93) up the street.

Lake Louise Backcountry Trails Office (☎ 403-522-1264; Lake Louise Visitor Centre) Dispenses specialist advice on exploring the backcountry area around Lake Louise.

Lake Louise Tourism Bureau (☎ 403-762-8421; Lake Louise Visitor Centre; ☉ 9am-7pm summer only) Can help with activities and accommodations in Lake Louise village.

Lake Louise Visitor Centre (Map p85; ☎ 403-522-3833; ll.info@pc.gc.ca; Lake Louise village; ☉ 9am-5pm spring & autumn, to 7pm summer, to 4pm winter) Next to Samson Mall, with Parks Canada staff who provide comprehensive information on trails, activities and sights around the Lake Louise area. There are some interesting interpretive displays – look out for a stuffed grizzly bear and a battered raincoat that possibly belonged to the park warden Bill Peyto (see the boxed text, p115).

USEFUL NUMBERS
In an emergency, contact the 24-hour number for the **Park Warden Office** (☎ 403-762-4506) or call ☎ 911. Wildlife sightings (especially bears, cougar, wolverines and lynx) and any unusual animal behavior should be reported to the Park Warden Office.

Avalanche Hazards (☎ 403-762-1460)
Park Warden Office (Map p94; ☎ 403-762-1470; PO Box 900, Banff, Alberta, T1L1K2)
Road Conditions (☎ 403-762-1450)
Trail Conditions (☎ 403-760-1305)
Weather Report (☎ 403-762-2088)

Park Policies & Regulations
It is illegal to remove any natural or cultural artifacts from the park, including rocks, stones, minerals and fossils as well as antlers, nests, bird eggs, plants, cones and wildflowers. Tree bark should also be left in situ to avoid the spread of the mountain pine beetle and other tree parasites. Pets must be kept on a leash at all times and are not allowed in backcountry shelters. Hunting and firearms are not permitted anywhere

in the park. Most importantly, stay on the maintained trails and avoid cutting across switchbacks, which causes unnecessary erosion and damages fragile plants.

Most permits and passes listed can be ordered in advance by calling the main **Parks Canada reservation service** (☎ 1-800-748-7275) or by contacting the visitor centers in Banff and Lake Louise.

BACKCOUNTRY CAMPING

The days of Bill Peyto and his bushwhacking pals have long passed, but you can still get a taste of the wilderness in one of the park's backcountry campgrounds. In most of the backcountry, you're required to camp in one of the designated campgrounds, although in some of the park's more remote areas, wild camping is still permitted – contact the Banff Information Centre for details. Wherever you sleep, you'll need a **wilderness pass** (per day/year C$10/70) for every night you intend to stay, and must reserve your chosen campgrounds with park staff. You don't necessarily have to submit a detailed trip itinerary when you purchase the pass, but it's often a good idea; if you're not back by the specified date, a search party will set out to look for you, so it's *vital* that you report back to park authorities once your trip is finished to avoid triggering a false alarm. For some possible backcountry routes, see p118.

BIKING

Biking is popular in Banff, but it's not without its opponents. Many people feel that mountain bikers cause more lasting damage to the park than other users, and many of the old cross-country trails have been closed in recent years despite howls of protest from the local mountain-biking fraternity. The Banff Information Centre can supply you with maps of designated trails. You need to wear a bike helmet in Alberta by law. There's also an unofficial rule that you should yield to hikers and horses; remember to slow down when you're overtaking to avoid kicking mud up into the faces of other trail users.

CAMPING

If you're looking to sleep under the stars without the backcountry hike, Banff has 13 frontcountry campgrounds catering for tents, recreational vehicles (RVs) and camper vans. Reservations for some campgrounds (including Tunnel Mountain and Lake Louise) can be made via the **Parks Canada campground reservation service** (☎ 1-877-737-3783; www.pccamping.ca/parkscanada; ☽ 7am-7pm), but most campgrounds are allocated on a first-come, first-served basis. Checkout is 11am and there's a maximum stay of 14 nights. You can have one tent and up to two vehicles at one campsite. Depending on the campground, you'll either need to pay at the kiosk or find a vacant site, self-register and drop your fee in the collection box.

Fires are usually allowed at campsites where there's a fire pit – you'll need to buy a fire permit (C$8, including wood) from the campground entrance. Watch for fire restrictions during dry periods. As in the backcountry, it's good practice to try and keep your campsite as clear as possible. Dump stations, bear-proof garbage containers and recycling bins are available at many campgrounds.

FISHING & BOATING

A national park **fishing permit** (per day/year C$9.90/34.65) is required for angling in Banff. In the contiguous mountain parks (Banff, Jasper, Kootenay and Yoho), one permit is valid for all the parks. Permits come with a *Fishing Regulations* summary detailing catch allowances and protected species. The usual catch-and-possession limit is two fish per day, but it's illegal to keep many endangered native species such as bull trout, kokanee salmon and cutthroat trout; park wardens will have little sympathy with claims of ignorance or misidentification, so return any species you can't identify, unless you're happy to face the fine. Better still, return everything you catch and use barbless hooks, which are less harmful to the fish.

Fishing seasons vary according to specific lakes and seasons. The main Bow River is open year-round (although ice fishing is always banned), while Ghost Lake, Johnson Lake, Lake Minnewanka, Two Jack Lake and the Vermilion Lakes are usually open mid-May to mid-September. Check with park authorities on the latest rules and regulations before you cast your line.

Nonmotorized boats are officially allowed on all the park's lakes, but there are only a few with proper boat access. Motorboats are only permitted on Lake Minnewanka, where there's a loading ramp specifically designed for larger vessels. Canoes and kayaks are allowed on most of the park's rivers, but it's a good idea to check your route beforehand with park staff – mountain rivers are notoriously unpredictable and rescue can be a long way away.

HORSEBACK RIDING

Most trails within Banff are open to horses, with a few exceptions, including most of the Healy Pass area, the Sunshine Creek watershed, the Sunshine Village Ski area and the upper watershed of Howard Douglas Creek from Brewster Rock to Citadel Pass. Watch out for high rivers in spring or after heavy rain, especially around Pipestone River, Mistaya River, Howse River, Clearwater River and Red Deer River. For full details about horseback riding in the park, pick up a copy of the *Horse Users' Guide* from visitor centers. It details trailheads and staging areas where you can leave your horse at the start and end of a trip. Try to minimize your impact on the park by traveling in single file, cleaning up manure, avoiding spillage of feed bags (which attracts bears) and avoiding grazing on wet and fragile areas.

Horses are also permitted on many backcountry trails; you'll need to purchase both a wilderness pass and a **grazing permit** (per day/month C$2/22). Make sure you check with park authorities that the trail is definitely open to horse use and reserve your route well ahead in summer. Chain saws, horse-drawn vehicles and (bizarrely) llamas are all banned, so bang goes that llama-powered chariot race you've set your heart on.

TRASH & RECYCLING

There are garbage bins at most frontcountry campsites, some of which also have limited recycling facilities. In the backcountry, you have to pack out all your garbage by law.

Garbage bins are located all over Banff town, often with accompanying bins for recyclable plastic bottles and glass. You'll also find recycling at the corner of Banff Ave and Caribou St, as well as outside Safeway.

Getting Around

The vast majority of visitors explore the park with their own wheels. It's not the greenest way of getting around but it's unquestionably the most convenient – try to share cars if you can to cut down on traffic, especially if you can find other people going to the same trailhead. The easiest option is to rent a car in Banff, Canmore or at Calgary airport, although regular shuttle services also travel to Banff and Lake Louise from the airport (p257).

There are no scheduled buses to the main sights and trailheads, other than those provided by private sightseeing companies, so you'll need your own car to reach more out-of-the-way locations.

BICYCLE

Bikes are a great way to experience the park, especially along scenic roads such as the Bow Valley and Icefields Parkway. Banff is well geared up for cyclists, with plenty of bike shops and rental companies dotted around the main town. Rather short-sightedly, few of the trailheads have cycle racks, but many rental companies offer shuttle services to the start and finish of main trails. You can also take your bikes on the Banff Public Transit. Downhilling and freeriding is not permitted in Banff; if you're into these activities you're better off heading for Canmore Nordic Centre (p145), Golden and Fernie.

See the Biking section on p120 for more on cycling in Banff.

CAR & MOTORCYCLE

Speed limits for major routes within the park are 90km/h (56mph), dropping to 60km/h (37mph) or 30km/h (18.6mph) on secondary roads. Wildlife activity, weather and road maintenance can result in temporary speed-limit reductions. Gas stations are sparse outside Banff town and Lake Louise village; the only other places to fuel up are at Castle Mountain Junction and The Crossing.

Trans-Canada Hwy 1 is the country's major thoroughfare, crossing the continent from east to west. The section passing through Banff National Park is surprisingly busy, both with tourists and local commuters. It has a bad reputation for collisions, so take care and, as always in the park, keep your eyes peeled for wildlife. The single-lane Bow Valley Parkway (Hwy 1A) runs parallel to Hwy 1 and is much quieter and slower than the main three-lane highway. Your chance of spotting elk and deer here is much greater. The eastern section (up to Johnston Canyon from Banff) is closed in spring from 6pm to 9am to give wildlife some peace and privacy.

There are parking lots at most major trailheads. Don't leave valuables in your car, as theft from parked vehicles is an increasing problem. It's also worth removing any rental-company stickers on the bumpers or panels, as these can make cars easy targets.

All of the parking lots in Lake Louise and Banff town are free, but some have time restrictions indicated on signs with a green circle. Driving RVs can be a headache in Banff town, so it's worth parking up at the RV lots beside the train station or at the northern end of Banff Ave and walking into town.

There are no official restrictions on vehicle lengths within the park, but it's worth remembering that some of the minor roads (especially the ones to trailheads at high elevations) can be narrow, twisty and quite steep, and may have patches of ice or snow during cold weather. In winter, you are required by law to have your vehicle equipped with snow tires or chains on all roads except Hwy 1. All roads are subject to closure due to winter weather conditions.

PUBLIC TRANSPORTATION
Bus
Banff's bus services leave a lot to be desired in comparison to more ecofriendly parks such as Glacier. Public transportation to the main sights is almost nonexistent, which goes a long way to explaining why there's so much traffic on the park's main roads.

Greyhound (Map p94; ☎ 800-661-8747; Gopher St, Banff), the venerable intercity bus service, travels four or five times daily between Banff and Canmore (C$9, 25 minutes), and three or four times daily between Banff and Lake Louise (C$14, 45 to 50 minutes) en route from Golden and Field (both across the border in British Columbia). Routes can get very busy in summer and winter high seasons, so it pays to reserve ahead.

For details on Brewster's airport and resort connector, see p258.

Banff Public Transit (☎ 403-762-1215) is the town's main bus service. Route 1 travels between the Fairmont Banff Springs Hotel along Spray Ave, Beaver St and the Banff Ave hotels. Route 2 travels from Beaver St northeast along Wolf St and past the

Tunnel Mountain Dr campgrounds and hotels. Route 3 travels south from Beaver St over the river along Mountain Ave to the Upper Hot Springs Pool and the gondola. All routes run every half-hour from around 6:30am to 11pm in summer, with a reduced service in winter. You'll need to give the driver the exact fare – adult tickets cost C$2, with children between six and 12 years charged C$1; kids under six are free. Multi-ticket booklets and monthly passes can be purchased from Banff Town Hall.

Sundog Tours (☎ 780-852-4056; www.sundogtours.com) offers a daily shuttle bus between Jasper and Banff. Southbound minibuses pick you up from your hotel in Jasper around 8am, stopping in Lake Louise (adult/child C$53/29) around 11am before arriving in Banff (adult/child $59/35) at 12:15pm. Northbound minibuses collect guests from Banff hotels around 1:30pm, stop at Lake Louise around 2:30pm and terminate in Jasper at 5:30pm. The service operates year-round and you'll need to reserve in advance.

Taxi
Due to the distances between sights, taxis aren't a terribly practical way of getting around, although they can make an economical way of getting to trailheads, especially for families and groups of more than three people. For transportation from Calgary airport, you're better off catching one of the airport shuttles.

In Banff, try **Banff Taxi** (☎ 403-762-4444), **Legion Taxi** (☎ 403-762-3353) and **Mountain Taxi** (☎ 403-762-3351). In Lake Louise, try **Lake Louise Taxi** (☎ 403-522-2020).

Train
Ironically for a town that owes its entire existence to the coming of the railway, regular passenger trains now speed right through Banff without stopping. The only train trips to Banff are run by **Rocky Mountaineer Rail Tours** (☎ 800-665-7245; www.rockymountaineer.com), which offers several luxury train trips through the Rockies, Banff and Jasper. Trips are available in two classes: Red Leaf (coach class, with reclining seats, picture windows and meal service) and Gold Leaf (1st class, with dome windows, rotating seats and luxury meals in a twin-level coach). Most of the travel is done during daylight hours for the best views, and prices include park

BANFF IN...

One Day
You'll be hard-pushed to do much more than scratch the surface of this natural wonderland in a day. Kick off with an early morning trip up to the crest of Sulphur Mountain aboard the **Banff Gondola** (p95), when hopefully the crowds will be at their lightest and you can drink in the views in peace. Grab a coffee, then head back down for a wander round Banff town: stop by the **Cave and Basin National Historic Site** (p96) and the **Luxton Museum** (p96), and take a short stroll down to **Bow Falls** (p97). Grab lunch at the **Bison Mountain Bistro** (p141) and have a mosey around the **Whyte Museum** (p92). If it's a sunny day, you might still have time to hop in the car and follow the **Minnewanka Meander** (p124) driving tour, stopping off at **Two Jack Lake** and **Johnson Lake** before winding up at **Lake Minnewanka** (p97) for glorious dusk views. Then celebrate the day's sightseeing at the **Maple Leaf Grillé** (p142).

Two Days
Follow the one-day itinerary and then hit the road for more distant sights. Head for the Bow Valley Parkway and aim to reach **Johnston Canyon** (p106) as early as possible. If the weather's good and you're up for a hike, continue on to the Inkpots. Otherwise trace the **Bow Valley** (p123) driving tour to **Lake Louise** (p98), which you should reach by late afternoon. Indulge in a classy afternoon tea at the **Deer Lodge** (p143) and then take a leisurely stroll along the lakeshore as the evening light hits the glaciers and illuminates the peacock-blue lake, or climb aboard the **Lake Louise Gondola** (p100), looking out for grizzly and black bears. Head back down to Banff, either via the Bow Valley Parkway or Trans-Canada Hwy 1, and try **Saltlik** (p142) or **Fuze** (p142) for dinner.

Four Days
With four days you'll have plenty of time to really get out and explore the park's natural attractions. Follow the first two itineraries and then choose a classic day hike for day three – good suggestions include the **Garden Path Trail** (p113), **Cascade Amphitheatre** (p108), **Larch Valley** (p111) or the **Plain of Six Glaciers** (p109). Then on day four you'll have time to set out early and drive up the **Icefields Parkway** (p125), explore **Yoho National Park** (p152) or try out an activity such as **white-water rafting** (p127) or **horseback riding** (p128). If you've got the cash, you might prefer a once-in-a-lifetime **helicopter trip** (p146).

passes, hotel accommodations and day trips by coach. The Western Explorer (Red Leaf C$2389 to C$5519, Gold Leaf C$3189 to C$6319) is a seven-day itinerary between Vancouver and Banff via Kamloops, Jasper, Yoho and the Icefields Parkway that leaves on Monday, Wednesday and Saturday. The Canadian Rockies Highlights (Red Leaf C$1979 to C$4039, Gold Leaf C$2799 to C$4839) trip follows a stripped-down version with sidetrips to Lake Louise and to a glacier by helicopter. The three-day Classic Rail Vacation (Red Leaf C$1129 to C$2029, Gold Leaf C$1929 to C$2829) just takes in Vancouver, Kamloops and Banff.

TOURS
If you're just planning to explore Banff through a few day hikes and driving tours,

then there's really no need to splash out on an organized tour. But if your time in the park is limited, or you're traveling without wheels, there are several companies that provide whistle-stop trips around the essential sights. Some of the posher hotels run minibus shuttles to the key sights, and for deep-pocketed travelers looking for a sky-high perspective, there are helicopter trips from Canmore (see p146).

The Brewster brothers, Bill and Jim, ran the first guided tours in Banff back in 1892, but these days the trusty steeds at **Brewster** (Map p94; ☎ 403-762-6750, 877-791-5500; www .brewster.ca; 100 Gopher St, Banff) are air-conditioned motor coaches rather than trail-hardened horses. There's a three-hour Discover Banff tour (C$71) that includes stops at the hoodoos, the Cave and Basin, Surprise Corner and a ride on the Banff Gondola. The marathon, 9½-hour Mountain Lakes and Waterfalls tour (C$105) takes in the Bow Valley Parkway, Johnston Canyon, Lake Louise, Moraine Lake, the Spiral Tunnels in Yoho, Emerald Lake and Takakkaw Falls. There are also several trips to the Columbia Icefield and Jasper from Lake Louise, including a trip onto the glacier with the Ice Explorer (p168).

The other big hitter is **Discover Banff Tours** (Map p94; ☎ 403-760-5007; www.banfftours.com; Sundance Mall, 215 Banff Ave, Banff), which operates much smaller buses than Brewster, so things feel a bit less regimented. In summer its guided trips include a three-hour Banff Tour (adult C$49, child eight to 12 years C$30), a four-hour tour of Moraine Lake and Lake Louise (adult C$59, child eight to 12 years C$35), and a nine-hour trip up the Icefields Parkway (adult C$145, child six to 15 years C$75) via Crowfoot Glacier, Bow Lake, Peyto Lake, Mistaya Canyon and the Athabasca Glacier. There's also a 10-hour Discover Grizzly Bears tour (adult C$119, child six to 12 years C$84) that visits Lake Louise, Takakkaw Falls and Kicking Horse Canyon, and includes a visit to a bear refuge inhabited by an orphaned grizzly cub. Banff Tours also runs morning and evening Wildlife Safaris (adult C$49, child eight to 12 years C$30), plus rafting (C$69 to C$126), horseback riding (C$41 to C$92) and all-terrain-vehicle (ATV) tours (C$269).

GyPSy (☎ 403-760-8200; www.gpstourscanada.com; per day/week C$39/219, per day for rentals of more than 8 days C$15) has audio guides offering a GPS-based tour around the Canadian Rockies that can be rented from Discover Banff Tours (above) or the Tourism Calgary desk at Calgary airport.

SIGHTS

If it's the quintessential Canadian landscape you're looking for, then Banff certainly lives up to the mark. Every twist and turn of the road reveals a fresh vista of jaw-dropping views: roaring rivers, iridescent glaciers, dense forests of fir, larch and pine and, of course, enough mountain trails to fill several lifetimes of hiking. It's a spectacular location whatever time of year you visit, with many of the Canadian Rockies' classic walks as well as a growing reputation for skiing and other winter sports. It's certainly no secret, however – with over 3.2 million visitors every year, it's far and away Canada's most popular national park.

BANFF

Nestled in a bowl-shaped valley bisected by the Bow River and framed on every side by glowering peaks, the town of Banff is for many people something of a surprise: a bustling mini-metropolis dropped smack bang into the center of Canada's flagship national park. Even a decade ago Banff was still something of a sleepy backwater, but over recent years the town has exploded into a year-round hub for the whole national park, crammed with upmarket hotels, shops, designer restaurants and museums. It's the main commercial and administrative center for the park, and you certainly won't be short of a companion or two on the town sidewalks – in high season Banff Ave does a passable, shopper-dense impression of Fifth Ave. Despite the seasonal traffic, Banff makes an excellent base for exploring, with most of the main sights (including Lake Louise) less than an hour's drive away, and plenty of after-dark distractions to keep you happy once the sun goes down.

Whyte Museum of the Canadian Rockies

Founded by the artists Peter and Catharine Whyte, who spent most of their lives living and working in Banff and the Canadian Rockies, the **Whyte Museum** (Map p94; ☎ 403-762-2291; www.whyte.org; 111 Bear St; adult/senior C$6/3.50, child 6yr & over C$3.50, family C$15; ☼ 10am-5pm) opened its doors in 1968 in a modest building shared with the Banff public library. The original displays were based around an assortment of local artifacts belonging to the Whytes, but over 40 years the museum has assembled a huge collection of paintings, artwork and cultural exhibits relating to the Rockies' heritage. The heart of the museum is the permanent display exploring the Whytes' fascinating life together. Among the exhibits you can see a reconstruction of their mountain cabin, Catharine's Paris-designed wedding dress, Peter's military uniform and an entrancing collection of First Nations costumes belonging to their friend, the Stoney Chief Walking Buffalo.

RETAIL THERAPY

Despite the profusion of ultra-tacky gift shops and Canadiana souvenir stores, there's actually some good shopping to be had in and around Banff – especially if you're after outdoors gear and trail maps.

Books

The quirky, much-loved **Banff Book & Art Den** (Map p94; ☎ 403-762-3919; www.banffbooks.com; 94 Banff Ave; ☼ 9am-9pm) is crammed floor-to-ceiling with fiction, nonfiction and local interest titles, as well as plenty of trail guides, maps and guidebooks to help you make the most of your Banff visit.

Viewpoint (Map p94; ☎ 403-762-0405; 201 Caribou St; ☼ 10am-10pm) is a top place for photo books, as well as geology, wildlife and Banff-themed titles.

Gifts

The **Bear & Butterfly** (Map p94; ☎ 403-762-8911; 214 Banff Ave) gift store, run by Friends of Banff, is streets ahead of the tourist tat shops along Banff Ave – local craftwork and pottery, mountain artwork, books and even moose-skin moccasins and buckskin purses find space on its shelves.

Trail Rider (Map p94; ☎ 403-762-4551; 132 Banff Ave) is *the* place in town to stock up on authentic Albertan trail gear – cowboy hats, breeches, belt buckles 'n' all.

Rocky Mountain Soap Company (Map p94; ☎ 403-762-5999; 204 Banff Ave) sells 100% natural soaps, lotions and creams handmade in Canmore, including body butters and foot lotions that are wonderful after a long day's hike.

Chocoholics will be in seventh heaven at **Chocolaterie Bernard Callebaut** (Map p94; ☎ 403-762-4106; 111 Banff Ave), a gourmet chocolate maker with over 48 flavors to choose from.

Founded by Norman Luxton as the Sign of the Goat, **Banff Indian Trading Post** (Map p94; ☎ 762-2456; cnr Cave & Birch Aves) is the place to head if you're after some First Nations crafts, including beadwork, deer-hide gloves, antler-handled hunting knives and authentic 'dreamcatchers.' Some of the stuff's pretty tacky, so choose carefully.

Outdoors Equipment

Monod Sports (Map p94; ☎ 403-762-4571; www.monodsports.com; 129 Banff Ave; ☼ 9am-9pm) is Banff's oldest outdoor-equipment supplier, and still the best. Women's and men's clothing from big brands such as Patagonia, Arcteyx, Icebreaker, Columbia and North Face, supplemented by good backpack, equipment and footwear sections.

Mountain Magic (Map p94; ☎ 403-762-2591; www.mountainmagic.com) is another big outdoors shop mainly geared toward climbers and cyclists; there are separate stores for technical clothing (220 Bear St) and sportswear across the street (225 Bear St).

There are also plenty of their paintings on display, alongside temporary exhibitions drawn from the museum's archives. Ask at the admissions desk for a 'museo-pack' to keep the kids entertained.

The museum also runs guided tours including the 1½-hour **Historic Banff** (C$7; ☼ 2:30pm Jun-Sep) walk and a 45-minute **Banff Heritage Homes** (C$7; ☼ 11am & 2:30pm Jun-Sep) tour. You can pick up a free self-guided *Banff Culture Walk* from museum staff.

Banff Park Museum

Taxidermy fans will be in seventh heaven at the **Banff Park Museum** (Map p94; ☎ 403-762-1558; 93 Banff Ave; adult/child C$4/2; ☼ 10am-6pm summer, 1-5pm winter). Housed in a striking wooden building built in 1903 in the fashionable 'railway pagoda' style, the museum was founded to explore the natural history of the park by preserving specimens of native creatures, but it's a long way from our idea of an environmentally friendly enterprise. A disturbing menagerie of stuffed animals stare out from the museum's walls, including elk, cougars, golden eagles, bears, pi' and a selection of enormous bison (look out for Sir Donald, the patr buffalo herd that once lived r Mountain). The museum

BANFF NATIONAL PARK

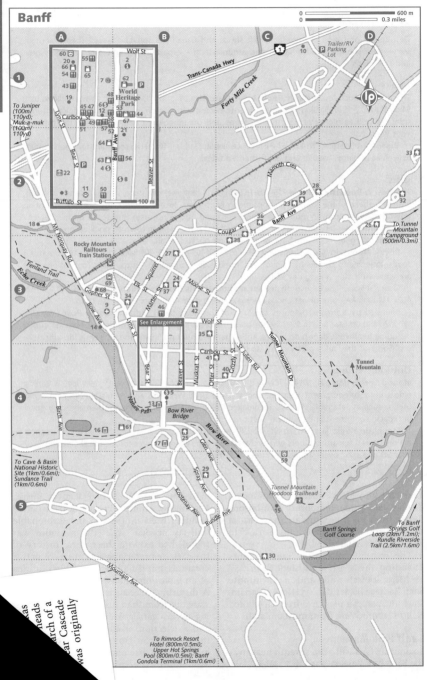

Banff

0 ——— 600 m
0 ——— 0.3 miles

curated by Norman Sanson, the self-taught naturalist and steel-legged weatherman who regularly climbed Sulphur Mountain to take weather readings from the observatory. You can still see his office on the 1st floor and the museum's original wood-paneled reading room is just behind the admissions desk.

Banff Gondola

Alright, it's a lazy way of getting to the mountaintops but for instant access to glorious views you can't beat the **Banff Gondola** (☎ 403-762-5438; www.banffgondola.com; Mountain Ave; adult C$25, child 6-15yr C$13; ☒ 7:30am-9pm summer, 10am-4pm winter, reduced hours spring & autumn, closed early Jan), which whisks you 2281m (7486ft) to the top of Sulphur Mountain in just eight minutes. The panoramic views on a clear day are pretty mind-blowing, with Banff town far below and 360-degree outlooks of the surrounding peaks. Trails lead away from the observation terrace to Sanson's Peak and the old weather station, or the much more challenging ridge walk to the top of Sulphur Mountain. There's a gift shop

and a couple of restaurants near the gondola station: the **Summit** (lunch $$, dinner $$$) and the slightly more formal **Regal View Garden** (lunch $$, dinner $$$; ☒ Jun-Sep), both serving café-style food with unsurprisingly fab views. They open the same hours as the gondola.

Route 3 on the Banff Public Transit climbs Mountain Ave to the Upper Hot Springs Pool, from where it's a five-minute stroll to the lower gondola station. Hardy souls can tackle the hike up the mountain (see p107), but don't expect any admiring looks at the top – everyone's much too busy drinking in the views.

Upper Hot Springs Pool

Banff quite literally wouldn't be Banff if it weren't for its hot springs, which gush out from 2.5km (1.5 miles) beneath Sulphur Mountain at a constant temperature of between 90°F and 116°F. It was the hot springs that drew the first tourists to Banff, and you can still sample the soothing mineral waters at the **Upper Hot Springs Pool** (☎ 403-762-1515; www.hotsprings.ca; Mountain Ave; adult/child/senior/family C$8/7/7/23; ☒ 9am-11pm summer, 10am-

THE BIRTH OF A NATIONAL PARK

Canada's present-day national park system can trace its origins back to the discovery of three geothermally heated springs near Banff in the fall of 1883. Although First Nations people had known about the hot springs around Banff for well over 10,000 years, the first white man to set eyes on them was James Hector, who recorded the springs on the Palliser expedition of 1859, probably following the advice of local Stoney Indians. Two surveyors working for the Canadian Pacific Railway revisited the springs in 1874, but it was the arrival of brothers Tom and William McCardell, and their partner Frank McCabe, that changed the history of the springs for good.

In the fall of 1883, they crossed the marshy area to the west of present-day Banff and stumbled across a series of deep chambers filled with naturally hot water. When William was lowered by his companions into one of the caves, he's reported to have described it as being 'like some fantastic dream from a tale of the Arabian Nights.' They quickly smelled much more than just the odor of the sulfurous water – with the fashion for spa bathing still in full swing in Europe, and hot water on tap still an undreamt-of luxury, there was the whiff of money to be made around the hot springs. The three companions staked a claim on the area, though ownership of the site soon degenerated into complicated legal wranglings over mineral rights and land claims, forcing the government to step in and declare the springs the property of all Canadian people – sowing the seeds for the birth of Banff National Park and the National Park Act, eventually enacted in 1930.

The springs themselves proved to be just the money-spinner the three companions had hoped, although none of them saw any of the proceeds. Victorians and First Nations peoples alike believed the waters had healing properties (supposedly good for everything from arthritis to stinky feet) and within a few short years resort spas had sprung up all across the foot of Sulphur Mountain. By the early 1900s, the precious water was being pumped to a health sanatorium on the site of present-day Canada Pl, while companies were bottling the water for export to the distant corners of Canada. There were even bars along Banff Ave where customers could take a tot of gin or rum along with a splash of mineral water. And though the medicinal properties of the waters have never quite been proved, there's no doubt that sinking into the superheated waters with a view of the surrounding mountains is a fantastically soothing experience. Though the original springs at Cave and Basin National Historic Site are now off-limits to bathers, you can still sample the hot water at the Upper Hot Springs Pool (p95).

10pm Sun-Thu, 10am-11pm Fri & Sat winter). Several hotels once occupied the site where the present-day Hot Springs Pool stands – Dr RG Brett's Grand View Villa, built in 1886, was joined by the Hydro Hotel in 1890 but both establishments burnt down and were replaced in the 1930s by a new bathhouse in the fashionable Art Deco style. Renovations have since masked some of the bathhouse's period elegance, but the hot springs still rank as one of those not-to-be-missed Banff experiences. Towels, lockers and swimsuits are available for hire, and the **Pleiades Spa** (per 30min/hr C$55/85) offers treatments such as shiatsu, hot stone massage and reiki.

Cave & Basin National Historic Site

The three original springs discovered by McCabe and the McCardell brothers now form the **Cave and Basin National Historic Site** (☎ 403-762-1566; adult/youth/senior C$4/3/3.50;

⊙ 9am-6pm summer, 11am-4pm Mon-Fri, 9:30am-5pm Sat & Sun winter). Although bathing in the hot springs here is no longer allowed, to safeguard the endangered Banff Springs snail, you can still view a replica of the original 1887 bathhouse, visit the interior basin and open-air mineral pool and follow a boardwalk around the museum from where you can peer into the upper vent holes and see the many species of algae, plants and wildflowers that thrive in the warm water. Below the museum, another boardwalk leads down to the Marsh Loop walking trail (p102), as well as a fish-viewing platform and a bird blind where you might be able to spot redwinged blackbirds, green-winged teals and yellowthroats (bring binoculars in case).

Buffalo Nations Luxton Museum

Built to resemble a wooden fort, **Buffalo Nations Luxton Museum** (Map p94; ☎ 403-762-2388;

1 Birch Ave; adult C$8, child C$2.50, senior & student C$6; ⊗ 9am-6pm) explores the culture of the First Nations from the Rockies and the Northern Plains. Some of the exhibits are fascinating, especially the collections of traditional costumes, weapons and tools – look out for the 'protection pouches' filled with sacred items, an intriguing gallery of peace pipes and some gloriously simple buckskin dresses, bags and rifle cases, all decorated with intricate beadwork. Some of the fiberglass reconstructions are a bit tacky (check out the 'sun-dance' tableau), but on the whole it's an interesting introduction to First Nations culture. The museum was founded by another of Banff's colorful characters, Norman Luxton, an amateur taxidermist, globe-trotting seaman, explorer and trader whose original goods outpost, the Sign of the Goat, now houses a gift shop selling native crafts, souvenirs and the like (see the boxed text, p93).

Canada Place

At the end of Banff Ave, across the Bow River, and surrounded by the flower-filled grounds of the Cascade Gardens, **Canada Place** (Map p94; ☎ 403-760-1338; www.pc.gc.ca/pn -np /ab/banff/visit/visit1a_E.asp; Mountain Ave; admission free; ⊗ 10am-6pm spring & summer, noon-5pm autumn) is a rather odd celebration of all things Canadian, with interactive panels on Canadian art, history and geography, as well as more esoteric exhibits, including a real birch-bark canoe and a 'Canucklehead' general knowledge computer game.

Fairmont Banff Springs

Looming up beside the Bow River, the **Banff Springs** (Map p94; ☎ 403-762-6860; Spray Ave) is a local landmark in more ways than one. Originally built in 1888, and remodeled in 1928 to resemble a cross between a Scottish baronial castle and a European chateau, the turret-topped exterior conceals an eye-poppingly extravagant selection of ballrooms, lounges, dining rooms and balustraded staircases that'd make William Randolph Hearst green with envy. Highlights include an Arthurian great hall, an elegant, wood-paneled gentleman's bar and the gorgeous hot-springs spa; even if you're not staying here, you're welcome to have a wander around, and it's worth splashing out on a coffee or a cocktail in one of the four (count 'em!) lounges. The hotel's best seen in winter, when the lights of its 700-odd rooms twinkle out from under a thick crust of snow. For information about staying here, see p134.

AROUND BANFF
Lake Minnewanka

Curving in a silvery-blue arc ringed by humpbacked mountains and green woodland, Lake Minnewanka is the largest lake in the national park, 24km (15 miles) long, 142m (465ft) deep and barely a few degrees above freezing. Known as the Lake of the Spirits to Stoney people, who believed its waters were haunted, and later as Devil's Lake to early Europeans, these days Minnewanka is a wonderfully peaceful place for strolling by the lakeshore and tucking into a waterside picnic. The lake was dammed three times at its western end – in 1895, 1912 and finally in 1941 – completely submerging the small lakeside settlement of Minnewanka Landing, which boasted several hotels, four avenues and three main streets. The drowned town is a popular spot for local scuba divers. For more information on diving in the area visit www.pc.gc.ca/pn -np/ab/banff/natcul/natcul4m1_E.asp.

If you fancy exploring the lake, **Lake Minnewanka Boat Tours** (☎ 403-762-3473; www.min newankaboattours.com; adult/child C$40/20; ⊗ 10:30am, 12:30pm, 3pm, 5pm & 7pm) offers 1½-hour cruises out onto the water, with a guided commentary on the history, geology and mythology of the lake, and a visit to the famous glacial pass known as the Devil's Gap. Minnewanka is also the only lake in Banff that allows motorboats; there's a landing where you can lower your vessel into the water, or a boathouse that rents motor launches (C$40 per hour) if you happen to have left the luxury yacht at home.

Bow Falls & the Hoodoos

A short walk from the town center, the surging rush of Bow Falls is more a rapid than a waterfall, but it's still an impressive sight, and gives you a good idea of the astonishing force of one of the park's great rivers. There are viewpoints on either side of the falls, along Glen Ave or at Surprise Corner.

Further east of Banff town are the otherworldly pillars known as the Hoodoos, tall columns of sandstone that have been carved out of the hillside by the combined forces of wind, rain and river water. There's a good viewpoint on Tunnel Mountain Dr, which leads to a short interpretive walk with wonderful views of the Bow Valley. Both the falls and the hoodoos can be reached on an easy morning hike from Banff (see p101).

Castle Mountain

Marking the end of the Front Ranges and the official start of the Rockies' Main Ranges, the majestic Castle Mountain claims the northern horizon as you head west from Banff town. Its crimson-hued slopes are stacked horizontally, sandwiching limestone layers between shale and quartz. The force of nature has weathered its top into buttresses and pinnacles, giving the mountain its fortresslike appearance. After WWII the mountain was briefly known as Mt Eisenhower in honor of the great general, but was renamed Castle Mountain in 1979; a pinnacle at the southern end is still known as Eisenhower Peak. Located halfway between Banff town and Lake Louise village, there are lookout points on Hwy 1 and the Bow Valley Parkway.

LAKE LOUISE & AROUND

If you were ever asked to imagine the quintessential Rocky Mountains view, chances are you'd come with something pretty close to Lake Louise. Favored by photographers, hikers and grizzly bears alike, and dotted with glacial lakes, overarching mountains, snowy slopes and vast glaciers, the area contains some of the park's most beautiful natural scenery – you'll need at least a day to explore the main sights, plus at least another day to tackle one of the area's fantastic day hikes.

Lake Louise

Arguably the most famous sight in Banff National Park – if not the whole Canadian Rockies – the gleaming blue bowl of Lake Louise, 8km from Lake Louise village, is an essential stop on every visitor's itinerary. Around 2.5km (1.5 miles) long and 90m (295ft) deep, the lake is bordered on either side by glowering mountains, and backed by the crystalline Victoria Glacier, which seems to tumble straight into the far shore. The lake is famous for its searingly blue water, caused by light reflecting off tiny particles of 'rock flour' (glacial silt) carried down from the mountain glaciers. On still days, the lake becomes a shimmering mirror for the surrounding scenery; it's best seen early or late in the day, when the vibrant colors of the lake are strongest. In winter, the scene is transformed into a wonderland of powder-white ice and snow-cloaked peaks. The surface of the lake often freezes over and skaters glide across its surface, wrapped up tight against the biting mountain cold.

Stoney people knew about the lake long before the first European settlers arrived, but

---

ICEFIELDS PARKWAY

The Icefields Parkway is often referred to locally as the 'world's most spectacular road,' and it's certainly tough to quibble with the nickname. Stretching for 230km (142.6 miles) north from Lake Louise all the way to Jasper, the road climbs through an amazingly diverse range of Rocky Mountain scenery, from surging rivers and high alpine glaciers to mountain passes and brilliant blue lakes. Much of the route was established in the 1800s by First Nations people and fur traders looking for easy trading routes through the mountains, and the road itself was constructed in several stages before opening in the 1940s and being improved in the early 1960s. The road's most famous sights include the **Crowfoot Glacier** (so called for its three-pronged face, although one of the toes has since disappeared), the turquoise sweep of **Peyto Lake** and **Bow Lake** and the enormous expanse of the **Columbia Icefield** (p169), the largest area of unbroken ice in North America, just across the border into Jasper over Sunwapta Pass.

About the only way to explore the parkway is by car; we've put together a special driving itinerary (p125) that strings together all the essential sights. Accommodations along the southern section of the parkway are limited; apart from campgrounds at Rampart Creek, Mosquito Creek and Waterfowl Lakes, and a historic lodge established by the famous Rockies character Jimmy Simpson, the only accommodations are a motel at The Crossing, and hostels at Mosquito Creek and Rampart Creek. You might be better off overnighting in Lake Louise and Jasper, both handily situated at opposite ends of the parkway.

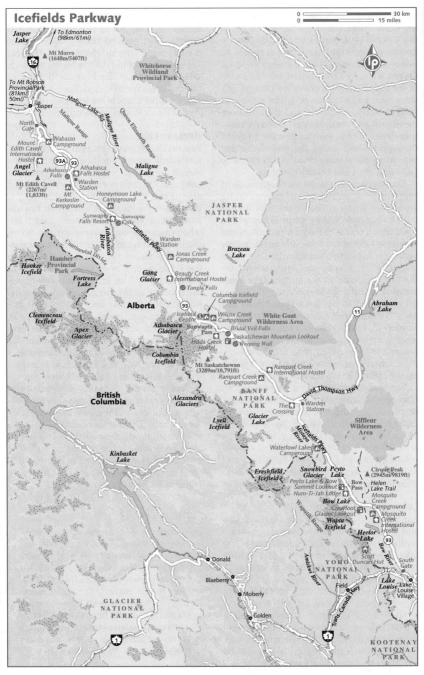

Icefields Parkway

0 — 30 km
0 — 15 miles

To Edmonton (98km/61mi)
Jasper Lake
Mt Morro (1648m/5407ft)
Whitehorse Wildland Provincial Park
To Mt Robson Provincial Park (81km/50mi)
Jasper
North Gate
Maligne Lake Rd
Maligne Range
Queen Elizabeth Range
Maligne River
Wabasso Campground
Mount Edith Cavell International Hostel
Angel Glacier
93A 93
Athabasca Falls
Athabasca Falls Hostel
Warden Station
Maligne Lake
Mt Edith Cavell (2267m/11,033ft)
Mt Kerkeslin Campground
Honeymoon Lake Campground
Sunwapta Falls Resort
Sunwapta Falls
Icefields Pkwy
Athabasca River
JASPER NATIONAL PARK
Continental Divide
Hooker Icefield
Hamber Provincial Park
Fortress Lake
Gong Glacier
Beauty Creek International Hostel
Tangle Falls
Warden Station
Jonas Creek Campground
Brazeau Lake
Alberta
Columbia Icefield Campground
Clemenceau Icefield
Apex Glacier
Icefield Centre
93
Wilcox Creek Campground
White Goat Wilderness Area
Abraham Lake
11
Athabasca Glacier
Sunwapta Pass
Bridal Veil Falls
Saskatchewan Mountain Lookout
Weeping Wall
Hilda Creek Hostel
Columbia Icefield
Mt Saskatchewan (3289m/10,791ft)
Rampart Creek Campground
Rampart Creek International Hostel
British Columbia
Alexandra Glaciers
BANFF NATIONAL PARK
David Thompson Hwy
Warden Station
Lyell Icefield
Glacier Lake
The Crossing
Siffleur Wilderness Area
Kinbasket Lake
Waterfowl Lakes Campground
Icefields Pkwy
Mistaya River
Freshfield Icefield
Snowbird Glacier
Peyto Lake
Cirque Peak (2945m/9819ft)
Peyto Lake & Bow Summit Lookout
Num-Ti-Jah Lodge
Bow Pass
Helen Lake Trail
Mosquito Creek Campground
Bow Lake
Mosquito Creek International Hostel
Crowfoot Glacier Lookout
Wapta Icefield
Hector Lake
93
Bow River
Donald
Waputik Range
Scott Duncan Hut
South Gate
Blaeberry
YOHO NATIONAL PARK
Amiskwi River
Lake Louise
Lake Louise Village
Moberly
Field
Trans-Canada Hwy
Golden
GLACIER NATIONAL PARK
1
1
KOOTENAY NATIONAL PARK

the first white man to see it was the pioneering guide Tom Wilson, who was taken to the 'Lake of Little Fishes' in 1882. Originally known as Emerald Lake, it was renamed in honor of Princess Louise Caroline Alberta, Queen Victoria's fourth daughter and wife of the then Canadian governor-general. It's since become one of the park's most famous (and busiest) attractions, and the lakeshore inevitably gets crushingly crowded on summer days – visit as early as possible to avoid the squash, and spend the rest of the day exploring the nearby attractions of Moraine Lake and the Lake Louise Gondola.

You can usually escape the coach-loads of snap-happy tourists and sightseers milling around in front of the Fairmont Chateau Lake Louise by following the paved lakeshore trail, which tracks through forest along the northern side of the lake, offering fabulous vistas of Fairview Mountain and the Victoria Glacier. A spur trail leads steeply up the mountainside to the famous **Lake Agnes teahouse** and the **Big Beehive** (see p110), but it's a long slog, so you'll need good shoes and some bottled water. Continuing on the lakeshore trail, you'll eventually reach a staircase leading up past a colorful **quartz wall**, much favored by gravity-defying rock climbers, from where you can continue up the valley on the **Plain of Six Glaciers walk** (p109).

For something more sedentary, you can hire canoes large enough for three adults or two adults and two kids from the **Lake Louise Boathouse** (per hr C$35; 🕑 10am-7pm Jun–mid-Oct). Sculling through the water, far from the crowds, you'll be rewarded with gloriously tranquil views and a sense of the silence and natural majesty that must have greeted Tom Wilson when he first laid eyes on the lake.

Lake Louise Gondola

For an aerial view of the Lake Louise area – and a good chance of spotting grizzly bears on the avalanche slopes – climb aboard the **Lake Louise Gondola** (☎ 403-522-3555, 800-258-7669; www.lakelouisegondola.com; adult/child C$24/12; 🕑 9am-5pm Jul & Aug, to 4:30pm May, Jun & Sep), which crawls up the side of Whitehorn Mountain via an open ski lift or enclosed gondola to a dizzying viewpoint 2088m (6850ft) above the valley floor. At the top of the mountain there are free hourly interpretive programs exploring grizzly bears and the history of the Lake Louise area, plus a

45-minute **guided nature walk** (C$5; 🕑 10:30am, 12:30pm & 3:30pm), or you can wander around several short marked trails – look out for the imposing fang of 3543m (11,621ft) Mt Temple piercing the skyline on the opposite side of the valley. Back at the bottom of the mountain, you'll find light meals and snacks at the **Lodge of the Ten Peaks** (mains $-$$; 🕑 8:30-11am & 11:30am-2:30pm May-Sep).

Moraine Lake

Reached by a twisting 13km (8-mile) road that's only open from June to October, the mountainous panoramas around Moraine Lake are arguably even more stunning than those at Lake Louise. Backed by the Wenkchemna Peaks – all of which top out over 3000m (10,000ft) – Moraine Lake is another sparkling blue reservoir that's fed by glacial runoff from the surrounding mountains. It's one of the best-known views in the Rockies, and once graced the back of the C$20 bill. The mountains were originally named in 1894 by the explorer Samuel Allen, using the numbers one to 10 in the Stoney language ('wenkchemna' means 10); all but two of the mountains have been renamed, but you'll still see some guidebooks and maps with the original Stoney names.

At the northern end of the lake is a massive pile of boulders, either left over from an ancient avalanche or a long-disappeared glacier. They're an irresistible challenge for amateur scramblers and there's a fine view from the summit. The lakeshore walk (p104) is a popular stroll, and there are other trails if you fancy something more strenuous, including the Consolation Lakes trail (p105) and the hike through Larch Valley (p111). Canoes are available for hire (per hour C$35).

THE TEN PEAKS

From east to west, the Wenkchemna Peaks (with the Stoney name in brackets) are: 3234m (10,607ft) Mt Fay (Heejee); 3140m (10,302ft) Mt Little (Nom); 3072m (10,079ft) Mt Bowlen (Yamnee); 3057m (10,030ft) Peak Four (Tonsa); 3051m (10,010ft) Mt Perren (Sata); 3310m (10,860ft) Mt Allen (Shappee); 3245m (10,646ft) Mt Tuzo (Sagowa); 3424m (11,233ft) Deltaform Mountain (Saknowa); 3237m (10,620ft) Neptuak Mountain; and 3206m (10,518ft) Wenkchemna Peak.

GUIDED HIKES

If you're looking for someone to help you interpret the scenery, there are lots of hiking guides in the Banff area. Make sure your guide is accredited by the Mountain Parks Heritage Interpretation Association (MPHIA) for that extra seal of quality.

One such accredited company is **Great Divide** (☎ 403-522-2735; www.greatdivide.ca; half-/full-day hikes C$50/75), run by a knowledgeable husband-and-wife team based in Lake Louise, and offering daily guided hikes from June to September; the first to book gets to choose the route for the day, but you're welcome to tag along on a trip if there's space available. The maximum group size is eight people or you can charter guides for a private hike. There are also tailored nature trips on the themes of grizzly bears, birdlife, glaciers and water features.

Mahikan Trails (☎ 403-609-2489; www.mahikan.com; half-/full-day hikes C$69/124) provides the full range of guiding services, from half- and full-day hikes to courses in map work, tracking and wood lore and even traditional skills programs such as rope-making, native medicine and navigation.

White Mountain Adventures (☎ 403-760-4403; www.whitemountainadventures.com; half-/full-day for 6 people C$270/420) is another well-regarded hiking and adventure guiding service, with charter guided trips along popular Banff trails.

HIKING

While you can see many of Banff's classic sights from an air-conditioned automobile, to really appreciate the park's beauty you'll have to strap on the hiking boots and take to the trail. Even if you're not a regular hiker, try to build at least one or two walks into your itinerary. While there are plenty of hardcore routes to delight mile-eaters, there are also lots of easy, level trails perfect for families, part-time walkers and wheelchair users. No matter what your level of fitness, there's a hike out there for you – and if you develop a taste for the wilds, you could always try one of the multi-day backcountry hikes (p118).

A national park pass is all you require for day hikes, but for backcountry trips you'll need a wilderness pass (see p88). Though you'll see plenty of people tackling the trails in T-shirts and sneakers, don't follow their example – even on the simplest trails, it pays to be prepared. Wear sturdy boots, take plenty of water and pack warm, layered clothing and waterproofs in case the weather takes an unexpected turn for the worse. For more information on hiking safety, see p37.

EASY HIKES

If you're keen to sample the mountain scenery but don't fancy braving blisters and backpacks, then these easy hikes are just the ticket. Most are easily within reach of

reasonably fit walkers and family groups, and as you won't have to tackle any serious terrain or elevation change en route, they're the ideal way of getting acclimatized to the mountains before taking on some of the more challenging routes detailed later in the chapter.

BOW RIVER FALLS & THE HOODOOS

Duration 4 hours round-trip
Distance 10.2km (6.4 miles)
Difficulty easy
Start/Finish Buffalo St, Banff
Nearest Town Banff (p92)
Transportation bus
Summary An easy, partly paved stroll, tracking the Bow River through woodland all the way to the Hoodoos.

Despite its proximity to downtown Banff, this easy ramble quickly leaves both traffic noise and tourists behind and delves into the forests and rivers west of the main town. Start out on Buffalo St and follow the road east to the start of the gravel trail beside the river, a popular jaunt for Banff cyclists and joggers. The flat trail tracks the Bow River for about 1.2km (0.7 miles), where it reaches a set of two staircases up to the Surprise Corner viewpoint and parking lot, looking out over the rushing white water of **Bow River Falls**. You could turn round and retrace your steps here, but it's worth carrying on to the Hoodoos.

From the parking lot, the trail descends through larch and pine woodland and again runs parallel to the river, passing several inlets and small beaches en route to a wide, open grass **meadow** at around 3km (1.9 miles), from where there are fine southerly views to Mt Rundle on the opposite side of the river. From here the trail climbs gently up onto the canyon-side above the river, with great views across the Bow Valley – make sure you stick to the main trail, as several faint subtrails veer off along the riverbank and are much tougher going. After 5.1km (3.2 miles) you'll reach the **Hoodoos interpretive trail**, from where you can view these weird rock pillars and look down across the snaking course of the Bow River below. Return along the same route or, if your legs are feeling the strain, catch a bus back to Banff from Tunnel Mountain Dr.

MARSH LOOP

Duration 1 hour round-trip
Distance 2.5km (1.6 miles)
Difficulty easy
Start/Finish Cave and Basin National Historic Site
Nearest Town Banff (p92)
Transportation bus
Summary Intriguing walk around one of the best-preserved marsh ecosystems near Banff, which can be combined with a visit to the Cave and Basin (p96) or a bike ride on the Sundance Trail (p121).

You'll see plenty of forests and mountains in Banff, but this is one of your only chances to see a natural river marsh. The leaf-litter-and-dirt trail is especially popular with horseback riders and walkers. Start out at the Cave and Basin site and follow the wooden boardwalk down to the marsh, where you'll find the **fish-viewing platform** and **bird hide**. On your way back up the boardwalk, turn left onto the forest trail, which joins up with the paved Sundance Trail after about 10 minutes. Look out for the trail signs on the right indicating the start of the Marsh Loop.

The trail meanders on a level course, with the **Bow River** (often filled with canoeists and kayakers) on the left-hand side and the reeds, grasses and plants of the marshy habitat on the right. It's a great place to spot butterflies, birds and dragonflies, as well as many native wildflowers, so bring along a nature guide to help you identify the various species. There are a couple of wooden bridges crossing outlets where the marsh water flows into the Bow River, and these are often a good place to spot marsh birds and beaver dams. You've reached the halfway point when you can see the bird hide directly opposite on the far side of the marsh. From here the trail winds past more pools, bogs and reed beds before heading back inland. At the end of the trail you can turn left into the car park or right to return to the Cave and Basin.

FENLAND TRAIL & VERMILION LAKES

Duration 30 minutes round-trip
Distance 2.1km (1.3 miles)
Difficulty easy
Start/Finish Forty Mile picnic area, Banff
Nearest Town Banff (p92)
Transportation private
Summary Quiet forest walk that follows the green Echo and Forty Mile Creeks through the fenlands.

Popular with Banff cyclists and joggers, this short trail travels through a variety of natural habitats: woodland, marsh, fen, riverbed and wetland. Begin the trail at the Forty Mile picnic area, just north of the 'Welcome to Banff' sign on Lynx St. If you're coming from downtown, there's a connecting trail on the left side of Lynx St, just over the rail tracks. Bring along some mosquito repellent as the biting bugs can be rampant along here, and pick up one of the free trail leaflets from the start of the trailhead.

The flat dirt trail travels through the trees and crosses several wooden bridges where you can view the river and the rich fenland; look out for wooden posts that match points of interest on the trail leaflet. It's a rich habitat for wildlife – listen for tapping woodpeckers, whistling chickadees, honking Canada geese and bugling elks in the fall. Try also to spot the many flowers and plants that thrive in the fenland – sedges, grasses, willows, poplars and dogwoods all flourish in the nutrient-rich groundwater.

The only drawback is the constant thrum of traffic traveling along Hwy 1 nearby, but it does at least give you a sense of how the local wildlife must feel about the racket on the main road.

If you're looking for a longer hike you can extend the walk by crossing the large bridge about halfway round the loop and heading left down the road to the **Vermilion Lakes**, a wetland that's popular with wildlife-spotting tours. The lakes are a 4km (2.5-mile) round-trip. Note that in late May and early June the trail is often closed due to aggressive female elk, which use the area for calving.

SUNDANCE CANYON

Duration 1 hour round-trip
Distance 2km (1.2 miles)
Difficulty easy
Start/Finish Sundance Trail
Nearest Town Banff (p92)
Transportation hike/bike
Summary A delightful route around a river canyon, with views of a gushing waterfall, rugged mountains and the Bow Valley.

To reach this lovely canyon walk, you'll need to hike or bike along the Sundance Trail (p121) from the Cave and Basin. There are some stiff uphill sections near the start of the canyon trail, and the route's mainly through thick forest so the views are fairly limited, but it's nearly always quiet since you can only reach the canyon on foot or by bike.

The trail starts at the bike lock-up and passes steeply up the left side of the canyon waterfall. After crossing the wooden bridge and scrambling up a section of rocks and boulders, you'll come out on the mainly flat, sun-dappled trail, which tracks a bubbling stream through the wooded canyon; in summer it's always filled with birdsong and butterflies. After crossing a couple more wooden bridges the trail loops back on itself and after about 1.6km (1 mile) reaches a lookout point from where there are views across the Bow Valley and distant mountain peaks – look closely and you can even see the twisting outline of Hwy 1. From here the trail descends through switchbacks back to the bike lock-up.

JOHNSON LAKE

Duration 45 minutes round-trip
Distance 3km (1.9 miles)
Difficulty easy
Start/Finish Johnson Lake parking lot
Nearest Town Banff (p92)
Transportation private
Summary An easy ramble around the shore of this popular recreational lake, mixing wooded and open-air sections and the option of a paddle in the water when the weather's warm.

Compared to many Banff lakes, most obviously, Lake Minnewanka, Johnson Lake is little more than a pond, but on warm summer days it's the nearest thing Banff has to a seaside getaway – sun worshippers and beach bums throng to the lake to lounge around in the sunshine. Ringed by dense fir forest and encircled by an easy trail with fine views of Cascade Mountain, Johnson Lake makes a lovely place to combine a lakeside picnic with a leisurely hike.

To reach the lake, follow Lake Minnewanka Rd north of Hwy 1 and take the first right. The next junction is signposted right to Johnson Lake.

From the parking lot, follow the trail past a few picnic tables down to the lakeshore, and pick up the trail on the lake's right (southern side). Initially you'll pass through a grassy section overlooked by power lines from the nearby hydroelectric dam, but the dirt trail soon passes into the fir and spruce woods by the lakeshore. **Johnson Lake** sits in the montane zone, a subalpine area that makes up just 3% of the park's landscape, but provides a crucial, vegetation-rich habitat for wildlife. The trail emerges at an earthen dike on the eastern edge of the lake after about 1.6km (1 mile); the forest to the east is one of the few areas of unmanaged woodland left in Banff National Park, with many ancient Douglas fir trees.

As you continue following the trail around the lake, peer into the water to see if you can spot rainbow trout or spotted frogs, and watch for water birds. On the northern side of the lake, the trail sticks close to the water and passes a small marshy section formed by a tributary off the main lake. Nearby is a shady area under the trees that makes an excellent spot to break the walk and tuck into your picnic. From here it's a short walk back to the parking lot.

STEWART CANYON

Duration 1½–2 hours round-trip
Distance 5.6km (3.5 miles)
Difficulty easy
Start/Finish Lake Minnewanka parking lot
Nearest Town Banff (p92)
Transportation private
Summary A good, level hike that takes in a section of the north shore of Lake Minnewanka plus an impressive river canyon.

With several of the trails around Lake Minnewanka closed during buffalo berry season due to grizzly activity – including the classic hike to Aylmer Lookout – the easy walk up to Stewart Canyon is the area's best option for a summer hike. The trail starts from the recreational area near the boat ramp on the west side of the lake, and travels for a few hundred meters along a flat, paved section past picnic tables and BBQ shelters. The trailhead proper is marked by an information panel where you'll find notices about trail closures during the buffalo berry season. From here the trail passes onto a wooded dirt track offering views of the turquoise lake; it's just about passable for sturdy wheelchairs, but becomes increasingly rooty and rocky the further you travel. At 1.6km (1 mile) the trail heads over a wooden bridge above the Cascade River, reaching a fork on the far side. The right-hand branch leads up to Aylmer Pass, so take the left fork. The trail follows the canyon-side for another 1.2km (0.7 miles) before reaching another fork. The route to the right leads down into a river gully where you can clamber across boulders and rocks to the bottom of the canyon and the edge

of the Cascade River. The **canyon** itself is named after George Stewart, first superintendent of Canada's first national park. The water level here has risen by about 25m (80ft) since Lake Minnewanka was last dammed in 1941. Retrace your steps back to the Minnewanka parking lot.

MORAINE LAKE SHORELINE TRAIL

Duration 40 minutes round-trip
Distance 2.4km (1.4 miles)
Difficulty easy
Start/Finish Moraine Lake
Nearest Town Lake Louise (p137)
Transportation private
Summary This walk offers a taster of the natural wonders around Moraine Lake, including soaring mountains and gleaming glaciers, but without the effort of a full-blown day hike.

For a glimpse of the glorious scenery of the Valley of the Ten Peaks, follow the wooded trail along the western edge of Moraine Lake. It's level and easy (although watch out for lots of knotted tree roots jutting up from the path) and affords amazing views of the first five Wenkchemna Peaks. From the rock pile, the forested path leads past the Moraine Lake lodges and crosses a series of bridges as well as the fork for the trail leading up toward Larch Valley (p111); stick left along the lakeshore unless you're heading up into the valley. At the end of the lakeside trail, you'll reach a short boardwalk with astounding views north across the glittering blue water and east to the jagged Wenkchemna Peaks.

MORAINE ROCK PILE TRAIL

Duration 30 minutes round-trip
Distance 1.4km (0.8 miles)
Difficulty easy–moderate
Start/Finish Moraine Lake
Nearest Town Lake Louise (p137)
Transportation private
Summary Big views for minimum effort on this easy trail along the Moraine Lake shoreline, taking in the famous rock pile en route.

Offering one of the most famous views in the Rockies, this short walk begins to the

TOP FIVE CANYON WALKS

- Johnston Canyon (p106)
- Stewart Canyon (above)
- Mistaya Canyon (p106)
- Sundance Canyon (p103)
- Marble Canyon (p157)

east of the Moraine Lake parking lot. The going is pretty easy, but a shady hat and sturdy walking shoes will definitely come in handy. Start out by walking down to the rock pile at the edge of the lake. Cross the bridge and follow the same initial route as the trail to the Consolation Lakes. At the top of the rocky hill, turn right and follow the steps as they wind their way up the rock pile. Signs along the way describe the area's past life as an ancient seabed, with **fossils** en route to prove it.

The views from the top of the **rock pile** inspired early adventurer Walter Wilcox to write in 1899: 'No scene had ever given me an equal impression of inspiring solitude and rugged grandeur.' Moraine Lake lies below you, while the Wenkchemna Peaks on the far side of the lake each rise to more than 3000m (10,000ft) in height. From **Twenty Dollar View** you can glimpse the scene that graced the Canadian $20 bill from 1969 to 1986.

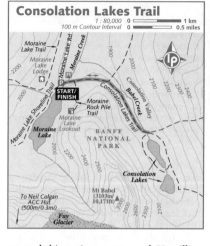

CONSOLATION LAKES TRAIL

Duration 2 hours round-trip
Distance 6km (3.8 miles)
Difficulty easy–moderate
Start/Finish Moraine Lake
Nearest Town Lake Louise (p137)
Transportation private
Summary For a true taste of the scenic Rockies, try this wonderfully rewarding and highly accessible trail, bizarrely ignored by the vast majority of visitors to Moraine Lake.

Though it's barely a two-hour walk from the Moraine Lake parking lot, this fantastic hike allows you to leave the tourist hordes well behind and experience at least a sliver of Banff's wilder side. The destination is a brace of sparkling mountain lakes backed by brooding cliffs. The walk is mostly straightforward, although you'll need proper hiking boots to avoid busting an ankle. Note that the Consolation Lakes are a popular bear hangout, and the trail falls under group access restrictions (see the boxed text, p108) in summer.

Heading east from the parking lot, the trail crosses a small bridge and then a small rocky hill, where you can see the effect of the currents left behind by the sea that covered this entire area around 50 million years ago. At the top of the hill, turn left and descend to the foot of a giant **rockslide**, which was left behind by a receding glacier. Only 10 minutes from the parking lot, you'll already find fabulous views up the side of Mt Babel and back over the shoreline peaks of Moraine Lake.

The trail crosses over the moraine, hopping from boulder to boulder and heading east in the direction of the trees. At around 1.6km (1 mile) the trail forks; take the right-hand path toward the clattering **Babel Creek**.

You'll reach the northern end of Consolation Lakes after 3km (1.9 miles), tucked into the base of a distinctive U-shaped glacial valley. The valley is dotted with boulders, scree and smashed rocks, and trammeled by Panorama Ridge to the east, Mt Bell to the southeast and the wolf-tooth peaks of Mt Quadra and Bident Mountain at the far northern side of the lake. The icy monsters to the east are Mt Fay and Mt Babel, both topping 3100m (10,170ft). Great crusts of snow and ice crown the mountains' summits, and if you're really lucky you might even glimpse a distant avalanche or two as the sun heats up and melts the upper layers of snow.

The trail on to the Upper Lake is rough and crosses some treacherous areas of boulders and scree, so it's best to settle for the views from the lower lake before heading for home.

BANFF NATIONAL PARK

MISTAYA CANYON

Duration 30 minutes round-trip
Distance 1km (0.6 miles)
Difficulty easy
Start/Finish Mistaya Canyon lay-by
Nearest Town The Crossing (p140)
Transportation private
Summary An excellent walk to one of the park's most picturesque canyons, where you'll find yourself above rather than inside the ravine.

This short trail barely even qualifies as a hike, but it's well worth taking the detour from the Icefields Parkway to discover this dramatic, potholed canyon. The level dirt track leads through forest for around 500m (0.3 miles), before emerging on the canyon wall high above the pounding swirl of the Mistaya River, which rises in Peyto Lake far to the south. From the bridge you can watch the river plunge impressively down into the curves and curls of the limestone ravine, and watch how the action of the water has carved out the canyon's tortuous shape. From the far side of the bridge the path leads on to two much more challenging trails, including the long slog up to the disused Sarbach fire lookout, a 10.6km (6.6-mile) round-trip; and the historic route to Howse Pass, the first fur trading route established through the Canadian Rockies – it's 4.3km (2.7 miles) to the Howse River.

DAY HIKES
Day hikes are a more challenging proposition, and though you'll have to expend some extra effort, the scenery more than makes up for the strain. You'll need to be prepared for some steep elevation changes, fickle weather and sections of unmaintained terrain: boots, emergency supplies and plenty of water are essential on any day hike.

TOP FIVE SCENIC LOOKOUTS

- Bow Summit Lookout (p116)
- Standish Ridge (p114)
- Sulphur Mountain (opposite)
- Big Beehive (p110)
- Parker Ridge (p117)

JOHNSTON CANYON & THE INKPOTS

Duration 5 hours round-trip
Distance 11.6km (7.2 miles)
Difficulty moderate
Start/Finish Johnston Canyon parking lot
Nearest Town Banff (p92)
Transportation bus
Summary A classic canyon hike past two of the park's most impressive waterfalls, with an optional add-on to five colorful springs in an alpine meadow.

The paved path through Johnston Canyon to its twin waterfalls is one of Banff's highlights, which means it's nearly always jammed with people – but don't let its popularity put you off. It's a must-see destination, and you can usually beat the worst of the crowds by turning up early – if you arrive before 9am you'll have the canyon practically to yourself. The asphalt trail cuts through the center of the lush canyon, traversing several suspended catwalks high above the surging waters of Johnston Creek, which has carved out the deep canyon from the soft surrounding limestone rock over countless millennia. Shaded by trees, the towering canyon walls are covered with dense mosses, lichen and ferns, and rare black swifts can often be seen darting around the treetops during their nesting season from late June to September. It's also a great walk to do in the rain, as a downpour only adds to the spectacular force of the falls.

The first paved section (suitable for wheelchairs) leads to the **Lower Falls** after 30 minutes; here you can duck through a natural cave right into the spray of the falls – be prepared to get wet, and bring a plastic bag to protect your camera. The route to the Upper Falls (about 45 minutes from Lower Falls) is steeper and crosses a few staircased sections, passing en route the mineral and algae-encrusted wall known as the Travertine Drape. You can descend to a platform viewpoint at the bottom of the **Upper Falls**, but it's worth continuing on up the trail for a reverse view of the falls as they plunge over the cliff edge into the canyon below.

Most people turn back at this point, but they're missing out on another nearby natural marvel known as the Inkpots. From the Upper Falls, the trail climbs fairly steeply through the forest for a couple of kilometers and then begins to descend before emerging into a vast mountain meadow encircled by snowcapped mountains and pockmarked by the five natural springs of the **Inkpots**, filled with brightly colored bluegreen water. If you look into the bottom of the pools you can see the water bubbling up from somewhere deep inside the mountainside. From the Inkpots, trails lead deep into the backcountry: northeast along Mystic Pass and Forty Mile Creek, and northwest along Johnston Creek (sometimes used by bears as a handy drinking hole). Both are challenging multi-day trips, so you'll need proper supplies and a wilderness pass if you fancy tackling either trail.

SULPHUR MOUNTAIN

Duration 4 hours round-trip
Distance 11km (6.8 miles)
Difficulty demanding
Start/Finish Banff Gondola terminal
Nearest Town Banff (p92)
Transportation bus
Summary Savor your superiority over the gondola-goers after climbing this challenging mountain, with outlooks on Banff town and Mt Rundle.

If you want to test your calf muscles, this tough route zigzagging up the side of Sulphur Mountain is just the ticket. While mere mortals ride to the top on the gondola (which you'll glimpse occasionally as you ascend the mountain), the sense of achievement you'll get by arriving on foot is well worth the climb. And when your lungs feel like they're fit to burst and you're still only halfway up, remember that meteorologist Norman Sanson made the ascent over 1000 times between 1903 and 1933 – so stop groaning and just get on with the climb.

The trail starts at the northwest end of the gondola parking lot, near the Upper Hot Springs Pool. You start climbing almost immediately on the well-marked trail (a daily workout for some of Banff's fitter residents), with occasional viewpoints of Mt Rundle and Banff far below. Most of the trail is along well-graded switchbacks and

becomes increasingly steep the further you go; the last section, where the trail arrows straight up the mountainside, is pretty hairraising. Once at the top, grab an ice cream at the gondola station as a reward and stroll along to **Sanson Peak**, where you'll find Norman's old weather station and great views over the whole valley.

Hikers used to get a free trip back down on the gondola, but now you'll have to pay half the standard fare, so it's probably more worthwhile just making the downhill trudge instead.

C-LEVEL CIRQUE

Duration 4 hours round-trip
Distance 8.8km (5.4 miles)
Difficulty demanding
Start/Finish Upper Bankhead picnic area
Nearest Town Banff (p92)
Transportation private
Summary Throw your own echo into the silent peaks at this amazing natural amphitheater – if you've still got the energy after the climb.

This popular trail starts out from the Upper Bankhead picnic area, 3.5km (2.2 miles) from Hwy 1 along Lake Minnewanka Rd. The route starts from the west side of the parking lot and climbs for about 20 minutes through green forest, often sprinkled with violets, calypso orchids and clematis in summer, before reaching the first remains of the old anthracite coal mine of **Bankhead**, which closed in 1922 (the C-Level in the hike's name refers to the level where the miners once worked). You'll pass more abandoned mine workings as the route continues, along with other mine shafts, buildings and vents that have been reclaimed by the forest; if you're here alone it can be a rather spooky place, even in blazing sunshine.

After 45 minutes of climbing, the forest thins out and you'll begin to catch glimpses back toward Banff town, Mt Rundle and the nearby lakes, and pass through a few sections with steep drop-offs. A little over an hour into the hike, you'll emerge into the **C-Level Cirque** amphitheater itself, created by a long-gone glacier and surrounded by jagged mountaintops, many of which remain snowcapped till summer. Let out a yell and it'll echo back around the cirque in a thoroughly satisfying fashion.

Pikas, golden-mantled ground squirrels and even the occasional hoary marmot can often be seen scurrying beside the path as you continue along the small trail along the edge of the theater, before joining up with the last steep, rubbly section up to the **lookout knoll**. Rest here and admire the fabulous views of Lake Minnewanka and the amphitheater.

CASCADE AMPHITHEATRE

Duration 5 hours round-trip
Distance 13.2km (8.2 miles)
Difficulty demanding
Start/Finish Mt Norquay parking lot
Nearest Town Banff (p92)
Transportation private
Summary Huge views and a technical hike make this trail a good option if you're after something challenging.

You'll start out high and keep on getting higher on this mountain trail into a hanging valley beneath Cascade Mountain, carved out by glaciers that melted away long ago. It's a favored hangout for marmots and pikas, and a well-known spot for appreciating alpine wildflowers in late July and early August, but it's tough going and

largely through forest, so you won't get too many views till the end.

Head up Mt Norquay Rd from Banff town all the way to the ski lodge parking lot; the trail starts near the entrance. You'll traverse a service road and pass several dormant ski lifts, before the trail branches north along Forty Mile Creek near the end of the fourth and final ski run. It's a bit tricky to find, so watch out for trail signs.

Following the trail right and over the bridge, you'll soon have views west to Mt Louis and Mt Edith. From here the real climb begins as the trail continues through the forest to a junction with the Elk Lake Summit Trail at 4.3km (2.7 miles). Keep right and catch your breath ahead of a series of brutal switchbacks that carry you 2.3km (1.4 miles) up the pine-forested western slope of the mountain.

Just before arriving at the valley, the trail levels off and a number of faint paths head to the right. These lead to the summit ridge, which is suitable for mountaineers only, so stick to the main path until you emerge at a lovely **alpine meadow**, dotted with white anemone and yellow lilies.

The trail becomes indistinct but continues for about 1km (0.6 miles) to the upper end of the **amphitheater**, where the vegetation thins out and boulders litter the ground. Rest here for a while and you'll be able to watch marmots and pikas scurrying between the rocks.

GROUP ACCESS

The Lake Louise area is one of three key grizzly bear habitats in Banff National Park, and supports a number of grizzly sows and their cubs. Following a series of serious bear encounters and several unplanned trail closures, park authorities have implemented new group access restrictions during the important berry season (from June to early September) on popular trails in the Lake Louise area, including the Consolation Lakes Trail, Larch Valley, Paradise Valley, Sentinel Pass and Wenkchemna Pass.

Under these new rules, hikers are legally required to travel in tight groups of at least four people and are advised to take extra precautions to avoid bear encounters (see the boxed text, p37, for further advice about bears). Some popular trails, notably the Aylmer Lookout above Lake Minnewanka, are closed altogether during berry season – a sure sign that the park is taking its duty to its grizzlies much more seriously. Other routes (including the Moraine Lake Highline Trail) may also be closed according to bear activity – check ahead with park staff.

If you can't muster up three chums, the Lake Louise Visitor Centre has a logbook where you can sign up with other hikers to form the necessary group, or you could tag along with an organized hike (see p101). It might be inconvenient, but it seems to be working, with the number of bear encounters decreasing markedly in recent years, protecting both people on the trail and the park's endangered bear population.

PLAIN OF SIX GLACIERS

Duration 4–5 hours round-trip
Distance 13.5km (8.4 miles)
Difficulty moderate
Start/Finish Fairmont Chateau Lake Louise
Nearest Town Lake Louise (p137)
Transportation private
Summary A once-in-a-lifetime trek along Lake Louise and into a striking mountain valley, ending up at a viewpoint across the side-by-side Victoria and Lefroy Glaciers – with the added bonus of afternoon tea on the way home.

Endless swarms of trippers pootle around the shoreline of Lake Louise, snapping photos of the duck-egg-blue lake and its dramatic backdrop, but most of them jump back in their cars without realizing that there's much more to discover than just the pretty lakeshore. This classic trek punches up the rubble-strewn glacial valley to the foot of Victoria and Lefroy Glaciers, twin tongues of glittering ice jammed between regal peaks. It's a jaw-dropper of a hike that'll leave you breathless in more ways than one. You'll need sturdy boots with plenty of tread, as well as warm layers and a good rain shell. Walking poles are useful for keeping yourself upright on the shifting moraines.

Follow the paved shoreline walk from the Fairmont Chateau Lake Louise for 2km (1.3 miles) to the lake's southwestern end, and then head along the edge of the river flats, watching as the glacial creek feeding the lake becomes a torrent. The trail climbs steadily through forest, emerging occasionally to give you views of the glacial ravine. At 3.3km (2 miles) and again at 4km (2.5 miles), you'll meet trails branching off to the right, leading to the highline trail to the Big Beehive and Lake Agnes (see p110). Ignore these and press on up the valley, as the tree cover gradually thins out and you emerge onto switchbacks. You'll have plenty of opportunity to stop and catch your breath, as well as gaze in wonder at the rapidly approaching glaciers to the southwest and the ice-strewn slopes of Mts Lefroy and Victoria. Keep your ears open for the rumble of avalanches crashing off the distant Victoria Glacier, especially late in the morning; if you're lucky you might even see one as you near the end of the switchbacking trail.

After two hours and 5.5km (3.4 miles) of climbing, you'll reach a tree-lined clearing and the **Plain of Six Glaciers Teahouse** (lunch $; ☺ 8am-6pm Jun–mid-Oct), constructed in 1927 as a way station for Swiss mountaineering guides leading clients up to the summit of Mt Victoria. Perched in a quiet glade, the rustic twin-level log chalet is crammed with chocolate-box charm, and dishes up hearty sandwiches, homemade cakes, gourmet teas and steaming hot chocolates to its clientele of puffed-out hikers. Bag a table on the 1st-floor balcony for the best views and try a slice of the chocolate fudge cake.

Despite its allure, sensible walkers leave the treats of the teahouse for the return walk, as the main hike isn't over yet. From the teahouse clearing the trail leads a further 1.6km (1 mile) uphill to the **Plain of Six Glaciers** itself, tracking along a rubbly ridge that can be slippery in wet weather and is exposed to vicious winds funneled up from the valley. Although there's nothing

---

THE DEATH TRAP

At the crest of Victoria Glacier on the Plain of Six Glaciers hike, look out for the tiny speck of Abbot Hut, a tiny refuge built in 1922 by the pioneering guide Edward Feuz Jr as a shelter for mountaineers. It's Canada's highest national historic site, and is now maintained by the Alpine Club of Canada. The pass (and the hut) are named after Philip Abbot, an experienced American mountaineer who set out with three friends to make the first successful ascent of Mt Lefroy in 1896, but tragically became the first climbing fatality in North America when he slipped on loose snow on the final section of the ascent and fell to his death. The narrowest section of the glacier up to the hut is known as the Death Trap, receiving its ominous name while Feuz and his companions were building the Abbot Hut; the entire construction team were caught in one of the frequent avalanches and swept back down the glacier. Despite having narrowly escaped with his life, Feuz is said to have been unruffled by the experience – his only complaint was that he had lost his favorite pipe in that 'damned avalanche.'

to mark it, you'll know you've reached the lookout when you have a grandstand view of the front edge of the Victoria Glacier and can see back down the valley to Lake Louise and the chateau. In the 1800s, the glacier covered most of the surrounding area. From the lookout, a path leads up the face of the moraine to the cliff edge and a small waterfall; it's very slippy, so only tackle it if you're a competent scrambler. You should see the cleft of Abbot Pass from the top.

Once you've admired the views, retrace your steps down the moraine to the teahouse, before heading back down the valley. If your legs are still up for a challenge, veer left onto the signposted highline trail on the way back down to combine this walk with the Lake Agnes & the Big Beehive trail.

Lake Agnes & the Big Beehive

LAKE AGNES & THE BIG BEEHIVE

Duration 3 hours round-trip
Distance 10.2km (6.4 miles)
Difficulty demanding
Start/Finish Fairmont Chateau Lake Louise
Nearest Town Lake Louise (p137)
Transportation private
Summary The walk that practically everyone who visits Lake Louise wants to do. It's crowded but the sights are unmissable, visiting a historic teahouse, two mountain lakes and a fantastic cloud-level lookout.

This is one of the most popular walks in the Lake Louise area, so it's worth doing early or late in the day to beat the crowds. You can either make it a stand-alone hike or combine it with the Plain of Six Glaciers walk (p109). It's a bewitching route taking in forest trails, hidden lakes and scenic viewpoints – as well as another landmark alpine teahouse – but there are some formidably steep sections (especially around the Big Beehive), so bring plenty of water and take regular rests.

Begin on the Lake Louise shoreline trail, and follow the trail to the right after about 800m (0.5 miles) as it ascends into forest. The path zigzags through the trees for about 45 minutes, with occasional views back over the lake to Mt Fairview, before meeting a horse trail. Take the left turn and continue for another five minutes to

the glassy surface of **Mirror Lake**, famous for its photogenic reflection of the Big Beehive. Mirror Lake is a good place to refuel before continuing on the steep climb to Lake Agnes itself.

The trail divides at Mirror Lake. You can reach the lake via the right-hand trail, but the most straightforward route is to take a left from the lake and then an immediate right after about 100m for the direct climb to the teahouse (left here leads on to the Plain of Six Glaciers walk). It's a steep slog through the forest for a further 15 minutes, but you'll have good views of the mountains as the trees begin to thin out. The final section passes a waterfall and traverses a near-vertical set of wooden stairs before emerging at the lake and the teahouse, nested in a bowl-shaped dell backed by scree-cloaked mountains and guarded on either side by the Big and Little Beehives. **Lake Agnes** itself is named after Lady Susan Agnes Macdonald (wife of former prime minister Sir John Macdonald), who made the climb to the lake in 1890.

It's a gorgeous setting, especially in the early morning, when the luminous blue lake throws back reflections of the peaks and the oranges, scarlets and smoke-grays of the rocks are at their most vivid.

The best place to appreciate the scenery is the open-air patio of the **Lake Agnes Teahouse** (teas $, meals $-$$; ☺ 8am–5pm Jun–Oct), a single-story alpine-style chalet that has been brewing up piping-hot tea and freshly baked scones for its guests for over a century, although the original 1901 structure was replaced by a replica in 1981. As you might expect, there's a comprehensive selection of teas, ranging from earl grey and Darjeeling to golden monkey, apple spice, Imperial Keernun sacred blend and even green, white and herbal teas. Sandwiches, soups and hot meals are also available on a daily basis.

Once you've fuelled up at the teahouse, it's time for the final challenge. Follow the track around the right side of the lake and then gird your loins for the 1.6km-long (1 mile), 40-minute hike through arduous switchbacks to the **Big Beehive Saddle**. Here there's a crossroads: straight on (south) leads to the Highline Trail to the Plain of Six Glaciers; right (southwest) leads to the unmarked Devil's Thumb trail; and left (east) leads to a small gazebo on the ridge of the **Big Beehive**, where you'll be rewarded with a sky-topping vantage of the entire area, with the Slate Range to the northeast, the Bow Valley southeast and Lake Louise and its surrounding peaks way below. It's an absolutely glorious lookout, but you'll need a head for heights.

Back at the crossroads, turn left along the dizzying Highline Trail to a T-junction, where you can head right toward the Plain of Six Glaciers or left back down to Mirror Lake and Lake Louise.

LARCH VALLEY & SENTINEL PASS

Duration 4–5 hours round-trip
Distance 11.6km (7.2 miles)
Difficulty moderate
Start/Finish Moraine Lake
Nearest Town Lake Louise (p137)
Transportation private
Summary A challenging but rewarding hike through larch forest, with wonderful views of the Wenkchemna Peaks and an optional add-on to the high mountain corridor of Sentinel Pass.

Another of Lake Louise's quintessential hikes, this wonderful route delves deep into the Valley of the Ten Peaks and travels through some of the park's finest larch forests. It's best visited in fall when the valley turns into a sea of autumnal colors. Strong hikers can extend the walk for an impressive mountain panorama at Sentinel Pass.

Start on the Moraine Lake Shoreline Trail and veer right at the signpost for Larch Valley into a thickly forested section, traveling along a lung-busting set of switchbacks, gaining over 350m (1148ft) in 2.5km (1.6m miles). At a T-junction, the left trail leads to the high mountain tarn of Eiffel Lake, so take a right and climb gently before making a descent into the fragrant larch forest and emerging after about 3.5km (2.2 miles) into

---

TOM BOYD, WAITER, PLAIN OF SIX GLACIERS TEAHOUSE

My parents are friends with the owners of the teahouse, so we used to come up here fairly regularly and it's a place I've always loved and felt a real affinity for. I graduated this summer from school in Calgary and decided to come up here to work for a while and see what it was like to live this far up the valley, living a much simpler and calmer existence than in the big city back home.

We live up here for five days at a time, working at the teahouse during the day and then sleeping in the little wooden outbuildings at the edge of the glade. We're 5.5km from Lake Louise and 2090m from the valley floor, so all the supplies for the teahouse have to be hiked in on foot, although we also have stocks of essential items such as sugar and flour helicoptered in once a year. There's no electricity and limited water supplies, so it's quite a rustic way of life up here – in fact, it's really not that different to how it must have been in the 1920s when the hut was first built by Swiss guides.

Once the last visitors hike back down in the late afternoon, it gets really quiet and peaceful and you can appreciate the sense of solitude and wilderness – the wind in the valley, the sound of the river, and the setting sun on the glaciers. My favorite time is during a thunderstorm; the sound of thunder up here is amazing, totally deafening and completely unforgettable. I'll definitely miss it when the season's over – the only things I won't miss are some of the daft questions I get asked. People are amazed that we don't have ice, beer and cold Coke, but it's hardly surprising really since we don't have any power…

Larch Valley & Paradise Valley

1 : 150,000

100 m Contour Interval

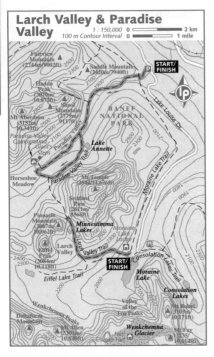

the wide-open spaces of **Larch Valley**. You should be able to see most of the 10 peaks here in a line to your left, as well as the massive, hulking Mt Temple on your right. The trail levels out briefly before climbing above the tree line toward the tiny **Minnestimma Lakes** at about 4.5km (2.8 miles), hemmed in by Eiffel Peak and Pinnacle Mountain to the left (west) and Mt Temple to your right (east); the route to Sentinel Pass is dead ahead. The trail crosses through talus and scree, which can be slippery in wet weather, before making the final half-hour push through zigzags into 2611m **Sentinel Pass**. It's a mind-blowing viewpoint, with the Minnestimma Lakes and Larch Valley to the south, Paradise Valley to the north and eight of the 10 peaks visible in the distance. The pass gets its name from the brooding spires of rock that stand guard above the pass. On a clear day the area seems benign, but when wind and rain set in on an inclement day, you can almost feel the mountain willing you to turn back. Bring layers and waterproofs as the weather can turn suddenly, and check the forecasts before you set out.

While it's possible to continue on to Paradise Valley and Lake Louise in the same day, it's a tough challenge and you'll be stranded unless you've got two vehicles, so most people return to Moraine Lake via the same route, with an optional sidetrip to Eiffel Lake. Note this route has group access restrictions (see the boxed text, p108).

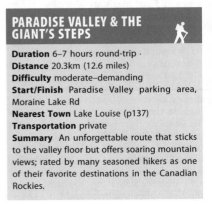

PARADISE VALLEY & THE GIANT'S STEPS

Duration 6–7 hours round-trip ·
Distance 20.3km (12.6 miles)
Difficulty moderate–demanding
Start/Finish Paradise Valley parking area, Moraine Lake Rd
Nearest Town Lake Louise (p137)
Transportation private
Summary An unforgettable route that sticks to the valley floor but offers soaring mountain views; rated by many seasoned hikers as one of their favorite destinations in the Canadian Rockies.

Paradise Valley goes head to head with Larch Valley in the scenic stakes; it's a showstopper, tracing a route past ice-crowned summits, delicate cornices, scree slopes and a natural rock cascade known as the Giant's Steps. You'll need to be properly equipped, and remember this is prime grizzly habitat, so group access restrictions (see the boxed text, p108) may be in force – take care and make extra noise. Trails have recently been rerouted to avoid bear encounters.

The trailhead starts at the parking lot about 2.5km (1.6 miles) along Moraine Lake Rd. The first section is uninspiring, winding gently through forest past a couple of junctions. Bear right after 1.1km (0.7 miles), ignoring the narrow trail to Moraine Lake, and soon after head left on a trail signposted to Paradise Valley. After 3.6km (2.2 miles) you'll arrive at a tree-lined meadow and cross a couple of bridges over the clashing tumult of Paradise Creek, both offering great views of nearby Mt Temple. After 4km (2.5 miles) there's another junction; head straight on toward Lake Annette and Paradise Valley (right heads over Saddleback Pass to Lake Louise). The trail moves into murky forest before reaching the start of the upper Paradise Valley Circuit at around

SUNSHINE MEADOWS

Straddling the Continental Divide, Sunshine Meadows is an expanse of high alpine meadowland stretching for 15km (9.3 miles) between Citadel Pass and Healy Pass. It's famous for its blazingly colorful display of summer wildflowers, and is equally well known as one of Banff's top snow-sports destinations during the winter. From around October to May the whole area is blanketed by a thick layer of snow, and Sunshine Village becomes a buzzy hub for skiers and snowboarders clambering aboard one of several gondolas that ratchet their way up the mountainsides. Once the snows thaw, Sunshine Village also marks the start of several fantastic hiking trails, but it's not an easy place to reach; it's at an altitude of about 2300m (7545ft) and the main gondola up to the village doesn't run in summer, so you'll face a steep 6.5km (4-mile) climb up the hillside before you even reach the start of the best trails. Thankfully, **White Mountain Adventures** (☎ 403-760-4403; www.whitemountainadventures.com) operates a shuttle bus along the mountain access road, departing from the Sunshine parking lot (adult/child C$24/14) every hour from 9am to 4pm, and from Sunshine Village back down the mountain every hour from 9:30am to 5:30pm. There's also an 8:30am bus from Banff (adult/child C$49/24), with return buses at 2:30pm and 4:30pm. Reservations aren't accepted, except for the morning bus from Banff. It might seem pricey, but trust us – once you've seen the practically vertical access road, you'll be glad you forked out the dough.

5.1km (3.2 miles); take the left fork to begin the clockwise trip.

After another rocky, steep section you'll emerge suddenly at the glittering sweep of **Lake Annette**, overlooked by the towering face of 3544m (11,626ft) Mt Temple – it's one of the most startling images of the whole hike, so have your camera ready. From the lake, take the trail signposted to Sentinel Pass and climb again for 15 minutes to a rocky slope directly beneath Mt Temple, with a fine view of all the glacier-cloaked peaks ringing the valley. The trail continues across the rock-slide through a couple of boggy, faint sections, offering fine reverse views of Sentinel Pass, Mt Temple and Pinnacle Mountain. Reach another junction at 8.4km (5.2 miles); the narrow left path leads across Sentinel Pass, so veer right across the boulder field, with stunning outlooks over Horseshoe Meadow, cut through by the silvery thread of Paradise Creek and backed by a ring of massive ice-cloaked mountains, including Mts Hungabee and Lefroy to the northwest. In warm weather, listen for the crack and thunder of avalanches breaking off the mountainside and allow extra time to just stand and marvel at the scenic spectacle.

From here the trail drops and passes along the edge of **Horseshoe Meadow** (watch for bears here), joining up with the connector trail back to Lake Annette at around 10km (6.2 miles). It's worth taking the left fork for a quick 1km (0.7-mile) loop around the relocated Paradise Valley campground and the **Giant's Steps**, a tumble of rock slabs stacked up along the mountainside (if you're planning on overnighting at the 11-site campground, check ahead, as it's often closed when there's a bear in the valley). Follow the loop round and travel straight on (southeast) along the connector trail, which joins up with the main route along the southern side of Paradise Valley. Turn left for the journey back to the parking lot.

GARDEN PATH TRAIL & TWIN CAIRNS MEADOW

Duration 3½ hours round-trip
Distance 8.3km (5.1 miles)
Difficulty easy–moderate
Start/Finish Sunshine Village
Nearest Town Banff (p92)
Transportation bus
Summary You don't have to break out the snowshoes and ice ax to explore the high mountains, with this simple trail visiting three lovely mountain lakes, wildflower-filled meadows and an amazing man-made viewpoint.

This is the least challenging of the three main trails from Sunshine Village, but just because it's easy doesn't mean it lacks world-class scenery. In fact, it's the best route of all if you're a lover of lakes and wildflowers, and there are two glorious lookouts overlooking the Continental Divide. Watch out for ground squirrels bounding around the

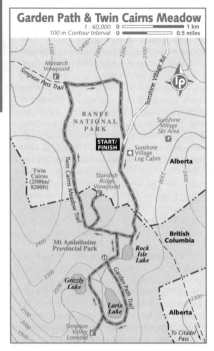

Garden Path & Twin Cairns Meadow

the trail and head left at the next junction. The path winds through larch trees and crosses pebble-filled streams en route to the Grizzly and Larix Lakes loop. Stay straight at the next junction for **Grizzly Lake** and continue along the lake's left edge to the **Simpson Valley Lookout**, where the land drops away under your feet into a jagged pass framed by peaks stacked like dominoes. The pass is named after George Simpson, governor of the Hudson's Bay Company, who made the first foray along the valley in 1841. From the viewpoint, the trail loops around greeny-blue **Larix Lake** and rejoins the main Garden Path trail; turn right to head back toward Rock Isle Lake.

You could now return to Sunshine Village, but for better views head back via the Twin Cairns Meadows. Turn left at the first junction after Rock Isle Lake, signposted to Standish Viewpoint. It's worth detouring 500m (0.3 miles) off the main trail to reach the **Standish Ridge** viewpoint. It's a steep, switchbacking climb to the wooden platform, but you'll be rewarded with a 360-degree panorama of Citadel Pass, Simpson Valley, the Monarch and Healy Pass, with Sunshine Village and the ski gondola directly behind you (be prepared for a stiff breeze).

Descend back to the main trail and turn right (north) across the flat, flower-filled **Twin Cairns Meadow**. After 2km (1.2 miles) you reach a T-junction; take a detour left to **Monarch Viewpoint** (100m) and excellent views of Mt Assiniboine on a clear day. Turn back from the viewpoint and follow the path back down to Sunshine Village, 1.6km (1 mile) away, via a lovely, winding trail through the woods.

pathway and take along a nature guide to help you check off the summer blossoms.

The trailhead starts on the southern side of the Sunshine Village area, passing underneath the line of the main gondola up to Standish Ridge (look out for the log cabin at the start of the trail). From here it's a gentle 10-minute climb up to the first fork, where you should stay right. At the top of the hill, you enter the rolling alpine meadows, sprinkled with mountain flowers and larch trees; you'll soon reach the summit of the Great Divide and cross over into British Columbia. At the next junction, keep right; the left fork leads to another classic alpine walk via Quartz Hill to the soaring Citadel Pass.

Over the crest of the hill, the terrain rolls downwards to **Rock Isle Lake**, so-called for the distinctive wooded islet that juts out from the middle of the water. Above the lake there's a good **lookout** with views of Standish Ridge to the right and Quartz Hill to the left, with a distant glimpse of the snowy pinnacle of Mt Assiniboine; be prepared to jostle for position if you're here at photography prime time. Once you've snapped your pictures, rejoin

HEALY PASS

Duration 6 hours round-trip
Distance 18.4km (11.4 miles)
Difficulty moderate–demanding
Start/Finish Sunshine parking lot
Nearest Town Banff (p92)
Transportation bus
Summary Wildflowers, forest and lofty mountain ramparts combine on this varied hike, which ascends from the valley floor right onto the rooftop of Sunshine Meadows.

If the Sunshine Meadows area has whetted your appetite, try this slightly more challenging route up Healy Pass, which traverses lush meadows with an uninterrupted vista of peaks and lakes. There are two ways to kick off the hike; you can start out at the Sunshine parking lot and hike the 5.5km (3.4 miles) up Healy Valley, or you can dodge the ascent, catch the bus up to Sunshine Village and hike up to Healy Pass via Simpson Pass.

If you choose the harder option, get ready for a punishing climb. From the Sunshine parking lot, the trailhead starts to the right of the gondola base station, traveling up a rocky service road to the Healy Pass trailhead, which heads right into forest after 800m (0.5 miles). From here the trail ascends steadily along **Healy Valley**, canopied by spruce and fir trees, passing Healy Creek after 3km (1.9 miles) and the Healy Creek campground after 5.5km (3.4 miles). Catch your breath; the 2km (1.2-mile) climb from here to the meadows is somewhat steeper.

The forest opens up and the trail levels off into a more gradual climb as it enters the open **meadows**, alive with wildflowers throughout July and August and dotted with alpine larch. The junction for Simpson Pass Trail will appear on the left; continue ahead for a further 1.5km (0.9 miles) to **Healy Pass**. At 2330m (7644ft), atop an escarpment called **Monarch Ramparts**, this pass offers truly magnificent views. Less than 1km (0.6 miles) from the Great Divide, mountains encircle

THE MOUNTAIN MAN

Driving into Banff you might notice a distinctive face staring out at you from the town-limits sign, sporting a jaunty hat, a drooping meerschaum pipe and a rather splendid handlebar moustache. Meet 'Wild' Bill Peyto, one of the great characters of the Canadian Rockies and the original wild man of the mountains.

Born in Kent, England in 1869, young William was the third eldest of a family of nine children. Having left the cramped environs of the Peyto household at 17, Bill set out to find his fortune in Canada, arriving in Halifax in 1887, where he initially found work as a railway laborer, part-time rancher and government employee. But it wasn't long before Bill found his true calling – as a mountain guide working for the packing and outfitting business owned by Tom Wilson (who discovered Lake Louise).

Over the next decade he proved himself a skilled trapper, huntsman and alpinist, exploring Mistaya Valley and Peyto Lake, making the first successful ascent of Bow Summit in 1894 and notching up the first (failed) attempt at Mt Assiniboine the following year (he eventually scaled it in 1902). He even found time for some fancy book-larnin', schooling himself in paleontology and geology using secondhand textbooks, and within a matter of years he had become one of the most skilled amateur naturalists in the Rockies.

He was also a notorious showman with an eye for a natty outfit. One of his clients, Norman Collie, painted a vivid picture of Wild Bill: 'Peyto assumes a wild and picturesque though somewhat tattered attire. A sombrero, with a rakish tilt to one side, a blue shirt set off by a white kerchief (which may have served civilization for napkin), and a buckskin coat with a fringe border add to his cowboy appearance. A heavy belt containing a row of cartridges, hunting knife and six-shooter as well as the restless activity of his wicked blue eyes, give him an air of bravado…'

As his reputation grew, so did the stories that surrounded him. According to one famous legend, Bill once strolled into a saloon with a wild lynx strapped to his back to scare off the other punters (apparently he liked to drink in peace). Another tall tale maintains that he had a habit of setting lethal man-traps inside his cabin in order to catch unscrupulous types helping themselves to his stores.

But he was also a man with a conscience. He fought in the Boer War, became one of the very first park wardens in 1913 and later served with the 12th Mounted Regiment in WWI, sustaining wounds at Ypres in 1916 and enduring a long convalescence in England before returning to his park duties. He continued to serve as a warden until he eventually retired in 1936 to care for his wife, Ethel Wells; she died in 1940, and Bill followed three years later.

You can still visit one of Bill's original log cabins on the grounds of the Whyte Museum (p92) in Banff, and his action-packed diary – which is appropriately titled *Ain't It Hell: Bill Peyto's Mountain Journal* – is available from the museum shop.

you. To your left (southeast) is the distinct peak of Mt Assiniboine, soaring above the surrounding summits. Ahead of you, and not nearly so far away, stands the Monarch, identifiable by its pyramid shape. To your right (west) you'll see Egypt Lake and Scarab Lake, shining brightly beneath the Pharaoh Peaks, and behind you looms the aptly named Massive Range. Grizzlies and black bears are occasionally seen around the open meadow areas.

BOW GLACIER FALLS

Duration 3 hours round-trip
Distance 7.2km (4.4 miles)
Difficulty easy–moderate
Start/Finish Num-Ti-Jah Lodge
Nearest Town Lake Louise (p137)
Transportation private
Summary An attractive, straightforward walk across river flats and moraine fields to a glacial waterfall, worth considering for a rainy day when the cascade is extra-strong.

When Jimmy Simpson used to lead his guests along this well-worn walk in the early 1900s, the Bow Glacier still filled much of the basin at the end of the trail. These days it's shrunk into the mountains, leaving a boulder-filled valley and a tumbling waterfall in its wake. It's an easy and rewarding jaunt, with just one steep section and a fine finish as you cross the moraine moonscape up to the face of the falls.

The trailhead starts just behind Num-Ti-Jah Lodge, 37km (23 miles) from the southern end of the Icefields Parkway. The first section winds along the lakeshore, with great views of Crowfoot Mountain and the Wapta Glacier. After 2km (1.2 miles) you reach the lake edge and the inlet, which the path follows southwest across a rock bed. To your right are two narrow **waterfalls** streaming down the cliff face. Follow the cairns across the rocky terrain, heading for a distant staircase and the canyon mouth.

After 3.5km (2.2 miles) the steep staircase leads you up a forested ridge alongside the canyon; watch your step if it's been raining, as there are no handholds and there's a long, damaging drop to your left. It's hard going, so take rests and gaze down the drop-off into the canyon. About halfway up you'll

pass a massive boulder jammed into the valley, which climbers have to cross in order to follow the route to the high-altitude Bow Hut, the starting point for many ascents.

After 10 minutes or so the staircase ends and the trail leads onto the edge of the huge moraine field, sprinkled with boulders, rocks and stones and backed by the distant crash of the **Bow Falls** plunging 100m (328ft) over the edge of the valley. Cairns mark the route across the valley to the falls themselves; walking poles will come in handy here, as it's usually slippery underfoot. Finish up with a drink and a picnic beside the cascade before retracing your steps back to the lake.

PEYTO LAKE & BOW SUMMIT LOOKOUT

Duration 2 hours round-trip
Distance 6.2km (3.8 miles)
Difficulty moderate–demanding
Start/Finish Peyto Lake parking lot
Nearest Town Lake Louise (p137)
Transportation private
Summary An old fire road passing the famous Peyto Lake viewpoint up to an abandoned fire lookout high above the Bow and Mistaya Valleys.

You'll have plenty of company along the first part of this trail; practically every visitor to the Icefields Parkway stops to take in the sights from the **Peyto Lake lookout**, which you'll reach after an easy 15 minutes through the forest from the main parking lot. Leave behind the crowds on the main wooden lookout and continue on to a three-way junction; left leads to the upper parking lot, while the right and middle trails continue on a forested loop with interpretive signs detailing various aspects of the alpine environment. Take the middle trail and look out for an unmarked dirt road on your left after about 1km (0.6 miles), zigzagging uphill toward the lookout. Soon you'll reach a **plateau** on the right with much better views across the lake than you'll get from the main viewpoint. Stop here for a while to appreciate the scenery, with mountain sentinels standing on either side of the glittering blue water and a string of smaller waterways leading off into the distance at the far end of the valley.

From here the trail continues to climb, with wildflowers replacing the increasingly scarce trees. At 2.5km (1.5 miles) the road dips into a rocky bowl, often frequented by sunbathing marmots and bisected by a tinkling stream. Cross the bowl and set out on the last ascent of 500m (0.3 miles), crossing two hills to the **Bow Summit Lookout**. North is Mistaya Valley rising up to Bow Pass; east is Cirque Peak, and southeast across the Bow Valley is the great sweep of Crowfoot Glacier.

HELEN LAKE

Duration 4 hours round-trip
Distance 12km (7.4 miles)
Difficulty moderate–demanding
Start/Finish Helen Lake parking lot
Nearest Town Lake Louise (p137)
Transportation private
Summary Steep route leading up to a hidden valley renowned for its glorious display of summer wildflowers.

Relatively few walkers tackle this trail, which is a real shame. They're missing out on one of the most beautiful high-altitude valleys along the Icefields Parkway and, in summer, they're also passing up the chance to see a technicolor wildflower display. You'll have a real sense of solitude at the top and the mountain panoramas of Cirque Peak and Dolomite Peak are outstanding. It's best done in good weather; you're quite exposed on the trail and at the top, and the views are disappointing if it's sheeting with rain.

The trailhead is 33km (20.5 miles) along the parkway, near the turnoff to the Crowfoot Glacier viewpoint. From the parking lot, follow the dirt trail through spruce and fir for the 3km (1.9-mile) ascent heading east. As the forest thins, you'll be able to look west toward Crowfoot Glacier and Bow Lake, before heading into subalpine slopes across a giant, boulder-strewn ridge; to the left, before the top, is a great outlook. Over the ridge, the trail heads back toward the west along a fairly level path into an ancient glacial valley with more mountainous panoramas, before crossing a rockslide at about 4km (2.8 miles) and traversing **Helen Creek** shortly afterward. The trail can be faint here; cross where it looks clearest and pick it up on the other side over the ridge.

The last section to the lake crosses open meadow and is usually one of the best areas for wildflowers; it's a blaze of color if you time the trip right. **Helen Lake** itself is reached after 6km (3.7 miles), hidden in a dip below Cirque Peak and encircled by thick alpine grass and tough heather. Break the hike here and savor the powerful aura of solitude. Few hikes give you such a sense of the age and silent power of the country; you'll even be rewarded with fantastic views along the parkway on the return walk.

PARKER RIDGE

Duration 2 hours round-trip
Distance 4km (2.5 miles)
Difficulty moderate
Start/Finish Parker Ridge parking lot
Nearest Town Lake Louise (p137)
Transportation private
Summary If you want to see a glacier in all its glory, you can't beat this steep ascent onto the crest of an impossibly scenic ridge near the Banff–Jasper border.

If you only do one hike along the Icefields Parkway, make it this one. It's short enough to crack in an afternoon, but leads to one of the most impressive lookouts of any of Banff's day hikes, with a grandstand view of Mt Saskatchewan, Mt Athabasca and the gargantuan Saskatchewan Glacier. Bring warm clothing and a decent coat, as the wind on the ridge can be punishing.

The first part of the walk is pretty uneventful. From the parking lot the trail runs through a narrow wood before emerging on the hillside and entering a long series of switchbacks. As you climb, you look down onto the main road as it recedes into the distance, and every step improves the panorama of mountains across the valley. Near the top, the trail turns briefly nasty, ascending sharply before you finally stumble over the **crest** of the ridge at 2km (1.2 miles), puffed out and panting, to be greeted by an explosive panorama of peaks and glaciers. On the right loom Mts Athabasca and Andromeda, and just to their left is the gleaming shimmer of the huge Saskatchewan Glacier, which lurks at the end of a deep valley pocked by more impressive peaks. For the best views, follow the trail southeast along the edge of the ridge and stop at one of the unmarked **viewpoints**. It's a real world-beater of a view, and you'll want to stop for a while to admire it. On the way back down the trail, swing left onto a narrow spur trail, which climbs for 15 minutes to another ridge crest, marked by rough cairn shelters where you can escape the wind and look down over the parkway. Retrace your steps and rejoin the main trail for the descent to the parking lot.

BACKCOUNTRY HIKES

While Banff's day hikes are pretty extraordinary, for a real appreciation of the park's wilder edge you've got to head into the backcountry. With a seemingly endless network of trails crisscrossing the high mountains, and a selection of routes ranging anywhere from two days to several weeks, there are enough backcountry trips here to satisfy the most mile-hungry hiker; the real challenge lies in choosing which one to do.

For information about camping and staying in the backcountry, see the boxed text, p134.

EGYPT LAKE

Duration 2–4 days round-trip
Distance 26.4km (16.4 miles)
Difficulty moderate–demanding
Start/Finish Sunshine parking lot
Nearest Town Banff (p92)
Transportation bus
Summary A great introduction to the world of the backcountry, crossing meadows and a mountain pass en route to a network of glittering lakes.

This backcountry classic starts out as a standard day hike to Healy Pass and just keeps on going. Rather than turning back once you've crossed the Continental Divide, you'll continue on for another 3km (1.9 miles) to reach the high mountain tarns around Egypt Lake. Time it right and you'll be greeted with a profusion of wonderful summer wildflowers or autumnal trees. Whenever you choose to come you'll have a sweeping panorama of the Monarch Ramparts, the Ball Range and the Alberta–British Columbia border. Best of all, the hike is surprisingly easy for a backcountry hike, which unfortunately also means it can get crowded in season.

Start out on the Healy Pass hike (p114) from the Sunshine parking lot and, once you crest over Healy Pass, continue northwest into forest, passing Pharaoh Creek at 3km (1.9 miles). A little further on, you pass a trail on the right to Egypt Lake Warden Cabin, then cross a bridged creek into a meadow, where you'll find your overnight spot of **Egypt Lake Campground** (as well as the Egypt Lake Shelter).

Spur trails radiate out from the campground and provide plenty of day-hike options. **Egypt Lake** itself, ringed by forest and the Pharaoh Peaks, is 800m (0.5 miles) southwest along the level Whistling Pass Trail, branching left after 500m (0.3 miles). The main trail becomes tough as it ascends through forest toward Whistling Pass. After crossing a number of rockslides, the trail rolls out into a meadow from which you can hang a left for a 2.8km (1.7-mile) sidetrip to **Scarab Lake** and **Mummy Lake**, or stick to the main route up to **Whistling Pass**, which you'll reach after a long 3.3km (2-mile) climb. The views are superb; on your right stands Haiduk Peak and on your left the Pharaoh Peaks, while dead ahead are the glacier-roofed Mt Ball and Haiduk Lake. The pass is apparently named for the hooting hoary marmots that you may hear echoing across the valley, although it could equally be named for the whistling wind that often whips across the top of the pass.

SKOKI VALLEY & MERLIN LAKE

Duration 4 days round-trip
Distance 62.8km (39 miles)
Difficulty moderate–demanding
Start/Finish Fish Creek trailhead
Nearest Town Lake Louise (p137)
Transportation private
Summary An extraterrestrial landscape of high mountains and lakes awaits around the Skoki Valley.

It might not have the lush greenery of some of Banff's other backcountry destinations, but for the desolate beauty of its high mountains and truly unparalleled views, Skoki Valley is a gem. The Skoki area has been a popular skiers' hangout since the 1930s, but these days it has also become a regular haunt of summer hikers, especially for those visitors itching to try out a night at the historic Skoki Lodge (see the boxed text, p134). You can expect a mix of mountain landscapes en route – meadow, peaks, lakes and barren rock – and a massive sense of achievement once you're done.

The trip starts out at an elevation of 1690m (5545ft), with the first steep, wooded section following Temple Fire Rd for 3.9km (2.4 miles). It reaches a trail lodge and crosses a ski slope before ascending to a meadowy area with great views of the Slate Range after around 6.5km (4 miles). At 7.1km (4.4 miles) you'll pass **Halfway Hut**, a day shelter once used by skiers heading for Skoki Lodge, and the Hidden Lake campground, where you can take an overnight break if you wish.

Most people push on to **Boulder Pass** at 8.5km (5.3 miles), situated above Ptarmigan Lake with a view of Ptarmigan Peak, Redoubt Mountain and Mt Temple to the southwest. Break for lunch then continue north via **Deception Pass**, looking out for the Skoki Lakes on your left (avoid the left-hand spur trail to Packer's Lake), before reaching **Skoki Lodge** after 14.6km (9.1 miles).

Most campers base themselves at nearby Merlin Meadows and spend the next day exploring the rocky 5km (3.1-mile) loop to **Merlin Lake**. On the third day you can push south of Skoki Mountain, along the Jones Pass Trail, for a night at **Red Deer Lakes**, a walk of 3.4km (2.1 miles), before retracing your steps on the fourth day. Hardier hikers head south for a walk through the glorious meadows along Cotton Grass Pass, overnighting at Baker Lake campground before rejoining the main trail just south of Deception Pass.

MT ASSINIBOINE & LAKE MAGOG

Duration 4–5 days round-trip
Distance 57.6km (35.8 miles)
Difficulty moderate–demanding
Start/Finish Sunshine Village
Nearest Town Banff (p92)
Transportation bus
Summary The *pièce de résistance* of Banff backcountry trips, carrying you far from civilization into the shadow of the Matterhorn of Canada.

This multiday hike ventures into the heart of Mt Assiniboine Provincial Park, an area famous not just for its pyramidal mountain but also for its meadows, lakes and glorious sidetrips.

The traditional route in is via Bryant Creek, accessed near the southern end of the Spray Lakes Reservoir, but its poorer views, heavy commercial use and foraging grizzlies have helped promote the route from Sunshine Village as an alternative. This route is far more scenic, offering wide-open views along the Great Divide, and you'll barely notice the extra 3km (1.9 miles) thanks to the eye-popping scenery.

The walk described here begins with a four- to five-hour first day and a six- to seven-hour second day, breaking open into a variety of sidetrips over the next two or three days.

Begin the hike along the Garden Path Trail (p113), but instead of continuing to Grizzly Lake, take the junction left at 1.3km (0.8 miles) toward Citadel Pass. The trail gives you a brief 1km (0.6-mile) jaunt through British Columbia before reentering Alberta. Head downhill through a thin forest, cross a small meadow and begin a steep climb that takes you up to the summit of **Quartz Hill** at 5.3km (3.3 miles). From here there's a long view of meadows and forest that lie between Citadel Peak to the right and Fatigue Mountain to the left. The trail descends to **Howard Douglas Lake**, on the shore of which you'll find Douglas Lake campground. The trail continues southeast to **Citadel Pass**, crossing between Citadel Peak and Fatigue Mountain before descending into **Golden Valley**. At 12.5km (7.8 miles) the trail meets a junction; to reach Porcupine campground (where most hikers spend their first night) head right, continuing down into the valley for a further 500m (0.3 miles).

From Porcupine campground head southeast, keeping to the left at the first junction. This path will bring you back onto the main trail and into the aptly named **Valley of the Rocks**. The enormous boulders that crowd this lengthy valley are left over from a long-ago rockslide. The valley ends at **Og Lake** at 22.2km (13.8 miles), where you'll find another campground. Continuing south, the trail gradually climbs through the open **Og Meadows**, scattered with wildflowers. You'll come to a junction with a trail heading left; keep to the right, where you'll be egged on by continuous views to Mt Assiniboine. A second four-way junction follows immediately after; again continue ahead.

From here there are a number of signposted trails taking you east to park headquarters and southwest to Lake Magog campground near the shores of the lake. There are a few accommodations options around Lake Magog; see p156.

Once you are in Mt Assiniboine Provincial Park, there are a number of day trips, including a 4.2km (2.6-mile) hike to **Assiniboine Pass**, a 21.4km (13.3-mile) round-trip to **Ferro Pass** and a 14.8km (9.2-mile) round-trip to **Wedgewood Lake**. Ask at the park headquarters for details. You can return from the area along the same route over Citadel Pass to Sunshine Village, or you can head back by way of the Bryant Creek.

BIKING

Despite the grumbles of Banff cyclists, who moan that park authorities are trying to shove them out of the park on the sly, Banff still has plenty of paved routes, singletrack and dirt trails to satisfy most two-wheelers. The free *Mountain Biking and Cycling Guide,* available at park offices, details the most popular routes, many of which are shared-use trails with horseback riders and hikers. In addition to the trails outlined below, other well-known routes include the family-friendly, 12.5km (7.8-mile) Spray River Loop, the 28km (17-mile) roller-coaster singletrack along Rundle Riverside and the super-challenging 30km (18.6-mile) Lake Minnewanka singletrack to Devil's Gap.

There are several places in the park that rent bikes and offer guided and self-guided trips, as well as trailhead transport.

Snow Tips/Bactrax (Map p94; ☎ 403-762-8177; www.snowtips-bactrax.com; Bear St, Banff; hire per hr C$7-13, per day C$22-44, tours C$20-60) is an excellent bike store and tour company, with organized trips to Vermilion Lakes, Tunnel Mountain Dr, Bow Falls, Lake Minnewanka and Johnson Lake. Rental bikes are mostly Norco hardtails and trail bikes. You'll need to reserve 24 hours in advance for tours, the cost of which includes guide, bike, helmet and lock. There's also a useful shuttle service to bike trailheads.

Ski Stop (Map p94; ☎ 403-762-5333; www.theskistop.com; Bear St, Banff; hire per hr C$5-13, per day C$28-45), just up the road from Bactrax, is another snowboard-cycling crossover store offering a smorgasbord of biking equipment plus a range of rental bikes, including town bikes, hardtails, full-suspension bikes, road bikes, kiddy trailers and bear trailers.

White Mountain Adventures (Map p94; ☎ 403-760-4403; www.whitemountainadventures.com; 122a Eagle Cres, Banff) provides guided tours in partnership with Ski Stop. The Backcountry Shuttle & Ride (C$95) service provides a minibus shuttle for a self-guided ride on the Goat Creek Trail (opposite), including bike and gear rental – you'll need to book before 10am with a minimum of two people. There are also guided trips to Sundance Canyon ($95), Banff ($75) and the Lake Minnewanka Loop ($75), plus self-guided tours to Storm Mountain via Moose Meadows, Johnston Canyon and Castle Mountain ($95, two-person minimum with 48-hour notice required), Sunshine Village Gondola via the Healy Creek Trail (C$55, 48-hour notice required) and an epic 230km haul from Banff to Jasper via the Icefields Parkway (price depends on trip duration and bike selection).

Banff Adventures Unlimited (Map p94; ☎ 403-762-4554; www.banffadventures.com; 211 Bear St, Bison Courtyard, Banff; ⏲ 7:30am-9pm summer, 9am-9pm winter) rents bikes with trail maps, helmets and locks, although they tend to be a bit more basic than those provided by the specialist bike stores.

Rebound Cycle (Map p145; ☎ 866-312-1866; www.reboundcycle.com; 902 Main St, Canmore; hire per day C$30-70) is a great bike store with clued-up staff and a range of rental bikes ranging from street hardtails to cross-country full-suspension bikes and downhill rigs. Kids' bikes, locks, helmets, road bikes and chariot carriers (for the kids) are also available.

Canmore Nordic Centre (Map p145; ☎ 403-678-2400; canmore.nordiccentre@gov.ab.ca; hire per hr/day C$15/45, kids' bikes C$5/15) has the area's best network of cross-country and mountain-bike trails, plus guided tours on various single and doubletrack trails (one to five hours C$60), a mountain-bike skills clinic (one to five hours C$60) and rentals.

Wilson Mountain Sports (☎ 403-522-3636; www.lakelouisewilsons.com; Samson Mall, Lake Louise) is the only place around Lake Louise to rent decent bikes, including hardtails (per hour/day C$15/39), full-suspension bikes (C$25/59), kids' bikes (C$10/20), road bikes (C$20/49), chariot trailers (C$15/29) and bike locks (C$4).

SUNDANCE TRAIL & HEALY CREEK

Duration 3 hours round-trip
Distance 17km (10.5 miles)
Difficulty easy
Start/Finish Banff
Nearest Town Banff (p92)
Transportation bus
Summary Paved, mixed-use trail that's perfect for families and riders of all abilities, tracking the course of the Bow River en route to Sundance Canyon and beyond.

This gentle trail is a perfect route if you're just up for a refreshing ride through the countryside. Start out in Banff town and cross the bridge over Bow River at the end of Banff Ave. Turn left and roll along the main road or the dirt trail all the way to the **Cave and Basin National Historic Site**, where the tarmacked Sundance Trail begins just beyond the museum. It's flat and easy riding, with views of the Bow River on your right and Sulphur Mountain to your left, passing through a few sections of marsh and wetland where you'll often spy wading birds and dragonflies. There's a dirt track on the left side of the trail reserved for horses, which is handy as it keeps the main trail free of horse manure. If you fancy taking a break, you'll find riverside benches dotted along the trail. After around 2km (1.2 miles) you'll reach a junction. Left climbs gently to **Sundance Canyon**, where there's a bike-rack where you can lock your wheels while you follow the canyon walk (p103). For a longer bike ride, turn right instead along the Healy Creek dirt doubletrack, which meets Hwy 1 after 4.8km (3 miles); follow the busy main road back to Banff, or reverse the route for a quieter return journey.

GOAT CREEK TRAIL

Duration 2–3 hours one way
Distance 19.1km (11.9 miles)
Difficulty moderate
Start Whiteman's Gap
Finish Banff
Nearest Towns Banff (p92), Canmore (p144)
Transportation private
Summary A great doubletrack between Banff and Canmore that crosses several types of terrain and winds its way between the Goat Range and Mt Rundle.

This much-recommended one-way route is best done with two vehicles, or on an organized tour that provides transportation

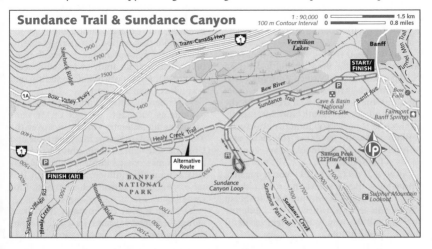

Sundance Trail & Sundance Canyon
1 : 90,000
100 m Contour Interval
0 — 1.5 km
0 — 0.8 miles

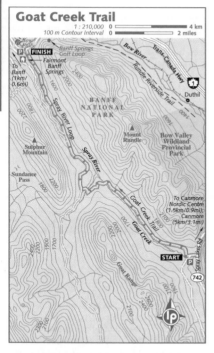

Goat Creek Trail

1 : 210,000
100 m Contour Interval

MORAINE LAKE VIA TRAMLINE

Duration 3–5 hours round-trip
Distance 30km (17 miles)
Difficulty demanding
Start/Finish Lake Louise village
Nearest Town Lake Louise (p137)
Transportation private
Summary Technically challenging but rewarding; experienced mountain bikers rate this as the best trail in the Lake Louise area. You can expect forest, lakes, peaks and exhilarating riding.

from either end of the trailhead. It's equally good in both directions, though most people tend to get dropped off at Canmore and head northwest to Banff. It's a pretty easy ride along dirt and gravel doubletrack, with a few climbs and steep sections, as well as a fiddly bridge crossing and a few blind corners – watch out for other trail users, especially cyclists coming in the opposite direction.

The trailhead is high above Canmore at **Whiteman's Gap**, up the dirt Smith–Dorrien road past Canmore Nordic Centre. The first section travels through pine and spruce forest along the course of **Goat Creek**, with the Goat Range to the south and Mt Rundle to the north. It feels wild and rewardingly remote and you can either roll along at a leisurely pace or pin back your ears and pick up the speed.

After 9.2km (5.7 miles) you'll reach a bridge over the **Spray River** near the old fire road. Turn right at the junction to begin the second section, which travels along the fire road all the way to the Fairmont Banff Springs parking lot.

The trail to Moraine Lake begins outside the old Laggan station (now the Station Restaurant, p143), and the first section follows the course of the old tram line that ferried visitors up to Lake Louise in the early 1900s. Cross the bridge and set out along the broad trail, climbing and dipping before crossing **Louise Creek** and eventually linking up with the busy Lake Louise road – take care crossing here, as traffic is fast and heavy.

Continue along a short section of track to Moraine Lake Rd, where you need to turn left for a brief pavement section to the start of the Moraine Lake Trail on the right. Here's where the fun really starts; the trail zips into rocky, rooty singletrack that's tough and technical. There are two junctions: one at 5.6km (3.5 miles), where you turn right briefly onto the Paradise Valley hiking trail, and then a left at 6.4km (4 miles) onto the Moraine Lake Highline Trail (note this section is a grizzly favorite, and is usually closed during the peak buffalo berry season from mid- to late summer – check with a park office before setting out, and take care at all times).

From here the views and the riding both explode as you climb the side of Mt Temple and encounter fantastic views over the Valley of the Ten Peaks, Moraine Lake and Consolation Valley. The route is rough, narrow and exposed in places – take it easy and admire the outlook. After 15km (9.3 miles) you'll roll down to the shore of Moraine Lake.

You can retrace the route or head back along the paved Moraine Lake Rd to complete the loop.

DRIVING

There aren't many places in the world where you can see so much natural grandeur without ever having to leave the comfort of your automobile. Banff has some of the world's most beautiful drives, and while it may be tempting just to cruise through the scenery, to really appreciate the show it's well worth breaking up the drive to stretch your legs and explore some of the sights close-up.

ON THE WILD SIDE

Duration 2–2½ hours one way
Distance 52km (32.2 miles)
Difficulty easy
Start Banff
Finish Lake Louise
Nearest Towns Banff (p92), Lake Louise (p137)
Summary A lovely spin along one of the park's most picturesque minor roads, with a fine chance of spying wildlife.

While most people zoom up busy Hwy 1 with nothing but views of truck tailgates and overtaking automobiles, wiser souls swing over onto the quieter and much more scenic Bow Valley Parkway, which runs parallel to the main highway practically all the way to Lake Louise. The entire route is hemmed in by thick fir forest and mountains, with regular viewpoints looking out across the Bow Valley. If you start out very early, you'll have a good chance of spotting elk, bighorn sheep and even the occasional moose moseying along the side of the road. Slow down and savor the sights – the Bow Valley Parkway is a hot spot for wildlife collisions, and the eastern section of the road between Fireside Picnic Area and Johnston Canyon is closed from 6pm to 9am during spring mating season (March to late June).

From Banff town, head west on the Trans-Canada Hwy toward Lake Louise, taking the exit for **Bow Valley Parkway** at 5km (3.1 miles). The road zips into forest, passing the **Muleshoe Wetlands** and the Sawback Range, which underwent a prescribed burn in 1993; interpretive panels along the route

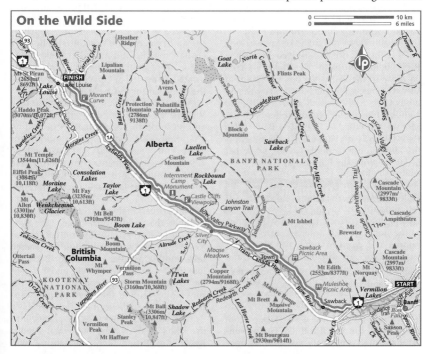

On the Wild Side

explain the science behind forest fires. At around 15km (9.3 miles) the road divides briefly (supposedly thanks to a lazy construction worker) before passing the Johnston Canyon trailhead (p106) at 18km (11.2 miles). Just west is a viewpoint overlooking the grassy **Moose Meadows** (once filled with the eponymous moose, but now more often frequented by elk).

Around 5km (3.1 miles) further west, look out for a panel marking the site of **Silver City**, which flourished briefly between 1883 and 1885 after silver was said to have been discovered here. Three thousand prospectors flocked to the site, but the rumor ultimately turned out to be nothing more than a money-making ruse propagated by unscrupulous local entrepreneurs.

At 24.5km (15.2 miles) you'll pass **Castle Mountain Junction** (where there's a small gas station and diner), directly opposite the fiery orange lump of **Castle Mountain** and the **Castle Cliffs** on the right. Another 6km (3.7 miles) on, you'll pass a small **monument** that marks the site of a former prison camp that housed Ukrainian immigrants during WWI. Nearby is another pullout with grand views of Mt Whymper and a crucial wildlife corridor known as the Vermilion Pass.

Traveling west toward Lake Louise, look out on the left for the rugged Panorama Ridge before crossing over Baker's Creek en route to the world-famous viewpoint at **Morant's Curve**, a site much favored by the famous Canadian Pacific Railway (CPR) and *National Geographic* photographer Nicholas Morant, who died in 1999. The Bow Valley Parkway ends at 47km (29.1 miles); right is the Lake Louise Gondola (p100), while left heads toward Lake Louise and Hwy 1.

MINNEWANKA MEANDER

Duration 1–1½ hours round-trip
Distance 16.5km (10.2 miles)
Difficulty easy
Start/Finish Banff
Nearest Town Banff (p92)
Summary A leisurely loop past a clutch of the park's finest lakes.

This quick loop is just a short hop from Banff town, but you'll feel like you've ventured through some truly wild country once the drive's done. There are great views of Cascade Mountain, the Palliser Range and the Fairholme Range and you can break up the drive with quick hikes along Lake Minnewanka and Johnson Lake. As with other high roads, this route is closed for snow cover from November to mid-April or May.

Heading west from Banff town along Banff Ave, follow signs for the Minnewanka Loop Drive. You'll cross under Hwy 1 and begin to ascend up the edge of **Cascade Mountain**, with small waterfalls streaming down its walls and rugged shapes and pinnacles carved along its top. On the right is the turnoff to **Cascade Ponds**, a picnic area around small pools of water.

Pass the right-hand turnoff to Johnson Lake and continue north through trees; the stacked-up spires of the Palliser Range will loom dead ahead. At 3km (1.9 miles) there is a turnoff on the right for **Lower Bankhead**, the site of a thriving coal-mining town from 1904 to 1922 and once home to over 1000 people as well as shops, saloons, a pool hall and even a church. The town was abandoned after a slump in coal prices and continuing labor disputes forced the closure of the mine in 1922. Bits of mining machinery and ruined buildings can still be seen around the site and a guided walk points out areas of interest. The actual mine was located up the hill at Upper Bankhead, now the trailhead for C-Level Cirque (p107).

After 6km (3.7 miles) you'll arrive at **Lake Minnewanka** (p97), popular with picnickers and powerboaters and often frequented by a resident population of grazing mountain goats. Time your arrival right and you'll be able to jump on a boat trip around the lake before continuing over the top of the lake dam toward **Two Jake Lake**, backed impressively by the humped Mt Rundle – watch out for horned highway jackers holding up traffic in the middle of the road.

A little further on, 11km (6.8 miles) along the route, is the junction for **Johnson Lake**, another popular getaway for Banffites looking to escape the bustle and buzz of the town. If it's sunny, you can join people sunbathing around the lakeshore, or wander around the lake trail on cloudier days. Brave souls sometimes take the plunge into the lake's chilly waters, but you'll need a steely constitution (and preferably a wetsuit) to join them. From here the road trundles downhill and rejoins the main loop road; swing left to head back to town.

ICY EXPLORER

Duration 3–4 hours one-way
Distance 230km (143 miles) from Lake Louise to Sunwapta
Difficulty easy
Start/Finish Lake Louise
Nearest Town Lake Louise (p137)
Summary A glorious journey along Canada's most scenic blacktop, with mountains, glaciers, lakes and much, much more to discover en route.

Strap yourself in – you're in for one of the most amazing drives of your life. This once-in-a-lifetime road trip starts in Lake Louise and follows the southern section of the Icefields Parkway up to The Crossing, where you can either break your journey before taking the return trip, or continue north into Jasper National Park. Either way, it's quite a long route, so set out early and leave yourself plenty of time to enjoy the drive, as you'll be stopping frequently for photo ops en route. Make sure you set out with a full tank and a well-stocked picnic, as the only gas station and shops en route are at The Crossing. Take care on the highway, too – wildlife is a fairly common hazard on the parkway, and what with all the scenic eye-candy, it can be easy to forget to keep your eyes on the road. The road is officially open year-round, but heavy winter snows frequently bring closures and most services are in hibernation between November and March.

Start out at Lake Louise and head north along Hwy 1 to the signed turnoff to Jasper and the Icefields Parkway. You'll reach a parks tollbooth 2km (1.2 miles) north of the junction; as you've probably already got your parks pass, you can zip through without stopping. You'll soon be greeted with your first taste of the scenic wonders that lie ahead, with the Waputik Range, dominated by 2755m (9039ft) Waputik Peak, looming from the west, on the far side of the snaking Bow River. Around 16.1km (10 miles) from the start of the parkway you'll reach **Hector Lake**, the second largest in Banff National Park, and, at 33km (20.5 miles), the glorious **Crowfoot Glacier**, sandwiched between mountain crests high above **Bow Lake**. The glacier was named for its three clawlike toes at the turn of the last century, but its third (lowest) toe had completely melted by the 1940s, almost certainly as a result of warming global temperatures. The first viewpoint, opposite the trailhead for Helen Lake (p117), is often crowded, but the Bow Lake viewpoint a little further on usually has a bit more space.

At the north end of Bow Lake is the historic **Num-Ti-Jah Lodge** (p140), founded by Jimmy Simpson, who arrived from England in 1896 and went on to become one of the Rockies' best-known explorers, adventurers and alpine guides. From the lodge you can follow the trail to the edge of **Bow Glacier** (p116), a great funnel of ice that carved out the entire Bow Valley over 10,000 years ago, but which has since retreated into the Wapta Icefield.

From Bow Lake the road climbs almost imperceptibly toward **Bow Pass**, which, at 2069m (6788ft), is the highest point on the

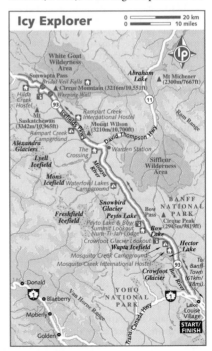

MONSTER BEAR

In the untamed land between Banff and Jasper, you may well expect to encounter a little wildlife. However, if you're anticipating elk or even a grizzly, what lurks beyond that next bend might surprise you.

In 1811, David Thompson was forging across the Rocky Mountains en route to Jasper. He was a surveyor for the Northwest Company and he recorded in his journal: 'When proceeding up the Athabasca River to cross the mountains…we came to the track of a large animal, which measured 14 inches in length by eight inches in breadth. Report from old times had made the head branches of this River, and the Mountains in the vicinity the abode of one, or more, very large animals, of which I never appeared to give credence. But the sight of the track of that large beast staggered me, and I often thought of it, yet never could bring myself to believe such an animal existed, but thought it might be the track of some Monster Bear.'

Thompson's Monster Bear was the M-s-napeo, more commonly known as Sasquatch or Bigfoot. Such a creature has been glimpsed by Stoney people around the Saskatchewan River throughout the past century. Big, hairy and supposedly preceded by a foul smell, the Sasquatch has reportedly been seen by locals and visitors around Banff and Jasper National Parks into the 1990s.

---

parkway. A little further on is the turnoff to **Peyto Lake**, named after the park warden Bill Peyto (p115) and always one of the parkway's busiest sights. A 400m (0.2-mile) wooded trail leads from the parking lot to a wood-decked viewpoint looking out over the cerulean-blue lake; it's bound to be crammed so it's worth continuing along the forest loop to emerge at a much quieter viewpoint just below the path up to Bow Summit Lookout. This is a great spot for a picnic, so remember to bring supplies.

Back in the car, head 6km (3.7 miles) further north to a pullout overlooking **Snowbird Glacier**, which clings to the edge of Patterson Mountain like an avalanche frozen in mid-motion. A little further north is the unmarked parking lot for **Mistaya Canyon** (p106), reached by a 500m walk from the pullout. Carved out by the Mistaya River, the curving limestone canyon is spanned by a wooden bridge from where you can look right down into the pounding white-water. A short distance to the northwest is **The Crossing**, first used by fur trappers crossing the Rockies en route to British Columbia and now home to a motel, restaurant and gas station. Nearby is the junction with Hwy 11, the David Thompson Hwy, named for the famous explorer and mapmaker. The road leads to Red Deer, 256km (159 miles) east.

From The Crossing the road winds through another impossibly scenic stretch, crossing an area of river flats (often frequented by elk and birdlife) en route to Cirrus Mountain, where snowmelt streams down the mountainside, creating a sheet of tiny waterfalls known as the **Weeping Wall** (frozen solid in winter). From here the road sweeps around a huge hairpin known as the Big Bend; at the top there's a fantastic viewpoint that looks back down the North Saskatchewan Valley and Mt Saskatchewan. Around the next bend is **Bridal Veil Falls**, named for the interlaced pattern of their cascade. Continuing on, you'll pass the trailhead for Parker Ridge (p117) about 13km (8 miles) from Bridal Veil, before breaching 2023m (6637ft) Sunwapta Pass, which marks the boundary with Jasper National Park.

Return to Lake Louise along the Icefields Parkway or join the Icefields Parkway drive (p186) to continue on to Jasper.

OTHER ACTIVITIES

Though hiking and biking are undoubtedly the firm favorites, Banff has a host of other ways for you to explore the great outdoors, from hurtling down a whitewater river to clambering up a cliff face. Most lakes and rivers are open to fishing and canoeing, horses are allowed on many trails and in winter the Banff area boasts some of the best snow slopes anywhere in the Canadian Rockies, so there's something to suit practically every brand of outdoor enthusiast. Most outdoor companies have lots of experience with younger clients and people who are new to the sports, so it's also a great place to try out something different.

Banff Adventures Unlimited (Map p94; ☎ 403-762-4554; www.banffadventures.com; 211 Bear St, Bison Courtyard, Banff; ⏰ 7:30am-9pm summer, 9am-9pm winter) is an excellent activity booking company that can help you arrange practically any type of outdoor adventure in Banff.

Inside Out Experience (☎ 403-949-3305; www.insideoutexperience.com; Bragg Creek) is another good multi-activity provider offering mountain biking, white-water rafting, hiking and winter sports, as well as exciting combination tours involving several activities (ride and raft, saddle and paddle…you get the idea).

SUMMER ACTIVITIES
Canoeing & Kayaking
Climbing into a canoe and gliding out onto the water is a fantastic way to escape the crowds and appreciate the stillness and beauty of the Banff scenery. Many lakes are frozen until mid-May, but don't ice over again until early October, so there's plenty of time to try out the sport. You can hire canoes from boathouses at Lake Louise (p100) and Moraine Lake (p100), or head for **Blue Canoe** (Map p94; ☎ 403-760-5465; Bow River Canoe Docks, cnr Bow Ave & Wolf St, Banff; per hr/day C$27/60), which rents out canoes and kayaks for paddles up the Bow River and Forty Mile Creek into the wildlife haven around Vermilion Lakes.

For experienced canoeists, the rest of the Bow River provides wonderful paddling – contact parks staff for a free guide-sheet or download it from www.pc.gc.ca/pn-np/ab/banff/activ/activ28c_E.asp.

White-Water Rafting
If canoeing's too sedate then the white-knuckle sport of white-water rafting is guaranteed to provide a few more thrills and spills. The best areas are along the aptly named Kicking Horse River, Red Deer River and the Kananaskis River; you can opt for a swift half-day hit (from C$45 to C$100) or a multi-day expedition (from around C$120 per day). All the companies below provide life jackets, instruction, experienced guides and full safety gear. Rapids are classed from I (easy) to V (expert) – the extreme Class VI is for rapids that have rarely been completed successfully.

Hydra River Guides (Map p94; ☎ 403-762-4554; www.raftbanff.com; 221 Bear St, Banff) is based in the Banff Adventures building, with an easy Class II–III rapids trip (C$69) and a popular 'Kicking Horse Classic' (C$99).

Wild Water Adventures (☎ 403-522-2211; www.wildwater.com) is based at the Chateau Lake Louise, with a selection of half- and multi-day package trips rated according to challenge and ability.

Canadian Rockies Rafting Company (☎ 403-678-6535; www.rafting.ca) offers floats and rafting trips that include extreme extras such as cliff jumping and river boarding.

Fishing
Casting a line and landing a catch is an enormously satisfying experience, and even if the fish don't play ball, just being out on the river is a real tonic for the soul. There are quotas and restrictions on particular fish, and several areas operate a catch-and-release policy, so it's worth making sure you can identify specific species before you set out. You'll also require a fishing permit for the stretch of water you want to fish – see p46 for more details.

Lake Minnewanka Boat Tours (☎ 403-762-3473; www.minnewankaboattours.com; up to 2 adults C$275; ⏰ mid-May–early Sep) offers charter fishing trips on Lake Minnewanka for lake trout, splake and whitefish, traveling aboard 22ft cabin cruisers.

Tightline Adventures (☎ 403-762-4548; www.tightlineadventures.com; up to 2 people from C$540) specializes in dry-fly fishing for rainbow and brook trout in the Bow River, with walk-and-wade packages to some of the more remote river stretches. There are reduced rates for larger groups.

Banff Fishing Unlimited (☎ 403-762-4936; www.banff-fishing.com) offers year-round fly-fishing, spin-casting and lake-trout fishing, plus ice fishing on Spray Lake in winter.

Alpine Anglers (☎ 403-762-8223; www.alpineanglers.com; day trips from around C$550) offers a selection of float trips and walk-and-wades, plus some much more adventurous multi-day excursions where you'll fish deep in the backcountry. All fishing is catch-and-release.

Climbing
Climbers have been flocking to Banff's sky-piercing peaks and dizzying rock faces since

the sport first took off in the late 1800s, and it's still hugely popular, with an array of challenging ascents that regularly crop up on climbers' wish lists. Consult an experienced local guide or one of the Canadian mountain associations (p49) if you're tackling anything even remotely challenging; unless you're an experienced climber it's definitely worth going with an organized climbing company.

CMH Mountaineering (☎ 800-661-0252; www.cmhmountaineering.com; per adult/child from C$1986/1655) is one of the best-known and most experienced mountaineering companies, specializing in multi-day heli-hikes and high-altitude guided trips. The company also maintains six mountain lodges for its clients, and provides mountaineering guides for C$747 per day. It's not cheap but it's an experience you won't forget in a hurry.

Yamnuska (☎ 403-678-4164; www.yamnuska.com; half-/full day from C$260/380) is a better option if you're just starting out, with lots of daily instruction courses for beginners, as well as more complex and challenging trips for intermediate and advanced climbers. Prices drop considerably if you can persuade a couple of friends to join you.

The head office of Canada's main mountaineering association, the **Alpine Club of Canada** (☎ 403-678-3200; www.alpineclubofcanada.ca; PO Box 8040, Indian Flats Rd, Canmore), can help arrange

mountaineering and ice-climbing trips and put you in touch with qualified guides all over the Canadian Rockies. Courses and mountaineering programs are also available from around C$900.

Horseback Riding

Even if you've never sat in the saddle, it's worth taking at least one guided horse trip in Banff. Without the help of the humble horse, it would never have been possible to open up the Canadian Rockies to visitors, and clopping along the trail will definitely give you a new appreciation and understanding of how the park must first have appeared to early settlers. Most trails are open to horses – see p89 for more information, or consult the free *Horse Users Guide*, available from park offices.

Warner Guiding and Outfitting (Map p94; ☎ 1-800-661-8352; www.horseback.com; 132 Banff Ave, Banff) operates from two stables, one in Banff and the other at Spray Creek, and runs a wonderful range of horseback tours, including easy rides along the Sundance Loop, Bow Valley, Spray Valley and on Mt Rundle (C$36 to C$170), a breakfast and evening cookout (C$98 on horseback, C$78 in a covered wagon) and multi-day backcountry trips.

Timberline Tours (☎ 888-858-3388; www.timberlinetours.ca; Lake Louise) has its corral near Lake Louise, with 1½-hour trips along the lake

---

JILL MOELLERING, WARNER GUIDING & OUTFITTING

I've been riding all my life, so when I saw an ad in the local paper for horseback trail guides I knew that I just had to apply. Six years later I'm still here, arranging pack trips and taking regular rides out into the backcountry.

Traveling through the mountains on horseback is indescribable unless you've done it. The bond that forms between horse and rider after climbing 2400m (8000ft) to the top of a mountain pass is really profound – anyone who tops out over Allenby Pass or Sawtooth Ridge has an immense sense of appreciation for the horse they're partnered with, and a new understanding of the landscape around them. Pack trips are a fundamental part of the history and heritage of the Rockies, and our trips take people out into a world that's hardly changed over the last century. We like to take people back to a simpler and purer way of life: rustic rail corrals for the horses, diamond hitches on the pack mules, no phones, no TV, no internet, just wood stoves, tents and campfires, with nothing but mountains on every side and the night stars over your head.

Fortunately for us, Parks Canada is very supportive of heritage tourism initiatives in the national park and, in my opinion, guided horseback trips are the best, safest and most moving way to experience the backcountry. When you're traveling by car or doing short day hikes you're walking in the footsteps of millions of visitors before you, but a horse trip allows you to travel into the far country most visitors will never have the opportunity to see. Sometimes I feel like my life is just one long vacation.

(C$55), day rides up to Lake Agnes Tea-house (C$75) and the Plain of Six Glaciers (C$90) as well as Paradise Valley, Skoki Lodge and Baker Lake (C$130). Overnight trips and pony rides are also available.

Ranger Programs

Friends of Banff (Map p94; ☎ 403-762-8911; www .friendsofbanff.com; Bear & Butterfly, 214 Banff Ave, Banff) runs a free summer program with guided walks and children's events and activities. Many of the evening events take place at Tunnel Mountain campground, Two Jack Lakeside campground and Johnston Canyon campground. Look out for 'roving interpreters' at other locations around the park.

Golf

Aim for the greens (and try to avoid the elk) on the renowned **Banff Springs Golf Course** (Map p94; ☎ 403-762-6801; www.fairmont.com; 18-holes/tunnel 9 C$200/60; ☼ May-Oct), laid out in 1928 and impressively located in the shadow of Mt Rundle and Sulphur Mountain. You'll need to dress up for the occasion; no denim, no sweats, dress shorts only and collared shirts required for men. Shoe and club rentals are available.

WINTER ACTIVITIES

Once the autumn leaves have fallen and the first snows have settled, the winter season in Banff begins in earnest. Not long ago, skiing was by far the most popular mountain sport on the slopes, but these days snowboarding is catching up fast – and if you fancy something a little more unusual, you can also try snowshoeing or the quintessentially Canadian sport of dog-sledding.

Skiing & Snowboarding

Banff certainly isn't just about hiking – it also has a growing reputation as one of Canada's top ski resorts. There are three main areas – Mt Norquay, Lake Louise and Sunshine Village – all covered by the **Tri-Area Lift Pass** (☎ 403-762-4561; www.skibig3.com; 3-day pass adult C$231, 6-12yr C$109, senior & 13-17yr C$206, season pass C$1559), which is priced according to how many days you want to spend on the mountain. Passes include gondolas, lifts and free shuttles to the mountains, but you'll usually get better value if you buy them as part of an organized package tour, which includes accommodations at local hotels. Boards, skis and mountain gear can be rented at all three resorts or from Snow Tips/Bactrax (p120) and Ski Stop (p120), both in Banff. All the resorts have good ski schools where you can pick up the basics or graduate to more advanced skills, as well as day-care facilities. The websites for each resort have regular snow reports and piste webcams so you can check the snow before you go.

Located 6km (3.7 miles) north of Banff town, **Mt Norquay** (☎ 403-762-4421; www.banff norquay.com; Mt Norquay Access Rd; full day adult C$49, 13-17yr C$38, 6-12yr C$16; ☼ Nov-May) is the smallest of the Banff resorts (just 30 runs), but what it lacks in size it makes up in speed – some of the double black diamond runs on the North American lift will turn your hair whiter than the mountain snow. There's also a good terrain park for snowboarders, and classes in advanced techniques are available at the Snow Sport Centre.

Lake Louise (☎ 403-522-3555; www.skilouise.com; full day adult C$69, 6-12yr C$22, 13-17yr C$48; ☼ Nov-May) has 139 runs scattered over four faces and 1700 skiable hectares (4200 acres), so there's more than enough here to keep you occupied for several seasons. There are runs of all levels from all the chairlifts. The longest run (8km) is on the Larch Face, and there are lots of beginner runs on the Front Side/South Face, especially around the base area. There's plenty of powder and off-piste skiing for advanced riders too, as well as a snowboard park.

Nearly all the runs at **Sunshine Village** (☎ 877-542-2633; www.skibanff.com; adult C$74, 6-12yr C$25, 13-17yr C$52) are at pretty high elevations, so snow conditions are nearly always good on the three mountains. The 3.2-hectare (8-acre) Rogers Terrain Park is a snowboarders' favorite, and the resort also boasts Banff's only ski-in, ski-out hotel at the Sunshine Inn.

Cross-Country Skiing

It might not have the adrenaline edge of downhilling, but cross-country skiing has a long mountain heritage and it's about the only way to explore the parks' trails in winter. Park authorities groom over 80km (50 miles) of trails, including the Spray River Loop, Cave and Basin Trail, Cascade Fire Rd and the Banff Springs Golf Loop. From

Lake Louise village, head out along Moraine Lake Rd or the Lake Louise Shoreline Trail. Check with Parks Canada to see which trails are currently open; it will also be able to recommend trails further afield. Gear can be rented at either of the outfitters in Banff town.

Other Winter Activities

They're devilishly difficult to get on, but **showshoes** have been used by First Nations people in the Rockies for hundred of years; Discover Banff Tours (p92) runs winter snowshoeing trips if you fancy trying out the sport. **Ice-skating** is often possible at various spots, depending on seasonal temperatures. The Fairmont hotels in Lake Louise and Banff both maintain small skating areas, as does the Banff Recreation Center. If you're skating in the wild, take extra care as ice thickness varies dramatically and your chances of rescue on a remote lake aren't terribly promising. Vermilion Lakes, Johnson Lake and Lake Minnewanka often have skateable ice, but check with a park office first. Local climbing schools and alpine guides can also arrange **ice-climbing** trips, although these are really for intermediate to advanced climbers. There are also two **dogsledding** companies based in Canmore (p145) that will take you on an amazing trip aboard a specially designed sleigh pulled by trained sled dogs.

SLEEPING

With enough hotel rooms to rival a city twice its size, finding a place to sleep in Banff certainly isn't a problem, but finding somewhere that'll suit your budget is an altogether trickier proposition. Banff's room rates are notoriously expensive and take a hefty upward hike in the peak seasons, especially between June and August. While there are usually discounts and package deals for stays of a week or more, accommodations will still be your biggest outlay during your stay in the park – which explains why so many visitors choose to cut costs by camping or bringing their own mobile sleeping quarters in a rented RV.

For full details on the facilities at Banff's campgrounds, see the camping chart on p138.

BANFF
Camping

Tunnel Mountain (Tunnel Mountain Dr; sites $) Banff's massive main campground is split over three separate areas at the top of Tunnel Mountain Dr and, all told, offers over 1000 sites. Despite its size, however, it often fills to capacity in summer thanks to its top-class facilities and proximity to downtown Banff. All three areas have flush toilets and showers, and wheelchair-accessible sites are available in each village. An evening interpretive program is run during July and August.

On a forested slope nearest to town is **Tunnel Mountain Trailer Court** (May-late Sep), dedicated to trailers and RVs with full hookups (water, power and sewage). Each site occupies its own terraced pullout and some are shaded by overhanging trees, so there's a bit of privacy and seclusion even between neighboring sites. Campfires aren't allowed.

Next door is **Village Two** (year-round), occupying an open, grassy field with space for tents and paved pullouts for RVs, as well as power-only hookups. There's not much tree cover and you'll need to get cozy with your neighbors during busy periods, but there's usually a fun and buzzy atmosphere around the place. **Village One** (May-late Sep) is 1.5km further up the road from Banff, and has 618 tent sites but no hookups. This one's the favorite for seasoned campers, but it can be a little noisy when it's full – campfires, singsongs and marshmallow-toasting are definitely the order of the day, so it's probably one to avoid if you're a light sleeper. Some sites have lovely outlooks on the mountains – try to bag one in section B if you can.

Hotels & Hostels

Banff has at least a few accommodations to suit all budgets and tastes, from home-stay B&Bs to full-blown pamper palaces with all the luxury trimmings. If your wallet's feeling the strain, don't fret – it's still possible to stay in Banff without taking out a second mortgage. There are three hostels in the town, all efficient, well run and surprisingly comfortable, though obviously for the cheapest rates you'll have to be prepared to sleep in communal dorms. Private rooms are available, however, and can be a good

STRESS-FREE CAMPING

There's no better way to experience Banff's natural charms than stretching out under an open sky with nothing but a canvas covering between you and the stars. The campgrounds around Banff, Lake Minnewanka and the Bow Valley have some of the best facilities of any of the park's sites and they're incredibly handy for exploring the main sights around the southern section of the park. Unsurprisingly, they're also very popular, so space is at a premium in summer. Unfortunately, the only sites currently accepting reservations are the three Tunnel Mountain campgrounds in Banff. Spaces can be reserved in advance by contacting the **Parks Canada campground reservation service** (☎ 1-877-737-3783; www.pccamping.ca/parkscanada; sites $; ⏰ 7am-7pm), but it's not currently possible to select a particular site.

Otherwise, sites are allocated on a first-come, first-served basis, so the best way to claim a spot is to turn up early (well before the official 11am checkout time) or check with parks staff about which sites currently have availability. Banff Park Radio (101.1FM) also releases regular bulletins on campgrounds with available sites. It's a good idea to stay in one place over weekends; sites are generally easier to come by on Thursday and Friday. Some campgrounds have a self-registration system in which you find an available site, note the number and drop your fees into the self-registration kiosk, remembering to fill out your name, site number, license plate and duration of stay on the envelope provided. If it's really late when you arrive, you can do this in the morning, or sometimes staff will come round and collect your fees in person in the morning.

Generally campgrounds with fewer facilities (ie no hookups, showers or shops) stay quieter than the showpiece ones around Banff town, and the lesser-known campgrounds in the neighboring areas of Canmore, Kootenay, Yoho and Kananaskis Country often still have sites when the rest of Banff's campgrounds are full.

Other than Lake Louise Tent & Trailer, Tunnel Mountain Village Two and Mosquito Creek, Banff's campgrounds are closed in winter. For general rules and regulations on camping in the park, including fire regulations, see p88.

option for families or groups of four or more. The other option is to stay in one of Banff's B&Bs; ask about weekly rates, and check their policy on pets and kids before booking. Doubles range between C$75 and C$175 – contact the Banff Information Centre for a full list.

Motels and hotels are strung all along Banff Ave, but you'll need to book well ahead to ensure the best rates at your chosen spot – the most popular places are often booked out well ahead in summer and winter. If you're stuck for a place to sleep, there are several organizations that can help winkle out that last elusive room:

Banff Central Reservations (☎ 403-277-7669; www.banffinfo.com) Commercial agency with links to preferred hotels.

Banff Tourism Bureau (Map p94; ☎ 403-762-8421; www.bannfflakelouise.com; 224 Banff Ave)

National Park Hotel Guide (☎ 866-656-7124; www.nationalparkhotelguide.com)

HI Banff Alpine Centre (Map p94; ☎ 403-670-7580; banff@hihostels.ca; 801 Hidden Ridge Way; dm/r $/$$; ⏰ ♿) The pick of Banff's hostels, run by Hostelling International in typically efficient style. Housed in a wood-clad building with bags of alpine atmosphere, this place is a haven for outdoors enthusiasts, with a bevy of organized hikes and activities (the hostel even has its own 11m-high ice wall). The rooms boast the standard hostel staples – pine bunk beds, identikit curtains and easy-clean colors – but they're all clean and modern and, for more luxury, there are log-cabin suites complete with TVs and Rocky Mountain views. Other facilities include a cozy log-fired lounge, the excellent Cougar Pete's kitchen-café and a lively pub, the Storm Cellar, with free pub games. If you're bored there are evening entertainments from twister tournaments to 'horizontal bungeeing' (don't ask).

SameSun Backpackers (Map p94; ☎ 403-762-5521; www.samesun.com/destinations/banff; 449 Banff Ave; dm/d $/$$; 🖥) This indie hostel is an altogether more chaotic affair than its HI cousin, halfway along Banff Ave in a rather drab, timber-fronted building that's showing its age despite recent refurbishment. Facilities are unsurprisingly basic – the bunk beds are packed in sardine-can-tight, four or six to a room, and the duvets have seen more hot washes than you've had hot dinners, but the jazzy color schemes at least keep things sunny. On the plus side, rooms have lockers and private bathrooms, there's wi-fi in the common area and there's a pleasant outdoor courtyard as well as a titchy hot tub for easing those aching bones.

Banff Y Mountain Lodge (Map p94; ☎ 403-762-3560, 800-813-4138; www.ymountainlodge.com; 102 Spray Ave; dm/d/f $/$$/$$$; ♿) Despite being run by the YWCA, this ex-hospital hostel is open to travelers of both sexes, but it's the least attractive of Banff's three hostels. It's mainly popular with seasonal workers, who flock to the hostel for its cut-price weekly rates. Casual backpackers will find themselves crammed into cramped, institutional rooms decked out in off-white shades and squeaky sheets. The private rooms are a bit smarter and some have private bathrooms.

Tarry-a-While (Map p94; ☎ 403-762-0462; www.tarry.ca; 117 Grizzly St; d $$$) You want history? You got it. Owned and operated by the Whyte Museum, this gorgeous little bolt-hole was hand-built in 1912 from local stone and timber and was once owned by the pioneering explorer Mary Schäffer. The three rooms are still stuffed with heritage trappings; choose from the dormer-roofed Sid Unwin Room, with twin beds and a claw-foot bath, the wood-paneled Billy Warren Room, or Mary's own bedroom, complete with hardwood floors, vintage fireplace and antique chairs. A real treat.

Rocky Mountain (Map p94; ☎ 403-762-4811; www.rockymtnbb.com; 223 Otter St; r/ste $$/$$$) This pretty little pale-blue timber house might lack the historical cachet, but it's wonderful value considering its proximity to town. Built for CPR workers in the 1930s, the house has rooms split over three levels: cut-price basement suites (with fridges and microwaves), standard doubles (some sharing bathrooms) on the 2nd floor and a roomy top-floor suite with full kitchen and wrap-around views. The decor's a touch spartan – neutral tones, modern fixtures and catalogue-style furnishings – but comfort's definitely the name of the game.

Poplar Inn (Map p94; ☎ 403-760-8688; www.thepoplarinn.ca; 316 Lynx St; d $$) Hospitality runs in the family at this delightful little home stay in downtown Banff. Run by a convivial land-lady whose parents ran one of the town's original guesthouses, this elegant B&B offers two swish rooms with deluxe touches such as Egyptian cotton sheets, silk throws and sliding doors onto private garden patios. Throw in sparkling bathrooms and a homemade breakfast of muffins, scones and chocolate croissants served in a mountain-view turret, and you've got one of the best B&Bs in town.

Treetops (Map p94; ☎ 403-762-2809; www.banfftreetops.com; 336 Beaver St; d $$) There are just a couple of fresh, inviting rooms at this homely B&B, so you'll need to plan ahead. Located in a smart wooden chalet just off Beaver St, the simple rooms are nicely furnished in crisp white, pine and pastel prints. The real selling point is the private guest dining room and fire-warmed lounge, not to mention the glorious mountain views from the house balcony.

Bumper's Inn (Map p94; ☎ 403-762-3386; www.bumpersinn.com; 603 Banff Ave; r $$) Alright, so it's a motel, and it might lack the character of Banff's B&Bs, but for the money this is one of the best deals in town. Luxury it ain't – expect boxy rooms, prefab furniture and dangerously outdated decor – but if all you're after is a basic Banff base, this motel is well worth considering. Try to bag one of the 2nd-floor balcony rooms, some of which have views of the forest and the looming specter of Cascade Mountain.

Rundle Manor (Map p94; ☎ 403-762-4496; www.bestofbanff.com; 337 Banff Ave; apt $$) It's not much to look at from outside, but this concrete condo block offers one- and two-bedroom apartments (complete with fully equipped kitchens) that are ideal if you're planning an extended stay. The two-bed apartments have queen-size beds in both rooms plus pull-out sofa beds in the lounge, and they're unbeatably good value if you're traveling in a large group or en famille – just don't bank on many frills.

Elkhorn Lodge (Map p94; ☎ 403-762-2299; www.elkhornbanff.ca; 124 Spray Ave; r $, ste $$-$$$; ☐ ♿) Rusticity and relaxation take top billing at this homely little forest-side lodge, which offers a mix of basic doubles and stand-alone suites with galley kitchens and separate sitting rooms. Rough wood, solid stone and '70s furnishings underpin the decidedly dated decor, but the lodges are top value – the best is super-spacious Suite 5, with fire lounge, twin bedrooms and picture windows onto the forest. The poky Suite 4 and a couple of the smaller rooms could do with a spruce-up, but it's not a bad Banff base by any means.

our pick **Juniper** (☎ 403-762-2281; www.thejuniper.com; 1 Juniper Way; r $$$; 🖳 ♿) This boutique new hotel feels reassuringly metropolitan compared to many of Banff's old stalwarts. Situated near the base of Mt Norquay, the hotel is arranged across a series of side-by-side chalets, and the decor throughout is sexy and stripped-back – more New York than national park. The standard rooms are smart bordering on spartan: all slate and cappuccino tones, designer lamps and arty photographic prints, backed up by touches such as wi-fi, minifridges and Rocky Mountain room sprays. For real luxury, opt for a king suite with gas fire and Jacuzzi tub, or a multi-room chalet with kitchen and giant flat-screen TV. A real looker.

Buffaloberry (Map p94; ☎ 403-762-3750; www.buffaloberry.com; 417 Marten St; d $$$; 🖳) You'll be hard-pushed to find as much character in any of Banff's big hotels as this fab little B&B squeezes into a single room. The four individually styled bedrooms are charming and cozy, blending rich fabrics and queen-size wooden beds with the down-home atmosphere of a mountain country lodge. Under-floor heating and nightly turn-down treats keep the pamper factor high, and the lovely wood-burner lounge, stocked with local literature, makes a great place to kick back after a hard day's hike.

Thea's House (Map p94; ☎ 403-762-2499; www.theashouse.com; 138 Otter St; d $$$) Soaring vaulted ceilings, pared-back pine and designer architecture characterize this 21st-century B&B. It's a real treat, run with flair and style by its owners Jami and Greg Christou. The two rooms are a mix of old-fashioned features (hand-built wooden beds, chaise lounges, glossy fir floors) and deluxe trappings (gas fireplace, spa, mountain-view balconies), while little extras such as fresh-brewed coffee, hiking guidebooks and homemade yogurts will keep you suitably spoiled until the time comes to tear yourself away.

Banff Ptarmigan Inn (Map p94; ☎ 403-762-2207; www.bestofbanff.com; 337 Banff Ave; d $$$; 🖳 ♿) It lacks the wow factor of Banff's top-end hotels, but for value the red-roofed Ptarmigan Inn is a top choice. Though it's right in the heart of the hotel-heavy ghetto on Banff Ave, most of the cheaper rooms are set back from the main road so they're surprisingly tranquil. There's not much to choose between the standard, superior and premium rooms (floral throws, framed watercolors and beige shades are standard throughout), though extra cash buys you more space and slightly flasher bathrooms. It's comfy if unavoidably generic, but dead handy for downtown.

Driftwood Inn (Map p94; ☎ 403-762-3577; www.bestofbanff.com; 337 Banff Ave; d $$$) Not the regal residence you were dreaming of, perhaps, but another cut-price hotel that will allow you to spend you hard-earned cash on more worthwhile activities than sleeping. Next door to the Ptarmigan Inn (and sharing use of its facilities), the Driftwood is a bog-standard motel with the usual cookie-cutter facilities – rectangular layouts, battered bathrooms, scuffed-up furniture and the occasional dustball under the bed – but its main attraction is the bargain-basement price tag. Ask nicely and you might even bag a room with a view.

Banff Caribou Lodge (Map p94; ☎ 403-762-5887; www.bestofbanff.com; 521 Banff Ave; r $$$-$$$$; 🖳 ♿) Despite its concrete-clad exterior, this popular Banff Ave hotel does its best to create a convincingly alpine feel with log fires, faux-stone walls and wood beams aplenty, but the majority of its rooms are only just above motel standard, with peach-and-cream finishes, puffy duvet–clad beds and maple furniture. The split-level loft suites are classier, with a small sofa lounge and fire downstairs, topped off by a Jacuzzi spa and sleeping area. The luxurious Red Earth Spa and complimentary shuttle bus are nice touches, but considering the price, you'd expect a bit more pizzazz.

Buffalo Mountain Lodge (Map p94; ☎ 403-762-4200; bmlmanager@crmr.com; 700 Tunnel Mountain Dr; lodges $$$-$$$$) If it's a mountain-getaway experience you're after, but you just can't bear to give up the mod cons, look no further than these detached lodges on the edge of Tunnel Mountain. Buffalo heads, antler chandeliers and stout wood beams in the main lobby and dining room set the rustic-chic tone, while the lodges mix old-fashioned touches (slate-floored bathrooms, bear-claw bathtubs, pine ceilings) with an elegant aesthetic that's straight out of an interior-design magazine.

Hidden Ridge Resort (Map p94; ☎ 403-762-3544; www.bestofbanff.com; 901 Coyote Dr; lodges $$$-$$$$; 🐾 ♿ 🐕) Tucked away among trees, this self-catering resort is a great option for families, with modern condos and old-world A-frame chalets in a range of configurations. The basic chalets boast wood-burning stoves, galley kitchens and mountain-view porches, while at the top end you can splash out on Jacuzzis and cozy loft bedrooms for the kids. There's even a forest hot tub if you're valiant enough to brave the mountain air.

Fairmont Banff Springs (Map p94; ☎ 403-762-2211, 800-441-1414; www.fairmont.com; Spray Ave; d $$$$; 🖥️ 🐾 ♿ 🐕) Slap down the platinum and prepare to be preened – you've just checked into one of Canada's landmark hotels. Built in 1928, the Banff Springs juts out above the tree line beside the Bow River like a fairy-tale European chateau. The hotel has always provided the last word in luxury for its discerning guests – it's not quite as exclusive as in its heyday, but the grand halls, stately staircases and balustraded landings are as impressive as ever. Guests can plunge into the indoor pool, wallow in the Willow Stream spa, sip cocktails in the Grapes bar or just wander around the ostentatious public rooms, which range from a Gothic great hall to a full-blown evening ballroom. As always with celebrity hotels, you'll pay through the nose for the privilege of staying here, and the plush rooms are criminally overpriced, so unless you've got greenbacks to burn, it might be best to just settle for afternoon tea.

Fox Hotel (Map p94; ☎ 403-760-8500; www.bestof banff.com; 461 Banff Ave; r $$$$; 🐾 🖥️ 🐕) This new

---

BACKCOUNTRY STAYS

Camping

There are over 50 campgrounds dotted around the Banff backcountry, but they're fairly rudimentary – cleared sites, tent pads and pit toilets pretty much sum up the facilities – so you'll need to pack in everything else (and pack everything out again once your trip's finished). Fish Lake, Egypt Lake and Aylmer Pass Junction are all popular destinations, but there are lots more to try if these are full (as they often are in season). You'll need to indicate which campgrounds you intend to use when you purchase your wilderness pass. Reservations are accepted up to three months in advance, and you *must* stick to these campgrounds once you've booked them. Trail and campground numbers are strictly limited, so you might well find your chosen route is booked out unless you plan ahead. The maximum stay at any one site is three days.

Beyond the backcountry, there are even more remote areas where there are no designated campgrounds at all. Here, random camping is still allowed. Make sure your campsite is 5km from any trailhead, 50m off the trail and 70m from any water source, and take the usual precautions to prevent forest fires and unnecessary damage to the environment.

Shelters

Parks Canada operates two backcountry **trail shelters** (per night $), one at Egypt Lake and another at Bryant Creek. Both are extremely rustic and offer little more than a roof over your head. You'll still need to be completely self-sufficient, with your own bedding, food and cooking equipment. Book the shelters when you purchase your wilderness pass. Reservations can be made up to three months in advance and there's a maximum stay of three nights.

Alpine Club of Canada Huts

Initially set up to provide overnight shelters for climbers and mountaineers tackling the park's peaks, the basic huts run by the Alpine Club of Canada have since become popular with other backcountry explorers. They range from basic portacabins to historic log huts and nearly all are perched in the kind of lofty location that's guaranteed to make vertigo sufferers go weak at the knees. Most have mattresses, cooking stoves and utensils, but you'll need your own sleeping bag, food and other supplies (including toilet paper and matches).

Reservations are required at all huts and can be made through the **Alpine Clubhouse** (☎ 403-678-3200; www.alpineclubofcanada.ca; PO Box 8040, Indian Flats Rd, Canmore; per night $, under 16yr half-price) up to a month in advance. You'll also need a wilderness pass.

pretender to Banff's luxury crown opened to much fanfare in 2007, and it's a real beauty. Water trickles over rock displays and a blazing fire burns inside the swish lobby, and the same deluxe detail runs throughout the upstairs suites. Gingham-check bedspreads, richly patterned wallpapers and artful prints conjure a warm, inviting feel inside the rooms. Some have small kitchen nooks, others lounge annexes, while the premium-rate suites have an ultra-romantic loft bedroom. This fox is fancy.

Rimrock Resort Hotel (☎ 403-762-3356, 800-661-1587; www.rimrockresort.com; 300 Mountain Ave; d $$$$; 🐾) Opposite the Upper Hot Springs Pool, near the gondolo station at the base of Sulphur Mountain, this is another top-class sleep, although the building itself is something of a concrete eyesore. The corporate rooms are stacked up like brick boxes on the mountainside and the hotel offers the usual high-end facilities: spas, saunas, a jazz lounge, a brace of swanky dining rooms and to-die-for views across the Bow Valley.

Other options:

Royal Canadian Lodge (Map p94; ☎ 403-762-3307; www.charltonresorts.com; 459 Banff Ave; d $$; ♿) An expensive, slightly stuffy, lodge-style hotel that's heavy on the Canadiana (think log fire and moose head in the lobby). The hotel offers three tiers of rooms with fairly standard features that don't quite justify the elevated price tag.

Spruce Grove Inn (Map p94; ☎ 403-762-3301; www.sprucegroveinn.com; 545 Banff Ave; d $$, ste $$$; 💻 📺 ♿) Lots of motel-standard rooms in this large, purpose-built hotel. Ask for one of the twin-level loft suites, three of which come with jet tubs.

The historic **Abbot Pass Hut** (Map p85; Mt Victoria; ☼ summer) sleeps 24 and is perched atop a difficult glacier climb at the end of the Plain of Six Glaciers (p109). The tiny **Castle Mountain Hut** (Map p85; Castle Mountain; ☼ summer) sleeps six and is located halfway up the mountain. It's mainly used by rock climbers. There's also a string of huts along the Wapta Icefield, allowing adventurers to complete the so-called Wapta Traverse. These include **Peyto Hut** (☼ summer & winter), which sleeps 18 in summer and 16 in winter; **Bow Hut** (☼ summer & winter), sleeping 30; and **Neil Colgan Hut** (Map p85; Valley of the Ten Peaks; ☼ summer & winter), the highest habitable structure in Canada, sleeping 18 in summer and 16 in winter. The Alpine Club also operates huts along the Icefields Parkway (see p139).

Lodges

There are two commercial lodges in Banff's backcountry, which both offer a much higher standard of accommodations than the backcountry huts and shelters (you'll even get afternoon tea!).

Skoki Lodge (Map p85; ☎ 403-522-3555; www.skoki.com; r $$, 2-night minimum stay) was the first ski lodge ever built in the Canadian Rockies and remains one of the most atmospheric places to stay in the whole national park. Built in 1931 overlooking a glorious high mountain valley and briefly managed by Peter and Catharine Whyte (who founded Banff's Whyte Museum), the lodge can only be reached after an 11km climb from Lake Louise via Deception Pass (see the Skoki Valley & Merlin Lake hike, p118), so traffic noise certainly isn't going to be a problem. As you'd expect, the decor's rough and ready – log walls and simple little beds in the cabins, kerosene lamps for lighting, water jugs for washing and mountain memorabilia dating back to the 1930s dotted all around the main lodge. Despite the rustic feel, you'll be thoroughly spoiled throughout your stay, with gourmet meals served buffet-style by the lodge chef, and everything from fireside reading to cribbage competitions once the sun goes down. Real adventurers can even snowshoe or ski here in midwinter.

Shadow Lake Lodge (Map p85; ☎ 403-762-0116; www.shadowlakelodge.com; cabins $$) has 12 cute little timber cabins just a stone's throw from Shadow Lake, 13.2km (8.2 miles) from the Redearth Creek trailhead. Though it lacks the heritage kick of Skoki, the cabins are a little roomier and more private (complete with solar-powered lighting and propane heating) and the mountain setting is just as fine. Meals are included in the price and you're near wonderful hikes to Gibbon Pass, Ball Pass and Haiduk Lake.

LAKE MINNEWANKA
Camping
The twin campgrounds around Lake Minnewanka are perennially popular thanks to their peaceful wooded setting.

Two Jack Lakeside (Map p85; Minnewanka Loop Dr; sites $; ☽ mid-May–mid-Sep) With just 74 sites, the lakeside campground is nearly always the most packed. There are fantastic views, particularly if you can grab a site overlooking the lake itself, and thanks to the comprehensive facilities (bear-proof lockers, flush toilets, showers) and the limited number of campers, it's one of the best Banff campgrounds.

Two Jack Main (Map p85; Minnewanka Loop Dr; sites $; ☽ mid-May–Sep) Offers lots more sites dotted liberally under the trees just up the road from the lakeside campground. This is where all the campers who can't squeeze in beside the lake end up. There are sites for RVs and tents, but no power hookups or showers.

BOW VALLEY
Set midway between Banff town and Lake Louise village, the lush Bow Valley gives you a chance to experience the wilderness and is also handy for an early start on day hikes.

Camping
Johnston Canyon (Map p85; Bow Valley Parkway; sites $; ☽ early Jun–mid-Sep; ⓐ) If you really want to get that backwoods camping feel, this excellent campground opposite the parking lot for Johnston Canyon is tough to top. It strikes just the right balance between facilities and camper freedom. The 132 sites are spacious and fairly private, especially along the wooded loops and the creek, and you certainly won't feel as hemmed in or overlooked as you would at the larger campgrounds around Banff. Flush toilets, showers and dump stations are all available.

Protection Mountain (Map p85; Bow Valley Parkway; sites $; ☽ Jun–Sep) Slightly more basic site further up the Bow Valley Parkway that's usually fairly quiet and surrounded by wonderfully scenic views. It's equally handy for heading on to Lake Louise and Banff, but there are no hookups, showers or laundry facilities, so RV campers tend to give it a wide berth.

Hotels & Hostels
Castle Mountain Wilderness Hostel (Map p85; ☎ 403-670-7580; cr.castle@hihostels.ca; Castle Junction; dm $) Take a step into the wilds at this rural cottage hostel secreted in the shadow of Castle Mountain. Like Rampart Creek (p140) and Mosquito Creek (p139), this is definitely a hostel from the old school; more a backcountry cabin than a facility-packed backpackers. There's just a simple kitchen, a couple of gender-sorted dorms and a snug common room set around a log-burning stove, with large windows looking out onto the unspoilt mountain countryside. Don't be surprised if you spy an elk or two grazing outside – it's all part of the backwoods vibe.

Johnston Canyon Resort (Map p85; ☎ 403-762-0868; www.johnstoncanyon.com; Bow Valley Parkway; cabins $$-$$$; ☽ May-Oct) Built in the late 1920s to accompany the nearby teahouse (now a restaurant), these dinky little log cabins are always booked out thanks to their lovely position right beside Johnston Canyon. Despite their heritage appearance (complete with porch and smoking chimneys), most of the cabins have been thoroughly renovated with modern furniture, patterned rugs and gas-flame fires, though there's the odd hardwood doorframe left over from the olden days. Choose from single-room layouts to the top-end classic bungalows with leather sofas and enamel bathtubs.

Castle Mountain Chalets (Map p85; ☎ 403-762-3868; www.decorehotels.com; Castle Junction; chalets $$$) If you're desperate for a log chalet and Johnston Canyon and Baker Creek are both full, then these timber-frame cabins make a decent back-up, though they offer a good deal less character and they're disappointingly close to the main highway. There are heritage trappings outside and motel furnishings inside, with dishwashers, Jacuzzis and walk-in showers at the top end.

Baker Creek Chalets (Map p85; ☎ 403-522-3761; www.bakercreek.com; d $$$-$$$$, q $$$$) These red-roofed chalets are a lot roomier than their neighbors at Johnston Canyon Resort, and rather smarter too. Set on a quiet glade near Baker Creek, there's a choice of single-story chalets, lodge-style doubles or deluxe twin-level loft cabins, with a living area downstairs and mezzanine bedrooms. The style is deliberately old-country – wood panels, porches, stoves – and there's even a trapper's cabin complete with antlers and animal skins.

> **TOP FIVE CABIN HIDEAWAYS**
>
> ▪ Num-Ti-Jah Lodge (p140)
> ▪ Storm Mountain Lodge (p159)
> ▪ Skoki Lodge (p134)
> ▪ Mt Assiniboine Lodge (p156)
> ▪ Cathedral Mountain Lodge (p154)

LAKE LOUISE

There's no getting around the fact that staying around Lake Louise is going to make a hefty dent in your wallet. On the whole, the hotels around Lake Louise village are fairly average but command premium prices. Generally the older properties around the lakes are cheaper, cozier and considerably more fun.

Camping

Lake Louise Tent & Trailer (Map p85; Lake Louise village; sites $; ⊙ trailer park year-round, tent park late Jun-late Sep; ☢) Despite the name, the Lake Louise campground (actually two campgrounds with one access gate) is a good distance from the lake, but as it's the only place for campers and RVs nearby, it's nearly always busy. It's not as pretty or private as some of Banff's other campgrounds; the best locales for campers are away from the perimeter toward the trees, where you're less exposed and the traffic noise is less obvious. The RV ground is a bit barren and nearer the highway. During busy periods there's a very basic overflow site a few miles south along Hwy 1.

Hotels & Hostels

HI Lake Louise (Map p85; ☎ 403-670-7580; www.hi hostels.ca; Village Rd, Lake Louise village; dm/d/f $/$$/$$; ▣) Another flagship HI hostel with more facilities than your average top-class hotel. Built in the chalet style that's *de rigueur* around Lake Louise, it's an absolute gem for everyone from backpackers to families looking to rein in the costs. Organized activities aplenty (plus sleigh rides and ski packages in the winter) keep the active types happy, while lesser mortals can relax in the lounge or tuck into hearty meals of chilies, soups and baked spuds in the on-site Bill Peyto's Café (p143). As always, the rooms are small, bland and basic, but for these prices they're a steal.

Paradise Lodge & Bungalows (Map p85; ☎ 403-522-3595; www.paradiselodge.com; 105 Lake Louise Dr; ste & bungalows $$$) Characterful and cozy, these sweet little 1930s cabins have been thoroughly smartened up and refitted. Best of the bunch are the log bungalows, still crammed with rickety furniture, wood-clad walls, cast-iron belly stoves and tiny gingerbread windows. The modern suites and lodge rooms are posher but a lot less fun, with hotel-style interiors and kitted-out kitchens.

Deer Lodge (Map p85; ☎ 403-522-3991, 800-661-1595; www.crmr.com; 109 Lake Louise Dr; r $$$-$$$$) One of Lake Louise's most historic lodges, with a legacy stretching back 90-odd years and still boasting plenty of old-fashioned atmosphere. Like its sister lodges in Banff and Moraine Lake, this is a sleek, chic place to stay, with smartly finished, TV-free rooms decked out in taupe bedspreads, burnished furniture and achingly tasteful tones. Try the heritage rooms in the new wing for the most space, or the higgledy-piggledy Tower Rooms for vintage radiators, antique brass lamp stands and a quirky layout.

Post Hotel (Map p85; ☎ 403-522-3989, 1-800-661-1596; www.posthotel.com; Village Rd, Lake Louise village; d $$$, cabins & ste $$$$) This sprawling hotel

> **PEAK EXPERIENCE**
>
> By 1898 the Canadian Pacific Railway (CPR) knew it had to do something to keep mountaineering enthusiasts boarding its trains for the Rockies. One climber had already fallen to a tragic death and it seemed inevitable that more would follow.
>
> Enter Edward Feuz Jr (1884–1981). Hailing from Switzerland, Edward and some of his fellow countrymen were hired by the CPR for their reputed ability to lead people skillfully and safely through the mountains. Edward was one of the first Swiss guides in the Rockies and was the first person to stand atop 78 Canadian peaks. During his 50-year career, he led over 100 new routes and never once lost a climber.
>
> When visiting Lake Louise, take a look across the water to the towering Mt Victoria; Edward scaled this peak one last time in 1965 and then hung up his hiking boots for good. Not that anyone could blame him – he was 81, after all.

BANFF NATIONAL PARK CAMPGROUNDS

Campground	Location	No of sites	Elevation	Open
Johnston Canyon	Johnston Canyon	132	1430m (4700ft)	Jun-Sep
Lake Louise Tent	Lake Louise village	210	1540m (5050ft)	May-Oct
Lake Louise Trailer	Lake Louise village	189	1540m (5050ft)	year-round
Mosquito Creek	Icefields Parkway	32	1850m (6070ft)	year-round
Protection Mountain	Bow Valley Parkway	89	1450m (4760ft)	Jun-Sep
Rampart Creek	Icefields Parkway	50	1450m (4760ft)	Jun-Sep
Tunnel Mountain Trailer Court	Banff	321	1440m (4725ft)	May-Sep
Tunnel Mountain Village One	Banff	618	1440m (4725ft)	year-round
Tunnel Mountain Village Two	Banff	188	1450m (4760ft)	May-Oct
Two Jack Lakeside	Lake Minnewanka	74	1460m (4790ft)	May-Sep
Two Jack Main	Lake Minnewanka	380	1460m (4790ft)	May-Sep
Waterfowl Lakes	Icefields Parkway	116	1650m (5410m)	Jun-Sep

Drinking Water | Flush Toilets | Great For Families | Wheelchair Accessible | Grocery Store Nearby | Fireplace | RV Dump Station

covers all bases, from fully catered hotel suites to a double-gabled family cabin with enough space in which to hold a cat-swinging championship. Idyllically situated on the banks of the Pipestone River, and originally founded by a team of Swiss brothers, it's a curious blend of countrified ambience and modern-day convenience. Most of the double rooms in the main building are disappointingly generic; for the most character, opt for one of the riverside cabins, which crank up the snugness levels and conjure a much more authentic mountain ambience.

Moraine Lake Lodge (☎ 403-533-3733; www.mo rainelake.com; d & lodges $$$$; ⦿ Jun-Oct) Scattered beneath trees beside Moraine Lake, this lodge complex is unquestionably the top option for lovers of great views. Steer clear of the main building and plump for one of the pocket-sized detached cabins that are stretched out behind the main shoreline trail. Upstairs you'll find a simple bedroom area leading onto a decked patio (with a

view of Moraine Lake if you're really lucky), while downstairs there's a cute little lounge with log-fire hearth. The rooms are tiny for the money, but once the day-trippers finally leave for home sometime around 5pm, you couldn't ask for a more peaceful sleep.

Fairmont Chateau Lake Louise (☎ 403-522-3511; www.fairmont.com; Lake Louise Dr; d $$$$) Despite its stellar reputation, this world-famous hotel has about as much exterior charm as a municipal car park, and the rooms are a lot less spectacular than the glossy brochures make out. Like its sister hotel in Banff, you're renting a slice of history when you stay here, but most of the hotel's original 1920s elegance has been swept away in successive renovations. There are boutique shops, grand public areas and chandelier-strewn rooms aplenty, and if plush beds, snooty service and fantastic views are what you're looking for, then book away; but you could do a lot better for a fraction of the price.

Reservations required?	Facilities	Description	Page
no	(icons)	One of the park's most scenic and best-equipped campgrounds, with lots of day hikes on your doorstep	136
yes	(icons)	Tent campground next door to the RV ground, protected by an electric bear-proof fence	137
yes	(icons)	RV-friendly site that keeps 30 sites open in winter	137
no	(icons)	Very basic, tree-lined campground in the shadow of Mt Hector, handily situated for the southern Icefields Parkway	below
no	(icons)	Popular with hikers thanks to its proximity to trailheads; amenities including recycling and kitchen shelters	136
no	(icons)	The last frontcountry campground south of the Jasper border; rudimentary but peaceful	below
yes	(icons)	Dedicated RV and trailer site with full hookups	130
yes	(icons)	Large, forested, tent-only campground, popular with families but can get overcrowded	130
yes	(icons)	Mixed-use campground that's handy for Banff town but feels a little exposed to the elements	130
no	(icons)	Beautiful and very popular lakeside campground with private, secluded sites	136
no	(icons)	Scattered under the trees; no showers but you're free to use the ones at nearby Lakeside	136
no	(icons)	The best equipped of the Icefields Parkway campgrounds, with recycling bins, piped water and food storage	below

ICEFIELDS PARKWAY
Camping

The campgrounds along the Icefields Parkway are a lot more basic than many in Banff, but they're ideal if you want to escape the campfire smoke and crowds of the busier sites.

Mosquito Creek (Map p125; sites $; ☽ Apr–mid-Sep) Tucked under Hector Mountain in a wooded creek-side setting, this campground is about as simple as they come – pit toilets and a hand pump for water just about sum up the facilities, but it's a lovely spot for those who are seeking seclusion. And despite the name, mosquitoes don't seem to be too much of a problem (hardly surprising given the nighttime temperatures!).

Waterfowl Lakes (Map p125; sites $; ☽ mid-Jun–late Sep; ♿) The best serviced of the parkway campgrounds, nicely situated at the head of the lake with lots of large, wooded, wheelchair-accessible sites and surprisingly luxurious facilities, including flush toilets and

BBQ shelters. The Ritz it ain't, but it's pretty plush for this neck of the woods.

Rampart Creek (Map p125; sites $; ☽ Jul-Sep) The northernmost campground in Banff is a pretty primitive affair, but handy for the Columbia Icefield. The mountain views are particularly grand and it's often a good spot for wildlife – don't be surprised if the odd elk or bighorn sheep putters past your tent. There's well water, dry privies and kitchen shelters on-site and there's a fire-free loop if you're sick of smelling other people's smoke.

Hotels & Hostels

Mosquito Creek International Hostel (Map p125; ☎ 403-670-7580; www.hihostels.ca; Icefields Parkway; dm $) Tucked away under trees near the camp-ground, this sweet little hostel makes the perfect retreat for hikers who don't mind getting cozy with their neighbors. The cabins were originally used to house German POWs during WWII, but they're far from prisonlike these days. There's a rustic sauna, a stove-lit lounge stuffed with cushions and bench seats and a pocket-sized (propane-powered) kitchen where you can cook up communal grub. Simple and sweet.

Rampart Creek International Hostel (Map p125; ☎ 403-670-7580; www.hihostels.ca; Icefields Parkway; dm $) These 12 gingerbread cabins collected around a wood clearing are much loved by hostelers and hikers. The facilities are similar to Mosquito Creek – plain dorm cabins, a shared lounge, a wood-fired sauna and a lively kitchen. It's a little shabby in spots but livened up by a great climbing library and a decidedly off-kilter chap in charge.

The Crossing (Map p125; ☎ 403-761-7000; www .thecrossingresort.com; cnr Hwy 11 & Icefields Parkway; d $$; ☺ mid-Mar–Nov) Apart from the Num-Ti-Jah, this drab and overpriced motel is your only option on the Icefields Parkway, but if you're stuck it makes a handy fallback. There are plenty of bog-standard motel units arranged around the courtyard, and there are a café, pub and shop if you get tired of staring at the goggle-box.

our pick **Num-Ti-Jah Lodge** (Map p125; ☎ 403-522-2167; www.num-ti-jah.com; Icefields Parkway; d mountain/ lake view from C$245/270, incl meals C$480/525; ☺ Dec–mid-Oct) After lots of pale pretenders, this is the real deal – a genuine historic mountain lodge, built by the pioneering backwoodsman Jimmy Simpson, a man who did much to popularize the Rockies and who laid the foundations for the modern-day practice of mountain guiding. Picturesquely plonked on the shores of Bow Lake, overlooking Crowfoot Mountain and the Wapta Icefield, it's the kind of place where every crevice and corner hides a historic secret. Huge animal skins, dog-eared photos and wonky bits of furniture litter the library and downstairs lounge, while elk heads and snowshoes hang from the walls, commemorating Simpson's life in the great outdoors. Haphazard staircases lead up to the plain, pine-paneled rooms, all free of TVs and phones and laid out in charming, higgledy-piggledy fashion.

EATING & DRINKING

BANFF

Banff is brimming with places to pamper your palette, from designer delis and wholefood cafés to top-notch dining emporiums boasting the best food this side of the British Columbia border. Choices are more limited the further you travel north along Hwy 1; Lake Louise has a few decent options, including a landmark restaurant in the old Laggan station, but around the Icefields Parkway you'd do well to take your own supplies.

Most of the nightlife centers on Banff town, so if you're staying in other parts of the park you'll have to settle for a good book and a hot mug of cocoa.

Cafés
Wild Flour Café (Map p94; ☎ 403-760-5074; 211 Bear St; mains $; ☺ 7:30am-6pm) Blueberry scones? Chocolate zucchini loaf? Homemade banana bread? This zingy little organic café is closer to the kind of place you'd find in some bohemian enclave of Greenwich Village than downtown Banff, and it's the town's top spot for coffee, cakes and light bites. Sun streams in through the windows onto little tables, and the chug of cappuccino machines echoes in the background as you peruse the complimentary papers. Whether it's sticky cakes, grilled paninis or steaming soups you're after, the Wild Flour is guaranteed to fit the bill.

Evelyn's Coffee Bar (Map p94; ☎ 403-762-0352; 201 Banff Ave; mains $; ☺ 7am-11pm Mon-Sat, 7:30am-11pm Sun) Another top-notch coffeehouse that also does a nice line in lunchtime wraps, sandwiches and soups, as well as gooey cakes and pastries for that essential mid-afternoon indulgence. There are other outlets in Wolf & Bear St Mall and at 119 Banff Ave.

Restaurants
Cascade Plaza Food Court (Map p94; 317 Banff Ave; meals $; ☺ 10am-10pm summer, 10am-7pm Mon-Fri, 10am-9pm Sat & Sun winter) The lower level of the Cascade Plaza mall has loads of options for budget bites, including noodles and sushi from Edo Japan, stir-fries and wok dishes from Lotus Chinese Foods, curries from Taste of Sri Lanka and fresh-made smoothies and milkshakes from Booster Juice.

Magpie & Stump (Map p94; ☎ 403-762-4067; 203 Caribou St; lunch/dinner $/$$; ☺ noon-2am; ⚇) Saddle up, pardners; this Tex-Mex cantina is all about down-home ranch food in a gin-u-wine wild-west setting. Sombreros, neon signs, beer bottles and mounted animal skins dot the rough-hewn timber walls and it's all good fun in a cowboy-kitsch kind of way – the kids are bound to love it. The menu's stuffed with Mexican favorites, including chimichangas, burritos and quesadillas, and the house drink obviously has to be margaritas – but with around 20 varieties to try, you might need to arrange for a cab home…

Coyote's Deli & Grill (Map p94; ☎ 403-762-3963; 206 Caribou St; breakfast $, lunch & dinner $$; ⏰ 7am-11pm) Southwestern spices and traces of Cajun and Mexican flavors underpin the food at this ever-busy little diner, where you can grab something quick from the counter or something heartier at one of the candlelit tables. The atmosphere's bright, buzzy and informal, with a hint of ranchero style, and there's chicken corn chowder, lamb zinfandel and goat's cheese quesadilla to get your teeth into.

Bumper's (Map p94; ☎ 403-762-2622; 603 Banff Ave; mains $$; ⏰ from 4:30pm; 🚼) For a solid prime-cut fillet, Banff diners make a beeline for this much-loved steakhouse diner at the top end of Banff Ave. It's refreshingly unpretentious, offering good solid steaks and all-you-can-eat salads in a family-friendly diner setting. Those in the know plump for the 'pile-o-bones' ribs or the ominously titled 'Man Mountain' steak.

our pick Bison Mountain Bistro (Map p94; ☎ 403-762-5550; Bison Courtyard, 211 Bear St; sandwiches $, meals $$-$$$; ⏰ breakfast, lunch & dinner) This brilliant bistro has stamped its authority on Banff's dining scene with its innovative cuisine, gourmet ingredients and unswerving dedication to home-sourced produce. Downstairs there's a fantastic sandwich bar serving up gourmet subs and artisan cheeses, while upstairs there's imaginative fare from smoked bison pizzas to elk burgers with brie and braised mushrooms. The feel throughout is light and contemporary – think polished wood, abstract art and huge picture windows, plus a rooftop terrace for sunny days. Quite a find.

Café Soleil (Map p94; ☎ 403-762-2090; 208 Caribou St; mains $$-$$$; ⏰ lunch & dinner) A little piece of Mediterranean sunshine comes to Banff at this fiery little brasserie, decked out in spicy reds and terracotta tones and filled with wicker chairs and twisted willow. Big plates of authentic tapas are the menu's mainstay, but more adventurous types could tuck into Moroccan chicken or finger-lickin' lamb lollipops.

Typhoon (Map p94; ☎ 403-762-2000; 211 Caribou St; lunch/dinner $$/$$$; ⏰ lunch & dinner) Pan-Asian food takes center stage at Typhoon, with a magpie menu that raids the classics of Thai, Malaysian and Indian cuisine. Globe lanterns and technicolor flower murals conjure up an oriental atmosphere and tiny candles flicker on every table, while the eclectic menu takes in everything from flash-fried prawns and seafood curries to codfish marinated in saké and maple syrup.

Muk-a-muk (☎ 403-763-6205; 1 Juniper Way; mains $$-$$$; ⏰ breakfast, lunch & dinner) With a name deriving from the First Nation word for 'feast,' this classy new restaurant at the Juniper hotel certainly serves up a banquet of unusual dishes, from a west-coast seafood hotpot to a wonderful plate of antipasto with elk pastrami, bison whiskey sausage and bannock bread. Like the hotel, the feel is funky and 21st century, with big windows overlooking the Bow Valley and a mountain-view terrace that's just about the finest in Banff.

Cilantro Mountain Café (Map p94; ☎ 403-760-3008; Tunnel Mountain Dr; mains $$-$$$; ⏰ 5-10pm, closed Mon & Tue in winter) A big wood-burning oven forms the centerpiece of this restaurant at the Buffalo Mountain Lodge, where the culinary cue comes from local produce laced with a hint of Canada's First Nations past. Rustic mains of game, chicken and Alberta-sourced steaks, plus a host of pastas and pizzas, are baked up in the oven while you gaze out at the Banff views. It's a lot less stuffy than many of Banff's more expensive eateries, but the food is just as fancy.

Grizzly House (Map p94; ☎ 403-762-4055; 207 Banff Ave; mains lunch/dinner $$/$$$; ⏰ lunch & dinner) With its weird pyramidal building and slightly skewwhiff tagline of 'For Lovers & Hedonists,' it's obvious from the outset that things are done a bit differently over at the Grizzly. It's a curious mix of tourist tat and quirky character – bear skins, totem poles and buffalo heads hover over your head as you dine, and every table still has a working phone beside it, left over from the restaurant's former incarnation as a '70s disco. But it's on the menu where things get really odd – there are 14 varieties of fondue to choose from, ranging from beef and buffalo to more outlandish options such as lobster, shark and rattlesnake. Whatever you make of the food, you won't forget this place in a hurry.

Saltlik (Map p94; ☎ 403-762-2467; 221 Bear St; starters $, mains $$$; ☽ dinner) Things are slik at the 'lik, which offers a contemporary take on the traditional steakhouse, both in design and dining. Shiny wood, polished floors, murals and tasteful mood lights create a ritzy dinner club atmosphere. You can sink some drinks at the semicircular lounge bar before delving into a menu that's packed with rancher salads, club sandwiches and enough varieties of steak to sate the most discerning carnivore. Top choices include the skirt steak with truffle oil or a classic New York–style sirloin in peppercorn sauce.

Maple Leaf Grillé (Map p94; ☎ 403-760-7680; 137 Banff Ave; lunch/dinner mains $$/$$$; ☽ 11am-11pm) Canada might not be renowned for its globe-beating cuisine, but this smartly furnished dining lounge does its level best to bring the country's very finest flavors to the table. A big birch-bark canoe dangles above the entrance, and the rest of the decor is suitably Canuck-themed (snowshoes, stained timber), while Canadian ingredients from Quebec foie gras to Albertan game and BC salmon crop up on the upmarket menu. It's swish and a touch stuffy, but a polished dining experience.

Fuze (Map p94; ☎ 403-760-0853; 110 Banff Ave; mains $$$-$$$$; ☽ dinner) Haute cuisine in a high mountain setting. Recycled fir, rich earthy colors and deep banquette seats match a refined menu that's all about innovation and invention – think pan-roasted sablefish, Indian-spiced steak and red snapper with a gazpacho sauce. It's a place that sets out to light up your taste buds with new flavors, and it has quickly garnered a devoted fan club among the local fooderati. It's pricey but worth the pennies.

Le Beaujolais (Map p94; ☎ 403-762-2712; 212 Buffalo St; mains $$$, 3-course menu $$$$; ☽ dinner) Ooh la la – for some authentic Gallic cooking, the long-standing Beaujolais is the only choice in Banff. Ice-white tablecloths, razor-sharp napkins and glittering cutlery litter the tabletops, while waistcoated waiters buzz around the dining room taking orders of lobster bisque, braised wild boar and, of course, *escargots* (snails) and *cuisses de grenouilles* (frogs' legs). As you'd expect, the wine list is first-class, the food is rich and delicious and the atmosphere is starchier than a nanny's apron – leave some

space for crème brûlée or the house-special 'raspberry *ballon*' for dessert.

Bars, Pubs & Clubs

Tommy's Neighborhood Pub (Map p94; ☎ 403-762-8888; 120 Banff Ave; mains $; ☽ lunch & dinner) Stout pub grub in the great British tradition, veering from shepherd's pie and fish and chips to crispy wings and a smorgasbord of burger choices. Wash down your chow with a pint of draft beer and then try your hand at a game of arrows (darts to the uninitiated).

Bruno's Bar & Grill (Map p94; ☎ 403-762-8115; 304 Caribou St; mains $$; ☽ breakfast, lunch & dinner) Named after the champion skier Bruno Engler, this cozy burger bar makes an excellent place for a slap-up breakfast or a super-sized lunch. Old beer signs and tatty posters adorn the walls, and meals are dished up to a soundtrack of jukebox music and clacking pool balls. Sink your chops into the house-special BBQ Classic burger or a crispy chicken wrap, or try the massive omelets or Eggs Benny breakfasts to keep yourself fuelled up till dinner.

Rose & Crown (Map p94; ☎ 403-762-2121; 202 Banff Ave; ☽ 11am-late) For a cold pint and a rack of pool, you can't beat this welcoming little Anglophile pub in the heart of town. There are lots of beers on tap, live bands at weekends and a rooftop patio that's tailor-made for a sunset tipple.

St James's Gate (Map p94; ☎ 403-762-9355; 205 Wolf St) Leprechauns in the window and draft Guinness behind the bar set the tone for this lively Irish boozer, with a formidable selection of over 30 beers and 50 scotches to sample.

Wild Bill's Legendary Saloon (Map p94; ☎ 403-760-0333; 201 Banff Ave; ☽ 11am-late) Break out the cowboy boots and slap on the Stetson – this saloon bar caters squarely for the cowboy crowd. Country tunes sing out from the jukebox while line dancers and two-steppers shuffle to the beat several nights a week. The saloon is also a popular venue for visiting bands.

Lik Lounge (Map p94; ☎ 403-762-2467; 221 Bear St; ☽ 11am-2am) Things are altogether smoother at the Lik Lounge, downstairs at the Saltlik and the venue of choice for Banff's well-heeled crowd. Expect plenty of stripped-back urban style, DJs after dark and a menu of criminally overpriced cocktails.

Hoodoo Lounge (Map p94; ☎ 403-760-8636; 137 Banff Ave; ☺ from 9pm) Banff's biggest club has nights to suit all tastes – house, dance and jungle at weekends, with themed party nights throughout the week. Don't expect anything too cutting edge; do expect cheap shooters and big cheesy choons.

Aurora Club (Map p94; ☎ 403-760-3343; 110 Banff Ave; ☺ 6pm-late) Another late-night hangout for the party people, with a lounge-room vibe in the Onyx Bar (complete with huge plasma TV, pool tables and banquette seats) and big beats, bright lights and guest DJs in the Club.

BOW VALLEY PARKWAY & LAKE LOUISE

Bill Peyto's Café (Map p85; ☎ 403-670-7580; HI Lake Louise, Village Rd, Lake Louise village; ☺ 7am-10pm summer, to 9pm winter; ♿) It might be in a backpackers' hostel, but the food at Bill Peyto's is anything but cheap and nasty. The varied menu dabbles in chilies, grilled fish, chicken tortillas and bison burgers, as well as a selection of fresh-made sandwiches, soups and baked spuds, all served in a cozy dining room crammed with the essential backcountry trappings of timber and slate. It's an old fave with hostellers and hikers, so pitch up early to be sure of a table.

Laggan's Mountain Bakery (☎ 403-522-2017; Samson Mall, Lake Louise village; ☺ 6am-8pm) Fine dining it certainly isn't, but this unpretentious little deli-bakery is still packed throughout the day thanks to its house-special hot pies, doorstop sandwiches, quiches and trademark apple fritters. Join the queue of RV drivers and trail walkers and prepare for a wait.

Trailhead Café (☎ 403-522-2006; Samson Mall, Lake Louise village; sandwiches & omelets $; ☺ 8am-5:30pm) If you get tired of the queues at Laggan's, zip across the courtyard to this fresh little sandwich bar, where music's always blaring on the stereo and hikers are tucking into stonking great breakfasts of piled-up pancakes or French toast. Sandwiches, bagels and wraps are made to order if you need some nosh to take out on the trail (the brownies are rather special, too).

Station Restaurant (Map p85; ☎ 403-522-2600; 200 Sentinel Rd; lunch/dinner $$/$$$; ☺ 11:30am-midnight) Back in the days when Lake Louise was still Laggan and steam trains chugged up the Bow Valley, this place was the village's main station, and the original CPR tracks still run right outside its windows. It's a wonderfully atmospheric place for a slap-up supper; you can dine in the old station or the painstakingly restored Delamere dining car, complete with wood paneling and Arts and Crafts furniture. The food's not quite as exciting as the historic setting, but pork, steaks and rack of lamb all feature and there are usually some veggie and seafood options.

Deer Lodge (Map p85; ☎ 403-522-3991; 109 Lake Louise Dr; mains lounge/dining room $$/$$$; ☺ lounge 11am-11pm, dining room breakfast & dinner) You'll find a brace of upper-crust eateries at the Deer Lodge. First up is the Caribou Lodge tea lounge, famous for its wonderful views of Victoria Glacier and a fine place for a light lunch or tea and scones. With its log ceiling, crackling grate and faintly old-world atmosphere, it's a charming refuge from the relentlessly modern feel of the rest of Lake Louise. Nearby is the more formal Mt Fairview Dining Room, with a similarly retro air and a menu revolving around classic fish and game.

Baker Creek Bistro (Map p85; ☎ 403-522-2182; Bow Valley Parkway; lunch/dinner $$/$$$; ☺ dinner) Some of the finest food in the Bow Valley finds its way onto the plates at Baker Creek's restaurant, where the chef mixes up French and Italian influences with a passionate devotion to Canadian fare. It's a real treat, crammed with country charm and idyllically situated in a forest setting. While the seasonal menu changes regularly, according to whatever takes the chef's fancy, local game and freshly fished trout and salmon are guaranteed to feature somewhere. Book well ahead and check opening hours in advance.

ICEFIELDS PARKWAY

The Crossing (☎ 403-761-7000; cnr Hwy 11 & Icefields Parkway; lunch/dinner $/$$; ☺ lunch & dinner Mar-Nov) The restaurants at The Crossing aren't anything to get excited about; there's a basic canteen dishing up chilies, fish and chips and burgers, or a tired old dining room with a selection of roasts, meats and poached fish. It's hardly nouveau cuisine, but since this is about the only restaurant within 20 miles, it's your only option if you're hungry.

Num-Ti-Jah Lodge (Map p125; ☎ 403-522-2167; www.num-ti-jah.com; Icefields Parkway; lunch/dinner $$/$$$; ☺ lunch & dinner) The Icefields Parkway

---

CULTURAL BANFF

The arts certainly take second billing to the great outdoors in Banff, but the cultural scene has its fair share of festivals, events and performances throughout the year – see the Festivals & Events boxed text, p28, for the lowdown on the town's annual events.

The **Lux Cinema** (☎ 403-762-8595; Bear St; adult/child C$10/6) is the town's main cinema, showing all the latest mainstream studio releases and hosting one-off films during the annual Banff Mountain Film Festival.

The **Banff Centre** (☎ 403-762-6301; www .banffcentre.ca/bsaf; 107 Tunnel Mountain Dr; tickets C$10-25) is the main arts and culture venue, with a program of concerts, lectures and events throughout the year, especially during the Banff International String Quartet competition.

---

is a little short on places to eat, but it hardly matters when you've got a gorgeous little hotel restaurant like this on your doorstep. In the best Jimmy Simpson tradition, it's all delightfully unstuffy, with hale and hearty food (steaks, pastas, fish and game) served in a gorgeous log dining room overlooked by the requisite moose heads and elk horns. Priority goes to guests, so if you're staying elsewhere make sure you reserve ahead.

AROUND BANFF NATIONAL PARK

Though Banff National Park receives most of the attention in the glossy tourist brochures (and a correspondingly large chunk of the visitors), it's well worth taking the time to venture out beyond the park's borders. Banff is surrounded by several other national and provincial parks, all blessed with the same kind of sky-topping scenery as their bigger and better-known neighbor, but with the added advantages of having far fewer visitors and much quieter trails. Kananaskis and Yoho are the locals' tips for spectacular hiking, Golden is the center for adventure sports and, for an unforgettable backcountry fix, trail junkies congregate on the remote trails around Mt Assiniboine Provincial Park.

CANMORE

Perched on the banks of the broad Bow River a few kilometers from Banff's eastern border, the little town of Canmore originally grew up as a bustling hub for the coal-mining industry. Over the last couple of decades, however, it's steadily reinvented itself as a busy gateway town for exploring the nearby national park, as well as a center for outdoor adventures. The future for Canmore looked pretty bleak following the closure of the last working mine in 1979, but it's currently enjoying a real renaissance, with plush apartment blocks and brand-new buildings springing up practically everywhere you look. It's quieter, cheaper and much more chilled than Banff town and makes the ideal springboard for exploring the eastern section of Banff and the mountains and lakes of Kananaskis Country (p148), a short drive to the south.

Orientation

Canmore is 25km (15.5 miles) east of Banff town and 6km (3.7 miles) from the park gates along Hwy 1. Many of the hotels are strung out along the Bow Valley Trail, which runs roughly parallel to Hwy 1. Most shops, services and restaurants are along 8th/Main St, which runs west from Railway Ave.

Information

Alberta Visitor Information Centre (Map p145; ☎ 403-678-5277; www.travelalberta.com; 2801 Bow Valley Trail; ☼ 8am-8pm summer, to 6pm winter) Regional visitor center just off the Trans-Canada Hwy west of town.

Bank of Montreal (Map p145; ☎ 403-678-5568; 701 8th St) Has an ATM.

Bow Valley Wash n' Dry (Map p145; ☎ 403-678-5085; 610 8th St; loads C$2-4; ☼ 8am-10pm)

Café Books (Map p145; ☎ 403-678-0908; 826 8th St; ☼ 9:30am-9pm Mon-Sat, 10:30am-5:30pm Sun) Good bookstore with fiction, nonfiction, trail guides and maps.

Canmore Visitor Centre (Map p145; ☎ 403-678-1295; www.tourismcanmore.com; 301 8th St; ☼ 8:30am-5pm Mon-Sat) The main tourist office, opposite the Canmore Civic Museum.

CIBC (Map p145; ☎ 403-609-6200; Unit 101, 730 8th St) Has an ATM.

Lost Sock Laundromat (Map p145; ☎ 403-678-6901; 113 7th Ave; loads C$3-5; ☼ 24hr) Cable TV and internet kiosk while you wait for your togs to dry.

Post Office (Map p145; ☎ 403-678-4377; 801 8th St)

Two Moose Internet Café (Map p145; ☎ 403-609-2678; Unit 100, 717 10th St; per 10min C$1; ☼ 8am-8pm)

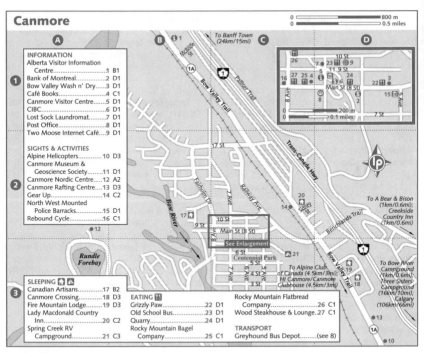

Canmore

Sights & Activities

Canmore has become a hub for all sorts of outdoor activities. Mountain biking is one of the most popular sports, thanks to the groomed trail system at **Canmore Nordic Centre** (Map p145; ☎ 403-678-2400; www.canmore .nordiccentre@gov.ab.ca; ste 100, 1988 Olympic Way) in the hills above town. There are loads of trails to choose from, including technical single and doubletracks and downhill sections; a 1½-hour guided trail tour costs C$60. There's also a 1½-hour daily **trail sports clinic** (C$60; 🕙 10:30am) where you can brush up on your skills, as well as bike rental (per hour/day C$15/45). Bikes can also be rented from **Rebound Cycle** (Map p145; ☎ 866-312-1866; www.reboundcycle.com; 902 8th St; rentals per day C$30-70; 🕙 10am-6pm Mon-Sat, to 5pm Sun) and **Gear Up** (Map p145; ☎ 403-678-1636; www .gearupsport.com; 1302 Bow Valley Trail; full-suspension bikes per hr/day C$15/45), which also rents out canoes and kayaks.

The **Canmore Rafting Centre** (Map p145; ☎ 403-678-4919; www.canmoreraftingcentre.com; 20 Lincoln Park; float trips from C$49, raft trips from C$75; 🕙 May-late Sep) runs lots of white-water trips on the

Red Deer, Kananaskis and Kicking Horse Rivers, and along the Bow River through Horseshoe Canyon. There are gentle floats geared for families as well as hardcore rapid rides for more experienced rafters. You can also take multi-day instruction and river safety courses.

Canmore is near a system of deep caves known as the Rat's Nest, hidden deep beneath Grotto Mountain. **Canmore Caverns** (☎ 403-678-8819; www.canadianrockies.net/wildcave tours) offers a number of trips into the maze of twisting passageways and claustrophobic caves, including an Adventure Tour (C$129), which includes a four-hour tour of the caves and an 18m (60ft) abseil down a sheer rock face, and an eight-hour tour (C$185) that adds on a hike into Grotto Canyon.

If you've always pictured yourself as a Grizzly Adams type, you could also try out the mountain sport of dogsledding, which has been a traditional mode of travel in the Canadian Rockies for centuries. **Snowy Owl Tours** (☎ 403-678-9588; www.snowyowltours .com) offers lots of sled trips on custom-built sleighs pulled by your own team of huskies. You can catch the two-hour Powder Hound Express (adult/child C$127/85) or plump for an unforgettable two-day camping trip in a Sioux teepee (C$1185). The sledding season is usually from November to April; if you're here in summer, you can meet the dogs on a kennel tour combined with a summer-style sled ride (C$35). **Howling Dog Tours** (☎ 403-678-9588; www.howlingdogtours.com) offers similar trips.

Alpine Helicopters (Map p145; ☎ 403-678-4802; www.alpinehelicopters.com; 91 Bow Valley Trail; sightseeing flights C$95-249, heli-hikes C$319-459) offers scenic flights over Mt Assiniboine, Spray Lakes and Kananaskis Country, as well as organized heli-hikes and charter trips for alpinists.

For the backstory on Canmore's heritage as a railway and mining town, swing by the displays at the **Canmore Museum & Geoscience Society** (Map p145; ☎ 403-678-2462; www.cmags.org; 907 7th Ave; adult C$3, under 9yr free; ⏱ noon-5pm Mon & Tue, 10am-6pm Wed-Sun summer, noon-5pm Mon-Fri, 11am-5pm Sat & Sun winter). The museum also runs the timber-fronted cabin housing the **North West Mounted Police Barracks** (Map p145; ☎ 403-678-1955; 601 8th St; ⏱ noon-4pm Mon & Tue, 10am-6pm Wed-Sun summer, 1-4pm Sat & Sun in winter), built in 1893 and now home to a small display of Mountie-themed memorabilia and a cute tearoom.

There are also plenty of trails within easy reach of town. Good short hikes include the 3.1km (1.9-mile) Grassi Lakes Trail, the 2.7km (1.7-mile) Ha Ling Trail and the 3km (1.8-mile) Cougar Creek Trail, but there are plenty more to discover, especially in nearby Kananaskis Country (p148).

Sleeping
CAMPING
Bow River Campground (☎ 403-673-2163; www .bowvalleycampgrounds.com; sites $; ⏱ May-Oct) The municipal campground in Canmore is pretty basic, so the best option if you want to camp close to town is this riverside site 1.6km (1 mile) down Hwy 1. It's sandwiched between the river and the highway, so it's not quite as peaceful as it could be, but it's pleasant enough if you can bag a spot by the water. Basic facilities include nonflush toilets and RV-accessible sites, although there are no hookups.

Three Sisters Campground (☎ 403-673-2163; www.bowvalleycampgrounds.com; sites $; ⏱ mid-Apr–

Oct) For prettier sites and a more peaceful atmosphere, head for this campground in the satellite town of Three Sisters, 16km (10 miles) east of Canmore. The tent spaces furthest from the highway are generally the quietest and you're handily positioned to plenty of hiking trails. RVs are welcome.

Spring Creek RV Campground (Map p145; ☎ 403-678-5111; www.restwelltrailerpark.com; 502 3rd Ave; sites $; ⏱ mid-Apr–mid-Oct) Dedicated entirely to motor homers, this open-meadow RV ground has fantastic mountain views but almost no privacy, though the hookups and handy town-edge location ensure it's always busy.

HOTELS & HOSTELS
Canmore's hotels and B&Bs generally offer much better value than most places inside the park. The **Canmore Bow Valley B&B Association** (☎ 403-609-7224; www.bbcanmore.com) keeps a comprehensive list of all the local B&Bs, and you'll find lots of motels and hotels along the Bow Valley Trail.

HI Canmore/Canmore Clubhouse (☎ 403-678-3200; canmore@hihostels.ca; Indian Flats Rd; dm $, r $$; 🖳) The old Canmore Clubhouse, run by the Alpine Club of Canada, is now affiliated with Hostelling International, and it's still the best budget bolt-hole this side of the Banff border. Split over two timber-clad buildings, both with fully equipped kitchens and spic-and-span dorm rooms, it's the ideal place to hook up with fellow hikers and mountaineers. You can browse the mountaineering guidebooks in the lounge, kick back in the sauna or just sit out on the deck and stare at the mountain views.

Canadian Artisans (Map p145; ☎ 403-678-4138; www.canadianartisans.ca; 1016 9th Ave; d $$) Run with off-kilter style by a couple of local artists, this homely B&B is crammed with individuality. The two suites are detached from the main house and back onto peaceful forest; the best is the upstairs Treehouse Suite, which has picture windows offering lovely wooded views, as well as arty touches such as stained-glass door panels, a futuristic shower pod and a lovely timber-log vaulted roof. The Forest House is a bit more cramped (especially in the bathroom-cum-bedroom department), but it's still a steal at this price.

Creekside Country Inn (☎ 403-609-5522; www .creeksidecountryinn.com; 709 Benchlands Trail; r $$-$$$;

🖥) This smart little property caters for all comers, with 12 simply furnished rooms in a choice of configurations (standard, family-size and twin-floored loft suite). It's a cross between a mountain-style inn and a motel; the decor's a bit bland, but you'll find fireplaces, fridges, soaker tubs and high ceilings in all the rooms, and the price includes a supersized breakfast of muffins, blueberry scones, bagels and cereals.

A Bear & Bison (☎ 403-678-2058; www.bearandbisoninn.com; 705 Benchlands Trail; r $$-$$$) An elegant, gabled lodge-hotel with lashings of Rocky Mountain atmosphere. The 12 rooms all have an individual feel; some boast hardwood floors, four-poster beds and antique dressers, while others have Jacuzzi tubs and private patios. Sink a drink in the A-frame piano lounge or indulge in a 31-jet therapeutic spa that's identical to the one Bill Clinton installed in the White House. Classy.

Lady Macdonald Country Inn (Map p145; ☎ 800-567-3919; www.ladymacdonald.com; 1201 Bow Valley Trail; d $$$) There's the cultivated air of an English country inn around this pleasant, prissy little hotel, with 12 dinky rooms furnished with a surfeit of feather beds, frilly cushions and patterned pelmets. Despite the Bow Valley Trail location, it's surprisingly peaceful. Ask for the top-notch turret room for wall-to-wall views of the Three Sisters mountains.

Canmore Crossing (Map p145; ☎ 403-678-9390; www.canmorecrossing.ca; 1120 Railway Ave; ste $$$) This condo complex is one of the best bases for families in Canmore, with a selection of multi-room apartments all featuring spacious sitting rooms, fully equipped kitchens and up to three bedrooms. It's designed to be a genuine home away from home, and the condos have all the mod cons you could ask for (DVD players, dishwashers, gas fires) and you'll even find a lovely rooftop hot tub where you can soak in style while you get to know your neighbors.

Fire Mountain Lodge (Map p145; ☎ 403-609-8204; www.firemountain.ca; 121 Kananaskis Way; 🍴🖥) Bringing a hint of big-city style to sleepy Canmore, this boutique beauty is the place for a chic sleep. The twin-story condos are dripping with designer flourishes – plate-glass windows, private balconies, stone-topped breakfast bars and minimal furniture – all finished in studiously

muted tones that feel more Manhattan than mountainesque.

Eating

Old School Bus (Map p145; 9th St; ice creams $; ☯ 9am-5:30pm) If it's ice cream you're after, this converted charabanc is definitely the place. The chalkboard menu is full of imaginative flavors, including white chocolate, blackberry and even green tea. For something different, try some Hawaiian-style shaved ice.

Rocky Mountain Bagel Company (Map p145; ☎ 403-678-9978; Unit 102, 830 8th St; mains $; ☯ 6:30am-10pm) The top spot in town for cappuccino and cake, with a correspondingly long queue at lunchtime. Deli sandwiches, salads and patisserie are all available to take out, or you can stick around and savor the New York coffeehouse vibe.

our pick Grizzly Paw (Map p145; ☎ 403-678-9983; 622 8th St; mains $$; ☯ lunch & dinner) This funky pub is one of the only microbreweries in the Canadian Rockies and it's a favorite hangout for Canmore's movers and shakers, especially on warm evenings when the outside patio is packed to bursting. The list of house-brewed beers includes Elk Red, Grumpy Bear and Honey Wheat, or you could try one of the homemade sodas (our tips are the cherry cola and the traditional creamy root beer). If you're feeling peckish there's good grub, including blackened chicken and Cajun burgers. Lively and lovely.

Rocky Mountain Flatbread Co (Map p145; ☎ 403-609-5508; 838 10th St; mains $$-$$$; ☯ dinner from 5pm) Once you've tasted one of the fantastic flatbread pizzas served up at this great little restaurant, you'll never quite be able to look at a boring old margherita in the same way. The 100% organic, wood-fired pizzas are a gourmet treat – try pork tenderloin with caramelized apple, perhaps, or organic tomato, seared mushroom and bocconcini cheese.

Wood Steakhouse & Lounge (Map p145; ☎ 403-678-3404; 838 8th St; mains $$$-$$$$; ☯ 11am-midnight) This beautifully restored lodge is the best steakhouse in Canmore. The interior is sexy and modern, with wood beams, black leather chairs and copper inlays, while outside you'll find patio heaters dotted around the smart outdoor deck. The menu's skewed toward the carnivores – think buffalo burgers and Alberta beef steaks – but you'll also find other treats such as BC sockeye salmon and pepper-crusted ahi tuna.

Quarry (Map p145; ☎ 403-678-6088; 718 8th St; mains $$$; ⏲ lunch Thu-Sat, dinner daily from 5pm) This swish brasserie has got the designer-dining aesthetic nailed. Rich wood furniture, skylights and natural stone create a suitably elegant setting for the stylish food, which adds a Canadian twist to French and Italian provincial dishes such as braised rabbit, duck breast and ricotta soufflé.

Getting There & Away
Canmore is easily accessible from Banff town and Calgary along Trans-Canada Hwy 1. All buses between Banff and Calgary stop in at the **Greyhound Bus Depot** (Map p145; ☎ 403-678-4465; cnr 8th St & 7th Ave; ⏲ 7:30am-midnight).

KANANASKIS COUNTRY
The area collectively known as Kananaskis Country (or K-Country to the locals) covers a vast area to the south and east of Banff National Park, comprising several side-by-side provincial parks and protected areas, including Peter Lougheed Provincial Park, the Elbow Valley, Sheep Valley, Ghost River Wilderness Area and Don Getty Wildland Provincial Park. While visitors and tourists make a beeline for Banff's trails, many Albertans choose to hike in the K-Country, where the routes are quieter, the scenery is just as impressive and that all-important sense of wilderness is much easier to come by. It's less well known than Banff, but with a bit of research you'll find some fantastic hikes and trails, as well as plenty of skytopping peaks, mountain lakes and outdoor pursuits.

Orientation
The Kananaskis Country begins just to the east of Canmore and stretches east as far as Bragg Creek and south to the small town of Highwood House. There are two main roads through the area, which link up near the Kananaskis Lakes to form a convenient loop: the Kananaskis Trail (Hwy 40) travels through the center of Kananaskis Valley, while the unpaved Smith-Dorrien Rd (Hwy 742) heads northwest all the way back to Canmore. There are gas stations at Deadman's Flats, Fortress Junction and Highwood House, and you can pick up sup-

plies at Kananaskis village. Several subroads are closed from December to May.

Information
There are several visitor centers where you can pick up the useful *Explore Kananaskis Country and the Ghost Area* brochure, which contains maps of the parks and useful visitor information, as well as purchase trail maps and wilderness passes for the area.

At the north end of Hwy 40 is **Barrier Lake Information Centre** (Map p149; ☎ 403-673-3985; ⏲ 8am-8pm Jun-Aug, 9am-5pm May & Sep, 9am-4pm Apr & Oct), while near the junction with Hwy 742, north of Kananaskis Lakes, is the **Peter Lougheed Information Centre** (Map p149; ☎ 403-591-6322; Kananaskis Lakes Rd; ⏲ 9am-9pm Jul & Aug, 9:30am-4pm Apr-Jun, Sep & Oct). There's also the **Elbow Valley Visitor Centre** (☎ 403-949-2461; ⏲ 9:30am-4:30pm Mon-Thu, 9am-6pm Fri-Sun summer, 9:30am-4pm or 5pm shoulder seasons) just west of Bragg Creek. An information booth, ATM and sub-post office are located in tiny Kananaskis village.

For general information visit the area's website at http://tprc.alberta.ca/parks/kananaskis/welcome.asp.

Sights & Activities
To the east of Barrier Lake, along Hwy 68 in the Sibbald recreational area, you'll find the **Jumpingpound Demonstration Forest** (☎ 403-297-8800; Hwy 68; ⏲ May-Sep). Covering 1110 acres (450 acres) of spruce, aspen and fir, this richly forested area explores the heritage of logging and forestry practices in southern Alberta, with old sawmills and modern logging machines to see en route. You can follow a 10km (6.2-mile) driving tour or explore several walking trails, many of which travel through reforested areas as well as a 200-year-old wood.

You're spoilt for choice of trails in the K-Country. The excellent guidebook *Where Locals Hike in the Canadian Rockies: The Premier Trails in Kananaskis Country* by Kathy and Craig Copeland has comprehensive descriptions of all the best trails, or you can pick up free guide leaflets from visitor centers. **Peter Lougheed Provincial Park** is a great spot for walkers. Recommended half-day hikes include the 3km (1.9-mile) trail to Boulton Creek (one hour) and the 5km (3.1-mile) hike to the natural bowl of Ptarmigan Cirque (three hours). Longer day

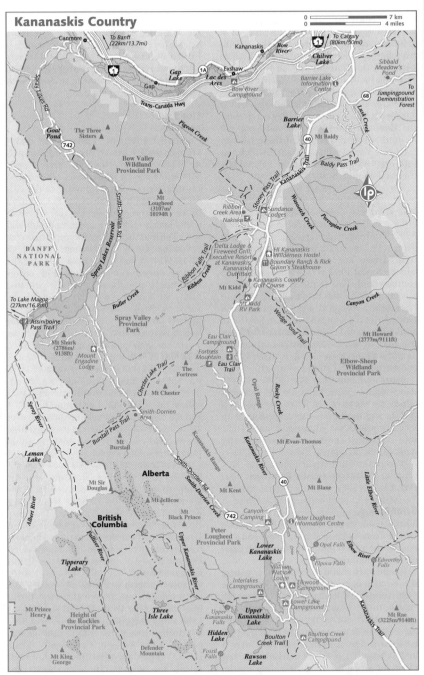

Kananaskis Country

0   7 km
0   4 miles

Canmore
To Banff (22km/13.7mi)
Kananaskis
Bow River
To Calgary (80km/50mi)
Chilver Lake
Sibbald Meadow's Pond
Exshaw
Gap Lake
1A
Lac des Ares
Barrier Lake Information Centre
To Jumpingpound Demonstration Forest
68
Gap
Bow River Campground
Trans-Canada Hwy
Pigeon Creek
Barrier Lake
Goat Pond
The Three Sisters
742
Mt Baldy
40
Baldy Pass Trail
Bow Valley Wildland Provincial Park
Mt Lougheed (3107m/ 10194ft)
Ribbon Creek Area
Nakiska
Stoney Pass Trail
Sundance Lodges
Kananaskis Trail
Winnock Creek
Porcupine Creek
BANFF NATIONAL PARK
Ribbon Falls Trail
Delta Lodge & Fireweed Grill; Executive Resort at Kananaskis; Kananaskis Outfitters
HI Kananaskis Wilderness Hostel
Boundary Ranch & Rick Guinn's Steakhouse
Ribbon Creek Trail
Mt Kidd
Kananaskis Country Golf Course
Buller Creek
Mt Kidd RV Park
Canyon Creek
To Lake Magog (27km/16.8mi)
Assiniboine Pass Trail
Spray Valley Provincial Park
Eau Clair Campground
Wedge Pond Trail
Mt Howard (2777m/9111ft)
Mt Shark (2786m/ 9138ft)
Mount Engadine Lodge
Chester Lake Trail
Fortress Mountain
Eau Clair Trail
The Fortress
Opal Range
Rocky Creek
Elbow-Sheep Wildland Provincial Park
Spray River
Mt Chester
Smith-Dorrien Area
Burstall Pass Trail
Mt Evan-Thomas
Leman Lake
Mt Burstall
Kananaskis Range
Kananaskis River
Little Elbow River
Alberta
Mt Sir Douglas
Smith-Dorrien Rd
Mt Jellicoe
Mt Kent
40
Mt Blane
British Columbia
Albert River
Palliser River
Mt Black Prince
Smith-Dorrien Creek
742
Canyon Camping
Peter Lougheed Information Centre
Opal Falls
Elbow River
Peter Lougheed Provincial Park
Lower Kananaskis Lake
Elpoca Falls
Edworthy Falls
Tipperary Lake
Upper Kananaskis River
William Watson Lodge
Interlakes Campground
Elkwood Campground
Lower Lake Campground
Mt Prince Henry
Height of the Rockies Provincial Park
Three Isle Lake
Upper Kananaskis Falls
Upper Kananaskis Lake
Boulton Creek Campground
Mt Rae (3225m/9140ft)
Hidden Lake
Boulton Creek Trail
Kananaskis Trail
Mt King George
Defender Mountain
Fossil Falls
Rawson Lake

routes include the 7.2km (4.5-mile) hike to Mt Indefatigable (four hours) and the 16km (10-mile) Upper Kananaskis Lake Circuit (five hours). The 10km (6.2-mile) hike to Chester Lake (four hours) and the 15km (9.3-mile) walk to Burstall Pass (five hours), near the border with Spray Valley Provincial Park, are also fantastic options. In the **Kananaskis Valley**, for a short leg-stretch try the 1km (0.6-mile) Wedge Pond Loop (30 minutes) around a popular fishing lake, or the Eau Claire Trail (one hour), which has interpretive signs exploring the natural history and wildlife of the K-Country.

For cyclists, there are lots of mixed-use trails shared with horseback riders and hikers. Popular options include the 16.5km (10.3-mile) round-trip ride on the Ribbon Falls Trail near Kananaskis village, the 31km (19.3-mile) Stoney Trail round-trip near Barrier Dam, and the hair-raising and very technical 19.2km (12-mile) round-trip route to Baldy Pass in the Sibbald area. The paved Evan-Thomas bike trail, just south of Kananaskis village, is a good option for a family-friendly spin, and you can hire bikes and child chariots from **Kananaskis Outfitters** (Map p149; ☎ 403-591-7000; www.kananaskisoutfitters .com; adult bikes per hr/day C$15/45, child bikes C$15/35, chariots C$9/19) in the village complex.

Boundary Ranch (Map p149; ☎ 403-591-7171; www.boundaryranch.com; Kananaskis Trail; short trips C$35-95, day trips from C$130; ☽ mid-May–mid-Oct) is the place to head for horseback riders, with lots of options for routes and pack trips, some of which combine with white-water trips and backcountry hikes.

The mountain-backed greens and fairways at **Kananaskis Country Golf Course** (Map p149; ☎ 402-591-7154; www.kananaskisgolf.com; green fees C$85) are almost as famous as those at Banff Springs, but they're much less snooty (and a good deal cheaper too). There are two courses to choose from, and you can rent all the gear (clubs, shoes and golf cart) from the clubhouse.

Kananaskis is also famous for its winter sports, thanks mainly to having staged the 1988 Winter Olympics at **Nakiska** (Map p149; ☎ 403-591-7777; www.skinakiska.com; day pass adult C$53, 6-12yr C$17, 13-17yr C$37), south of Kananaskis village. It's a lot smaller than the better-known resorts in Banff, but it's often a lot less busy. There are 28 marked runs, but plenty of scope for off-piste riding on the

slopes of Mt Allan. Snowboarders can also tackle the dedicated terrain park. Two more skiable faces are available to the south at **Fortress Mountain** (Map p149; ☎ 403-591-7108; www .skifortress.com), though the resort was closed for renovations at the time of research, with no scheduled reopening date.

Sleeping
CAMPING
Compared to Banff, Kananaskis' campgrounds are a haven of peace and tranquility. If you're off into the wilds, you'll need a wilderness permit (C$8 plus a C$8 administration fee per party) from one of the visitor centers; book well ahead, as K-Country's backcountry trails are very popular. There's a useful listing of all the main campgrounds at www.kananaskiscountrycampgrounds.com.

Boulton Creek Campground (Map p149; ☎ 403-591-7226; sites $; ☽ May-Nov) One of the best-equipped campgrounds and correspondingly popular, beautifully situated just to the south of Lower Kananaskis Lake. Showers, flush toilets and summer interpretive programs, plus power and water hookups, mean that it's nearly always full. There are some pull-through sites for RVs.

Mt Kidd RV Park (Map p149; ☎ 403-591-7700; www .mountkiddrv.com; Mt Kidd Dr; sites $; ☽ year-round) Halfway along the Kananaskis Valley, and handily placed for the facilities around Kananaskis village, this place is the best option for trailer and RV campers, with full hookups and over 200 sites, plus a fantastic range of facilities: tennis courts, laundry, grocery store, games rooms and even a sauna.

McLean Creek (☎ 403-949-3132; Elbow Valley; sites $; ☽ year-round) Another large and efficient campground near to McLean Pond and the Station Flats, just off Hwy 66 from Bragg Creek. The sites are crammed in pretty close together (especially on Loops C and D), but the facilities are comprehensive (campground theater, flush loos, showers) and you're well placed to explore the plentiful trails nearby.

Canyon Camping (Map p149; ☎ 1-866-366-2267; sites $; Kananaskis Lakes Rd; ☽ mid-Jun–Sep) Just a few short steps from Lower Kananaskis Lake and a gorgeous little picnic area, this is another lovely mountain-view campground. Loop A has just a few sites, while Loop C is furthest from the lakeshore but usually the quietest. There are horse pits, trailer pull-throughs and a bike trail that's handy to the visitor center.

Sundance Lodges (Map p149; ☎ 403-591-7122; www.sundancelodges.com; Kananaskis Trail; trapper's tents & teepees $$, campsites $; ☽ mid-May–Oct) For that authentic Canadian experience, try the hand-painted teepees and basic trapper's tents at this imaginative and organized campground. As you'd expect, facilities are basic – sleeping platforms and a lantern are about all you'll find inside – so bring along all the usual camping gear.

Other options:

Elkwood Campground (Map p149; ☎ 1-866-366-2267; sites $; ☽ May-Sep) The 130 sites here, near Lower Kananaskis Lake, are fairly private, scattered around four well-spaced loops.

Lower Lake Campground (Map p149; ☎ 1-866-366-2267; sites $; ☽ May-Nov) Lovely, quiet and secluded sites with mountain and lake views dotted along a single trail, with a few pull-through loops for trailers.

HOTELS & HOSTELS

HI Kananaskis Wilderness Hostel (Map p149; ☎ 403-521-8421; www.hihostels.ca; Kananaskis village; dm $) The rustic exterior might fool you into thinking you'll be roughing it at this back-woods hostel, but inside you'll find shiny pine floors, plush sofas, a fire-lit lounge and a kingly kitchen. The large bunk-bed dorms are a bit institutional, but on the plus side you probably won't be spending much time inside. There are discounts on horseback trips and rafting expeditions in summer.

William Watson Lodge (Map p149; ☎ 403-591-7227; Kananaskis Lakes Rd; cabins $; ☽ year-round; ⓑ) This excellent cabin complex is specially designed for disabled visitors, with fully accessible lodges in a quiet wood, as well as organized activities to help guests get out and explore. You'll need your own food and bedding.

Delta Lodge (Map p149; ☎ 403-591-7711; kan .reservations@deltahotels.com; d $$, ste & f $$$; ▣) Across the pond from the Executive Resort, this is another slick but rather soulless hotel catering mainly for business travelers and well-heeled golfers, with two buildings (a standard lodge and luxury 'manor') linked by a covered walkway.

Mt Engadine Lodge (Map p149; ☎ 403-678-4080; www.mountengadine.com; r $$, lodges & cabins $$$) For a lot more charm and character, head for this pleasant little country lodge, which has a selection of lodge suites (complete with balcony and sitting room), as well as peaceful rooms and rustic lodges with wooden deck overlooking a delightful meadow. Rates include four hearty meals, including afternoon tea and a slap-up brekkie. The easiest way to reach the lodge is to continue south along Hwy 40 past Kananaskis Village and the golf course, and take the right turn onto the Smith-Dorrien/Spray Trail turnoff (Hwy 742). Continue north for about 30km (18.6 miles) to Mt Shark Rd and the lodge.

Executive Resort at Kananaskis (Map p149; ☎ 1-888-388-3932; resortinfo@royalinn.com; Kananaskis village; d from $$$; ▣) One of the two corporate-style complexes in Kananaskis village, this big, spacious hotel has condo-style rooms set back from a bubbling fishpond. The decor is elegant if slightly anonymous, with mon-ochrome mountain photos and the usual palette of regal blues, yellows and creams. The loft suites, with fireplaces and twin bubble tubs, are worth the extra outlay.

Eating

Self-catering supplies are available from the small stores at Fortress Junction, Mt Kidd RV Park, Boulton Creek Trading Post and Kananaskis village.

Rick Guinn's Steakhouse (Map p149; ☎ 403-591-7171; Boundary Ranch; mains $-$$; ☽ 11am-7pm mid-May–mid-Oct) Ranchero-style cooking goes hand in hand with the ambience of a working corral at Rick Guinn's, where you can tuck into the usual standards of flame-cooked burgers, inch-thick T-bone steaks and smoked pork chops, all washed down with draft beer.

Mt Engadine Lodge (Map p149; ☎ 403-678-4080; breakfast buffet $, lunch/dinner $/$$$) For dining with a view, this is far and away the best choice in K-Country, with a pretty din-ing room overlooking the lush country meadow where you'll often spy moose and caribou through the windows while you're chowing down. The food is hale and hearty, cooked on the premises every day. Expect fresh-baked bread, lamb and beef dishes, stews and casseroles and a good range of veggie-friendly dishes. Reservations are es-sential.

Fireweed Grill (Map p149; ☎ 888-244-8666; Delta Lodge; lunch/dinner $$/$$$; ☽ lunch & dinner) A pretty swish affair, dabbling in global cuisine combined with Albertan standards such as grilled steaks and baked river fish.

Getting There & Away

Kananaskis Country can be reached off Trans-Canada Hwy 1 along the gravel Smith-Dorrien Rd (Hwy 742) from Canmore or the Kananaskis Trail (Hwy 40), just east of Canmore. From southern Alberta, you can reach the area in summer along Hwy 40 from Highwood House.

YOHO NATIONAL PARK

Just west of Lake Louise, Banff slips over into the neighboring province of British Columbia and Yoho National Park, much less visited than its larger neighbor but arguably just as spectacular. From the Banff border the park winds down into the Kicking Horse Valley, following the course of the surging Kicking Horse River. Hulking mountains rise up on either side of the road as you drop down toward the valley floor, and spur roads veer off to the area's most beautiful attractions – the crashing cascade of Takakkaw Falls and the glittering, green-blue pool of Emerald Lake.

Most of Yoho is still wild, remote country, and you'll find little in the way of visitor facilities; the only real settlement is the old CPR service station of Field, a quaint, attractive little town dotted with clapboard buildings and tumbledown outhouses that feels a world away from the hustle and hum of Lake Louise, 27km (16.7 miles) to the east.

Yoho National Park Visitor Centre (☎ 250-343-6783; yoho.info@pc.gc.ca; ☯ 9am-7pm summer, to 4pm winter) is just across the railway tracks from Field on the edge of Hwy 1. It's the main source of information on hikes and sights around the park, with the usual range of activity leaflets and accommodations booklets, as well as a small Friends of Yoho gift store and a Parks Canada desk where you can pick up wilderness passes.

Sights

TAKAKKAW FALLS

The Cree people were spot on when they named the 245m-high (804ft) waterfall of **Takakkaw** – the word means 'magnificent' in the Cree language. In fact, it's one of the highest waterfalls in Canada, with a thundering torrent of water that tumbles down from the nearby Daly Glacier into a small, mist-shrouded pool. It's equally impressive seen in rain or shine and the noise at any

time is quite deafening; don't miss it, even if you're only spending a day in Yoho. The road up to the falls veers north off Hwy 1 just after the Lower Spiral Tunnel lookout; you'll pass the second spiral tunnel lookout and the confluence of the Yoho and Kicking Horse Rivers on the way up to the falls.

EMERALD LAKE

For most visitors to Yoho, this extravagantly colored **lake** is top of the must-see list, and with good reason. Like its sister lakes of Peyto, Moraine and Lake Louise, Emerald Lake gains its otherworldly color from sunlight bouncing off rock particles suspended in the water – the brighter the light the more vivid the color, although early morning and evening are usually the best times to visit. It's a beautiful, soothing place, ringed by forest and silhouetted by impressive mountains. Trails lead around the lakeshore en route to the high **Yoho Pass** and **Emerald Basin**, and there's an 800m (0.5-mile) woodland walk up to the small **Hamilton Falls** from the main parking lot. Turn right (north) off Hwy 1 just south of Field, and continue for 10km (6.2 miles); stop for a peek at a **natural rock bridge** over the Kicking Horse River just after the turnoff.

BURGESS SHALE WORLD HERITAGE SITE

Hard as it may be to believe, 400 million years ago much of the Canadian Rockies area was submerged beneath a deep sea that was home to all kinds of exotic marine creatures. Eventually the sea disappeared and geological activity forced up the earth's crust into the spiky peaks and mountains we know today, but proof of the area's underwater history stayed in the fossilized remains of creatures perfectly preserved in the mountain rock. In 1909, a huge **field of fossils** was discovered by archaeologists on the slopes of Mt Field, now known as the Burgess Shale World Heritage Site. It has become one of the world's most important resources for the study of the origins of life on earth, and due to its delicate nature it can only be visited on a guided hike led by naturalists from the **Yoho-Burgess Shale Foundation** (☎ 800-343-3006; www.burgess-shale.bc.ca; ☯ Jul–mid-Sep). You can see a small exhibit exploring the various discoveries made in the Burgess Shale outside the Yoho National Park Visitor Centre in Field. This

Yoho National Park

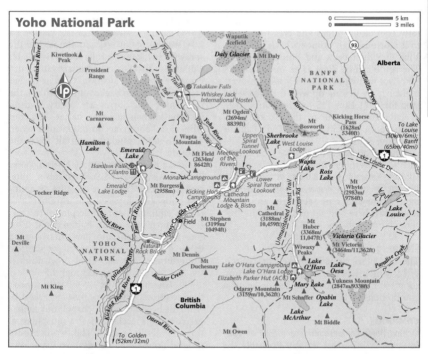

hike is around 20km there and back, so it's a full day on your feet. See the website for other hikes in the area. All are pretty long, with some steep elevations and strenuous sections, so you'll need to arrive suitably prepared.

SPIRAL TUNNELS & KICKING HORSE PASS
Upon completion of the railway in 1885, trains struggled up the challenging **Kicking Horse Pass**, the steepest railway pass in North America. Wrecks and runaways were common until 1909, when the **Spiral Tunnels** were carved into Mts Cathedral and Ogden. If you time it right, you can see a train exiting from the top of the tunnel while its final cars are still entering at the bottom. The main viewing platform (the Upper Lookout) is off the Trans-Canada Hwy, 8km (5 miles) east of Field.

LAKE O'HARA
It might be a little more difficult to reach than most of Yoho's other sights, but Lake O'Hara is more than worth the effort you'll expend on getting here. Hidden away in

a glorious amphitheater of mountains, the lake is home to some of the park's best wildflower meadows, backcountry campgrounds and high-altitude hikes, including the classic routes to **Lake Oesa** and **Yukness Ledge**. The only way into the area is via the 11km (6.8-mile) access road from the parking lot just off Hwy 1. The road is closed to public vehicles, so you'll either have to walk it or try for a spot on one of the hugely oversubscribed **shuttle buses** (☎ 250-343-6344; adult/child C$15/7.50; ◷ mid-Jun–Sep); reservations are available up to three months in advance for a C$12 fee. The four daily buses are always full, so book as early as you can; six seats per day are reserved for 24-hour bookings, but they're snapped up lightning-fast.

Activities
If you can't manage to bag one of the elusive seats on the Lake O'Hara bus, don't fret; there are plenty of other wonderful walks to explore in Yoho. One of the best is the tough but enormously rewarding network of trails from Takakkaw Falls. The most famous route is the 12.8km (8-mile)

high-altitude **Iceline Trail**, which follows a lofty trail along ridges and crests en route to a glorious high point with views of the Vice President peak and Emerald Glacier. The route can be done as an out-and-back hike, but many people turn it into an overnight trip by linking up with the **Yoho Valley Loop** for a 21.1km (13.1-mile) round-trip, overnighting at one of the backcountry campgrounds at Little Yoho, Twin Falls or Laughing Falls.

You can go **fishing** on Emerald Lake from July to November. Rent canoes from the lakeside **Emerald Sports & Gifts** (☎ 250-343-6377; 1hr C$20; ☯ 9am-7pm summer, noon-4pm winter). In winter you can rent **snowshoes** and **cross-country skis** here and set out across the frozen lake.

Sleeping

The best place to base yourself in Yoho is Field, which has lots of private B&Bs and rooms for rent; the visitor center keeps a comprehensive list.

CAMPING

Kicking Horse Campground (Map p153; Yoho Valley Rd; sites $; ☯ late Jun-late Sep; ☖) Probably the most popular campground in Yoho, in a nice forested location with plenty of space between sites, as well as all the deluxe facilities (hookup, flush toilets and wheelchair-accessible showers). The riverside sites (especially 68 to 74) are the pick of the bunch.

Monarch Campground (Map p153; Yoho Valley Rd; sites $; ☯ mid-May–Sep) Around 3km east of Field, and a stone's throw from Kicking Horse Campground, this is a more basic site situated in a large open meadow. Water is sourced from an on-site well and there's an outdoor BBQ shelter for alfresco cookouts.

HOTELS & HOSTELS

Fireweed Hostel (☎ 250-343-6999; www.fireweedhostel.com; Field; dm $) This spankingly posh little hostel in Field is a real find, beautifully finished with lashings of stripped pine, glossy wood and a country-cozy sitting room, complete with snowshoes above the hearth and hiking books for perusal. The dorms are small but smart; each room has two pine bunk beds and a shared bathroom off the hallway.

Whiskey Jack International Hostel (Map p153; ☎ 866-762-4122; cr.wj@hihostels.ca; Yoho Valley Rd; dm $; ☯ mid-Jun–mid-Oct) You can almost feel the spray from Takakkaw Falls at this simple HI wilderness hostel, so what it lacks in luxury it makes up for in location. Clad in timber and decked out in backcountry fashion, the three nine-bed dorms are pretty spartan and the kitchen has seen better days, but who cares about accommodations when you can see a mighty waterfall from the front deck?

Kicking Horse Lodge (☎ 250-343-6303; Kicking Horse Ave, Field; d $-$$, f $$$) This cabin hotel makes a decent bolt-hole if you're on a limited budget, with pleasant if unremarkable rooms equipped with basic pine furniture, simple furnishings and battered old TVs. The family rooms are particularly good value, with kitchens and space for six. The Roundhouse Pub and Grill downstairs is the heart of Field's modest nightlife.

Old Church Inn (☎ 250-343-3645; www.oldchurchguesthouse.ca; 308 Kicking Horse Ave, Field; d $$) It might be a converted chapel, but there's precious little ecclesiastical atmosphere at this friendly little B&B. The two-bedroom ground-floor suite is modern and spacious, equipped with lots of little touches to make you feel at home: books in the lounge, cute little lamps by the beds and a nice galley kitchen where you can whip up some tucker. It's a bit on the chintzy side, but good value.

Mt Stephen Guesthouse (☎ 250-343-6356; www.mountstephen.com; 304 Kicking Horse Ave, Field; d $$) Two smart self-catering suites in a quirky clapboard house, both with their own private entrance and a refreshing absence of frills and floral bedspreads. The tones are neutral, the decor's contemporary and there's a comfy queen-size bed plus a pull-out sofa bed in the lounge. There's no breakfast but you'll find complimentary coffee, tea and hot chocolate in the cupboards.

our pick **Cathedral Mountain Lodge** (Map p153; ☎ 250-343-6442; www.cathedralmountain.com; Yoho Valley Rd; lodges $$$$) If you're looking for wow factor, this place has got it in spades. Idyllically situated beneath the spire of Cathedral Mountain, the luxury log cabins ooze decadence and designer style: cedar-stocked fireplaces, soft down duvets, antique knickknacks and furniture crafted from native woods. The best cabins have a loft sleeping area above the main lounge, as well as lavish soaker tubs, and you'll find handmade chocs and Canadian cheeses in the fridge. Oh, and did we mention free guided hikes and lectures with the in-house naturalist?

Lake O'Hara Lodge (Map p153; ☎ 250-343-6418; www.lakeohara.com; lodges $$$$; ☻ mid-Jun–Oct & mid-Jan–mid-Apr) Things are altogether more countrified at this historic 1920s lodge, but then that's all part of the appeal. Despite the fact that you're miles from the outside world, you can still expect hot tubs, attentive service and slap-up meals, not to mention character-packed cabins finished off with shiny hardwoods and crackling hearths. The lake-view cabins command a hefty premium.

Emerald Lake Lodge (Map p153; ☎ 403-410-7417; www.crmr.com; lodges $$$$) Nestled beside Emerald Lake and accessed by a wooden bridge, this has long been Yoho's poshest place to stay, but it's looking tired considering the elevated price tag. The main lodge is as atmospheric as ever, stuffed with evocative photos, alpine memorabilia and antique furniture, but the old-fashioned color schemes and uninspiring furniture in the units themselves are disappointingly run-of-the-mill. As ever, you'll have to pay extra to secure a lake view.

Eating

Truffle Pigs Café (☎ 250-343-6462; Stephen Ave, Field; sandwiches & lunches $, mains $$; ☻ 9am-9pm, shorter hours in winter) Political fridge magnets, chaotically stocked shelves and a genuine dose of quirky Canadiana characterize this oddball café, which dishes out stonking great sandwiches and paninis at lunchtime and an ever-changing choice of home-cooked grub (think Malaysian chicken, beef bourguignon, teriyaki salmon) every evening. There are also comprehensive supplies for self-caterers.

Kicking Horse Lodge (☎ 250-343-6303; Kicking Horse Ave, Field; lunch $, dinner $$; ☻ breakfast, lunch & dinner) Simple staples from grilled burgers to Cajun chicken make up the menu at the Kicking Horse, served in a welcoming log-walled dining room that's part-shared with the in-house pub. The food's rough and ready but the atmosphere is all smiles.

Cilantro (☎ 250-343-6321; lunch & dinner $$-$$$; ☻ 11am-9pm mid-Jun–Oct, 11am-5pm May–mid-Jun) Right beside the bridge to Emerald Lake Lodge, with a wooden patio overlooking the river, Cilantro makes a delightful spot for an upmarket meal. The main dining room boasts a smart timber-vaulted ceiling, crisp white tablecloths and candlesticks. The menu's similarly cultured, taking in everything from lake fish to Albertan game.

Getting There & Away

Some Greyhound buses stop in Field on their way to/from Banff National Park; see p90 for details.

MT ASSINIBOINE PROVINCIAL PARK

With its ice-encrusted slopes and distinctive skyrocket profile, the pointy pinnacle of Mt Assiniboine is one of the most recognizable landmarks of the Canadian Rockies (and, at 3618m, or 11,870ft, one of the tallest) and you'll often catch distant glimpses of the mountain as you hike around some of Banff's higher trails. Dubbed the Matterhorn of Canada for its pyramidal shape, the mountain is surrounded by its very own provincial park, much favored by backcountry hikers and hardcore mountaineers, and only accessible on foot or (for moneyed-up hikers) by chartered chopper. If it's a wilderness hit you're craving, Mt Assiniboine is definitely the place; the high-altitude trails around the mountain and nearby Lake Magog are just about the most remote you'll find in the whole Canadian Rockies, and civilization certainly feels a world away.

Most people make the trip into Assiniboine in three days; one in, one out and one to explore the trails and mountain country around Lake Magog. Campsites in Assiniboine cost C$5 and are first-come, first-served. If you're overnighting at a campground in Banff on the way in, remember you'll need a wilderness pass and reservations at the appropriate campground. You'll find more information on the park at http://env.gov.bc.ca/bcparks /explore/parkpgs/mtassini.html.

Activities

You won't be surprised to hear that the main reason people make the trip to Assiniboine is to access its secluded backcountry trails. The core area centers on **Lake Magog**, with lots of easy day hikes nearby, including the 6km (3.8-mile) **Nub Peak Trail** to the twin hills known as the Nublet and Niblet, the 9km (5.6-mile) loop trail to **Sunburst**,

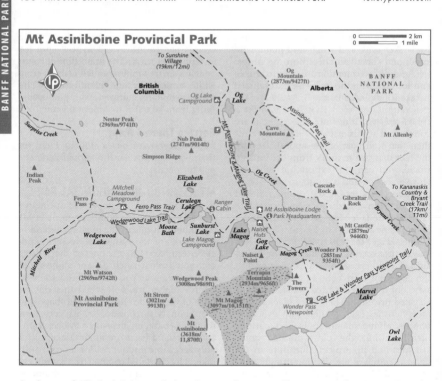

Mt Assiniboine Provincial Park

Cerulean and **Elizabeth Lakes** and the glorious 5.6km (3.5-mile) hike up to **Wonder Pass** via Gog Lake. The hike into the park is an event in itself; the traditional route is via Bryant Creek from the Mt Shark trailhead in K-Country, but there's a second, highly scenic route from Sunshine Village via the Valley of the Rocks (see the Mt Assiniboine & Lake Magog hike, p119).

Rock climbing and **mountaineering** in Assiniboine are for experienced alpinists only. The rocks are treacherous, the routes are challenging and the drops are very, very long, so you need to know what you're doing. **Cross-country skiing** is another way to explore the park in winter; telemarkers mostly arrive via Assiniboine Pass and need to be prepared for emergency camping and carry an avalanche beacon.

Sleeping

There are over 75 backcountry campgrounds in Assiniboine, but most people end up pitching their canvas at the main site on Lake Magog. Fires in all campgrounds are banned and the only sites with

bear-proof bins are at Lake Magog, Og Lake and Porcupine. Grizzlies and black bears often trundle through the area, so it's important to take precautions.

For a bit more shelter you can book a bunk in one of four **Naiset Huts** (bed $), which offer simple wooden beds, mattresses and a woodstove, as well as a newly added cooking shelter with propane lights and a stove. Reservations are a good idea in summer and mandatory in winter. There's also a 15-person climbing shelter called the RC Hind Hut nestled near the northern face of Mt Assiniboine. Reservations for all huts are made through the Mt Assiniboine Lodge.

Mt Assiniboine Lodge (Map p156; ☎ 403-678-2883; www.assiniboinelodge.com; lodge r & cabins $$$$; ☽ mid-Jun–Oct & mid-Feb–mid-Apr) – the first ski lodge built in the Canadian Rockies – is a Norwegian log cabin straight out of a storybook, gloriously backed by Mt Assiniboine and surrounded by mountain meadow. It's a real family affair – rates include home-cooked meals eaten at communal tables and there's a separate sauna and gender-specific shower house, so you're guaranteed to make some chums. The six lodge rooms (complete with flickering light bulbs and mountain decor) each sleep two people, so you might have to share if you're a solo traveler. Lodge staff lead personally guided hikes into the mountains.

Getting There & Away

Forget public transportation – your only chance of a lift into Assiniboine is aboard a helicopter from the Mt Shark heliport, booked through Mt Assiniboine Lodge (C$125, Sunday, Wednesday and Friday).

KOOTENAY NATIONAL PARK & RADIUM HOT SPRINGS

Stretching for just 8km (5 miles) to either side of Hwy 93 (sometimes known locally as the Kootenay Hwy or the Banff–Windermere Rd), Kootenay was founded in 1920 as a by-product of the construction of the first automobile highway across the Canadian Rockies. In exchange for helping out with the financial costs of building the road, the Canadian government claimed the slender sliver of land that now makes up the national park. Kootenay is another haven for hikers and outdoor enthusiasts, with plenty of trails to explore as well as several mustsee attractions, including the natural ochre beds known as the Paint Pots, the imposing bulk of the Stanley Glacier and the naturally heated pools around Radium Hot Springs.

Due to its unusual geography, Kootenay is one of the most fire-prone areas in the Canadian Rockies – the southern section of the park toward Radium Hot Springs has been dubbed 'lightning alley' thanks to its frequent summer thunderstorms. In 2003, 17,409 hectares (43,020 acres) of forest in the northern part of the park were damaged by a huge wildfire sparked off by lightning, forcing the closure of several popular areas around Tokumm Creek and Marble Canyon. The scars left by the fire are still plain to see, and while it looks severe, it's worth remembering that natural forest fires play a crucial role in ensuring the continued health of wild woodland.

Orientation & Information

Along the western ranges of the Rockies, Kootenay Park runs from the Alberta–BC border in the north, along the Continental Divide to the town of Radium Hot Springs

in the south. The 94km (58.3-mile) Hwy 93 is the only road through the park.

Radium is the main visitor hub, while you can pick up trail information and maps from the **Kootenay Park Lodge Visitor Centre** (☎ 403-762-9196; info@kootenayparklodge.com; 9am-6pm Jul-Sep, to 5pm May & Jun, to 4pm Sep & Oct) at Vermilion Lakes, 68km north of Radium Hot Springs, and the **Kootenay National Park Visitor Centre** (☎ 250-347-9505; kootenay.info@pc.gc.ca; 7556 Main St E, Radium Hot Springs; 9am-7pm mid-Jun–Sep, to 5pm mid-May–mid-Jun, Sep & Oct). In winter, tourist information is available from the Yoho National Park Visitor Centre (p152).

Sights

Traveling south along Hwy 93 from Hwy 1, you'll soon start to see the effects of the 2003 forest fire, with blackened trunks and ash-gray land coating the mountainsides on either side of the road, dotted with lush green patches where the forest has started to regenerate. The Vermilion Pass area, right on the edge of the Continental Divide, was the scene of another devastating fire in 1968 and you can now take a scenic 15-minute, wheelchair-accessible walk around the **Fireweed Trail**, with signs explaining the vital role fires play in maintaining a healthy ecosystem. Nearby is the trailhead for the 11km (6.8-mile) round-trip hike up to **Stanley Glacier**, a great white tongue of ice sandwiched by the crests of Storm Mountain and Stanley Peak. A little further southwest, the popular trail around **Marble Canyon** has been revamped after a long closure to repair bridges and walkways damaged by the fire. The easy 1.6km (1 mile) loop crosses Tokkum Creek and offers great views down into the plunging limestone canyon, sculpted and shaped by the surging force of the river.

A further 3km (1.9 miles) down Hwy 93, a short wheelchair-friendly trail leads to the rust-red **ochre ponds**, once used by First Nation tribes, including the Ktunaxa (Kootenay), Stoney and Blackfoot, as a source of decorative paint for adorning teepees, clothing and bodies. European settlers later used the ochre as a base for paint manufacture and a thriving mining operation was in full swing here in the early 1900s; you can still see bits of machinery scattered around the mineral beds. The **Paint Pots** themselves are three cold mineral springs with blue-green water that contrasts with the crimson crust of iron oxide decorating their edges.

Further south, you'll travel along the valley floor, traversing the Vermilion River at **Vermilion Crossing** around 31km (19.3 miles) from the Alberta border. Shortly afterward, look out for the **Sir George Simpson Monument and viewpoint**, which commemorates the trailblazing explorer and Hudsons Bay Trading Company supremo who pioneered the first trail over the mountains to Banff in 1841; the historic route he followed heads west from here along the Simpson River. Beyond the **Kootenay Crossing**, the road begins to climb again, rising to a wonderful **viewpoint** of the Kootenay Valley and Sinclair Pass 16km (10 miles) from Radium Hot Springs. From here the roller-coaster road winds along canyons and mountainsides all the way to Radium, just inside the park's southern border.

Like its sister town Banff, Radium is famous for its natural **hot springs** (☎ 250-347-9485; www.hotsprings.ca; Hwy 93; adult/child C$7/6; ☺ hot pool 9am-11pm mid-May–early Oct, noon-9pm Sun-Thu, noon-10pm Fri & Sat early Oct–mid-May, cool pool 1-8pm Sep-early Oct, 6-9pm Fri, noon-9pm Sat & Sun Oct–mid-May), which boasts the largest outdoor hot spring (39˚C) in Canada, gorgeously situated beneath the cliffs of Sinclair Canyon, as well as a 'cool pool' (27˚C) where you can chill out. Spa facilities, lockers and bathing gear are available and you might even glimpse a bighorn sheep while you're taking a dip in the pool. In case you're wondering, there is a trace of radium in the water, but it's about as much as in a luminous watch dial, so you're pretty safe.

Activities

Kootenay is crammed with day hikes. As well as the trail up to Stanley Glacier, you could try the 9.6km (6-mile) **Kimpton Creek Trail** round-trip and the 20km (12.4-mile) **Kindersley Pass Trail** round-trip, or the 21.4km (13.3-mile) backcountry hike to **Floe Lake** and the 55.6km (34.5-mile) **Rockwall Trail**. Wilderness passes and trail maps are available from parks offices.

Several local operators offer rafting trips on nearby rivers, including the peaceful Columbia River and the much wilder Kicking Horse. Contact **Kootenay River Runners** (☎ 250-347-9210; www.raftingtherockies.com; Hwy 93), just outside Radium, which offers several

trips on class I–III rapids, as well as peaceful twilight floats and river cruises. **Toby Creek Adventures** (☎ 250-342-5047; www.tobycreekadventures.com; Panorama), 32km from Radium, offers daily ATV tours around local trails and the abandoned Paradise Silver Mine, as well as snowmobile trips in winter.

Radium is also famous for its beautiful 18-hole golf courses run by **Radium Resort** (☎ 250-347-6266; www.radiumresort.com; ☺ May-Oct). There are two to choose from – the **Springs Course** (McKay St; Mon-Thu C$75, Fri-Sun C$100-115) and the **Resort Course** (Hwy 93/95; Mon-Thu C$45, Fri-Sun C$55) – with combined green fees if you want to play both.

Sleeping

Apart from the campgrounds along Hwy 93, most of Kootenay's accommodations are in Radium, with lots of bog-standard motels lining the main road into town. The visitor center can help out with suggestions if you're stuck for a bed, or just cruise around looking for the 'vacancy' signs. Redstreak is the only campground that accepts advance reservations.

CAMPING

Redstreak Campground (☎ 1-877-737-3783; www.pccamping.ca/parkscanada; Stanley St East, Radium Hot Springs; sites $; ☺ May-Oct; ♿) Kootenay's largest campground tops the list for facilities, with everything from flush toilets and hot-and-cold running water to full hookups, playground and a small theater. It's a big, busy site, partially wooded but crisscrossed by lots of access roads; it's probably not the place if you're looking for peace and quiet, but it's only a 30-minute walk from Radium.

McLeod Meadows Campground (Hwy 93; sites $; ☺ mid-May–mid-Sep; ♿) You'll find more natural splendor at this 98-pitch campground, peacefully located on the banks of the Kootenay River just a 2.6km (1.6-mile) walk to the shores of pretty Dog Lake. Plentiful trees and spacious, grassy sites make this a fine place to pitch your canvas; try Loop K for the best views. Flush toilets, bear-proof bins, fire rings, kitchen shelters and RV dumps are all on-site.

Marble Canyon Campground (Hwy 93; sites $; ☺ mid-Jun–Sep) This high-country campground is situated near the Marble Canyon trail, with similar facilities to McLeod

Meadows. Most sites have tree cover to keep you out of the wind. The eastern side has the best views.

HOTELS

Chalet Europe (☎ 250-347-9305; www.chaleteurope .com; Madsen Rd, Radium Hot Springs; d $$) Impressively perched on a spur high above Radium Hot Springs, this Swiss-style hotel is rather dated but the rooms boast the best views in town. Don't be fooled by the 'Suite' tags – inside, the color schemes and furniture are about as up-to-date as bell-bottoms and kipper ties, but you can't argue with the outlook. Corner suites (complete with private balconies) are the pick.

Alpen Motel (☎ 250-347-9823; www.alpenmotel .com; Hwy 93, Radium Hot Springs; d $$) Geraniums and window boxes are strewn all across the front of this three-story motel – one of several along Radium's motel strip – but the rooms don't quite live up to the floral display. Inside, you'll find the usual motel-standard furniture, well-worn bathrooms and boxy layouts. Rooms with a combi-bath and minifridge are better value.

Cedar Motel (☎ 250-347-9463; www.cedarmotel .ca; 7593 Main St W, Radium Hot Springs; r $$) Clean, competitively priced and (as its name suggests) cedar-clad, this is another pleasant budget bolthole with small, brightly colored rooms. Some have teeny kitchenettes and interjoining doorways, making them a good bet for families.

Kootenay Park Lodge (☎ 403-762-9196; www .kootenayparklodge.com; Vermilion Crossing, Hwy 93; d cabins $$-$$$; ☽ mid-May–late Sep) The pick of the places to stay inside the park, with a range of cute log cabins complete with verandahs, massive fridges and two-burner hot plates to warm through your beans and trail stews; think rusticity rather than refinement. The quiet wooded site is at Vermilion Crossing, so you're perfectly placed for exploring the rest of the park and there's a restaurant, gift store and information center on-site.

Village Country Inn (☎ 250-347-9392; www.vil lagecountryinn.com; 7557 Canyon Ave, Radium Hot Springs; r $$-$$$) After Radium's endless nondescript motels, this fine little gabled and turreted house comes as a real breath of fresh air. Inside it feels a little like a dressed-up doll's house; the rooms have heaps of country frips and frills, from potted plants to rose-print bedspreads, wicker chairs and dried flowers, and the same pastoral atmosphere runs into the downstairs tearoom, with its cobblestone fireplace, pine floor and spindle-back chairs.

ourpick Storm Mountain Lodge (☎ 403-762-4155; www.stormmountainlodge.com; Hwy 93, Castle Junction; cabins $$-$$$) Our favorite cabin complex has a collection of timber outhouses that have been painstakingly restored and yet still retain their original 1920s trappings. One of several 'Bungalow Camps' built by the CPR to attract tourists to Banff, the lodges are brimming with period curios: wooden snowshoes, bison heads and hand-crafted mirrors adorn the walls, beds are crafted from native timber, and hand-carved country trinkets are stacked up on the slate fire surround. Rocky Mountain Soaps, deep, freestanding tubs and twinkling lights outside the cabins just add to the experience, and if you don't feel like cooking there's a country kitchen and the chef will even whip you up a hiker's picnic if you're setting out on the trail. A true down-home delight.

Eating

Higher Ground (☎ 250-347-0089; Hwy 93, Radium Hot Springs; mains $; ☽ 6am-6pm) This great little metropolitan-style coffeehouse does the frothiest cappuccinos in town, as well as a great line in banana muffins, sour-cream coffee cake and deli sandwiches. Sink into one of the scruffy armchairs and read the morning papers as the coffee machines chunter in the background.

Backcountry Jack's (☎ 250-347-0097; Hwy 93, Radium Hot Springs; lunch/dinner $/$$; ☽ 11:30am-10pm Mon-Thu & Sat, to midnight Fri, to 9pm Sun) Honest country cookin' is the order of the day at this friendly, laid-back diner, decked out in cowboy fashion with a menu of spicy beans, grilled burgers, fillet steaks à la Big Guy and chicken wings to match. Our tip? Try the 'cowboy caviar' (otherwise known as beans and nachos).

Helna's Stube (☎ 250-347-0047; 7547 Hwy 93, Radium Hot Springs; mains $$$; ☽ dinner) Radium's curious Austrian connections reach their apogee at this gut-busting gourmet restaurant, where the Gothic-lettered menu is crammed with calorie-heavy staples such as trout Müllerin and authentic Wiener schnitzel. The atmosphere is authentically alpine and the house specialty is Mozart dumplings (filled with nougat, marzipan and chocolate-strawberry sauce). Time to let out that belt.

Getting There & Away

From Banff, head south along Hwy 93 from Castle Junction. You can also reach the park from the south by heading north from Cranbrook on Hwy 93 to Radium Hot Springs. In Radium Hot Springs, the Greyhound bus depot is on Hwy 93, next to the Esso station and near the junction with Hwy 98.

GOLDEN

The little community of Golden might not have the mountainous charm of the nearby national parks, but what it lacks in good looks it makes up for in adrenaline. There's no end of activities to occupy your time in Golden – stop by the tourist office and you'll be bombarded with an avalanche of leaflets offering all manner of extreme sports and outdoor pastimes. With everything from downhill mountain biking to white-water rafting on its doorstep, it's a fantastic base for thrill seekers and is handily placed for further forays into Kootenay and Banff. The town's divided in two by the Kicking Horse River, with the northern side, near the Trans-Canada Hwy, having most of the facilities. For visitor information, seek out the **Golden Visitor Information Centre** (☎ 250-344-7125; www.go2rockies.com; 500 N 10th Ave; ☒ 9am-5pm summer, 10am-4pm Tue-Fri winter), on the main highway into town. For a useful overview of accommodations options, check out www.stayingolden.com.

Sights & Activities

NORTHERN LIGHTS WOLF CENTRE

This fascinating **wildlife center** (☎ 250-344-6798; www.northernlightswildlife.com; adult/child C$10/6; ☒ 9am-9pm Jul & Aug, 10am-6pm Sep-Jun) is dedicated to the welfare and preservation of Canada's native wolves and houses a small pack of gray wolves and wolf-husky crosses, all born and bred in captivity. Visits include a tour of the wildlife facility, with lots of time to meet the resident wolves and learn about this fascinating and much-misunderstood animal.

BIKING

Mountain biking is one of the most popular sports in Golden, thanks to several nearby trail networks that are famous with the Ca-

nuck MTB fraternity. The Mount 7 system is mainly for downhillers, while Moonrakers has lots of easy and intermediate singletrack routes that are perfect if you just want a quick spin in the saddle. The **Golden Cycling Club** (www.goldencyclingclub.com) produces a trail map that's sold all over town. Bikes can be rented from **Summit Cycle** (☎ 250-344-6600; 11th Ave) and **Selkirk Sports** (☎ 250-344-2966; 504 9th Ave).

The fantastic **Kicking Horse Resort** (☎ 250-439-5400; www.kickinghorseresort.com; full-day bike & lift C$100, mountain ticket adult/child C$32/30), part boutique resort and part outdoor activity center, also operates its own trail system accessed via the **gondola** up to the top of the mountain, with plenty of routes to follow on the way down. Its on-site rental company, Canyon Creek Outfitters, can equip you with bikes and all the other necessary gear. Visit the website for full details.

RAFTING & CANOEING

With the Kicking Horse running right through the middle of town, it's hardly surprising that white-water trips are another favorite Golden activity. As usual, all the local operators offer a variety of runs to suit all abilities, ranging from sedate floats to heart-stopping roller-coaster rides down the rapids; all equipment, including helmets and paddles, is provided. Many operators also offer canoe trips onto the Blaeberry, Kicking Horse, Blue Water and Spillimacheen Rivers.

Alpine Rafting (☎ 888-599-5299; www.alpinerafting.com; Golden View Rd; trips C$65-149) offers several afternoon and day trips on nearby rivers, plus a 'Kicking Horse Challenge,' taking on 32km (20 miles) of white water on the Kicking Horse River.

Wet & Wild (☎ 800-668-9119; www.wetnwild.bc.ca; trips C$60-145) is another experienced local company with a range of tours on the Kicking Horse, plus jet-boat trips, canoe expeditions and a shuttle service to/from Banff, Canmore and Lake Louise.

The multi-activity **Adrenalin Descents** (☎ 250-344-4679; www.adrenalindescents.com; 735 Hefti Rd) puts the extreme in extreme sports – high-altitude ski touring, ski mountaineering, hardcore rapid rafting and even heli-biking, where you're dropped off by chopper and make your own two-wheeled descent. It mainly caters for experienced riders and skiers looking for that extra thrill factor.

Columbia River Safaris (☎ 250-344-4931; www .columbiariversafaris.ca; Hwy 1) specializes in 'river safaris,' which combine a guided river expedition with wildlife-watching trips. If you just want the white-water part, ask for the two-hour Columbia River Safari (adult/child C$90/70). There's a good chance of spotting elk, eagles and ospreys.

HANG-GLIDING

The Mount 7 site is one of the world's top spots for paragliders and hang-gliders, and hosts regular national and international competitions. If you fancy a bird's-eye view over the Rocky Mountain scenery, you can take tandem flights with an instructor – contact **Canadian Rockies Heli-Paragliding** (☎ 250-344-3214) or **Golden Eagle Tandem Paragliding** (☎ 250-344-7325), or consult the comprehensive website at www.flygolden.ca.

WINTER SPORTS

Skiing, snowboarding and cross-country skiing are all huge around Golden. The Kicking Horse Resort is the main focus of activity, and in winter its mountain-bike trails transform into a network of downhill runs covering over 164 hectares (405 acres) of skiable terrain, plus the second-highest vertical descent in Canada. Snowboarding packages, lessons and lift tickets are available at the resort, or if you're after something a bit more outlandish, how about cat- and heli-skiing with **Chatter Creek Mountain Lodge** (☎ 250-344-7199; www .catskiingbc.com; per day incl meals, accommodations & guide C$500, plus helicopter C$305) or snowmobiling with **Snowpeak Rentals** (☎ 888-512-4222; www.snowpeak rentals.com; 1025 10th Ave N; per day C$215-265).

Sleeping

Golden Eco-Adventure Ranch (☎ 250-344-6825; www.goldenadventurepark.com; tents & RVs $, yurts $$; 🖳) Spread over 160 hectares (395 acres) of mountain meadow, this great campground-cum-outdoors center feels a world away from the cramped world of municipal camping. Sites are spacious, there are full RV hookups and you can even kip in a Mongolian yurt if you're tired of your tent. The owners can help you book practically every outdoor sport you can dream up.

Kicking Horse Canyon B&B (☎ 250-344-6848; www.kickinghorsecanyonbb.com; 644 Lapp Rd; d $$)

Steer clear of Golden's cookie-cutter motels and book yourself into this endearingly offbeat B&B, where you're taken into the bosom of the family the minute you cross the threshold. The rooms all have their own oddball character – think log-frame beds, vintage railway photos and mountain-themed trinkets – and meals are eaten at a communal table that's straight out of the Waltons. Pancakes, muffins and scrambled eggs for breakfast, too.

Hillside Lodge & Chalets (☎ 250-344-7281; www .mistaya.com/hillside; Hwy 1; d & cabins $$, ste $$$) Goldilocks would feel right at home in these dinky little cabins, pastorally set around a forest glade and equipped with potbellied stoves, hand-carved wooden furniture and sweet little porches for that pioneer feel. If your budget can stretch to it, the summer suite has its own outdoor hot tub and steam sauna.

Copperhorse Lodge (☎ 250-344-7644; www.cop perhorselodge.com; ste $$$) Part of the Kicking Horse complex, this groovy little number combines the ambience of a ski lodge with the amenities of an upmarket hotel. You'll find luxurious fabrics, picture windows, huge beds and sexy bathrooms with multijet showers. Downstairs there's an elegant lounge-bar and gourmet brasserie brimming over with slate, stone and native hardwoods.

Vagabond Lodge (☎ 250-344-2622; www.vaga bondlodge.ca; 158 Cache Close; d $$$) Ten rooms with boutique trappings in a grand mountain mansion. Old-fashioned sinks and mismatched wardrobes sit alongside muted colors, varnished wood and quietly elegant furnishings. Six rooms have mountain-view balconies, but the best are the two split-level rooms with their own snug little sleeping loft. None have phones or TVs – the focus here is on the stunning setting.

Eating

Eleven 22 (☎ 250-344-2443; 1122 10th Ave S; mains $$$; 🕓 4pm-late) Part supper lounge, part chic bar, this funky four-roomed eating emporium is housed in a heritage building but is all about cutting-edge food. Abstract art and fiery colors cover the walls, while the chefs dabble away with pan-Asian and fusion dishes.

Kicking Horse Grill (☎ 250-344-2330; 1105 9th St S; mains $$$; 🕓 dinner) For a less outré atmosphere, you can't top this bustling little grill house, where Stetsons, candles and fairy lights conjure up a delightful down-home feel. While the surroundings are 100% Canadian, the menu's eclectic: tiger prawns, Dutch meatballs and Greek souvlaki reflect the chef's pan-global interests.

Cedar House (☎ 250-344-4679; 735 Hefti Rd; mains $$$; ✪ dinner) Organic gardens and locally sourced produce provide the fundamentals for this inventive restaurant off Hwy 95, just south of town, offering fine, fresh bistro food in a lovely mountainside setting.

Eagle's Eye Restaurant (☎ 250-439-5400; mains $$$$; ✪ lunch Mon-Sat, dinner Fri-Sun Jun-Sep) At 2350m (7700ft) above sea level, the Kicking Horse Resort's flagship bistro is one of the highest restaurants in Canada and it's been getting fittingly sky-high reviews. Mixing classic Gallic dishes with lots of characteristically Canadian flair, and with a dining room dripping with designer touches, it's a studiously sophisticated experience – but the unbelievable views from the panoramic terrace are the real draw. Access the restaurant aboard the Eagle's Eye Gondola from the Kicking Horse Mountain Discovery Centre, 14km from Golden.

Getting There & Away

About 25km (15.5 miles) west of Yoho National Park, Golden is situated next to the Trans-Canada Hwy, at the junction of Hwy 95 south. Greyhound buses pass through town twice a day.

Jasper National Park

'I'll take my oath, my dear friends, that God Almighty never made such a place,' opined an early Northwest Company trader as he surveyed the hostile, yet haunting scenery that makes up present-day Jasper National Park. He wouldn't be the last enraptured visitor to struggle for superlatives. Jasper's potent mix of crenellated mountains and landscape-shaping glaciers has been tempting daredevils and dreamers into its midst for well over a century. It's a procession that shows no signs of abating. Armed enthusiastically with skis, mountain bikes, binoculars and crampons, an estimated two million thrill-seeking visitors continue to descend annually on the Rocky Mountains' largest national park, searching wistfully for memorable adventures and life-changing experiences. Few leave disappointed.

While less foreboding than the unmapped wilderness of colonial folklore, modern-day Jasper has lost little of its rugged, back-to-nature appeal. Blessed with one of the most extensive trail networks in North America and loaded with a feast of possibilities for hikers, bikers, kayakers and cross-country skiers, visitors can plunge directly into a multifarious outdoor playground within minutes of leaving their cozy townsite hotel.

Larger than Banff, but with markedly fewer facilities, Jasper prides itself on its vastness and dramatic sense of scale. Maligne Lake is the Canadian Rockies' largest and most spellbinding body of water; the gargantuan Columbia Icefield covers an area larger than the city of Vancouver, while Miette Hot Springs churns out what is considered to be the hottest natural spring water in western Canada.

HIGHLIGHTS

- Enjoying timeless views of Spirit Island on sparkling **Maligne Lake** (p172) – tranquil, serene and postcard perfect
- Hurtling on a bike over roots, rocks and rough terrain on the hair-raising **Valley of the Five Lakes trail** (p184)
- Standing toe to toe with the colossal **Athabasca Glacier** (p168)
- Hitting the heights on the spectacular **Skyline Trail** (p180)
- Enjoying the ultimate North American road trip with a scenic drive down the **Icefields Parkway** (p186)

▓ Total area: 10,878 sq km (4200 sq miles)	▓ Elevation Jasper town: 1061m (3480ft)	▓ Average high/low temperature in July: 72/46°F

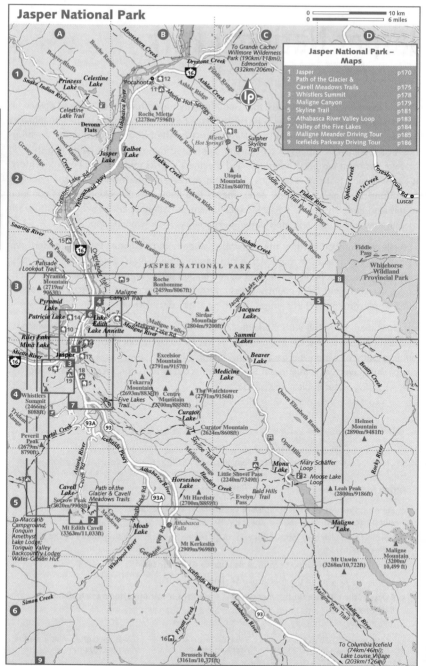

Jasper National Park

0 — 10 km
0 — 6 miles

**Jasper National Park –
Maps**

1	Jasper	p170
2	Path of the Glacier & Cavell Meadows Trails	p175
3	Whistlers Summit	p178
4	Maligne Canyon	p179
5	Skyline Trail	p181
6	Athabasca River Valley Loop	p183
7	Valley of the Five Lakes	p184
8	Maligne Meander Driving Tour	p185
9	Icefields Parkway Driving Tour	p186

When You Arrive

All visitors intending to stop off in Jasper National Park must purchase a **parks pass** (adult/youth/senior/family day pass C$8.90/4.45/7.65/17.80), even if it's just for a picnic or a short leg-stretch. Passes can be procured at the Jasper Information Centre (p166), or at one of three different road entrances (right). All visitors receive the *Mountain Guide*, a magazine with maps and information on local sights. If you're spending a week, an annual pass (p26) will work out cheaper and can be used in all national parks across Canada, including Banff and Yoho.

The park is open year-round, though many activities and services are closed in the winter.

Orientation

Jasper National Park, some 200km (125 miles) long and 80km (50 miles) wide, lies along the Continental Divide and the border between Alberta and British Columbia. The eastern Rockies span its length, topped with an amazing number of ice fields that drain into a web of rivers and lakes. In the southeast, Maligne River flows into Medicine and Maligne Lakes. In the north, the Athabasca River rages into Jasper Lake and continues south along the Icefields Parkway, following the wide Athabasca and Sunwapta Valleys. The northern third of the park is very remote, accessible only by hiking trails and rivers.

ENTRANCES

There are three main road entrances to Jasper National Park. The East Park gate is on Hwy 16 between Jasper and Hinton, just east of Pocahontas. The West Park gate is on the same highway, 24km (15 miles) west of Jasper town, near Yellowhead Pass and the border with British Columbia and Mt Robson Provincial Park. The Icefields Parkway gate is south of Jasper town on Hwy 93, on the way to Lake Louise. You must either buy or show a park pass at all entry gates.

JASPER NATIONAL PARK

JASPER IN...

Two Days

Get geographically orientated on day one with an early morning hike around the **Discovery Trail** (p170). Rejuvenate afterwards over a steaming cup of coffee at **Co-Co's Café** (p195) before hitting the **Jasper-Yellowhead Museum** (p171) for an impromptu history lesson. In the evening ride the **Jasper Tramway** (p170) to the top of Whistlers Mountain before returning to town for wine and escargot at **Andy's Bistro** (p196). On day two drive over to **Miette Hot Springs** (p173) for a soak in the pool and a quick foray to **Sulphur Pass** (p180). Return to Jasper in the afternoon and hire a bike to take you around the **Athabasca Valley loop** (p182). Stop for a beer and dinner at the **Fairmont Jasper Park Lodge** (p171).

Four Days

Follow the two-day itinerary and on day three head out to **Maligne Lake** (p172), stopping on the way at **Maligne Canyon** (p172). Make a day of it at the lake with a ramble around the **Mary Schäffer Loop** (p174) and a scenic boat trip out to **Spirit Island** (p172). On day four, head off early along the **Icefields Parkway** (p186), making spontaneous pit stops at **Athabasca Falls** (p169) and **Horseshoe Lake** (p169). Transfer onto a **Snocoach** (p168) at the Icefields Center for a trip onto the **Columbia Icefield** (p169). If there's time on the way back, stop off at **Mt Edith Cavell** (p169) and venture up into the resplendent flower meadows.

MAJOR ROADS

Jasper's major highways are in excellent condition and all have wide shoulders. The two main roads are Hwy 16 running east–west and Hwy 93 (the famed Icefields Parkway) running north–south. The roads meet in a 'T' in Jasper town. The well-paved Maligne Lake Rd runs south from Hwy 16, starting 5km (3.2 miles) east of Jasper town.

The 17km (10.5-mile) Miette Hot Springs Rd runs south from Pocahontas off the same highway, 42km (26 miles) further east. Other important spur roads around Jasper town include the 4km (2.5-mile) Whistlers Rd to the Jasper Tramway, the 11km (7-mile) Marmot Basin Rd to the ski resort, and the winding 12km (7.5-mile) Mt Edith Cavell Rd.

Information

BOOKSTORES

Jasper Camera & Gifts (Map p170; ☎ 780-852-3165; 412 Connaught Dr) Has a small but decent selection of books, including specialist guides on climbing and mountaineering.

Tangle Creek Gifts (Map p170; ☎ 780-852-5355; 640 Connaught Dr) Has books on local history and wildlife.

RETAIL THERAPY

Gifts

Stuffed bears, scented candles, flimsy trinkets and slogan-bearing t-shirts; shopping in Jasper is invariably of the incidental variety. For Canadian-made gifts try **Pine Cones & Pussy Willows** (Map p170; ☎ 780-852-5310; 308 Connaught Dr). **Tangle Creek Gifts** (Map p170; ☎ 780-852-5355; 640 Connaught Dr) has local and regional crafts as well as books.

Equipment & Supplies

Jasper has some great outdoor outfitters selling everything from camping gear to topographical maps. Most also rent ski gear and other supplies. Be sure to pop into one of the following:

Everest Outdoor Store (Map p170; ☎ 780-852-5902; 414 Connaught Dr)

Jasper Source for Sports (Map p170; ☎ 780-852-3654; 406 Patricia St)

Totem Ski Shop (Map p170; ☎ 780-852-3078; 408 Connaught Dr)

INTERNET ACCESS

Internet access is available in the park, primarily in Jasper town. A growing number of hotels and cafés also offer free wi-fi. Try any of the following:

More Than Mail (Map p170; Connaught Sq, Connaught Dr; 9am-10pm; per min C$0.10)

Soft Rock Café (Map p170; ☎ 780-852-5850; 622 Connaught Dr; per 15min C$2, wi-fi C$3)

Video Stop (Map p170; ☎ 780-852-5593; 607 Patricia St; per 15min C$2)

LAUNDRY

The best place to get your clothes washed is at **Coin-op Laundry** (Map p170; 607 Patricia St; 9am-9pm Mon-Fri, 10am-9pm Sat & Sun) beneath Video Stop; you can also buy coffee and pastries.

MEDICAL SERVICES & EMERGENCY

For emergencies dial ☎ 911. The 24-hour park warden can be contacted on ☎ 780-852-6155. For hospitals see p265.

MONEY

Most of your monetary needs can be dealt with at **CIBC** (Map p170; ☎ 877-777-3912; Connaught Dr), next to the information center.

POST

Jasper maintains one bona fide **post office** (Map p170; 502 Patricia St).

TELEPHONE

All park hotels, lodges and nonprimitive campgrounds have public phones. Courtesy phones (local calls only) are located in the information center (below). Cell (mobile) phone reception is patchy.

TOURIST INFORMATION

Built in 1913, the attractive **Jasper Information Centre** (Map p170; ☎ 780-852-6176; www.parkscanada .ca; 500 Connaught Dr; 9am-7pm summer, 9am-4pm winter) is the park's best-surviving example of environmentally congruous rustic architecture. After admiring it from the outside, pop inside to pick up maps, brochures and up-to-date trail information. Parks Canada also has a desk at the **Icefields Centre** (Map p186; ☎ 780-852-6288; 9am-6pm May-Oct), 103km (64 miles) south of Jasper town on the Icefields Parkway.

In the Jasper building, **Jasper Tourism & Commerce** (Map p170; ☎ 780-852-3858; www.jasper canadianrockies.com) carries lots of brochures on accommodations and services within the park. **Friends of Jasper** (Map p170; ☎ 780-852-4767; www.friendsofjasper.com) also has a shop here with maps and specialist guides to the park. Proceeds from sales are re-invested via grants and volunteer services back into the park.

Park Policies & Regulations

You must have a parks pass to stop anywhere in the park, including viewpoints and short day hikes. For wilderness permits, which are required for backcountry hiking, see below.

It is illegal to take anything from the park – from picking flowers to pocketing stones. Pets must be kept on a leash at all times and are not allowed in backcountry shelters.

Hunting and firearms are not permitted within the park.

BACKCOUNTRY CAMPING

Overnight stays in the backcountry require a **wilderness pass** (per person over 16yr per night C$9.90). Reservations are recommended, as Parks Canada limits the number of hikers on each trail; these can be made up to three months in advance and cost C$11.85. You must pick up the permit within 24 hours of heading out, at which time you'll receive updated information on trails. You will be required to show your pass to any wardens you encounter on the trail.

BIKING

In marked contrast to other parks, bikes are allowed on a large number of Jasper's trails. Pick up a clearly marked map from the information center. Helmets are mandatory and cyclists are required to stick to designated trails and avoid skidding. Due to the speed and silence of bike travel, cyclists are particularly susceptible to bear encounters. It is wise to make plenty of noise on blind corners and in heavily wooded sections.

CAMPING

Reservations (☎ 877-737-3783; www.pccamping.ca) are taken for the Whistlers (p192), Pocahontas (p194) and Wapiti (p192) campgrounds only. All other campgrounds operate on a first-come first-served basis. Checkout time is 11am.

Camping permits are mandatory in Jasper National Park and are available at all campground kiosks. Campers should be bear aware and safely store all food and garbage. Wapiti is the only campground open year-round.

DRIVING

Driving in Canada is on the right-hand side of the road, and seatbelts are mandatory. You cannot pass on a solid yellow line and cannot cross the highway to reach a pullout on the opposite side unless there is a break in the center line. Speed limits in the park are 90km/h (56mph) on major roads and 60km/h (37mph) on secondary roads. Motorists should regularly scan for wildlife either on or crossing the road. Also beware of other cars stopping or slowing down to view wildlife. Fickle weather conditions can create treacherous driving conditions, even in the summer. Free parking is available at most trailheads, if you display your park pass.

FISHING & BOATING

Fishing is permitted in many of the park's lakes and rivers, including parts of the Athabasca, Maligne and Miette Rivers and Maligne Lake, as long as you are in possession of a valid permit. Most of these waters are only open for short seasons, and many others are closed throughout the year. Visit the Parks Canada website or drop into one of its offices for opening dates and fishing restrictions.

Rowboats and canoes are allowed on many ponds and lakes within the park; electric boats are permitted on some; and gas-powered boats are generally restricted.

Getting Around

The easiest way to get around the park is by private vehicle, though, with a bit of patience and flexibility, car-less travel is also possible (p168).

BICYCLE

With a plethora of bike outlets in Jasper, it's easy to rent a bike to get you around the town and its main sights (see p182). Alternatively, you can bring your own.

Fortuitously, the park also has one of most extensive bike-trail networks in Canada. Wide highways with ample shoulders and strict speed limits make road biking easy. The truck-free Icefields Parkway south to Lake Louise and Banff is a particularly popular ride.

CAR & MOTORCYCLE

Jasper town has a number of gas stations. Car rental is available at the VIA railway station with **Thrifty** (Map p170; ☎ 780-852-4506; 607 Connaught Dr; per day from C$49).

PUBLIC TRANSPORTATION

Bus

Brewster Bus & Tour Company (☎ 780-852-3332; www.sightseeingtourscanada.ca) runs a coach south along the Icefields Parkway once a day to Lake Louise (C$60, four hours), Banff (C$70, six hours), and Calgary (C$120, 7½ hours). The coach leaves Jasper daily at 1:30pm arriving in Calgary at 9pm. The northbound coach leaves Calgary at 12:30am and arrives in Jasper at 8pm. It also stops at the Columbia Icefield and, by prior arrangement, at HI-Athabasca Falls (p191).

Maligne Lake Shuttle Service (☎ 780-852-3370; www.malignelake.com; 627 Patricia St) runs a daily shuttle bus from Jasper town to Maligne Lake (May to late September, to Maligne Lake/Canyon C$17/12), stopping en route at the Jasper Park Lodge, Maligne Canyon, the Skyline trailhead (north and south) and the Jacques Lake trailhead. The service runs four times daily in peak season.

The **Jasper Tramway Shuttle** (☎ 780-852-4056) runs a bus from the train station to the Jasper Tramway, also stopping at Jasper International Hostel (p192; up to eight times a day, 9:30am to 6:30pm in the summer). Cost is C$5, or C$29 including tramway ticket.

TOURS

Jasper Motorcycle Tours (☎ 780-931-6100; www.jaspermotorcycletours.com) Runs chauffeured Harley Davidson sidecar tours around the park's main sights; they'll even dress you up in the full Canadian leather garb. Three-hour trips start at C$300. A full day will set you back C$900.

Sundog Tours (Map p170; ☎ 888-786-3641; www.sundogtours.com; 414 Connaught Dr; ☒ 8am-8pm) Offers sightseeing tours of the Maligne Valley (adult/child C$53/32), helicopter sightseeing tours around Mt Robson (C$199) and a guided hike around Mt Edith Cavell (C$65/33). Other tours include Columbia Icefield (C$65/42) and half-day trips by train (C$89/59).

Thompson Tours (☎ 780-852-7269; tomtour@telusplanet.net) Takes small tour groups along Maligne Valley to Mt Robson (C$90) and to Miette Hot Springs (C$50). Guides speak French and German and offer up lots of information about the geography and wildlife in the area.

SIGHTS

ICEFIELDS PARKWAY

Icefields Centre

Situated on the Icefields Parkway, close to the toe of the Athabasca Glacier, the green-roofed **Icefield Centre** (Map p186; ☎ 1-877-423-7433; Icefields Parkway) contains a hotel, cafeteria, restaurant, gift shop, Snocoach ticket booth and Parks Canada information desk. Downstairs you'll find the fascinating Glacier Gallery, explaining the science of glaciers and providing a comprehensive snapshot of the area's history.

Athabasca Glacier

North America's most visited glacier (Map p99) is also one of its most majestic. Covering an area of 6 sq km (2.5 sq miles), the hulking Athabasca is a relic of the last ice age, and spills stealthily off the Columbia Icefield at the rate of several centimeters per year. As recently as the 1840s this immensely powerful river of ice reached as far as the modern-day Icefields Parkway, but it has retreated over the last 150 years by more than 1.6km (1 mile), leaving behind a stony moonscape part-filled by emerald Sunwapta Lake. To reach the glacier drive or walk 1km (0.6 miles) from the Icefields Centre to a small parking lot and the start of the short **Forefield Trail**, which takes you up to the toe of the glacier. While it is permitted to stand on a small roped section of the ice, do not attempt to cross the warning tape. Many do, but glaciers are riddled with crevasses, and almost every year there is an avoidable fatality.

Snocoach

Operated by Brewster Inc, Jasper's famous **Ice Explorers** (☎ 1-877-423-7433; www.columbiaicefield.com; adult/child C$36/18; ☒ 10am-5pm Apr-Oct) enable visitors to get up close and personal with the massive Columbia Icefield (you can even walk on it, under supervision). Ninety-minute tours leave from the Icefields Centre every 15 to 30 minutes in peak season. You are first taken a short distance by standard coach before transferring onto specialized Snocoaches that drive out across the ice. Dress warmly and wear good shoes. Tickets can be procured in the Icefields Centre (above) or purchased online.

THE COLUMBIA ICEFIELD

Situated atop the triple Continental Divide on the border of Alberta and British Columbia, the Columbia Icefield feeds eight major glaciers and covers an area larger than the metropolitan district of Vancouver. Said to be the northern hemisphere's biggest accumulation of ice south of the arctic circle, the Columbia's melt-waters empty into three separate oceans, the Pacific, Arctic and North Atlantic, and provide vital water supplies for millions of people across western Canada.

First spied by Canadian geologist and mountaineer AP Coleman in 1892, this 10,000-year-old leftover of the last ice age was obscured from public view until the construction of the Icefields Parkway in the 1930s and the subsequent inauguration of the first Icefield Chalet by Jack Brewster in 1939. In the early days, access to the ice field was infinitely easier, with the toe of the famous Athabasca Glacier reaching almost to the road; it has retreated significantly in the years since and now sits more than 1.6km (1 mile) away.

Cocooned on a high mountain plateau and surrounded by some of the highest peaks in the Canadian Rockies, the Columbia Icefield traps moist air from the Pacific, which then falls as snow on its huge central massif. Lacking a sufficient melting season, the snow gradually accumulates and forms ice before spilling through the gaps in the plateau via giant glaciers such as the Saskatchewan and the Athabasca. Despite its ongoing retreat, the Columbia Icefield still receives an annual snowfall of over 7m (23ft) and plays host to more than one million visitors per year, making it the most visited glacier in the world.

Athabasca Falls

A deafening combination of sound, spray and water, Athabasca Falls (Map p186) is Jasper's most dramatic and voluminous waterfall. Copious visitors crowd the large parking lot and short access trail to catch a glimpse of this enduring park emblem, which is just off the Icefields Parkway, 28km (17 miles) south of Jasper town, and at its most ferocious during the summer. Despite being only 23m (75ft) high, the heavy flow volume of the Athabasca River has cut deeply into the soft limestone rock, carving potholes, canyons and various water channels. Interpretive signs explain the basics of the local geology.

Sunwapta Falls

Meaning 'turbulent water' in the native tongue, 18m (60ft) Sunwapta Falls (Map p186) resulted when the glacial melt-waters of the Sunwapta River began falling from a hanging valley into the deeper U-shaped Athabasca Valley. Close to the Icefields Parkway and the Sunwapta restaurant and resort, the falls are a popular stop for travelers plying this scenic highway. They're also the start of a 25km (15.5-mile) biking and hiking trail to remote Fortress Lake in Hamber Provincial Park (p197).

Horseshoe Lake

This idyllic blue-green, horseshoe-shaped lake (Map p186), just off the Icefields Park-way, is missed by many visitors, making a stopover here all the more alluring. A choice spot for a bracing summer swim or a short stroll around the perimeter, the lake is surrounded by steep cliffs and is hence occasionally frequented by ill-advised cliff divers. Don't be tempted to join them.

Mt Edith Cavell

Rising like a snowy sentinel over bustling Jasper town, 3363m (11,033ft) Mt Edith Cavell (Map p186) is one of the park's most eye-catching and physically arresting peaks. What it lacks in height it makes up for in stark, ethereal beauty. Accessed via a winding, precipitous road that branches off the Icefields Parkway 6km (3.7 miles) south of Jasper, the mountain is famous for its vibrant flower meadows and wing-shaped Angel Glacier. First climbed in 1915, it was named the following year in honor of a humanitarian British nurse who was executed by a German firing squad during WWI, after helping to smuggle over 200 wounded allied soldiers into neutral Holland.

JASPER & AROUND

Nestled at the confluence of three wide river valleys, Jasper is surrounded by cathedral-like mountains and blessed with one of the most easily accessible trail systems in North America. Characterized by a mish-mash of low-rise shops and residential properties –

not all of which are attractive – the town these days maintains strict development laws, meaning its tenure as an expanding urban hub is well and truly over. Worthy of a day or two of casual exploration, the settlement boasts a heritage walk, an excellent museum, railway memorabilia and some decent outdoor outfitting stores. Added to this, you're never more than a hop, skip and a jump from the cusp of a vast and dream-evoking wilderness.

Jasper Tramway

Ascending 973m (3243ft) in a mere seven minutes, the **Jasper Tramway** (off Map p186; ☎ 866-850-8726; www.jaspertramway.com; Whistlers Mountain Rd; adult/child C$24/12, under 5yr free; ☟ 9:30am-6:30pm late Apr-late Jun & late Aug-late Sep, 8:30am-10:30pm Jul & Aug) carries you up a gondola (cable car) to an eagle's-eye lookout over the eastern Rockies, complete with café and boardwalk. From here you can hike a steep 1.5km (0.9 miles) to the summit of Whistlers Mountain or enjoy the views from the café. Dusk sees fewer crowds and is arguably the most beautiful time for the trip. Trams depart every 10 minutes. To reach the tramway, follow Hwy 93 south and turn right into Whistlers Rd after 3km (1.9 miles). Alternatively, you can catch the Jasper Tramway Shuttle (p168).

Discovery Trail

An interesting mix of interpretive walk, heritage trail and outdoor museum, the Jasper

Jasper

To Patricia Lake Bungalows (7km/4.3mi); Patricia Lake (7km/4.3mi); Pyramid Lake (7km/4.3mi);

To Marmot Lodge (500m/0.3mi);

To Whistlers Campground (2km/1.2mi); Whistlers Outdoor Theatre (2km/1.2mi); Wapiti Campground (4km/2.5mi); Jasper International Hostel (7km/4.3mi); Jasper Tramway (8km/5mi); Mt Edith Cavell (29km/18mi); Mount Robson (90km/56mi); Lake Louise Village (232km/144mi)

To Tekarra Lodge & Restaurant (800m/0.5mi); Fairmont Jasper Park Lodge (5km/3.1mi); Lake Annette (5km/3.1mi); Lake Edith (5km/3.1mi); Maligne Lake (48km/30mi); Edmonton (365km/226mi)

Jasper-Yellowhead Museum & Archives	15 B2
Maligne Rafting Adventures	(see 16)
Maligne Tours	16 A2
Old Fire Hall	(see 10)
On-Line Sport & Tackle	17 A2
Raven Adventures	(see 34)
Rocky Mountain River Guides	18 A2
Sundog Tour Company	19 A1
Vicious Cycle	20 A2
Walks & Talks Jasper	(see 18)

SLEEPING 🛏
Athabasca Hotel	21 A2
Mount Robson Inn	22 B3
Park Place Inn	23 A2

EATING 🍴
Andy's Bistro	24 A2
Bear's Paw Bakery	25 A1
Cassio's Trattoria	26 A2
Co-Co's Café	27 A2
Denjiro	28 A1
Jasper Pizza Place	29 A1
L&W Restaurant	30 C3
La Fiesta	31 A2
Other Paw Bakery	32 A2
Soft Rock Café	33 A2
Spooners Coffee Bar	34 A2

DRINKING 🍷
Jasper Brewing Company	35 A2

ENTERTAINMENT 🎬
Chaba Cinema	36 A2
Downstream Bar	37 A2
Pete's Night Club	(see 34)

SHOPPING 🛍
Jasper Camera & Gifts	38 A1
Pine Cones & Pussy Willows	39 C2
Tangle Creek Gifts	40 C3

TRANSPORT
Bus Depot	41 A2
Thrifty Car Rental	(see 41)

INFORMATION
CIBC	1 A1
Coin-Op Laundry	2 A2
Everest Outdoor Store	(see 19)
Friends of Jasper	(see 3)
Jasper Information Centre	3 A2
Jasper Source for Sports	4 A1
Jasper Tourism & Commerce	(see 3)
More Than Mail	5 A2
Police Station	6 B2
Post Office	7 A2
Seaton General Hospital	8 B3

Soft Rock Café	(see 33)
Totem Ski Shop	9 A1
Video Stop	(see 2)

SIGHTS & ACTIVITIES
Alpine Art-Eco Tours	(see 19)
Bush Fire Gallery	10 A1
Freewheel Cycle	11 A2
Gravity Gear	(see 11)
Jasper Activity Centre	12 B2
Jasper Adventure Centre	13 C2
Jasper Aquatic Center	14 B2

Discovery Trail completely circumnavigates the town via an 8km (5-mile) part-paved, part-unpaved pathway. Split into three sections highlighting the town's colorful natural, historical and railroad legacies, the trail makes a worthwhile evening stroll or breathless early morning jog. Interpretive boards en route provide an educational introduction to both town and park and, on the northwestern side, the trail dips in and out of montane forest, offering excellent views over the surrounding mountains. The train station is a good place to start.

Patricia & Pyramid Lakes

Of the plethora of small lakes that lie to the north and northeast of Jasper town, Patricia and Pyramid Lakes (Map p164) are the most striking and oft-visited. Lying in the imposing shadow of rust-colored **Pyramid Mountain**, these two bejeweled bodies of water sit on the higher expanses of Pyramid Lake Rd and offer great opportunities for recreation and escape. In 1943, Patricia Lake was the site of a bizarre WWII project known as Operation Habbakuk, which attempted – unsuccessfully – to build a prototype aircraft carrier out of ice and sawdust. The plan was abandoned when the ship, unsurprisingly, melted and the wooden supports sank to the bottom of the lake, where they remain a favorite haunt for visiting scuba divers.

The slightly larger Pyramid Lake is popular for picnicking and boating (p187), with rental available from a jetty opposite the upscale Pyramid Lake Resort. Further up the road, the pin-prick–sized **Pyramid Island** is joined to the shore by a quaint wooden footbridge. This gorgeous island has picnic tables, a shelter and a wheelchair-accessible path with stunning views of Mt Edith Cavell across the calm water.

Lake Annette, Lake Edith & Lac Beauvert

Jasper's most popular swimming lakes lie to the northeast of the town and are easily accessible by car and bike, or on foot. Sporting a small beach, Lake Annette can be circumnavigated by a wheelchair-accessible 2.4km (1.5-mile) trail (no bikes) with peek-a-boo mountain views. If you're brave, try dipping your toe in the water, or alternatively run in up to your waist (summer only) for a quick glacial-fed bath. Come

back in the winter and you'll more likely be skating across the lake than jumping in it, after the water turns to ice.

Next door, deeper and colder Lake Edith is surrounded by private log cabins built in the 1930s. You get more kayakers than swimmers here, and the adjacent trails and roads are popular with joggers and families out cycling.

Dominated by the Fairmont Jasper Park Lodge (below) and golf course, crystal-clear Lac Beauvert (literally 'beautiful green' in French) is the third picturesque glacier-fed lake in this area. It's a popular place for boating in the summer and ice-skating in the winter.

Fairmont Jasper Park Lodge

Part of a select chain of historic national-park lodges built in the early 20th century, the Jasper Park Lodge (Map p164) started life as a tent city set up by two pioneering railway workers, the Brewster brothers, on the shores of Lac Beauvert in 1915. Opened as a proper hotel in 1921, the property was summarily taken over by the newly inaugurated Canadian National Railway, which marketed it as the largest single-level log building in the world. The current lodge dates from 1953 and was built to replace the original structure, which burned down in a fire the previous year. Illustrious former guests include Marilyn Monroe and Bing Crosby, who is pictured inside practicing his putting on the adjoining 18-hole golf course with a black bear as his caddy. For hotel information, see p194.

Jasper-Yellowhead Museum & Archives

Furnished with a well-laid-out chronology of Jasper's brief but compelling history, the **Jasper-Yellowhead Museum & Archives** (Map p170; ☎ 780-852-3013; Pyramid Lake Rd; adult/student/senior/family C$4/3/3/10, under 6yr free; ☾ 10am-5pm daily summer & autumn, 10am-5pm Tue-Sun winter) brings to life the nomad hunters, fur traders, travelers, explorers, artists, mountaineers, gold prospectors and pioneers who shaped both the town and park of Jasper. It's worth an hour or two of quiet contemplation.

Bush Fire Gallery

Housed in the Old Fire Hall, the **Bush Fire Gallery** (Map p170; ☎ 780-852-3554; Old Fire Hall, cnr Elm Ave & Patricia St; ☾ 10am-1pm & 5-9pm Thu-Mon

Jul & Aug) is a nonprofit venue for Jasper's resident artists. Run by the Jasper Artists' Guild, it displays eclectic paintings and sculptures depicting local life and landscape. You can also pick up a self-guided walking-tour map of businesses displaying local artwork.

MALIGNE LAKE AREA
Maligne Canyon
As dramatic as Maligne Lake is placid, Maligne Canyon (Map p185) is one of the deepest canyons in the Canadian Rockies. Formed when the Maligne River cut back through the ancient limestone in its effort to reach the Athabasca Valley at the end of the last ice age, the gorge is over 15m (50ft) deep at its deepest point and, measuring only 2m (6.5ft) across in places, is extraordinarily narrow. Other interesting features include eroded potholes, fossils, frost-affected rock, mossy canyon walls and evidence of resourceful rock-dwelling wildlife. Crossed by six different bridges, various trails lead out from the parking lot on the Maligne Lake Rd. You'll also find a standard café and gift shop here.

Maligne Lake
Though it was first spotted as early as 1875 by Canadian Pacific Railway surveyor Henry McLeod, Maligne Lake (Map p185) will forever be synonymous with feisty Pennsylvania-born explorer Mary Schäffer, who was a female ahead of her time and the park's first tourist. Schäffer originally arrived here in 1908, guided by a map drawn from memory by Assiniboine Aboriginal Sampson Beaver, who had himself visited the area 16 years previously.

In the years since, the lake has enjoyed a place of pride on most tourists' itineraries. Stretching 22km (14 miles) north to south and surrounded by a craning circle of rocky, photogenic peaks, the lake is a stunner, and has caused many an enraptured visitor to take a step back in amazement. The real draw is **Spirit Island**, a speck of an island with spiritual significance for First Nations people and a regular feature on every postcard and photo-calendar this side of Calgary.

Unless you feel up to some long-distance kayaking (perfectly doable given that there are two lakeside campgrounds), the only way to catch sight of the island is by **tour boat** (p187). Summer schedules run 10am

to 5pm in peak season, but the boats get busy and reservations are recommended. Maligne Lake also has some fantastic trailheads (p174) and is a wonderful spot for oar-powered forays around the shimmering shoreline (p188).

Medicine Lake
A geological rarity, Medicine Lake (Map p185) is perhaps best described as a sinking lake that has holes in the bottom and functions rather like a plug-less bathtub. In summer, when the run-off is high, the lake fills more quickly than it can drain away and the body of water appears deep and expansive. In winter, as the run-off slows, the water empties, causing the lake to shrink to the size of a small stream. What bewildered Aboriginals and other early visitors was the apparent lack of any water outlet. In fact, the water actually flows out of the lake via a series of small holes on its floor, before passing into a complex underground cave system. The river then reemerges 16km (10 miles) downstream near Maligne Canyon. In the 1950s a ferry service across the lake was briefly attempted, but efforts to plug the holes with sandbags, mattresses and bundles of magazines all proved futile.

NORTH OF JASPER
Pocahontas
A one-time mining community that produced heaps of poor quality, smokeless coal for the allied war effort during WWI (1914–18), Pocahontas (Map p164) was once the largest settlement in Jasper National Park and home to hundreds of miners. When the market price for coal fell in 1921 the town fell into a rapid decline, becoming a veritable ghost town nine years later when the 1930 National Parks Act banned mining in the park for good. All that remains of Pocahontas today are some overgrown ruins, an antiquated superintendent's home and a set of rather plush tourist facilities, otherwise known as the Pocahontas Cabins (p194). Visitors can amuse themselves on a 1km (0.6-mile) wheelchair-accessible interpretive trail that meanders around the old mining site, re-creating the days when the government encouraged resource extraction from the park in return for handsome royalties. To get here take the Miette Springs Rd off Hwy 16 and turn first right into the parking lot.

> **JASPER WHO?**
>
> In 1813 a Northwest Company trading post was first built on Brûle Lake, near present-day Pocahontas, to act as a way station for fur traders plying their way west over the Athabasca Pass. Known originally as Rocky Mountain House, the post was renamed 'Jasper's House' in 1817, after its then-manager Jasper Hawse, to avoid confusion with another Rocky Mountain House located on the Saskatchewan River in western Alberta. A diligent yet unremarkable clerk who ran one of the best paying posts in the Saskatchewan district, Hawse was still presiding over the station in 1829 when the Hudson Bay Company (which had amalgamated with the Northwest Company in 1821) moved it several kilometers west to a trail crossing on the Athabasca River. Declining in importance over the ensuing decades, the post eventually ceased operation in 1884, long after Hawse's death, though, for some inexplicable reason, the name Jasper endured – and was soon being used to refer to the whole district. When the national park was inaugurated in 1907, the authorities promptly christened it Jasper Forest Park and, six years later, the burgeoning railway settlement of Fitzhugh was conferred with the same title. Somewhat ironically, the name of a little known and relatively insignificant trading clerk has subsequently become synonymous with a town, a park and a world-famous Rocky Mountain wilderness.

Miette Hot Springs

While the discovery of healing waters at Banff triggered the development of Canada's first national park, the founding of **Miette Hot Springs** (Map p164; ☎ 780-866-3939; Miette Hot Springs Rd; adult/child/senior/family C$6.15/5.20/5.20/18.55; ☼ 10:30am-9pm May 19-Jun 22, 8:30am-10:30pm Jun 23-Sep 4, 11am-7:30pm Sep 5-Oct 9) was slightly less dramatic. A rough trail to the Rockies' hottest natural mineral springs, long known to First Nations people, was first bushwhacked in 1909. A log bathhouse was slung together four years later and from 1934 to 1938 Depression-era workers constructed a hugely popular aquacenter at the end of Jasper's first paved road. Bursting from the earth at a scalding 54°C (129°F), the modern-day springs are cooled to 39°C (103°F), with a cold pool to plunge yourself into afterward – if you're brave enough. The latest bathing facility, built in 1986, is situated outdoors and surrounded by tree-covered mountains. Visitors can rent lockers, swimsuits and towels, and have lunch in the adjoining café.

Situated 17km (10.5 miles) down a winding road from Pocahontas, a couple of trails lead out from the Miette Springs parking lot. One takes you up to the top of Sulphur Mountain while the other leads 1km (0.6 mile) to the **source** of the underground springs, now overlooked by the ruins of the original aquacenter. If you have time en route, be sure to take in the giant, vertical **Ashlar Ridge** from the viewpoint at 8.9km (5.5 miles) from Hwy 16.

HIKING

With more than 1200km (660 miles) of hiking trails, Jasper National Park has enough well-maintained paths to satisfy the most inexhaustible of hikers. Better still, many of the trails leave directly from Jasper town, meaning shuttles or time-consuming drives to trailheads are not always necessary.

EASY HIKES

Aside from the ever-popular Discovery Trail (p170) that encircles the town via a part-paved, part-unpaved loop, Jasper boasts a decent number of easy hikes, one of which, Lake Annette Loop, is wheelchair accessible in its entirety.

LAKE ANNETTE LOOP

Duration 40 minutes round-trip
Distance 2.4km (1.5 miles)
Difficulty easy
Start/Finish Lake Annette parking lot
Nearest Town Jasper (p169)
Transportation Maligne Lake Shuttle
Summary Bring a picnic, swimsuit and Frisbee, and incorporate this short hike into a day out by the lake.

Surrounded by well-known peaks, this paved stroll around Lake Annette can be rounded off with a quick dip in the relatively warm water. The trail is wheelchair accessible, with benches and a shelter en route. From Hwy 16, turn right onto Maligne Rd and right again onto Lodge Rd. Take the left turn for Lake Annette; the trailhead is at the first parking lot on the right.

Head right along the western side of the lake first. The lake's berry bushes often draw deer and elk. You'll soon spot the rocky summit of Roche Bonhomme to the northeast and, after rounding the southern bend, the rust-colored Pyramid Mountain comes into view to the northwest. As you reach the northern shore, the trail runs between the lake and an unlikely but quite real pond of **quicksand** before bringing you to a sandy **beach**, from which you can take in views of the snowcapped **Mt Edith Cavell**. From here, continue along the lakeshore path to the trailhead.

MARY SCHÄFFER LOOP

Duration 45 minutes round-trip
Distance 3.2km (2.2 miles)
Difficulty easy
Start/Finish Maligne Lake parking lot
Nearest Facilities Maligne Lake area (p172)
Transportation Maligne Lake Shuttle
Summary View the lake through the eyes of one of Jasper's earliest 'tourists' on this easy waterside ramble.

Following the eastern shoreline of Maligne Lake before dipping into the surrounding forest, this trail gives you a chance to take in the view seen by the first European explorer to cross this body of water. When Mary Schäffer stepped off her raft in 1908, she wrote, 'There burst upon us…the finest view any of us had ever beheld in the Rockies.'

To reach **Mary's viewpoint** (Map p164), follow a paved, wheelchair-accessible path past **Curly's historic boathouse** for about 800m (0.5 mile) to where a quartet of informative signs tell the story of the lake's early-20th-century 'discovery.' Beyond the lookout, the trail continues inland through a spruce, pine and fir forest, with copious roots underfoot barring any further access to wheelchairs and strollers. After passing through a meadow, stay left at two junctions.

Along this path you'll see **kettles**, which are giant depressions left by glacial ice trapped beneath sand and silt. At the third junction, head right to return to the boathouse.

MOOSE LAKE LOOP

Duration 45 minutes round-trip
Distance 2.6km (1.6 miles)
Difficulty easy
Start/Finish Maligne Lake parking lot
Nearest Facilities Maligne Lake area (p172)
Transportation Maligne Lake Shuttle
Summary Escape from the crowds on this short, but surprisingly untrampled, path, which leads to a tranquil lake renowned for its moose sightings.

Offering a quick escape from the Maligne Lake hordes, this short, easy loop delivers you to a gorgeously placid lake framed by craning trees and embellished by the glacier-chiseled summit of Samson Peak. A moose sighting along the trail is another distinct possibility.

The trail starts in the parking lot at the end of the Maligne Lake Rd and follows the Bald Hills fire road for the first few hundred meters. Turn left at the first signpost and you'll quickly enter dense forest with the lake and its attendant boat cruisers a distant memory.

This new path is the Maligne Pass Trail, but a left at the second junction will divert you in the direction of **Moose Lake** and, if you're extremely lucky, a glimpse of one of those giant Eeyores of the forest swimming, foraging or hanging out near the shoreline. Moose or no moose, the scenery here is lovely.

With your curiosity satisfied, head north through the woods to the western shore of Maligne Lake and back to the trailhead parking lot.

DAY HIKES
Jasper's comprehensive trail network contains a wide variety of day hikes, many of which offer turnarounds or add-ons enabling walkers to either lengthen or shorten their journeys. Grab a map from the information center and meander as the mood takes you.

PATH OF THE GLACIER & CAVELL MEADOWS TRAILS

Duration 3 hours round-trip
Distance 9.1km (5.6 miles)
Difficulty moderate–demanding
Start/Finish Cavell Meadows parking lot
Nearest Facilities Icefields Parkway (p168)
Transportation private
Summary Angelic glaciers and heavenly scenery give this recently restored mountain trail a distinctly ethereal quality.

With its wings spread celestially between Mt Edith Cavell and Sorrow Peak, Angel Glacier gives the appearance of hovering over a small sapphire lake that is afloat with icebergs. The lake's ice-blue sheen is made all the more dramatic for the barren, stony surroundings that were created by the glacier's not-so-long-ago flight across the valley.

The Path of the Glacier Loop is the most popular hike in the area but, for greater solitude and a brilliant wildflower display

(in July), head further up the peak to Cavell Meadows.

To reach the trailhead from Jasper, follow Hwy 93A south to Cavell Rd and then drive 12km (7.4 miles) to a parking lot. Interpretive signs along the route tell the story of both Edith Cavell and the glacier.

Beginning with a climb through rocky moraine you'll pass the Cavell Meadows Trail turnoff after 0.5km (0.3 mile). The Path of the Glacier Trail continues ascending another 1km (0.6 mile) to a fantastic viewpoint of Angel Glacier, reflected in tiny Cavell Pond. Although the trail descends to the water, approaching the famous ice caves here is extremely hazardous. Keep your distance from the caves and beware of falling ice.

From the lake, the path levels out and loops back to the parking lot. This area was covered by the glacier until the 1950s, and small trees and plants are only just beginning to reappear.

A loop around **Cavell Meadows** will treat you to fantastic views and an even better workout. Take the left turn off the Path of

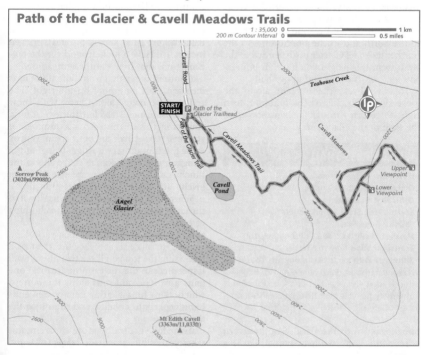

Path of the Glacier & Cavell Meadows Trails

1 : 35,000
200 m Contour Interval

0 —————— 1 km
0 —————— 0.5 miles

the Glacier trail at 0.5km (0.3 miles) and begin a steep ascent north. The trail soon levels off with clear views of the glacier to the right. This area is strewn with boulders up to 4m (13ft) high, left behind by the glacier. After crossing a stream, switchbacks take you north into the forest; keep right at the junction – 2.2km (1.4 miles) – crossing two more streams before entering an open, flowery meadow. At 3km (1.9 miles) a side trail branches right to the **Lower Viewpoint**.

Returning to the main trail, a brief climb brings you to another junction. If you've had enough, head left to meet up with the Path of the Glacier trail; if you've still got some energy and a penchant for climbs, turn right for the Upper Viewpoint.

The way is steep, and the rock-strewn trail becomes fainter and slippery. Continuing uphill to the right brings you to a high subalpine **meadow** with an explosion of flowers. The path runs along a bank of loose shale with a steep drop on the left; then it turns right, where it becomes incredibly steep and rather treacherous.

You'll know you've reached the **Upper Viewpoint** by the yellow marker; the views are also something of a giveaway. Southwest is Mt Edith Cavell; Pyramid Mountain lies to the north and Roche Bonhomme to the northeast. Angel Glacier is suspended to the west; from this height you have an impressive view of its wings and upper half.

Heading back, the descent along the loose shale is tricky. At the junction, turn right to return through lush meadows to the Path of the Glacier trail.

WILCOX PASS TRAIL

Duration 3½ hours one way
Distance 11.2km (6.9 miles)
Difficulty moderate
Start Wilcox Creek Campground
Finish Tangle Falls
Nearest Facilities Icefields Parkway (p168)
Transportation Brewster bus
Summary With minimal climbing, this old First Nations transportation route gets you into seriously high alpine terrain fast – it also offers unforgettable views of the Columbia Icefield.

Shoehorned into the park's southwestern corner, this lofty point-to-point hike is a ranger favorite that rockets you almost immediately up into a high alpine moonscape with exceptional views over the Columbia Icefield and some of the Canadian Rockies' highest peaks. Some hikers treat it as a round-trip excursion up to Wilcox Pass and back but, with a pre-arranged pick up, you can quite easily forge on to Tangle Falls, 7.2km (4.5 miles) further up the Icefields Parkway.

From the trailhead parking lot, the path climbs up steeply through the woods for 1km (0.6 miles) gaining 120m (394ft) in elevation. On the left watch for views to Athabasca Glacier as you travel through a patchwork of forest and flower-sprinkled meadows. At 2.5km (1.6 miles) you leave the forest behind, emerging into rocky, exposed terrain. To the right, Nigel Peak rises up 3212m (10,535ft).

At the junction head left, following the eastern ridge of a valley before turning north for a steep ascent. From the top there are fantastic views that take in Athabasca Glacier, Mt Athabasca and Mt Kitchener. At the next junction head right, veering away from the valley and heading between Wilcox Peak and Nigel Peak. Stepping stones lead you across a stream quickly after you reach **Wilcox Pass** at 4km (2.5 miles), marked by a cairn. Have a look around for the bighorn rams that frequent these meadows.

Continuing north, go straight at the next junction, passing a pool on the right. The trail can be boggy along here, with snow into midsummer. Head left at the next fork, following the cairns across a number of streams. About half an hour from Wilcox Pass, the trail crosses a ridge, bringing the Winston Churchill Range into view to the northwest. You'll notice the giant 3200m (10,499ft) Mushroom Peak resting like a beached U-boat. Follow the cairns down to the right, away from the range and climbing into the moraine.

From here the trail becomes very faint, turning to shale as it nears the crest of a hill. From the top you'll see two hills ahead; don't mistake the rock on the furthest one as a cairn. The trail runs along the western foot of these hills, bearing left and descending steeply into a valley and then into the woods.

From here the trail is more apparent, traversing the hills alongside **Tangle Creek** and

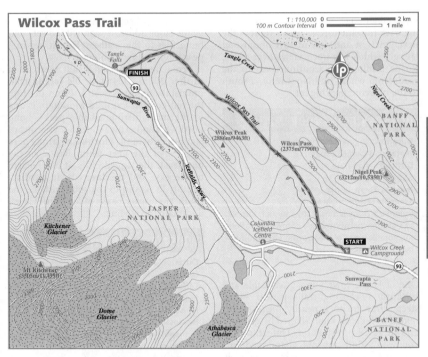

Wilcox Pass Trail

1 : 110,000
100 m Contour Interval

with a viewpoint to Stutfield Glacier. The final descent brings you to **Tangle Falls**.

MINA & RILEY LAKES LOOP

Duration 3 hours round-trip
Distance 9km (5.6 miles)
Difficulty easy–moderate
Start/Finish Jasper-Yellowhead Museum
Nearest Town Jasper (p169)
Transportation private
Summary A straightforward tramp to a trio of peaceful lakes that will give you a tantalizing taste of the scope of Jasper's surrounding wilderness.

A whole network of trails heads west from Jasper town into the forest-covered foothills of the Athabasca Valley. Venture less than 1km into this lake-speckled mini-wilderness and you'll quickly leave the hustle and bustle of the townsite behind.

Considered a good first-day orientation hike, the Mina & Riley Lakes Loop leaves from the northwest corner of the Jasper-Yellowhead Museum parking lot. Following trail No 8, climb gently up behind the town before turning rather abruptly into the forest. Keep to the right at the next three junctions, heading west through a mixture of pine, fir and spruce trees until the path widens out into a man-made meadow and fire break.

After crossing the gravel Cabin Creek Rd, the route plunges quickly back into a thick forest sprinkled with stands of closely packed birch trees. Swampy **Lower Mina Lake** will appear within minutes on your left-hand side, a large pond guarded by ptarmigan and Barrow's goldeneye ducks. Just beyond is the larger **Upper Mina Lake**, where you'll often spot loons gliding across the green surface.

At the western edge of the lake, turn right and climb up and down some gentle hills to a second junction. Foot-sore first timers can short-cut back to town here via trail No 8c. Old stalwarts, meanwhile, can descend the long hill down to **Riley Lake**, which glimmers ethereally with Pyramid Mountain framed behind it. The trail briefly skirts the moss-green edge of the lake before tracking back into the forest. Take a right at the next junction and ascend to Cottonwood Slough, which has open views over to the Roche Bonhomme. Continue east to the road, from where trail No 2 returns south to the museum parking lot.

OLD FORT POINT LOOP

Duration 1½ hours round-trip
Distance 3.5km (2.2 miles)
Difficulty moderate
Start/Finish Jasper
Nearest Town Jasper (p169)
Transportation private
Summary A rewarding early morning ramble to a peculiar hill just outside of town that offers memorable views of the town and its surrounding mountains.

One of Jasper town's most accessible and instantly rewarding trails is this short, steep climb up to a nearby *roche moun-tonnée* (a bedrock knob shaped by glaciers) known as Old Fort Point. Unfortunately, you won't find any old abandoned fort here. Instead, the name refers to the likely site of a one-time fur trading post known as Henry House that was built near here in 1811 by William Henry, a colleague of Canadian-British explorer David Thompson (p79).

The best way to reach the trailhead is by foot; simply follow Hwy 93A out of town to Hwy 16, cross the road and then pick up trail No 1b on the other side. This will bring you out by a bridge across the Athabasca River with the Old Fort trailhead situated on the other side.

The quickest way up to Old Fort Point is to take the wooden steps from the small parking lot. At the top of the staircase a steep ascent continues across an open slope to the **lookout** with panoramic views over Jasper town and the Athabasca Valley.

An alternative route is to follow trail No 1 from the parking lot up a gradually sloping wooded path into a small meadow and then on through a birch forest. After 1.3km (0.8 miles) the climb gets steeper, taking you up past a giant chunk of **pink limestone**. Dating back 750 million years, this is the oldest rock found in Jasper National Park.

At the top keep right, progressing up a gentle slope adorned with wildflowers and butterflies to the **Southeast Summit**, set in a peaceful meadow with great views.

From here, the trail heads west for a further 300m (984ft) to **Old Fort Summit**, unmistakable for its cairn. From the top, the red-colored Pyramid Mountain is one of the most distinguishable peaks, lying northwest and crowned with a microwave station. Turning clockwise from here you'll spot the gray Colin Range to the northeast, the jagged cliffs of Mt Tekarra to the east and the layered Mt Hardisty and Mt Kerkeslin to the southeast. To the south, the snowy peaks of Mt Edith Cavell dominate the skyline.

WHISTLERS SUMMIT

Duration 3½ hours one way
Distance 7.9km (4.9 miles)
Difficulty demanding
Start trailhead on Whistlers Rd
Finish summit of Whistlers Mountain
Nearest Town Jasper (p169)
Transportation Jasper Tramway Shuttle
Summary A long walk up a steep hill – with a wicked 360-degree view at the top.

If you're a peak bagger, this arduous climb through three different life zones to the top of Jasper's most visited summit – and a handy energy-refueling café – could be

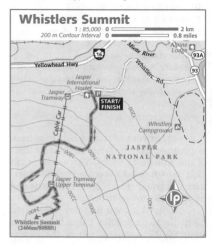

Whistlers Summit

1 : 85,000
200 m Contour Interval

0 ___ 2 km
0 ___ 0.8 miles

Miette River

Alpine Lodge

Yellowhead Hwy

Whistlers Rd

Jasper International Hostel

Jasper Tramway

START/ FINISH

Cable Car

Whistlers Campground

JASPER NATIONAL PARK

Jasper Tramway Upper Terminal

Whistlers Summit (2466m/8088ft)

the lung-bursting wake-up call you've been waiting for. While most sane people get the tramway (p170), there are always one or two masochistic maniacs punishing themselves on this 7.9km (4.9-mile) uphill slog, which logs a total elevation gain of 1200m.

To get to the trailhead, proceed 2.8km (1.7 miles) down the Whistlers Rd to a short, unpaved spur road on the left, which dead-ends in a small parking lot. The hike begins in what is known as the montane life zone of the mountain, consisting of thick forest and healthy aspen growth but, within a couple of kilometers, your uphill endeavors will be rewarded with a rich display of colorful wildflowers. Progressing up toward the tree line, the crippling switchbacks ease momentarily as you pass underneath the mid-point tower of the **Jasper Tramway** at approximately 1640m of elevation.

Above the tree line the landscape becomes ever more stony and barren, with eagle-eye views of the Athabasca Valley and Jasper town unfolding like a satellite map beneath you. For the final 1.5km (0.9 miles), from the tramway's upper terminal to the top, you should have plenty of company as annoyingly fresh tramway riders join in for the relatively undemanding dash for the 2466m (8088ft) **summit**. The stupendous views of lake-speckled valleys and row after row of endless snow-coated peaks are spellbinding.

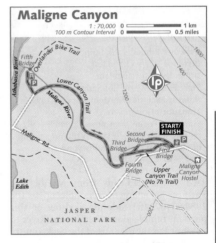

MALIGNE CANYON

Duration 1½ hours round-trip (to Fifth Bridge)
Distance 4.2km (2.6 miles) to Fifth Bridge
Difficulty moderate
Start/Finish Maligne Canyon parking lot
Nearest Facilities Maligne Lake area (p172)
Transportation Maligne Lake Shuttle
Summary Experience canyons, potholes, waterfalls and underground springs, in one spectacular and compact trail.

One of the park's geological highlights, Maligne Canyon is an awesome sight, and one best appreciated with a hike along the meandering riverside trail that traverses five narrow bridges.

Starting from the parking lot situated 7km (4.3 miles) along Maligne Rd from Hwy 16, the trail heads directly down to **Second Bridge**, where the narrow 51m (170ft) deep canyon falls away like a rocky crevasse into eerie darkness. From here, the paved Upper Canyon Trail takes you back to **First Bridge** and the park's highest **waterfall** at 23m (75ft), an angry torrent that is reduced to a mere trickle in the winter months. The canyon decreases in depth above First Bridge, revealing a water-eroded web of potholes, channels and lichen-covered rocks. You'll also spy **fossils** on the ground and **sunken gardens** where the water's spray has brought to life small pockets of ferns deep within the gorge.

To lengthen the hike, follow the Lowe Canyon Trail from Second Bridge down through a shady forest to **Third Bridge** and more waterfalls. **Springs** en route are outlets for one of the largest underground rivers on the continent, traveling from Medicine Lake, 17km (10.5 miles) away, and feeding most of the small lakes in the Athabasca Valley. The trail follows the course of the broadening water, crossing **Fourth Bridge** and eventually **Fifth Bridge**, a suspension bridge at the 2.1km (1.3-mile) mark. From here there are three options: retrace your steps on the Lower Canyon Trail, return via the multipurpose No 7h trail on the river's northern bank, or continue an extra 1.5km (0.9 miles) downriver to the Sixth (and final) Bridge.

JASPER NATIONAL PARK

JASPER NATIONAL PARK

SULPHUR PASS VIA FIDDLE RIVER TRAIL

Duration 2 hours round-trip
Distance 5.2km (3.2 miles)
Difficulty easy–moderate
Start/Finish Miette Hot Springs parking lot
Nearest Facilities North of Jasper (p169)
Transportation private
Summary Follow your nose – quite literally – on this sulfur-infused trail to the original site of Miette Hot Springs and beyond.

Two hikes lead out from Miette Hot Springs: an energetic scramble up to the 2050m (6724ft) Sulphur Skyline; or this pleasant ramble along the Sulphur River to Sulphur Pass at the start of the backcountry Fiddle River Trail.

Pick up the trailhead at the far end of the Miette Springs parking lot and proceed along a paved path for 500m, until you reach the ruins of an old bathhouse. This is all that remains of the original **Miette Aquacenter**, a building that served as the main spa facility between 1938 and 1985. Following the all-pervading smell of rotten eggs 200m further upstream along a wooden boardwalk, you'll quickly come to the **spring** itself, an innocuous-looking rock pool where 54°C (129°F) mineral-rich water comes spurting out of the earth from a depth of 3km (1.8 miles).

Beyond the springs the path becomes a narrow dirt track that hugs the river for another 1km (0.6 miles) before it crosses over via a makeshift wooden bridge onto the opposite bank. From here you climb 150m (0.1 miles) through the trees to **Sulphur Pass**, where a break in the forest provides a hidden haven for numerous species of wildflower.

If you fancy forging on further, the path continues another 1km (0.6 miles) to the Fiddle River, which it follows for 20km (12.5 miles) along a relatively primitive trail to 2135m (7000ft) Fiddle Pass on the park border.

BACKCOUNTRY HIKES

If you hate crowds, you're lukewarm about tour groups, and you frequently harbor an itching desire to run off into a vast and untamed Rocky Mountain wilderness,

then backpacking through Jasper National Park could be just your bag. Studded with great sights and crisscrossed by trails, the backcountry options here are practically unlimited.

For more information on backcountry hiking and safety, see the Activities chapter (p37).

SKYLINE TRAIL

Duration 2 days one way
Distance 45.8km (28.7 miles)
Difficulty moderate–demanding
Start Maligne Lake
Finish Maligne Canyon
Nearest Facilities Maligne Lake area (p172)
Transportation Maligne Lake Shuttle
Summary Enjoy challenging terrain and splendiferous views on what is, quite simply, one of the most rewarding backcountry hikes in Canada.

The crème de la crème of backcountry hiking in the Canadian Rockies, the Skyline Trail (Map p164) is a North American classic that hovers on or above the tree line for nearly 46 serendipitous kilometers. Some hikers spread the expedition over three days, others tackle it in two, while the odd gung-ho trail runner has been known to knock it out in just one. But don't get too ambitious. With a notable lack of trees and little natural shelter en route, the Skyline is notoriously open to the elements and fickle weather has taken the wind out of many an experienced hiker's sails.

A good, comfortable overnight option for two-day hikes is to reserve a room at the historic Shovel Pass Lodge (p193) at the halfway point. Alternatively, there are half-a-dozen backcountry campgrounds en route (campfires though are prohibited), and for a comfortable three-day outing you could camp at Snowbowl and Tekarra Campground, leaving the final descent for the third morning. Transportation to both trailheads is easy via the Maligne Lake Shuttle (p168).

DAY 1

For this walk – seven hours, 20.4km (12.6 miles) – most hikers start at the Maligne Lake trailhead and follow the Lorraine and

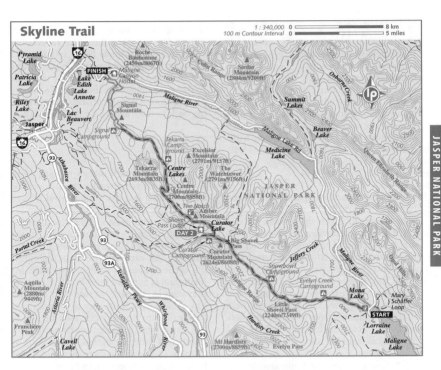

Skyline Trail

JASPER NATIONAL PARK

Mona Lakes Trail through the woods for the first 5km (3.1 miles). Beyond the turnoff for Mona Lake, switchbacks leave the trees behind, passing Evelyn Creek Campground – keep right at the junction – and bringing you into meadows. Upon the slopes of Maligne Range, **Little Shovel Pass**, at 10.2km (6.3 miles), gives you views back over Maligne Lake and to the gray Queen Elizabeth Range, to the east.

From here the trail dips down into the **Snowbowl**, a lush if somewhat boggy meadow crisscrossed with streams and stretching 7.3km (4.5 miles) along the Maligne Range. Snowbowl Campground is at 11.8km (7.3 miles).

At the end of the Snowbowl, a short climb brings you up to **Big Shovel Pass**, which has more great views. Keep left at the junction, continuing northwest for 2.1km (1.3 miles) and taking the trail left to Curator Campground and **Shovel Pass Lodge**.

DAY 2

Begin the day – eight hours and 25.2km (15.6 miles) – with a brisk climb up to the tiny **Curator Lake**, which is surrounded by vast, windswept terrain. The trail becomes steep as it climbs to the **Notch**. At 2510m (8733ft), this is the high point of the trail, with breathtaking views along the Athabasca Valley and, if you're lucky, all the way to Mt Robson in the northeast. Continue on to the summit of **Amber Mountain**, below which the trail switchbacks down to **Centre Lakes**, with the sentinel Centre Mountain to the northeast. The trail heads through a small valley to **Tekarra Lake** and then follows around the north side of Tekarra Mountain, amid the first trees you'll have seen all day. Tekarra Campground lies at 11.3km (7 miles), between the peaks of its namesake and Excelsior Mountain.

Coming back out of the trees, you'll have views of Pyramid Mountain to the northwest and the Roche Bonhomme to the north. It's worth taking the short detour left at 16.9km (10.5 miles) to **Signal Lookout** for even better views. Signal Campground is just beyond this junction, and from here the old fire road descends through the forest to Maligne Canyon Hostel.

TONQUIN VALLEY

Duration 2–3 days round-trip
Distance 53.2km (33 miles)
Difficulty demanding
Start/Finish Marmot Basin Rd
Nearest Facilities Icefields Parkway (p168)
Transportation private
Summary A true wilderness experience, hiking through archetypal Jasper terrain with the crenellated Ramparts glowering in the background.

Wildlife, lush meadows, sparkling lakes and gorgeous views make the road-less Tonquin Valley a mecca for hikers and horseback riders alike. The valley's crowning glory is the Ramparts, a collection of 10 peaks that tower like giant Gothic fortresses over the network of backcountry trails. According to First Nations people, they harbor supernatural spirits.

The trail (Map p164) begins from Marmot Basin Rd, off of Hwy 93A and about 16km (10 miles) south of Jasper town. While there is a shorter, less-grueling approach to Amethyst Lakes from the south, this route is far more scenic.

The hike to Amethyst Campground is a full day's hike; you can break the journey by staying at one of the two campgrounds en route, or stretch it to a three- or four-day trip by continuing along one of the trails from Amethyst Lakes. Campfires are not permitted at any of the campgrounds.

From Marmot Basin Rd, the trail follows **Portal Creek** southwest and climbs into the **Portal**, a narrow canyon amid the Trident Range. The path crosses large rockslides beneath Peveril Peak and then descends into a forested valley. A gradual climb takes you past Portal Campground and up toward **Maccarib Pass** at 11.7km (7.3 miles). As you ascend above the tree line, you can't help but notice Oldhorn Mountain to the south.

Beyond the pass, you begin your descent into the meadowland of **Tonquin Valley** with ever-impressive views of the Ramparts to the west. Maccarib Campground is next to a small creek at 17.8km (11 miles). The trail heads southwest for 6km (3.7 miles) to the northern shore of the glistening **Amethyst Lakes**. At the junction, head right if you've reserved a bed at **Tonquin Valley Backcountry Lodge** (p193), or continue along the shoreline

to Amethyst Campground at 26.6km (16.5 miles). On still days, the water reflects the snow-cloaked Ramparts like a mirror.

Either pack up camp the following day and make the return journey along the same route or, if you have the time, spend a day exploring around Amethyst Lakes before heading back to the trailhead on the third day.

BIKING

Jasper is a mountain biker's nirvana, with a comprehensive network of multi-purpose trails fanning out from the central hub of Jasper town. Bikers experience few limitations here, in contrast to US national parks, resulting in some of the most scenic, varied and technically challenging rides in North America. An excellent trail map highlighting cycling routes is available from the information center and most hotels. Bears are prevalent in the park, so ride with caution. The season runs from May to October.

If you didn't bring your own bike, you can easily rent a decent machine from a number of different outlets. Prices start at C$8/20/30 per hour/three hours/day for front-suspension mountain bikes.

Freewheel Cycle (Map p170; ☎ 780-852-3898; www
.freewheeljasper.com; 618 Patricia St; ⏰ 9am-10pm)
Freewheel also rents chariots to pull young children.
Jasper Source for Sports (Map p170; ☎ 780-852-3654; 406 Patricia St)
On-Line Sport & Tackle (Map p170; ☎ 780-852-3630; 600 Patricia St)
Vicious Cycle (Map p170; ☎ 780-852-1111; www.viciouscyclecanada.com; 630 Connaught Dr; ⏰ 9am-6pm)

ATHABASCA RIVER VALLEY LOOP

Duration 3 hours round-trip
Distance 18km (11.2 miles)
Difficulty easy
Start/Finish Jasper
Nearest Town Jasper (p169)
Summary A paved but traffic-light sojourn around the verdant Athabasca River Valley that should whet your appetite for further biking adventures elsewhere.

If you're looking for a safe, flat family bike ride, or just prefer the certainty of a paved

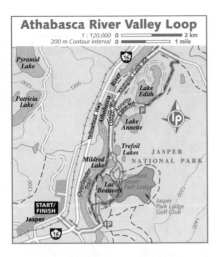

Athabasca River Valley Loop

1 : 120,000
200 m Contour Interval

road to single-track, this 18km (11.2-mile) spin around three luminous lakes on the southeast side of the Athabasca River Valley is an ideal option.

Start by tracking south from Jasper town on Hwy 93A, crossing both the railway line and busy Hwy 16 before turning left into Old Fort Rd. Follow the road east down to a narrow bridge across the Athabasca River and past the Old Fort trailhead. Another 1km further on you'll come to the shores of beautiful **Lac Beauvert** with the **Fairmont Jasper Park Lodge** perched on its opposite shoreline. Circumnavigate the lake via the

scenic golf course – listening out for shouts of 'fore!' – to the lodge itself, which is well worth closer inspection, before proceeding past the entrance gate and branching off onto the **Lake Annette** Rd. With its picnic tables, small beach and paved **lake loop**, this is a great place for lunch. Almost adjacent to Lake Annette is **Lake Edith**, and an old road, now closed to cars, leads along its south shore. Ultimately this will bring you out onto the busier Maligne Lake Rd. Turn left here and speed back to the Jasper Park Lodge Rd at 3.2km (2 miles), where you can either retrace your route or tack onto trail No 7 (the Overlander Trail) back to Old Fort Point and – ultimately – Jasper town.

PYRAMID LAKE LOOP

Duration 1½ hours round-trip
Distance 13km (8.1 miles)
Difficulty moderate
Start/Finish Jasper
Nearest Town Jasper (p169)
Summary Climb high up above the townsite to Pyramid Lake before blasting back down to earth on a bumpy single-track trail.

Half on the road and half off, this intermediate loop forges northeast up the Pyramid Lake Rd before careering back into town on the bone-rattling trail No 2. It's a great ride

---

MANABU SAITO, BIKE STORE OWNER & STAR CYCLIST

How does Jasper compare to other parks for cycling terrain? In my opinion, it's got the best single-track off-road cycling terrain in any Canadian national park. There are over 200km of bike paths that start minutes from the town center. There's also a very sophisticated mapping system with clear signage and good trail maintenance. People rarely get lost. **What's the ultimate hair-raising, adrenaline-filled trail?** The Valley of the Five Lakes, without a doubt. In fact, for me, this trail is one of the best rides in North America, and I've done quite a few! It's varied, scenic and there are areas when you can really let rip. **What's the best trail for beginners?** Trail No 7 around the Athabasca River and close to the town is a good bet. It's got two levels, low and high, so you've got options. **Any close encounters with wildlife?** I once hit a black bear on the Wabasso Lake trail. I came belting around a corner on my bike and there it was; I had no time to stop. I whammed it in the rear and the bear went screaming up a tree, far more frightened than I was. Some of its fur got stuck in my front wheel, meaning the bike went clunk, clunk, clunk, all the way home. **What other obstacles are riders likely to encounter?** Accommodation. Book early, or even better, come in April or September. The weather's also incredibly fickle. **Any other cycling recommendations?** The Icefields Parkway through Jasper and onto Lake Louise is a great ride for road bikes. Aside from the fantastic scenery, there are no trucks and changes in elevation are minimal.

for fit road bikers who want to mix in a bit of daring – but doable – single-track.

From Jasper town take the winding Pyramid Lake Rd from near the Jasper-Yellowhead Museum and head off into the woods. While the road plies ever upwards, the gradient is generally manageable, although you may feel the effects of altitude if you have just flown in from sea level. Leading to a sizable resort at Pyramid Lake, this route isn't a major highway, although delivery trucks occasionally whiz past, so be careful on the bends. You'll pass **Patricia Lake** at 5km (3.2 miles) and then **Pyramid Lake** at 7km (4.4 miles), where you can stop and admire calming views out across the blue-green water, often speckled with boats.

Continue along the road another 1km (0.6 miles) to a small parking lot adjacent to **Pyramid Island**, where a trailhead on the right will take you onto the roughish track that comprises trail No 2. This upper part of the trail is riddled with stones, roots and (often) mud, but stick with it and the path will soon even out. Downhill all the way, the route is generally nontechnical, although plenty of twists and turns will get the adrenaline charging. At **Cottonwood Slough** you'll cross the Pyramid Lake Rd and from here it's a short, but quite steep, 1.6km (1-mile) drop into town.

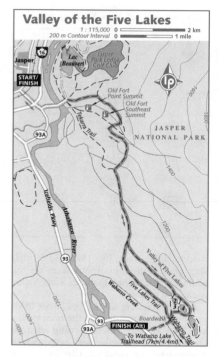

VALLEY OF THE FIVE LAKES

Duration 3 hours round-trip
Distance 27km (17 miles)
Difficulty demanding
Start/Finish Jasper
Nearest Town Jasper (p169)
Summary The holy grail for Jasper cyclists, riders travel from far and wide to test their mettle on this tough but scenic two-wheeled odyssey.

A hair-raising but gloriously scenic spin through the attractive Athabasca Valley to five turquoise mountain lakes, this trail has it *all,* including sweeping single-track, bone-rattling rocks and roots, sudden downhills and tough, technical inclines. No wonder serious cycling junkies rate it as one of the best off-road rides in North America.

Accessible via trail No 1, which cuts around the back of Old Fort Point, Valley of the Five Lakes is popularly tackled as an out-and-back trip from Jasper town. Linking up with trail No 9 after 2km (1.2 miles), the ride gathers pace with a narrow but nontechnical path meandering seamlessly through quiet tracts of sun-dappled forest to the lakes themselves, approximately 10km (6.2 miles) to the south. With **Lake 1** in sight things start to get hairy and, if you can make it around all five of these bejeweled watery havens without getting off to push (at least once), consider yourself an aficionado.

After looping around **Lake 4** with its resident loons and shimmering emerald coloration, the trail winds up at a crossroads that offers bikers three distinct options. The first is to double back on the opposite side of the lakes and link up again with trail No 9 for a return ride to Jasper. The second is to cross the plank bridge over the **Wabasso Creek Wetlands** and make for the trailhead and parking lot on Hwy 93. The third is to head south toward **Wabasso Lake** and a second Hwy 93 trailhead 9km away. Look out for wildlife if you elect to follow this last trail, and be particularly aware of bears and deer.

DRIVING

Driving along Jasper's well-maintained and uncrowded roads, amid rugged mountains and seemingly endless forests, is one of life's simple pleasures. Keep your eyes peeled for wildlife foraging by the roadside.

MALIGNE MEANDER

Duration 45 minutes one way
Distance 46km (28.5 miles)
Difficulty easy
Start Maligne Lake Rd turnoff on Hwy 16
Finish Maligne Lake
Nearest Town Jasper (p169)
Summary A necessarily slow drive through some of the Rocky Mountains' prime wildlife habitat to the region's largest natural lake.

The Maligne Lake Rd is as scenic as the destination. Wildlife is rife and with luck you'll spot a wolf, a bear or a moose. Each year, animals are killed on this road by vehicles,

so obey speed restrictions and watch for animals bounding across the road.

Begin the tour 2km (1.2 miles) north of Jasper town; follow Hwy 16 to the turnoff for Maligne Rd, crossing the **Athabasca River** and following the road left. Ahead are views of Roche Bonhomme, with its Old Man summit, and to the west lies the rust-colored Pyramid Mountain. At 3km (1.9 miles), the **Fifth Bridge** crosses the powerful **Maligne River**; if you're feeling ambitious, you can head over this suspension bridge and climb the trail into **Maligne Canyon**, one of the deepest in the Rockies. An easier way to see this dramatic canyon is via the **Upper Canyon Trail**; the trailhead is 7km (4.3 miles) along the route.

The road continues east between the Colin Range to the north and the Maligne Range to the south. At 22km (13.6 miles) there's a pulloff to Maligne River, though it only carries water here if Medicine Lake floods. Instead, the water flows downstream in an underground waterway. Aboriginals in the area believed the water was whisked away by magic (or bad medicine) and feared it.

JASPER NATIONAL PARK

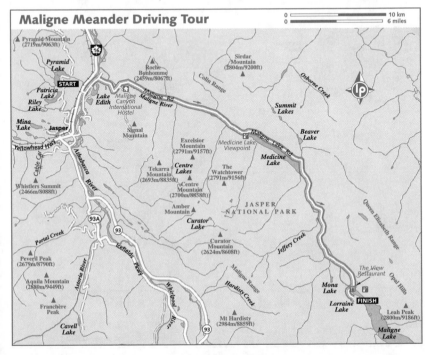

Maligne Meander Driving Tour

The next turnoff, on the northwest corner of **Medicine Lake**, offers superb views across the water. Along the north side of the lake, the craggy Colin Range leans flat-faced toward the road, and a delta on the far eastern side of the lake often hosts caribou in early spring and late fall.

At 32km (19.8 miles), look up. Above you, you'll see limestone arches cut into the summit of the Queen Elizabeth Range, caused by water that's freezing in the crevices, expanding and shattering the rock. If you've packed along a picnic and are hoping for a little peace, try the rest stop at 40km (24.8 miles), where you can relax beside the river before reaching the more hectic **Maligne Lake** (p172), 6km (3.7 miles) up the road.

ICEFIELDS PARKWAY

Duration 2 hours
Distance 103km (64 miles)
Difficulty easy
Start Jasper
Finish Icefields Centre
Nearest Town Jasper (p169)
Summary Frequently described, but rarely done justice, the Parkway is the drive of a lifetime that has to be seen to be believed.

Considered one of the most scenic drives in North America, the Icefields Parkway – or the 'road through the clouds' – is a kaleidoscopic mélange of cascading waterfalls

Icefields Parkway Driving Tour

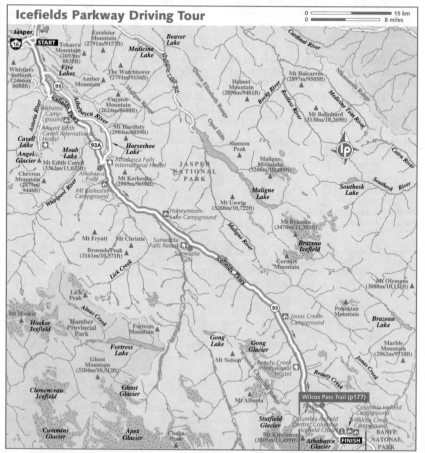

and spectacularly carved peaks, whose crowning glory is the glistening Columbia Icefield on the park's southern limits. Measuring 230km (144 miles) from Jasper town down to Lake Louise, a bejeweled 108km (67-mile) segment of the route traverses Jasper National Park, incorporating some of the region's star attractions.

Driving south out of Jasper, the first highlight is **Mt Edith Cavell**, the town's snow-capped guardian, accessible via a winding spur road off Hwy 93A. Stop here to stroll through flower-filled meadows and catch a glimpse of the peak's wing-shaped **Angel Glacier**. Rejoin the main parkway for 20km (12.4 miles) and you'll pass **Horseshoe Lake**, with its steep-sided cliffs and clear, bracing waters, followed quickly by the **Athabasca Falls**, the park's most voluminous waterfall, which throws its frigid glacial melt-water over a 21m (70ft) limestone cliff.

Look out for wildlife on the next section of the route as you head south through a wide corridor of mountains that runs parallel to the Continental Divide. At **Honeymoon Lake** there's a good viewpoint over the Athabasca River, while 2km (1.2 miles) further on, at **Sunwapta Falls**, you can refuel at the homey restaurant or stretch your legs on the short hike to the waterfall. This is also the start of an excellent hiking and biking trail to Fortress Lake at 25km (15.5 miles).

As the tree cover thins and the river becomes a confusing maze of different channels you'll start to notice the glaciers. Stop at the **Stutfield Glacier viewpoint** just past Beauty Creek to admire this outlying tentacle of the Columbia Icefield; 2km further on you'll pass **Tangle Falls** and the start of the scenic Wilcox Pass Trail. The drive's apex is the green-roofed Icefields Centre and the world-famous **Athabasca Glacier**, which slides like an icy river down toward the road. Stop here for interpretive displays, a walk around the Forefield Trail and an excursion on one of the unique Snocoaches.

OTHER ACTIVITIES

SUMMER ACTIVITIES
White-Water Rafting & Float Trips
Charging rivers course their way through Jasper National Park with rafts full of thrill-seeking adventurers. You won't run short of options for white-water rafting, whether you're after a relaxing float trip, a novice white-water trip for the family, or a wild adventure. The season is from mid-May to the end of September.

Maligne Tours (Map p170; ☎ 780-852-3370; www.mra .ab.ca; 627 Patricia St; novice/intermediate from C$55/85) Lots of options including paddle rafting, overnight trips and float trips.

Raven Adventures (Map p170; ☎ 780-852-4292; www.ravenadventure.com; 610 Patricia St; novice/ intermediate from C$55/75)

Rocky Mountain River Guides (Map p170; ☎ 780-852-3777; www.rmriverguides.com; 626 Connaught Dr; novice/intermediate C$55/85) Experienced rafters can sign up for multi-day Class IV trips.

Rock Climbing
Despite its preponderance of sedimentary rock, Jasper is a popular destination for ambitious rock climbers. Located up the trail from Fifth Bridge, off Maligne Lake Rd, Rock Gardens is the most popular crag and has the easiest approach. For climbers with experience (and preferably a guide), Mt Edith Cavell offers incredible vistas for climbers, while Ashlar Ridge and Morro Ridge are strictly the terrain of the experts.

Peter Amann (☎ 780-852-3237; www.incentre.net /pamann) can introduce you to the art of rock climbing with two-day beginner courses (C$214) and he also offers personal guiding. Daily courses on rock scrambling and glacier travel start at C$150. If you already know what you're doing, **Gravity Gear** (Map p170; ☎ 888-852-3155; www.gravitygearjasper.com; 618 Patricia St) has all the equipment to get you to the summit.

Boating
The Athabasca Valley is speckled with hidden lakes and misty ponds, most of which allow rowboats, kayaks and canoes. Of the bodies of water around Jasper town, Pyramid Lake is the most popular spot, and an oasis of tranquility caught in the distinctive shadow of Pyramid Mountain. **Pyramid Lake Boat Rentals** (☎ 780-852-4900; www.pyramidlakere sort.com; Pyramid Lake Rd) has canoes, rowboats, kayaks and paddleboats for hire.

As the largest lake in the Canadian Rockies, Maligne Lake offers visitors the archetypal Jasper experience. **Maligne Lake Cruises** (☎ 780-852-3370; www.malignelake.com; adult/child C$43/21.50; ☿ high season 10am-5pm, operates May-Oct) is the holy grail for most visitors intent on witnessing the much-photographed sight of Spirit Island with the craning Rockies stacked up in the background. Boats cruise down the lake up to eight times daily in the height of summer, but be warned – they're popular. To escape the crowds and get a bit of arm-powered exercise, head to the vintage **Maligne Lake Boathouse** (☎ 780-852-3370; www.malignelake.com; canoes & rowboats per hr/day C$25/75, kayaks C$30/90), first opened in 1928 by the charismatic Donald 'Curly' Phillips, for canoe or kayak rental. For longer backcountry kayaking trips on the lake, it is possible to overnight in the lakeside Fisherman's Bay (four-hour trip) and Coronet Creek (six-hour trip) campgrounds. Camping passes and reservations are necessary for both.

Fishing

Fishing is popular throughout the park, with both locals and visitors. Waters frequented by anglers include Celestine, Princess, Maligne and Pyramid Lakes – though there are many smaller nooks. Make sure you're up-to-date on regulations (p167) before you set out.

Maligne Tours (Map p170; ☎ 780-852-3370; www .malignelake.com; Maligne Lake; full/half-day per person from C$225/180; ☀ May-Sep) will guide you around Maligne Lake in search of rainbow and eastern brook trout. **On-Line Sport & Tackle** (Map p170; ☎ 780-852-3630; 600 Patricia St) rents gear, teaches fly-fishing and runs lots of fishing trips, including 10-hour marathons.

Horseback Riding

With horseback riders sharing trails with hikers and bikers, Jasper is able to trump most other parks when it comes to equestrian adventures. Rival stables on either side of the Athabasca Valley ply routes around Lake Patricia and Lake Annette, while further afield stunning backcountry trips can be organized in the Tonquin Valley, Maligne Pass, Jacques Lake and Bald Hills. Permits and regulations apply.

Skyline Trail Rides (☎ 780-852-4215; www .skylinetrail.com; 1hr rides from C$23) leads daily scheduled rides, as well as overnight trips that include meals and accommodations. **Tonquin Valley Adventures** (☎ 780-852-3909; www .tonquinvalley.com) specializes in rustic five-day jaunts around the Tonquin Valley, staying at the backcountry Tonquin Amethyst Lake Lodge; prices start at C$1050 per person, including meals and accommodation.

Watching Wildlife

With 69 different mammals, 277 species of bird and 16 amphibians and reptiles, your chances of spotting wildlife in Jasper National Park are pretty high. A trip down Maligne Rd or Miette Hot Springs Rd may score you a bear, wolf or mountain-goat sighting, and elk tend to linger just south of Jasper town, at the end of Hwy 93. About 0.5km (0.3 miles) north of Jasper town, on the eastern side of the road, a salt lick is frequented by goats and sheep in summer.

Alpine Art-Eco Tours (Map p170; ☎ 780-852-3709; www.alpineart.net; Rocky Mountain Unlimited, 414 Connaught Dr; half-day per person C$59) runs year-round safaris in search of elk, grizzlies, moose and the like. In summer it takes in the wildflowers, and in winter you can trek along on snowshoes. **Jasper Adventure Centre** (Map p170; ☎ 780-852-5650; www.jasperadventurecentre.com; 306 Connaught Dr; 3hr per adult/child C$50/25) also runs wildlife searches, with a chance to see animals up close through a spotting scope; and **Walks & Talks Jasper** (Map p170; ☎ 780-852-4945; c-walktalk@incentre.net; 614 Connaught Dr; adult/child C$50/25) will take you on a morning Birding & Wildlife Watch.

If birds are more your thing, **On-Line Sport & Tackle** (Map p170; ☎ 780-852-3630; c-online @incentre.net; 600 Patricia St; intro/half-day/by boat per person C$69/99/129) will help you see rosy finches, bufflehead ducks and ptarmigans. Species-specific tours are also available.

Golf

Fairmont Jasper Park Lodge Golf Club (Map p164; ☎ 780-852-6090; www.fairmont.com; hotel guest/nonguest C$150/200, incl power cart; ☀ mid-May–mid-Oct) overlooking the shores of shimmering Lac Beauvert is one of the most prestigious courses on the continent. Designed in 1925 by Stanley Thompson, the 18-hole course is as stunning as it is challenging. There's also a driving range, and you can rent shoes and clubs.

Ranger Programs

Each summer, Parks Canada sponsors live theater and free family-geared interpretive programs nightly at **Whistlers Outdoor Theatre** (Whistlers Campground; ☀ 9pm), 3km south of Jasper town. Noncampers are welcome. Topics vary from bear tips to park history.

Friends of Jasper (Map p170; ☎ 780-852-4767; www.friendsofjasper.com; 415 Connaught Dr) hosts a nightly historical walking tour at 7:30pm throughout the summer, leaving from the information center. Groups are limited to 30 and tickets are available in advance from the information center (p166). Other interpretive walks include a Saturday stroll in Pocahontas, departing at 2pm, and a **Junior Naturalist program** (🕙 5pm Wed-Sun) for six to 10 year olds at the Whistlers Campground. . Occasional theatrical events take place during the evenings on the lawn outside the Jasper Information Centre.

Gyms
If the weather isn't cooperating, hit the pool and gym at the **Jasper Activity Centre** (Map p170; 780-852-3381; 303 Pyramid Av; 🕙 9am-10pm).

WINTER ACTIVITIES
Boasting a bona fide ski resort at the Marmot Basin (Map p164), Jasper is very much a year-round destination. Far from shivering in their hotel rooms, stalwart winter visitors hit the wilderness for such varied cold-weather activities as ice skating, downhill and cross-country skiing and ice climbing.

Skiing
Active since the 1960s, the **Marmot Ski Resort** (☎ 780-852-3816; www.skimarmot.com; day pass C$58.50) showcases 84 trails and over 3000 vertical feet of skiing, split 30% novice, 30% intermediate, 20% advanced and 20% expert (double black diamond). Served by nine lifts and three mountain day lodges with cafés and sundecks, the season generally runs November through March, or until the snow lasts. A daily ski shuttle links the resort directly with most of Jasper town's hotels. For snow

---

> **TOP FIVE NOVEL WAYS OF GETTING AROUND**
>
> ▪ By heli-hiking (p197)
> ▪ By dogsled (right)
> ▪ By chauffeur-driven Harley Davidson motorbike and sidecar (p168)
> ▪ By train (p168)
> ▪ By Snocoach (p168)

---

conditions and other details, check out the resort's excellent website.

Cross-Country Skiing & Snowshoeing
True to its ethos of 'multipurpose trails for all,' Jasper's hiking and biking paths are largely given over to cross-country skiing and snowshoeing in the winter. Favorites around town include the Lake Annette Loop (p173), the Mina and Riley Lakes Loop (p177) and the longer Saturday Night Lake Loop. Maligne Lake is another cross-country skiing nexus with a good mix of novice and expert routes such as the Moose Lake (p174) and Bald Hills Loops. For the more adventurous, there's cross-country skiing to the remote Tonquin Valley.

For equipment rental see the boxed text, p166.

Other Winter Activities
Ice skating is possible on a number of the park's smaller lakes. Lac Beauvert and Pyramid Lake are the best maintained. You can rent skates at **Jasper Source for Sports** (Map p170; ☎ 780-852-3654; 406 Patricia St).

The area around Pyramid Bench is maintained for winter hiking. Along these trails you'll be sheltered by the woods and have a good chance of spotting wildlife. If you'd prefer to move a little faster, drive your own **dogsledding** team with **Jasper Adventure Centre** (Map p170; ☎ 780-852-5650; www.jasperadventurecen tre.com; 306 Connaught Av; per person C$175).

To see frozen waterfalls and stunning ice formations, take a trip into a frozen Maligne Canyon (adult/child C$60/30, December to late March) with Jasper Adventure Centre. For a spectacular setting, join one of the moonlight tours.

Ice climbing is another winter draw. Though not a sport for novices, those with experience can rent equipment from **Gravity Gear** (Map p170; ☎ 888-852-3155; 618 Patricia St). Maligne Canyon is an ice-climbing hot spot.

SLEEPING

Aside from its one historic lodge, Jasper boasts countless hotels, motels, hostels, cabins, B&Bs and campgrounds. Notwithstanding, in July and August you'd be wise to make reservations a long way in advance. Jasper town is the operations center for the park's various accommodation establishments, with a handful of economical hotels and a good smattering of privately run B&Bs. The park's biggest campground, Whistlers, is a veritable giant situated 3km to the south of town, while the region's rustic quintet of HI youth hostels provides cheap beds for travelers on a budget.

ICEFIELDS PARKWAY
Camping
Columbia Icefield (Map p186; Icefields Parkway; sites $; ☾ mid-May–mid-Oct) While somewhat exposed to the elements, these sites are set back from the loop, making them some of the most secluded on the parkway. Views of the area are fantastic. Facilities are limited to dry toilets and a water pump. Tents and vans only.

Wabasso (Map p186; Hwy 93A; sites $; ☾ Jun-Sep) Peaceful and remote, this campground is conveniently located, relatively near to sights and Jasper town. Despite having 228 sites, the grounds are spread out and fairly private. Walk-in tent sites along the river are wooded and lovely. Sites A74, 76 and 78 are drive-in sites next to the water.

Amenities include hot water, flush toilets and wheelchair-accessible sites.

Honeymoon Lake (Map p186; Icefields Parkway; sites $; ☾ mid-May–mid-Oct) With lake access, these campsites are fairly popular. Sites 26 to 28 are right next to the water, and the rest of the 35 sites are wooded and fairly large. Sites four to 20 are the most private. Dry toilets and a water pump are the only home comforts.

Mt Kerkeslin (Map p186; Icefields Parkway; sites $; ☾ late Jun-Sep) Across from its towering namesake, this campground has 42 sheltered sites. The first half of loop 14 to 42 are larger and good for RVs, although not all are entirely level. Facilities are limited to dry toilets and a water pump.

Wilcox Creek (Map p186; Icefields Parkway; sites $; ☾ early Jun-late Sep) If you score a site away from the road, you'll find trees and privacy here. Sites No one to seven are exposed but have great views, and site 21 is wheelchair accessible. All 48 sites are roomy enough to pull in an RV. Facilities are minimal; there is a dry toilet, a water pump and payphones.

Jonas Creek (Map p186; Icefields Parkway; sites $; ☾ May-Oct) The park's smallest campground

JASPER NATIONAL PARK CAMPGROUNDS

Campground	Location	No of sites	Elevation	Open
Columbia Icefield	Icefields Parkway	33	2012m (6600ft)	May-Oct
Honeymoon Lake	Icefields Parkway	35	1310m (4300ft)	May-Oct
Jonas Creek	Icefields Parkway	25	1500m (4920ft)	May-Oct
Mt Kerkeslin	Icefields Parkway	42	1200m (3936ft)	Jun-Sep
Pocahontas	Miette Hot Springs Rd	140	1200m (3936ft)	May-Oct
Snaring River	off Hwy 16	66	1050m (3445ft)	May-Sep
Wabasso	Hwy 93A	228	1125m (3690ft)	Jun-Sep
Wapiti	Hwy 93	362	1070m (3510ft)	year-round
Whistlers	Whistlers Rd	781	1070m (3510ft)	May-Oct
Wilcox Creek	Icefields Parkway	48	2012m (6600ft)	Jun-Sep

Drinking water | Flush toilets | Great for Families | Wheelchair accessible | Grocery store nearby | Restaurant nearby has 25 sites, half of which are walk-in tent sites. Unserviced and with no electricity or dump station, the place has a real back-country feel, despite its location just off the Icefields Parkway.

Hostels & Hotels

Athabasca Falls International Hostel (Map p186; ☎ 780-852-3215; www.hihostels.ca; Icefields Parkway; dm $; ☙ closed Tue Oct-Apr) A super-friendly hostel in the woods with an ingenious watering-can shower (summer only), a big, alpine-style kitchen-sitting area, table tennis and heated dorms in separate wooden cabins. There's no running water (just an outdoor pump) and the loos are in outhouses, earning the place a 'rustic' tag. The Brewster bus (p168) will drop you outside on the Icefields Parkway, if you give advance notice.

Mt Edith Cavell International Hostel (Map p186; ☎ 780-852-3215; www.hihostels.ca; Icefields Parkway; dm $; ☙ mid-Jun–mid-Oct) Rustic with a capital R – don't expect basic luxuries such as flush toilets, running water or electricity here. However, you can draw strength from the knowledge that your small but congenial

dorm sits pretty in the foothills of one of the Rockies' most sublime mountain peaks. Enjoy the scenery from the deck or the outdoor firepit, before retiring for the night to a communal cabin – and your snoring companions.

Beauty Creek International Hostel (Map p186; ☎ 780-852-3215; www.hihostels.ca; Icefields Parkway; dm $; ☙ Apr-Oct) Only 87km (54 miles) south of Jasper and 17km (10.5 miles) north of the Columbia Icefield, Beauty Creek is a wilderness hostel with no electricity or running water. Lights, stoves and heating are powered by propane, loos are outside and water is from a well. If none of this whets your appetite, then the C$5 all-you-can-eat pancake breakfast with real Quebec maple syrup undoubtedly will. The hostel makes a great stopover for cyclists laboring along the Icefields Parkway.

Sunwapta Falls Resort (Map p186; ☎ 888-828-5777; c-info@sunwapta.com; Icefields Parkway; r & ste $$$$; ☙ May-Nov) A handy pit-stop on the Icefields Parkway with comfortable rooms and suites cocooned in pleasant natural surroundings, though once you've seen the falls and done the adjoining Fortress

JASPER NATIONAL PARK

Reservations required?	Facilities	Description	Page
no	🗑📞	Tents only and basic facilities, but campground is secluded and views are tremendous	above
no	🗑	Small and quiet with some sites on lakeshore	above
no	🗑📞	Close to highway with some seclusion if you choose the right site	above
no	🗑📞	Basic campground with sheltered sites close to Athabasca Falls	above
available	🗑🚻♿🚾📞	Quiet and wooded; close to eastern park entrance	194
no	🗑	Rustic with no RVs; situated off highway 15km (9.5miles) north of Jasper town	194
available	🗑🚻🎣♿📞📦	Well-serviced but relatively remote campground off main highway and close to Mt Edith Cavell hikes	above
available	🗑🚻🚾📞📦	The park's only year-round campground offers 40 serviced site and showers; numbers limited in winter	192
available	🗑🚻♿🔥🚾📞🔥📦	A mini-town with every facility imaginable. Great for families	192
no	🗑📞📦	Close to Icefields Centre and Wilcox Pass trailhead	above

📞 Payphone   🔥 Fireplace   📦 RV dump station

Lake hike, you'll need wheels to get to anywhere else. There's a homey restaurant on site, though it's popular with the tour-bus crowd.

Columbia Icefield Chalet (Map p186; ☎ 877-423-7433; Icefields Centre, Icefields Parkway; r $$$$; 🏵 May-Oct) Forget the chalet tag, this rather businesslike hotel is on the 3rd floor of the Icefields Centre and offers exceptional views over the surrounding glaciers. But despite the rather plush and modern interior, the 32 rooms in the center lack character and, as a result, feel a little antiseptic. Your dinner options are also limited to the mediocre on-site restaurant (the next-nearest facilities are 108km to the north). It's worth a sleepover if you're tired of driving, but two nights would be pushing it.

JASPER & AROUND
Camping
Wapiti (Map p164; Hwy 93; sites $; 🏵 late Jun-early Sep & mid-Oct–early May) In summer, this campground has full facilities and fills up very quickly. All of its 362 sites are wooded; the ones that back onto the river are the most private. In winter, only 91 sites remain open and facilities are limited to flush toilets.

Whistlers (Map p164; Whistlers Rd; sites $; 🏵 early May–mid-Oct) Verging on a camping city, this huge campground supports 781 sites. A full list of amenities, including showers, wheelchair access and an interpretive program, keeps it packed through the summer. Sites are wooded but not particularly private. Loops 50 and 67 have good pull-through spots for RVs, and tents are best on the northern side of the campground. Fires are only permitted at campsites without hookups.

B&Bs
Jasper gets chock-a-block in the summer and finding a room on the spur of the moment can be extremely difficult. Fortunately, aside from the standard clutch of hotels, motels and campgrounds, the town – which has a permanent population of 4500 – boasts over 100 B&Bs in private houses. The **Jasper Home Accommodation Association** (www.stayinjasper.com) maintains an excellent website of inspected B&Bs inside the park, complete with descriptions, contact details

and web links. Prices range from C$60 to C$150 in high season and facilities often include kitchenettes, private entrances and cable TV. Reserve ahead.

Hostels & Hotels
Jasper International Hostel (Map p164; ☎ 780-852-3215; www.hihostels.ca; Whistlers Rd; dm $) Jasper's most 'luxurious' hostel has hot showers, plenty of lounging space and a big kitchen. Large male/female dorms sleep around 40 and there are three private rooms for those after a bit more privacy. Other bonuses include internet, a laundry, bike rental, vending machines and a cheap shuttle link to Jasper town (p168).

Athabasca Hotel (Map p170; ☎ 780-852-3386; www.athabascahotel.com; 510 Patricia St; r $$) Built in 1929, the Athabasca has a rather traditional English-pub feel downstairs, though stuffed animal heads quickly remind you that you're still definitely in Canada. Upstairs, small rooms are comfortable and well-equipped with sinks and TVs. Some of the rooms have (clean) shared bathrooms. Others are perched above a rather noisy nightclub. At the height of summer, this is one of the few places that might still be able to offer rooms at short notice.

Mt Robson Inn (Map p170; ☎ 780-852-3327; www.mountrobsoninn.com; 902 Connaught Dr; r $$$$; 🖵) Though it's a good 80km from Mt Robson, this hybrid Jasper motel-lodge on the west side of town spins no tricks with its facilities and service. Indeed, the ambience in this large edge-of-town inn is both congenial and friendly, and the accommodations surprisingly luxurious. Myriad rooms range from standards to suites, while communal facilities include two outdoor whirlpools, free wi-fi access and a rather tasty steakhouse.

Park Place Inn (Map p170; ☎ 780-852-9770; www.parkplaceinn.com; 623 Patricia St; r $$$$) Giving nothing away behind its rather drab exterior above a parade of downtown shops, the Park Place is a head-turner as soon as you ascend the stairs to its plush open lobby. Exhibiting 14 luxurious rooms decked out in marble, fine art and fluffy bathrobes, the inn's self-proclaimed heritage tag is well earned, with an intimate atmosphere and professional yet friendly staff welcoming you as soon as you cross the threshold. The heftier price tag is worth every penny.

Lodges

Patricia Lake Bungalows (off Map p164; ☎ 780-852-3560; www.patricialakebungalows.com; Pyramid Lake Rd; cottages $$$; ☺ May–mid-Oct) Situated 500m off the Pyramid Lake Rd, and often overlooked by drivers whizzing past, these choice bungalows could have been plucked innocently out of a quiet, upscale city suburb. Melting imperceptibly into the surrounding forest and located right next to the shores of placid Patricia Lake, these comfy cottages sleep up to six people and are equipped with kitch-ens, bathrooms, fireplaces and TVs. With a hot tub, playground, bike and boat rental and on-site laundry, the atmosphere here is relaxed and family-oriented.

Tekarra Lodge (Map p164; ☎ 780-852-3058; www.tekarralodge.com; Hwy 93A; cabins $$$; ☺ mid-May–early Sep) The most atmospheric cabins in the park are set next to the Athabasca River, amid tall trees and splendid tranquility. Hardwood floors, wood-paneled walls, a fireplace and kitchenette inspire a warm, cozy feeling. You might only be a kilometer

---

BACKCOUNTRY HUTS & LODGES

If the thought of camping out in bear country sends you running for the nearest hot tub, why not consider staying in the relative comfort of one of Jasper's half-dozen-or-so huts and lodges. All situated a good day's hike from the nearest road, these venerable backcountry retreats offer a unique wilderness experience without the hassle of tent erection or listening to strange noises go 'bump' in the night.

Huts

The Alpine Club of Canada maintains three rustic backcountry huts in Jasper National Park. The **Wates-Gibson Hut** (Map p164; Tonquin Valley) is a beautiful log cabin built in 1959 with a wood-burning stove, sleeping mattresses (30/24 in summer/winter) and a propane-powered cooking system (utensils available). In summer you can hike here via the 18km (11.2-mile) Astoria River Trail from the Mt Edith Cavell International Hostel (p191). Add on another 12km (7.5 miles) in winter when the Mt Edith Cavell Rd is closed. Used mainly by climbers, the six-bed **Mt Colin Centennial Hut** (Map p164; Colin Range) is accessed by a demanding six- to eight–hour hike off the Overlander Trail. It has a Coleman stove, mattresses and cooking utensils, and is closed in winter. The 12-bed Sydney Vallance (Fryatt) Hut (Map p164), situated 24km (15 miles) up the Fryatt Valley from the Icefields Parkway, is perhaps the most isolated hut and was given a complete renovation in 1999. It's open year-round and facilities include propane cooking and lighting and a wood-heating stove.

For all three huts, you must bring your own bedding, food, matches, toilet paper and dish-cloth and must pack out all of your garbage. Reservations (C$32) are required and can be made through the **Alpine Clubhouse** (☎ 403-678-3200; www.alpineclubofcanada.ca) in Canmore. You are also required to have a Parks Canada wilderness pass.

Lodges

In Tonquin Valley, **Tonquin Amethyst Lake Lodge** (off Map p164; ☎ 780-852-1188; www.tonquin adventures.com; per person incl meals Jun–Oct $$$, 4-bed cabins Jan–Apr $$$) and **Tonquin Valley Backcountry Lodge** (off Map p164; ☎ 780-852-3909; www.tonquinvalley.com; per person incl meals $$$) provide rustic accommodations in historic cabins with views of the lake and Ramparts, approximately 24km (15 miles) from the nearest road. Both lodges run multi-day horse treks to and around the lake, and in winter you can cross-country ski to the lodges.

Built in 1921 and rebuilt in 1991, the **Shovel Pass Lodge** (Map p181; ☎ 780-852-4215; www.sky linetrail.com; r $$$), situated halfway along the emblematic Skyline trail (p180), is the oldest lodge in the park. Boasting seven guest cabins plus a main chalet and dining room, the lodge can accommodate up to 18 people. Meals, bed linen and propane lights and heating are provided, though you'll have to bring your own towel. The price includes accommodations, three meals and transportation of up to 6.8kg (15lb) of gear (by horse). Three-day horse-trekking trips are also available. It's open June to September; reserve well in advance.

or two outside town but you'll feel as if you're years away.

Jasper House (Map p164; ☎ 780-852-4535; www
.jasperhouse.com; Hwy 98; r $$$) A friendly, quiet escape just 3.5km (2.2 miles) south of Jasper town, rooms here have an alpine feel, with all-wood interiors. Standards are simple, and suites have kitchens and sleep two to six. Bungalows are a bit flashier, with Jacuzzis, fireplaces and river-view balconies.

Fairmont Jasper Park Lodge (Map p164; ☎ 780-852-3301; www.fairmont.com; Old Lodge Rd; r $$$$) Jasper's 'parkitecture' classic resides on the quiet shores of Lac Beauvert and is surrounded by one of the nation's most picturesque golf courses. Once the haunt of royalty, artists and members of the international jet set, the original lodge burnt down in 1952, and was replaced by the current building, with its fancy underground shopping mall, the following year. Rambling across several hectares, the outlying log cabins and cedar chalets offer wonderful views across the small lake, but tired furnishings and slightly wooden service don't always justify the astronomical price tag.

Pyramid Lake Resort (Map p164; ☎ 780-852-4900; www.pyramidlakeresort.com; Pyramid Lake Rd; r $$$$) Jasper's second-grandest (and second most expensive) lodge, after the Fairmont, is this tastefully renovated mini-resort perched on a knoll above placid Pyramid Lake. Despite the on-site bustle and attendant pub, the amenity-packed rooms here are quiet and have pleasant views of the lake. The top-end loft rooms come with kitchenettes and can sleep four. Overall, the resort is relatively deluxe but, at this price tag, you can't help thinking it could do better.

MALIGNE LAKE AREA

Maligne Canyon International Hostel (Map p164; ☎ 780-852-3215; www.hihostels.ca; dm $) Well positioned for cross-country skiing and summer sorties along the Skyline Trail, this very basic hostel is poised a little too close to the road to merit a proper 'rustic' tag. Die-hards can get back to nature with six-bed dorms, outhouse toilets and regular visits to the water pump.

NORTH OF JASPER
Camping

Pocahontas (Map p164; Miette Hot Springs Rd; sites $; mid-May–mid-Oct) You'd never know this has 140 sites; spacious and densely

wooded, the campground is actually very peaceful and private. Loop F is the most pleasant. Facilities are minimal, with flush toilets and wheelchair-accessible sites, though they're very well maintained.

Snaring River (Map p164; off Hwy 16; sites $; ☺ May-Sep) The park's most isolated and primitive campground is located 16km north of Jasper town. There are 66 unserviced sites beside a river, along with a water pump, pit toilets and picnic tables.

Lodges

Miette Hot Springs Bungalows (Map p164; ☎ 780-866-3750; Miette Hot Springs Rd; motel r $$, bungalows $$$) Right next to the bathhouse, motel rooms here are old fashioned and charming, with a cabin feel to them. The quaint wooden bungalows were built in 1938, sleep up to four people and fill up quickly. The adjoining restaurant has reasonably priced standard meals.

Pocahontas Cabins (Map p164; ☎ 780-866-3732; www.mtn-park-lodges.com; cnr Hwy 16 & Miette Hot Springs Rd; cabins $$$; ☒) Once a thriving mining community, the settlement of Pocahontas now consists of this single recently renovated resort at the junction of Hwy 16 and Miette Hot Springs Rd, and boasts cozy log cabins, a small restaurant, a hot tub and an outdoor swimming pool. The refurbished cabins are amply furnished with wood stoves, kitchenettes, microwaves and black-and-white photos of the Pocahontas area in its heyday. Older cabins lack the character of the newer ones but are cute nonetheless. Both are pet-friendly and ideal for family use.

EATING & DRINKING

While Jasper's culinary scene is a long way from the bright lights of Calgary and Edmonton, budding gastronomes needn't starve. Aside from a small cluster of sterile fast-food franchises and a plethora of post-hike refueling joints, fine diners can travel the world in cosmopolitan Patricia St, touching down in such exotic locales as Spain, Korea, China, Greece and Japan.

ICEFIELDS PARKWAY

Sunwapta Falls Resort (Map p186; ☎ 888-828-5777; Icefields Parkway; lunch/dinner $/$$; ☺ deli 11am-6pm, dining room 6-9pm May-Nov) One of the better tourist-orientated restaurant–gift shop combos on the Icefields Parkway, the Sunwapta does homey ranch-style breakfasts and tasty salads, sandwiches and soups. Arrive early for lunch before the daily tour-bus invasion.

Icefields Centre Dining Room (☎ 877-423-7433; Icefields Centre, Icefields Parkway; breakfast/dinner $/$$; ☺ 8-10am & 6-9pm May-Oct) Fantastic views of Athabasca Glacier will likely keep you from noticing the lack of atmosphere here. Fill up on pancakes, omelets or oatmeal before heading out on the trail. For dinner there's a bit of everything, including lots of Chinese cuisine. You'll also find a hectic canteen (open 9am to 6pm April to October) at the Icefields Centre, good for hot dogs, noodles and not a lot else.

JASPER & AROUND

Bear's Paw Bakery (Map p170; ☎ 780-852-3233; 4 Cedar Ave; pastries $; ☺ 7am-6pm) This unsuspecting bakery outlet rustles up insanely addictive breads, scones, cookies and muffins along with equally gratifying coffee.

Other Paw Bakery (Map p170; ☎ 780-852-2253; 610 Connaught Dr; ☺ 7am-10pm) Not surprisingly, the queues are often long at Bear's Paw, but you can always pop around the corner to its sister café, the aromatic Other Paw, which also stays open later.

Soft Rock Café (Map p170; ☎ 780-852-5850; 622 Connaught Dr; meals $; ☺ 7am-7:30pm) A bakery, sandwich bar, internet café and all-day breakfast joint. Far from being a haven for ageing Bryan Adams fans, the Soft Rock is a busy nexus for hungry hikers and loquacious locals. Even better, the café turns into the Same Same (But Different) Thai restaurant after 5pm, allowing patrons to sprawl around low-slung tables over green curry and phad Thai noodles.

Co-Co's Café (Map p170; ☎ 780-852-5444; 608 Patricia St; meals $) Organic fair-trade coffee, vegan options, delicious breakfast wraps and fresh scones to write home about, Co-Co's is another popular Jasper wake-up call. Small, relaxed and trendy, it's a great place to sip a coffee and plan a hike or two.

Spooners Coffee Bar (Map p170; ☎ 780-852-4046; Patricia Plaza, Patricia St; mains $) A light, airy café perched above Patricia St, Spooner's specializes in fortifying breakfasts, slick smoothies and delicious soups. An excellent selection of sandwiches and salads make it a favorite spot for both breakfast and lunch.

Jasper Pizza Place (Map p170; ☎ 780-852-3225; 402 Connaught Dr; pizza for two $$, free delivery; ☺ 11:30am-10pm) Loud, boisterous and seemingly disorganized, there's a method to the madness here if you're prepared to stick around long enough to fight for a table. While queuing for pizza might not be everyone's idea of an authentic wilderness experience, the food here is surprisingly good when it finally arrives, and you can diversify with ribs, burgers and salad, if your taste buds can't take any more cheese and tomato. Love it or hate it, it's a Jasper institution.

Denjiro (Map p170; ☎ 780-852-3780; 410 Connaught Dr; lunch/dinner meals $$; ☺ noon-2:30pm & 5-10:30pm) With fresh fish sent in regularly from Vancouver, and rainbow rolls prepared with salmon, tuna, shrimp and scallops, this long-standing Japanese dining room has been tempting refined palates for nearly two decades. For those who prefer their food cooked there's teriyaki chicken, curry, noodles and tempura.

L&W Restaurant (Map p170; ☎ 780-852-4114; cnr Patricia St & Hazel Ave; meals $$; ☺ 10am-midnight) A family restaurant with a Greek twist, the L&W (not to be confused with the A&W situated opposite) has been in Jasper for donkey's years, knocking out steaks, souvlaki and the famous 'Gus' burger named after the original owner. A light, airy décor is stuffed with foliage and staffed by plenty of keen summer-job waiting staff. Enjoy a delicious après-hike feast and be sure to nab the dessert tray, which includes a wickedly sweet baklava.

A NIGHT OUT IN THE WILDERNESS

Big enough to brandish a (tiny) club scene, Jasper is home to **Pete's Night Club** (Map p170; Patricia St; ☺ 5pm-3am), an upstairs nightclub that boasts a pool table, bottled beers and plenty of scarily concocted theme nights hosted by the local branch of the Black Sabbath appreciation society.

Downstream Bar (Map p170; ☎ 780-852-3032; 620 Connaught Dr; drinks $; ☺ 4pm-late) is another comfy pub that hosts open-mike sessions, jazz, blues or reggae.

Plenty of popcorn, pop and dating potential is available at the two-screen **Chaba Cinema** (☎ 780-852-4749; 604 Connaught Dr; adult/child C$7/4).

La Fiesta (Map p170; ☎ 780-852-0404; 504 Patricia St; lunch $$, dinner $$$, tapas $; ☻ noon-11pm) A delicious tapas restaurant with a Mexican slant, this Mediterranean-styled place behind the Jasper Information Centre offers tasty tapatizers and tempting mains – if you ever get that far. Have fun mixing up a variety of tapas plates, including baked calamari, artichoke dip, grilled lamb and rosemary sausage, and tortilla crusted chorizo and goat's cheese cakes. It's not particularly Spanish, but who cares?

Cassio's Trattoria (Map p170; ☎ 780-852-4070; 602 Connaught Dr; meals $$$; ☻ 8am-11pm) Jasper's newest restaurant is situated inside the longstanding Whistler's Inn where the Cassio family concentrates on presenting *real* Italian fare as opposed to the cheap imitation stuff that haunts pizza parlors and pasta imitators elsewhere. You can feast here on gnocchi, meatballs, veal masala and pasta marinara and – yes – there's also a well-stuffed antipasto plate that'll quickly replenish hike-depleted appetites.

Andy's Bistro (Map p170; ☎ 780-852-4559; 606 Patricia St; meals $$$; ☻ 5-10pm) Jasper's most lauded fine-dining experience boasts a European menu with various Indian and Asian influences. This is where you go to forget about the hiking hoo-hah as you sup from one of 70 assorted wines and tuck into rare tuna, escargot in vol-au-vents and pan-fried veal *emince* Zurich-style.

The Pines (Map p164; ☎ 780-852-4900; Pyramid Lake Resort, Pyramid Lake Rd; meals $$$; ☻ lunch noon-4pm, dinner 5-9pm) Big windows give lovely views over the lake, while high ceilings and simple décor make this a classy place to dine. For dinner try seafood ragout, maple quail, chicken masala or rock fish. The re-

---

TOP FIVE RAINY-DAY ACTIVITIES

- **Chaba Cinema** (p195) – it's dry and there's popcorn
- **Miette Hot Springs** (p173) – it's wet, but it's warm
- **Fairmont Jasper Park Lodge** (p171) – see how the 'other half' vacation
- **Jasper Activity Centre** (p189) – go cycling – in the gym!
- **Discovery Trail** (p170) – grab an umbrella, or a raincoat – or just get wet!

---

sort remains enduringly popular despite its out-of-town location; reservations are recommended.

Jasper Brewing Company (Map p170; ☎ 780-852-4111; 624 Connaught Dr; drinks $; ☻ 11:30am-1am) A welcome recent addition to the après-hike scene with a good range of home-brewed Europhile beers, from Irish-style stout to English-tasting IPA. The food menu has a spicy Southern twist.

MALIGNE LAKE AREA

The View Restaurant (Map p185; ☎ 780-852-3370; Maligne Lake Lodge; meals $$; ☻ 9am-7pm) On first impressions this aptly named restaurant, perched on the bejeweled shores of Maligne Lake, is just another overpriced Jasper cafeteria decked out for tourists and staffed by summer jobbers. But, beyond the usual sandwiches, soups and machine-dispensed hot chocolate, this place serves up some of the best pastries, muffins, Nanaimo bars and cinnamon buns in the park.

AROUND JASPER NATIONAL PARK

Outdoor recreation doesn't end at Jasper National Park's border. For drivers heading south toward Vancouver, Mt Robson Provincial Park, home of the Canadian Rockies' highest summit and the headwaters of the mighty Fraser River, is well worth a stopover. Nestled to the north and west, meanwhile, Hamber Provincial Park and Willmore Wilderness Park lure travelers with a penchant for utter solitude.

MT ROBSON PROVINCIAL PARK

Bordering Jasper National Park in the east and flanked by the Selwyn Range to the west, the drive through Mt Robson Provincial Park follows a historic pathway of fur traders. Rejected by the Canadian Pacific Railway as a route through the Rockies, it was later adopted by Grand Trunk Pacific and Canadian Northern Pacific Railways and is today a major railway route. The views of snowy mountains and glacial lakes are magnificent.

Bisected by Hwy 16 on its way between Jasper and Prince George, Mt Robson Provincial Park abuts Jasper National Park at the **Yellowhead Pass**, 24km (15 miles) west of Jasper town. Covering 224,866 hectares (555,420 acres), the park's main hub is an excellent **information center** (☎ 250-566-4325; www.elp.gov.bc.ca/bcparks; ◐ 8am-5pm Jun & Sep, 8am-8pm Jul & Aug) near the western border. Here you can pick up trail information, register for hikes with Parks BC staff and take in exhibits on local geography and history – including a short interpretive trail. You'll also find a gas station and café situated next door. On clear days the neck-craning views of ice-glazed Mt Robson, glowering like a fiery beacon overhead, are truly amazing.

Sights & Activities

The tallest mountain in the Canadian Rockies, **Mt Robson** towers like a misplaced Everest over the surrounding peaks and valleys, dwarfing other rugged giants in its 3954m (12,969ft) shadow. Approaching from the east, no words can prepare you for the sight of its craggy southern face, which rises like a vertical wall over 2439m (8000ft) above Berg Lake. Visible for less than 14 days a year, the mountain has left onlookers awestruck for centuries; Aboriginals called it 'Mountain of the Spiral Rd' and trappers and explorers revered it as unconquerable. It wasn't until 1913 that the mountain was first officially climbed, and, even today, only approximately 10% of summit attempts are successful.

Hiking is what draws most visitors to the park. The famous 22km (13.6-mile) **Berg Lake Trail** takes you through the Valley of a Thousand Falls, next to Mt Robson and past the stunning, glacier-fed lake itself, filled with shorn-off chunks of ice. You must register to undertake the hike, which takes two to three days, and while the majority of spaces are filled on a first-come, first-served basis, **reservations** (☎ 800-689-9025) are accepted for particularly busy periods. Seven backcountry campgrounds are located en route (C$5 per person per night). Trail information, permits and maps can all be found at the information center.

For those with less time, the first segment of the Berg Lake Trail (bikes allowed) can be taken as far as the **Kinney Lake** picnic site and viewpoint at 9km (5.6 miles). Look out for mountain goats, black bears, caribou and porcupine. Alternatively, you can heli-hike, ie take a helicopter into the Berg Lake area and hike out. For more details enquire

with **Robson Helimagic Inc** (☎ 250-566-4700; Hwy 5 N, Valemount, BC; per person from C$179)

Boating is popular within the park, although fishing isn't particularly good. Launch your boat in the green waters of Moose or Yellowhead Lakes. Rearguard Falls, just west of the information center, is known for its salmon viewing (mid-August to early September).

Sleeping & Eating

Lucerne Campground (☎ 800-689-9025; Hwy 16, Yellowhead Lake; sites $) With large, wooded sites, the spacious Lucerne is a great place to set up home for the night. A number of the 36 sites are level and have pull-through for RVs; others are built up for tents. There are two walk-in, lakeside tent sites and a water pump.

Mt Robson Mountain River Lodge (☎ 250-566-9899; www.mtrobson.com; cnr Hwy 16 & Swift Current Creek Rd; r incl breakfast $$$) On the western border of the park, this friendly lodge commands stunning views of the giant peak – when it's visible. There's a main lodge and a couple of cabins that share a cozy, away-from-it-all atmosphere.

HAMBER PROVINCIAL PARK

Tiny Hamber Provincial Park is cocooned in an alcove on the western border of Jasper National Park. It is the domain of black and grizzly bears, but recent years have seen an influx of backpackers. While there is no road access into the park, an improved 22km (13.6-mile) trail from Sunwapta Falls along the Icefields Parkway leads to **Fortress Lake**, on the park's eastern border. Fishing for brook trout is popular here, and an air-accessed commercial fishing camp is located on the southern shore.

Along the lake's northeast shore are three basic campgrounds, each with a pit toilet and bear pole. You do not need a permit to camp, but you must register your vehicle with Parks Canada if you plan to leave it at Sunwapta Falls.

For more information about the park and current trail conditions, contact **BC Parks** (☎ 250-566-4325; www.env.gov.bc.ca/bcparks).

WILLMORE WILDERNESS PARK

Spreading across the foothills and mountain ranges north of Jasper National Park, Willmore Wilderness Park has more wildlife passing through it than people. If you really want to get off the beaten track, consider the 750km (465 miles) of trails crossing this park. Access is by foot only from Rock Lake, Big Berland or Grande Cache. At 95km (59 miles), **Mountain Trail** is the longest and most continuous route through the park, from Rock Lake to Grande Cache. The scenic 33km (20.5-mile) **Indian Trail** is popular for hunting and wildlife watching and is in better condition than many of the other trails.

Very little trail maintenance is done here, and while there are designated camping areas, you'll find nothing at them. Water is from lakes and rivers only and must be treated before you consume it. Permits to hike or camp in the park are not required. Be sure to tell someone where you're going and when to expect you back, and be prepared to deal with any emergencies or wildlife you meet on the trail.

For more information on Willmore Wilderness Park, contact **Travel Alberta** (☎ 800-661-8888; www.travelalberta.com). From Jasper town, the closest source of information is at the **Hinton Visitor Information Centre** (☎ 780-865-2777; Hwy 16, Hinton), 77km (28 miles) north.

Glacier National Park

National park, international peace park, World Heritage Site and protected Unesco biosphere; Glacier National Park's mantle as the aptly named 'Crown of the Continent' is backed up by plenty of illustrious titles. Rising like a ghostly apparition above the windswept prairies of western Montana, the region's sharp, snow-sprinkled ridges and precipitous, glacier-sculpted horns stand like huge Gothic cathedrals astride America's lofty Continental Divide, inspiring awe in all who pass.

Lauded for its remote backcountry hiking opportunities and spectacular big-sky scenery, Glacier is often looked upon as one of America's best protected and most pristine parks. A unique habitat for grizzly bears, bighorn sheep, myriad birdlife and a colorful pastiche of high alpine plants and flowers, the region's rich natural ecosystem has been barely altered since the days when Blackfeet Native Americans hunted in its forest-covered eastern valleys. But it's not all fresh air and hard-won green credentials. High up on the subalpine slopes of the dramatic Rocky Mountains, amid aquamarine lakes and glistening snowfields, a dwindling collection of melting glaciers provide scientists with a disturbing countdown on climate change.

First earmarked as a national park in 1910, Glacier owes much of its early existence to the Great Northern Railroad that penetrated the region in the 1890s, bringing with it carriage-loads of curious and adventure-hungry tourists. With the coming of the motor car in the 1930s, the park got its engineering emblem, the legendary Going-to-the-Sun Rd, a hair-raising, heart-in-your-mouth roller-coaster ride that climbs past weeping waterfalls and vertiginous drop-offs up to the Continental Divide at 2026m (6646ft) Logan Pass.

GLACIER NATIONAL PARK

HIGHLIGHTS

- Spying grizzly bears, mountain goats, bighorn sheep and swooping eagles on a **Two Medicine Valley** (p214) hike
- Harking back to the grand old days of the Great Northern Railroad in historic **Many Glacier Hotel** (p225)
- Learning about the spirituality and traditions of the Blackfeet people at a **Native American Speak** (p226)
- Tucking into buffalo meatloaf and homemade huckleberry pie at **Eddie's Cafe** (p225) in diminutive Apgar village
- Feeling the adrenaline rush of a white-knuckle (free!) shuttle-bus ride on the vertiginous **Going-to-the-Sun Road** (p206)

- Total area: 4046 sq km (1562 sq miles)
- Elevation Apgar: 960m (3153ft)
- Average high/low temperature in July: 78/48°F

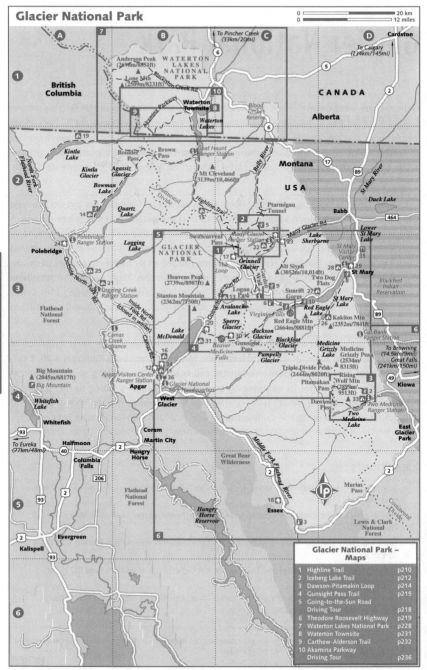

Glacier National Park

When You Arrive

The park is open year-round, though summer is by far the most popular season. Entry per car, or RV, costs US$25. People arriving on foot, bicycle or motorcycle pay US$12 per person. Both tickets are valid for seven days. Entrance fees are reduced in winter. Fees for Glacier do not include entrance to Waterton Lakes National Park. For information on annual passes see Entrance Fees & Passes, p26.

The park offers free entry on Founder's Day, August 25.

Staff at the entrance stations hand out free detailed Glacier-Waterton maps, a quarterly newspaper and the *Glacier Explorer,* a schedule of events and activities, including ranger-led day trips.

Orientation

Cocooned in northwest Montana and abutting the border with the Canadian provinces of Alberta and British Columbia, Glacier is bisected by the Continental Divide and contained within the 'Crown of the Continent' natural ecosystem. The 4046-sq-km (1562-sq-mile) park's natural delineators are the North Fork of the Flathead River (west), Marias Pass on US 2 (south), US 89 and the Blackfeet Indian Reservation (east), and the Canadian border (north).

The park's main areas, clockwise roughly northeast to northwest, are Goat Haunt; Many Glacier, a popular hiking valley; St Mary, best known for its photogenic namesake lake; Two Medicine, a rugged but secluded valley replete with wildlife; Logan Pass, at the apex of the Going-to-the-Sun Rd; the Lake McDonald Valley, home to Apgar village; and the North Fork Valley, the most remote and least visited corner of the park.

ENTRANCES

Glacier National Park has six official entrance gates. The two busiest are the West Entrance, just north of West Glacier, and the East Entrance, near St Mary at the opposite end of the iconic Going-to-the-Sun Rd. The other entrances are the Camas Creek Entrance and the Polebridge Ranger Station, both off the North Fork Rd on the park's western side, and the Two Medicine Entrance (on Two Medicine Rd, west of Hwy 49) and the Many Glacier Entrance (on Many Glacier Rd, west of US 89) over on the eastern side.

Boards at entrances indicate which park campgrounds are open or full.

MAJOR ROADS

The park's main thoroughfare is the scene-stealing Going-to-the-Sun Rd, which is also the only paved road that cuts directly across the park. This 80km (50-mile) engineering marvel climbs from forest-filled valleys to the stark subalpine meadows of Logan Pass in the blink of a camera shutter. US 2, which is 92km (57 miles) long, wraps around the southern boundary of the park, winding through national forest, Blackfeet

GLACIER NATIONAL PARK

GLACIER IN...

Two Days
Fortify yourself with a hiker's breakfast at the **Park Café** (p240), before dropping by the **St Mary Visitor Center** (opposite) for up-to-date information on trails, weather and bears. Next, take a free (yes – free!) shuttle bus west to **Logan Pass** (p206), where you can hike up to the **Hidden Lake Overlook** (p209). Curiosity satisfied, career west down the **Going-to-the-Sun Road** (p206) in another shuttle and spend the night at the **Lake McDonald Lodge** (p224). On day two take a boat out onto the lake before passing the afternoon exploring **Apgar village** (p206) and **West Glacier** (p241). In the evening enjoy a Native American Speak or an educational ranger talk in the lodge's auditorium.

Four Days
Follow the two-day itinerary, and on day three transfer to the **Many Glacier Hotel** (p225), ready to embark on a classic two-day backpacking excursion. Stride out in the morning along the **Swiftcurrent Pass Trail** (p212) and spend the night at the historic **Granite Park Chalet** (p224), just across the Continental Divide. On day four, rise early and tackle the panoramic **Highline Trail** (p210) to Logan Pass. Catch a shuttle back down to St Mary and spend the evening enjoying tasty food and friendly Montanan ambience in the rustic **Glacier Park Lodge** (p241).

reservation land and the park's southwestern tip. Camas Rd, which is 18km (11 miles) long, links the Apgar area with the beginning of the 21km (13-mile) stretch of the Outside North Fork Rd to Polebridge. The paved, but rutted, Many Glacier and Two Medicine Rds dead-end inside the park at various trailheads and lodges.

Information

BOOKSTORES

All three of the park's main visitor centers, at Apgar, Logan Pass and St Mary (opposite), stock an excellent selection of park-related books and literature, including maps and guidebooks. A more limited selection can be found in gift stores at the Many Glacier (p225) and Lake McDonald Lodges (p224).

EQUIPMENT & SUPPLIES

Minimal camping and equipment supplies can be found at stores at the Lake McDonald Lodge (p224), Many Glacier Hotel (p225), Swiftcurrent Motor Inn (p225) and Rising Sun Motor Inn (p224). Just outside the park, in West Glacier, the **Glacier Outdoor Center** (☎ 406-888-5454; 11957 US 2 E; ☼ 7:30am-9pm) rents and sells gear for rafting, fishing, mountain biking, camping and backpacking.

INTERNET ACCESS

Internet service in the park is almost non-existent. Laptop users may be able to plug in and dial up their own service long-distance from the Lake McDonald Lodge. If you're desperate, head to internet cafés in St Mary (p240) or West Glacier (p242).

LAUNDRY & SHOWERS

The camp stores at Rising Sun (p224) and Many Glacier (p225) have **showers** (per 8min US$1.25; ☎ 6:30am-10pm). The latter also has laundry facilities.

MEDICAL SERVICES & EMERGENCIES

Basic first aid is available at visitor centers and ranger stations in the park. For the nearest hospitals, see p265. For emergencies dial ☎ 911.

MONEY

Canadian currency is not widely accepted in Glacier. The nearest banks are in Columbia Falls and Browning. The lodges at Many Glacier and Lake McDonald have 24-hour ATMs. There's an ATM at the camp store at Eddie's Cafe (p225) in Apgar village.

POST

All Glacier hotel sites have mail boxes. There's a summer-only postal substation at the Lake McDonald Lodge (p224) where you can post mail and buy stamps.

TELEPHONES

All park lodges and nonprimitive campgrounds have public phones. Cell (mobile) phone reception in the park is sporadic and unreliable.

TOURIST INFORMATION

The park has three informative visitor centers and three fully staffed ranger stations scattered within its midst. All are overseen by knowledgeable and helpful rangers during peak season. Visitor centers usually offer other amenities such as restrooms, drinking water, bookstores, maps and interpretive displays. Call in at any of the following:

Apgar Visitor Center (☎ 406-888-7939; ☽ early May-late Oct, Sat & Sun only in winter) A small information center in the village, close to all amenities.

Logan Pass Visitor Center (☽ usually early Jun–mid-Oct) Opens when the Going-to-the-Sun Rd is fully functional. Books, toilets, water and interpretive displays, but no food.

Many Glacier Ranger Station (☎ 406-732-7740; ☽ late May–mid-Sep) Call here for local hiking information and details of recent bear activity.

Polebridge Ranger Station (☎ 406-888-7842; ☽ late May–mid-Sep) A small historic station with North Fork information.

St Mary Visitor Center (☎ 406-732-7750; ☽ early May–mid-Oct) Holds interesting geological exhibits and an auditorium featuring slide shows, ranger talks and Native American Speaks.

Two Medicine Ranger Station (☎ 406-226-4484; ☽ late May–mid-Sep) A good source for Two Medicine area hikes.

Infrequently staffed ranger stations are also situated at Goat Haunt, Cut Bank, Walton, Belly River, Logging Creek and Kintla Lake.

For information on the Glacier National Park Headquarters, see p242.

Park Policies & Regulations

Glacier supports a delicate natural ecosystem and various rules and regulations have been formulated to keep it that way. No fireworks or firearms are allowed in the park, and all litter and garbage must be packed out, or disposed of in bear-proof bins. It is illegal to collect environmental souvenirs such as rocks, flowers and plants.

Pets are prohibited from all park trails and backcountry campgrounds. Elsewhere, they must be leashed at all times to prevent them from provoking wildlife.

Hikers should always keep to designated trails and refrain from taking shortcuts across fragile soils and vegetation.

Park regulations allow visitors to collect up to a pint of berries per person per day, but think twice before going on a picking binge. Bears and other creatures depend on this food for sustenance.

BACKCOUNTRY CAMPING

No permits are required for day hikes, but you must have a permit to camp in the backcountry; they go for US$5 per adult per night and US$2.50 per child aged nine to 16. A season pass is US$60. Kids eight years old and under get free permits. Once in the park, permits can be arranged less than 24 hours ahead of time at the **Apgar Backcountry Office** (☽ 7am-5pm May-late Oct), which is near the Apgar Visitor Center, at St Mary Visitor Center or at the ranger stations at Many Glacier, Two Medicine or Polebridge. See left for season openings.

Planners can reserve backcountry sites in person at the Apgar Backcountry Office or at St Mary Visitor Center, or by writing to **Backcountry Reservations** (fax 406-888-5819; Glacier National Park, West Glacier, MT 59936). Applications postmarked before April 15 are not accepted.

Permits are required for backcountry camping in winter (late November to late April), though no fees are charged.

Backcountry campers are encouraged to bring their own cooking stoves and water purification system.

BIKING

Bikes are prohibited from all park trails. From June 15 through Labor Day cyclists are restricted from using the Going-to-the-Sun Rd between Apgar village and Sprague Creek Campground, and Logan Creek to Logan Pass, between 11am and 4pm.

CAMPING

Glacier National Park operates 13 campgrounds. Sites at Fish Creek and St Mary Campgrounds can be **reserved** (☎ 800-365-2267; www.recreation.gov) up to five months in advance. All other sites are first-come, first-served. Campgrounds generally open mid-May to the end of September. Only Apgar Picnic Area and St Mary Campground offer primitive winter camping (US$7.50).

RVs are allowed at all sites except Sprague Creek, though footage regulations vary. Large units are not recommended at those accessed via dirt road, ie Bowman Lake, Cut Bank, Kintla Lake, Logging Creek and Quartz Creek.

Drive-in campers should store their edibles in a hard-sided vehicle or in a bear-proof food locker. Stoves, coolers, containers and utensils (even if clean) and scented toiletries should never be left out unattended. Garbage should be disposed of in the bear-proof bins available in all front-country campgrounds.

Most stores within and around the park sell wood for campfires.

DRIVING

The speed limit is 72km/h (45mph) on all park roads, dropping to 40km/h (25mph) at the upper part of the Going-to-the-Sun Rd and 16km/h (10mph) in campgrounds. Vehicle restrictions are imposed on Going-to-the-Sun Rd only. Vehicles or combinations wider than 2.4m (8ft) or longer than 6.4m (21ft) are prohibited between Avalanche Creek to just east of Sun Point. State law requires motorcycle operators and passengers under 18 years old to wear helmets. Limited parking is available at most trailheads.

FISHING & BOATING

A Montana state fishing license is not required within Glacier National Park. Anglers are generally limited to possession of five fish daily, with caps varying by species. Some waters, including Hidden Lake and the North and Middle Forks of the Flathead River, are purely catch-and-release zones. Read the park's *Fishing Regulations* pamphlet. Portions of the North Fork and Middle Fork of the Flathead River outside the park are subject to Montana state fishing regulations. Part of Lower Two Medicine Lake is on reservation land and subject to Blackfeet reservation regulations.

Motorboats are permitted on Sherburne, St Mary and McDonald Lakes. On Bowman and Two Medicine Lakes, motorcraft must be 10HP or less. Read Glacier's *Boating Regulations* pamphlet. Jet skis are not allowed on Glacier's waters. Water-skiing is permitted only on St Mary Lake and Lake McDonald, and only during daylight hours.

TRASH & RECYCLING

Brown bear-proof containers for garbage are available all over the park. There are designated recycling bins at the St Mary Visitor Center (p203) and campground. All Glacier Park, Inc–owned lodges and motels have recycling receptacles for aluminum and cardboard. A redeemable deposit can be procured at park lodges and stores on returned cans and bottles.

Getting Around

BICYCLE

Getting around by bike is feasible on the Going-to-the-Sun Rd at certain times of day – although the ride is tough. With all trails out of bounds, cyclists are confined to plying the park's scant road network. For more cycling ideas see p217.

CAR & MOTORCYCLE

The only paved road to completely bisect the park is the 80km (50-mile) Going-to-the-Sun Rd. The unpaved Inside North Fork Rd links Apgar with Polebridge. To connect with any other roads, vehicles must briefly leave the park and re-enter via another entrance.

Car rentals are available at Glacier Park International Airport and in the nearby town of Whitefish.

PUBLIC TRANSPORTATION
Bus

Public transportation has improved exponentially in the park since the introduction of free shuttles on the Going-to-the-Sun Rd in July 2007 (see the boxed text, opposite). As a result, all of the park's major trailheads (bar those in the remote North Fork area) are well served by public transportation. On the park's eastern side, the East Side shuttle runs a less comprehensive paying service between East Glacier and Waterton (Canada), calling at Two Medicine, Cut Throat Creek, St Mary, Many Glacier and Chief Mountain. Journeys cost US$8 per trip segment and are rarely full; contact **Glacier Park, Inc** (☎ 406-892-2525) for reservations and more details. Shuttle buses generally run late June through early September.

Train

Largely responsible for opening up the region in the 1890s, the train has been a

THE GOING-TO-THE-SUN-ROAD SHUTTLE

Plagued by a burgeoning convoy of summer cars, traffic control on the scenery-studded Going-to-the-Sun Rd has long been a recurring park headache. But with the highway listed as a national historic landmark, altering the structure of this remarkably durable ribbon of asphalt isn't really an option.

Instead, in the summer of 2007, Glacier's forward-thinking park officials came up with an environmentally friendly solution. From July of that year, the park introduced a free shuttle service that offered motorists the opportunity to park at two newly amplified transit centers in Apgar and St Mary and grab a bus to ferry them across the Continental Divide. Linking various campgrounds, trailheads, lodges and viewpoints, the new shuttles run on three separate but interlinking routes. The Apgar (green) route tackles the short run between Apgar village and the Fish Creek campground; the Lake McDonald Valley (blue) route plies the western section of the Going-to-the-Sun Rd from Apgar to Logan Pass; while the St Mary Valley Route (red) runs from Logan Pass down to St Mary Visitor Center at the park's eastern gate (the green and blue routes use 12-seat buses while the red route uses 24-seaters). Join up the dots and you'll quickly discover that you can get just about anywhere on or around the Going-to-the-Sun Rd without once having to step inside your car.

Shuttle services run every 15 to 30 minutes between 7am and 11:30pm, from July 1 to Labor Day. The buses are wheelchair accessible and run on biodiesel. The larger buses can also accommodate bicycles. Clear route maps are provided at every shuttle stop or can be viewed on the park website at www.nps.gov/glac.

popular method of transport to Glacier since the park's inception in 1910. Amtrak's *Empire Builder* continues to ply the Great Northern Railroad's historic east–west route from Chicago to Seattle once daily (in either direction) stopping in both East Glacier (6:45pm westbound, 9:54am eastbound) and West Glacier (8:23pm westbound, 8:16am eastbound). The same train also connects with Whitefish.

TOURS

Bus

Run by **Glacier Park, Inc** (☎ 406-892-2525), Glacier's stylish red 'jammer' buses (a legacy of when drivers had to 'jam' hard on the gears) are synonymous with the park and a nostalgic reminder of the pioneering days of early motorized transportation. Introduced on the Going-to-the-Sun Rd between 1936 and 1939, the buses have been serving the park loyally for over 70 years, save for a two-year sabbatical in 1999 when the fleet was briefly taken out of service to be reconfigured by the Ford Motor Company. Sparkling afresh after an extensive makeover that has made the buses safer, sturdier and 93% more environmentally friendly (they now run off propane gas), jammers are once again transporting visitors along a dozen memorable routes interspersed with

plenty of scenic stops. As much a part of the scenery as the glaciers themselves, it is difficult to imagine the park without them.

Jammer tours range from the **Western Alpine Tour** (adult/child US$30/15), a 3½-hour trip between Lake McDonald Lodge and Logan Pass, to the **Big Sky Circle Tour** (adult/child US$65/32.50) an 8½-hour journey that circles the park via US 2. The International Peace Park Tour departs Many Glacier (US$50/25) and Glacier Park Lodge (US$75/37.50) daily, rumbling through the east side of the park before heading to Waterton Lakes National Park in Canada in time for an optional high tea at the Prince of Wales Hotel.

Blackfeet tribal members lead interpretive tours (adult/child under 13 US$40/15) of Going-to-the-Sun Rd, run by **Sun Tours** (☎ 406-226-9220, 800-786-9220). Air-conditioned buses leave from various points in East Glacier, St Mary and Browning; tours last approximately six hours, including a one-hour lunch break.

Boat

Glacier Park Boat Co (☎ 406-257-2426; www.montanaweb.com/gpboats) offers boat tours (US$11 to US$17, 45 minutes to 1½ hours) departing at least five times daily from the docks at Lake McDonald Lodge, Two Medicine, Many Glacier Hotel (for Swiftcurrent and

GLACIER NATIONAL PARK

Josephine Lakes) and Rising Sun (for St Mary Lake). All trips are on boats dating from the 1920s and '30s and are narrated by an interpretive (and often witty) guide; some include an optional short hike. Cocktail cruises depart the Rising Sun (6:30pm) and Lake McDonald (7pm) docks.

To get a view from above the eagles' nests, consider the helicopter tours run by **Kruger Helicop-Tours** (☎ 406-387-4565; www.kruger helicopters.com); hourly rates start at US$188 per person.

SIGHTS

GOING-TO-THE-SUN ROAD

St Mary Lake

Located on the park's dryer eastern side, where the mountains melt imperceptibly into the Great Plains, St Mary Lake lies in a deep, glacier-carved valley famous for its astounding views and ferocious winds. Overlooked by the tall, chiseled peaks of the Rockies and scarred by the devastating effects of the 2006 Red Eagle Fire, the valley is spectacularly traversed by the Going-to-the-Sun Rd and punctuated by numerous trailheads and viewpoints. Plying east from Logan Pass, the first notable highlight is the **Jackson Glacier Overlook**, a popular pull-over located a short walk from the Gunsight Pass trailhead, where you can steal telescopic views of the park's fifth-largest glacier. A few miles further east sits **Sunrift Gorge**, a narrow canyon carved over millennia by the gushing glacial melt-waters of Baring Creek. Look out here for picturesque Baring Bridge, a classic example of rustic Going-to-the-Sun Rd architecture, and follow a short, tree-covered trail down to misty Baring Falls. Another trail leads to **Sun Point**, a rocky promontory that overlooks St Mary Lake and was the site of some of the park's earliest and most luxurious chalets (now demolished). Further east, **Rising Sun** boasts a plethora of useful tourist facilities, including a motel, restaurant and boat launch while, at peculiarly named **Two Dog Flats** nearby, thick trees give way to grassy meadows replete with bears, coyotes and elk.

Logan Pass

Perched above the tree line, atop the wind-lashed Continental Divide, and blocked by snow for most of the year, 2026m (6646ft) Logan Pass – named for William R Logan, Glacier's first superintendent – is the park's highest navigable point by road. Two trails, Hidden Lake Overlook and Highline, lead out from here, the latter cutting like a deep scar into the side of the velvety **Garden Wall**, a steep-sided arête whose western slopes are covered with an abundance of summer wildflowers. A couple of thousand feet below, the glistening **Weeping Wall** creates a seasonal waterfall that was formed when Going-to-the-Sun Rd construction workers drilled their way across a network of mountain springs. The water has subsequently been diverted over the lip of a 9m (30ft) man-made cliff, and frequently gives unwary cars and motorbikes a good soaking. For a more natural waterfall, look across the valley at distant **Bird Woman Falls**, a spectacular speck of spray that drops 152m (500ft) from one of Glacier's many hanging valleys. **The Loop** is one of the road's few hairpin bends and a popular trailhead for hikers descending from the Granite Park Chalet and the Highline Trail; consequently it's normally chock-a-block with cars.

Lake McDonald Valley

Greener and wetter than the St Mary Valley, the Lake McDonald Valley harbors the park's largest lake and some of its densest and oldest temperate rainforest. Crisscrossed by a number of popular trails, including the wheelchair-accessible **Trail of the Cedars**, the area is popular with drive-in campers, who frequent the Sprague Creek and Avalanche Creek campgrounds, and winter cross-country skiers who use McDonald Creek and the Going-to-the-Sun Rd as seasonal skiing trails. On the south shores of the lake, the rustic **Lake McDonald Lodge**, first built in 1895 as the Glacier Hotel, is the park's oldest hotel. Replaced by a newer Swiss-style structure in 1913, before any roads had penetrated the region, the current lodge's imposing entrance was built facing the lake, meaning modern-day road travelers must enter via the back door.

Apgar

In contrast to townsites in Canadian national parks, **Apgar village** is miniscule, supporting little more than a couple of lodges,

PARKITECTURE

A loose term used to describe a unique form of rural architecture known as 'National Park Service Rustic,' parkitecture was first formulated in the US in the 1870s in response to a growing public interest in wilderness areas and their role in the nation's recreation and education. Designed to provide top-class visitor facilities without infringing upon the fragile natural environment, pioneering parkitecture buildings were first constructed in the early 1900s under the auspices of railroad companies in newly established national parks such as Yellowstone and Yosemite.

Glacier's early experimentation with the style came soon after the park's inception in 1910 with the construction of the Glacier Park Lodge, a 400-room rustic beauty – 191m (628 feet) long and four stories high – with a vast open-plan lobby supported by two dozen 900-year-old Douglas fir timbers imported from Washington State. Adorned with Native American art and finished in attractive local stone, the building was designed to bring the feel of the forest into the hotel where tourists, park rangers and Blackfeet chiefs gathered nightly around a huge crackling fireplace.

Quickly absorbing the new architectural zeitgeist, other Glacier lodges at Many Glacier and Lake McDonald soon followed, each employing similar irregular handcrafted designs reminiscent of popular Swiss and art-and-crafts architectural styles. Designed to blend in with the natural environment as much as they were to catch the eye, the lodges were located in the park's scenic hot spots, allowing privileged guests a stunning snapshot of the dramatic landscapes that the region had to offer.

Aside from two motor inns that were added in the 1940s, little has changed architecturally in Glacier since the groundbreaking days of the early 20th century. Indeed, not only have the historic lodges successfully stood the test of time, they have also managed to protect their old-fashioned rustic image, refusing to allow such modern-day luxuries as TVs, private phones, air-conditioning or elevators.

a gift shop and a restaurant, all of which nestle quietly on the western shores of Lake McDonald. Dimon Apgar, for whom the settlement is named, built the first road from Belton to the lake in 1895, allowing a handful of early homesteaders to make this choice spot their dream home. The original **schoolhouse**, dating from 1915, is now a gift shop.

SOUTH OF GOING-TO-THE-SUN ROAD
Two Medicine Valley

Before the building of the Going-to-the-Sun Rd in the 1930s, the Two Medicine Valley was one of the park's most accessible hubs, situated a mere 19.2km (12 miles) by horseback from the Great Northern Railroad and the newly inaugurated Glacier Park Lodge. Famous for its healthy bear population and deeply imbued with Native American legends, the region is less visited these days, though it has lost none of its haunting beauty. Hikers can grab a picnic at the historic **Two Medicine Campstore**, once the dining hall for the now defunct Two Medicine Chalets and the venue for one of President FD Roosevelt's famous 'fireside chats.' Towering authoritatively over sublime **Two Medicine Lake** is the distinctive hulk of **Rising Wolf Mountain**, named for Canadian-turned-Peigan Indian, Hugh Monroe, who was the first white person to explore the region in the mid-19th century.

A few miles to the northwest, 2444m (8020ft) **Triple Divide Peak** marks the hydrologic apex of the North American continent. Empty a bucket of water on its summit and it will run into three separate oceans: the Pacific, the Atlantic and the Arctic.

NORTH OF GOING-TO-THE-SUN ROAD
North Fork Valley

Glacier's most isolated nook is a riot of grassy meadows and regenerated forest that protects the park's only pack of wolves and hides some of its best backcountry trails and campgrounds. North and east of Polebridge, bone-rattling roads lead to a couple of secluded lakes. Due east, **Bowman Lake** is Lake McDonald without the tourists, an ideal spot to enjoy a picnic, launch a canoe, or scan the horizon for wildlife. Meanwhile, 22.5km (14 miles) further north, **Kintla Lake** is a secret haven for solitude-seeking fishermen. Stalwart hikers venture out from here along the backcountry Boulder Pass Trail.

Many Glacier Valley

Dubbed the 'heart and soul' of Glacier by park purists, Many Glacier Valley is a magical mélange of lush meadows and shimmering lakes, where the pièce de résistance is the strategically positioned **Many Glacier Hotel**, constructed by the Great Northern Railroad in 1915. Known traditionally for its 'rivers of ice' – though there aren't quite so *many* of them these days – the valley nurtures some of the park's most accessible glaciers, including the rapidly shrinking Grinnell Glacier, first spotted by conservationist and naturalist George Bird Grinnell (see the boxed text, p213) in 1885. Other curiosities include **Iceberg Lake**, where the turquoise waters are fed from a surrounding snowfield, and the **Ptarmigan Tunnel**, a 56m (183ft) corridor through the rock, blasted out of the mountain in the 1930s to cut several kilometers off the hike to Belly River Valley (an environmental anomaly that would win few backers today).

HIKING

EASY HIKES

You don't have to be an aspiring Everest climber to enjoy the well-tramped trails and scenic byways of Glacier National Park. Indeed, two of the park's most popular hikes are wheelchair accessible while countless more can be easily tackled by parents with children, vacationing couch potatoes or nervous novices.

TRAIL OF THE CEDARS

Duration 30 minutes round-trip
Distance 1.3km (0.8 miles)
Difficulty easy
Start/Finish Avalanche Creek shuttle stop
Nearest Facilities Lake McDonald Valley (p206)
Transportation Going-to-the-Sun Rd shuttle
Summary A wheelchair- and stroller-accessible hike that's on raised boardwalks and offers a tantalizing taste of the Lake McDonald Valley's dense old-growth cedar forest.

A must for families with strollers and travelers in wheelchairs, this easily negotiated interpretive trail (Map p200) is a worthwhile pit stop for any time-poor traveler with an interest in the park's diverse natural ecosystems. Plunging almost immediately into the McDonald Valley's dense old-growth rainforest, the trail starts next to the Avalanche Creek campground on a raised boardwalk that carries hikers past springy moss, dripping ferns and 30m-tall (100ft) Douglas fir and Red Cedar trees. For visitors from Washington or British Columbia it is a scene more redolent of the Pacific Northwest than glacier-sculpted northern Montana.

Various perches en route encourage quiet contemplation, including a strategically positioned bench overlooking swift-flowing **Avalanche Creek** at the loop's turnaround. Meander slowly back to your car or bus on the opposite side of the creek on a pine cone–covered paved path.

AVALANCHE LAKE TRAIL

Duration 2½ hours round-trip
Distance 6.4km (4 miles)
Difficulty easy–moderate
Start/Finish Avalanche Creek shuttle stop
Nearest Facilities Lake McDonald Valley (p206)
Transportation Going-to-the-Sun Rd shuttle
Summary A pleasant, family-friendly stroll through shady forest to the park's most accessible alpine lake, replete with glacier-strewn boulders and cascading waterfalls.

A handy stop on the new shuttle route, the Avalanche Lake Trail provides quick and easy access to one of Glacier National Park's most gorgeous alpine lakes – and you don't have to bust a gut to get there. As a result, the trail is invariably heaving in peak season with everyone from flip flop–wearing families to stick-wielding seniors making boldly for the tree line. But don't be deceived; while the walk itself might be relatively easy, it is highly recommended you come prepared with bottled water, layered clothing and the appropriate footwear.

Starting from the Going-to-the-Sun Rd, the path meanders for 800m (0.5 miles) along the paved Trail of the Cedars to a signposted three-way junction. Bear right here, diverting into thick rainforest and follow the path along a scenic section of narrow **Avalanche Creek**. Shaded from the summer sun by mature, old-growth cedar and western hemlock trees, the forest floor is strewn with huge moss-covered boulders, the remnants of a once-powerful glacier.

After half an hour of hopping over tree roots and fording trickling creeks, you'll emerge, as if by magic, at luminous **Avalanche Lake**, a mirror-like circle of water fed by cascading waterfalls and overlooked by the steep, rocky escarpments of Bearhat Mountain. The surrounding scenery is sublime and well worth the moderate 3.2km (2-mile) march to get here. Relax on the lakeshore with a pair of binoculars, keeping a lookout for birds and other wildlife (there's a pit toilet nearby) before heading back down.

squirrels and mountain goats are not shy along this trail. The elusive ptarmigan, whose brown feathers turn white in winter, also lives nearby. Up-close mountain views include Clement Mountain north of the trail and Reynolds Mountain in the southeast.

A few hundred metres before the **overlook**, you will cross the Continental Divide – probably without realizing it – before your first stunning glimpse of deep-blue Hidden Lake (and a realization of what all the fuss is about), bordered by mountain peaks and rocky cliffs; look out for glistening Sperry Glacier visible to the south.

Hearty souls continue on to Hidden Lake via a 2.4km (1.5-mile) trail from the overlook, steeply descending 233m (765ft).

HIDDEN LAKE OVERLOOK TRAIL

Duration 2 hours round-trip
Distance 5km (3.2 miles)
Difficulty easy–moderate
Start/Finish Logan Pass Visitor Center
Nearest Facilities Logan Pass (p206)
Transportation Going-to-the-Sun Rd shuttle
Summary An über-popular hike that's part boardwalk and part path, bisecting lush meadows and melting snowfields before descending to a translucent glacial lake.

SUN POINT TO VIRGINIA FALLS

Duration 4 hours round-trip
Distance 11.5km (7 miles)
Difficulty easy
Start/Finish Sun Point shuttle stop
Nearest Town St Mary (p239)
Transportation Going-to-the-Sun Rd shuttle
Summary Shelter from the famous St Mary Lake winds on this shady but sun-dappled trail that takes you to a tempestuous trio of waterfalls.

For many Glacier visitors this relatively straightforward hike (Map p200) is the one occasion in which they step out of their cars and take a sniff of the sweet-scented alpine air for which the area is famous. Starting at the busy Logan Pass Visitor Center, the hike ascends gradually along a raised boardwalk (with steps) through expansive alpine meadows replete with monkeyflower and pink laurel. Melting snowfields add a mild challenge for those who decided, misguidedly, to wear flip flops but, rain or shine, this trail is a hit with everyone – from tiny babies to spry septuagenarians – and the people-watching is almost as interesting as the wildlife.

After about 1km (0.6 miles), the boardwalk gives way to a gravelly dirt path. If the snow has melted, the diversity of grasses and wildflowers in the meadows around you is breathtaking. Resident trees include old Engelmann spruce, subalpine fir and whitebark pine. Hoary marmots, ground

Handily served by the free park shuttle, the myriad of trailheads along the eastern side of the Going-to-the-Sun Rd offers plenty of short interlinking hikes, a number of which can be pooled together to make up a decent morning or afternoon ramble.

This particular variation (Map p200) starts at the Sun Point shuttle stop, where you can track down a 400m (0.25-mile) trail to a rocky (and often windy) **overlook** perched above sparkling St Mary Lake. In the 1910s the Great Northern Railroad built some of Glacier's earliest and showiest chalets here in an accommodation chain that stretched from Many Glacier to the Sperry and Granite Park Chalets. Falling into neglect after WWII, the Sun Point chalets were demolished in 1949, though the view remains timeless.

Take the path west through sun-flecked forest along the lake toward shady **Baring Falls**, at 1km (0.6 miles), for a respite from the sun and/or wind. After admiring the

GLACIER NATIONAL PARK

gushing cascades, cross the river and continue on the opposite bank to link up with the busy **St Mary Falls Trail** that joins from the right. Undemanding switchbacks lead up through the trees to the valley's most picturesque falls, set amid colorful foliage on St Mary River. Beyond here, the trail branches along Virginia Creek, past a narrow gorge, to mist-shrouded (and quieter) **Virginia Falls** at the foot of a hanging valley.

Retrace your steps to Sun Point for the full-length hike or, if your legs start to tire, short cut to the St Mary Falls or Sunrift Gorge shuttle stops (follow the signs) and hop onto a bus.

DAY HIKES

Sally forth on a day hike and you'll soon leave the crowds and commotion of Logan Pass and Lake McDonald far behind. Classics like the relatively flat but spectacular Highline Trail still see a lot of foot traffic, but delve deeper into Two Medicine Valley or the isolated North Fork region and serendipitous solitude is yours for the taking.

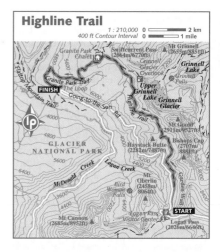

Highline Trail

1 : 210,000
400 ft Contour Interval

HIGHLINE TRAIL

Duration 7½ hours one-way
Distance 18.7km (11.6 miles)
Difficulty moderate
Start Logan Pass Visitor Center
Finish The Loop
Nearest Facilities Logan Pass (p206)
Transportation Going-to-the-Sun Rd shuttle
Summary A vista-laden extravaganza that cuts underneath the Garden Wall ridge just below the Continental Divide to the famous Granite Park Chalet.

A Glacier classic, the Highline Trail cuts like an elongated scar across the famous Garden Wall, a sharp, glacier-carved ridge that forms part of the Continental Divide and the summer slopes of which are covered with an abundance of alpine plants and wildflowers. The stupendous views here are some of the best in the park and, with little elevation gain throughout its 12km (7.6-mile) course, the treats come with minimal sweat.

Cutting immediately into the side of the mountain (there are handrails for those with vertigo), the trail presents stunning early views of the Going-to-the-Sun Rd and snowcapped Heaven's Peak. Look out for the toy-sized red 'jammer' buses motoring up the valley below you and marvel as the sun catches the white foaming waters of 152m (500ft) Bird Woman Falls opposite.

After its vertiginous start, the trail is flat for a mile or two before gently ascending to a ridge that connects Haystack Butte with Mt Gould at the 5.6km (3.5-mile) mark. From here on it's fairly flat as you bisect the mountainside on your way toward the Granite Park Chalet. At approximately 10.9km (6.8 miles), with the chalet in sight, a spur path (on your right) offers gluttons for punishment the option of climbing up less than 1.6km (1 mile) to the **Grinnell Glacier Overlook** for a peek over the Continental Divide.

The **Granite Park Chalet** (p224) appears at around 12km (7.6 miles), providing a welcome haven for parched throats and tired feet (stock up at the chalet on chocolate bars and soda or water).

TOP FIVE PEACE PARK HIKES

GLACIER NATIONAL PARK

From here you have three options: you can retrace your steps back to Logan Pass; head for Swiftcurrent Pass and the Many Glacier Valley; or descend 6.4km (4 miles) to the Loop, where you can pick up a shuttle bus to all points on the Going-to-the-Sun Rd.

RED EAGLE LAKE TRAIL

Duration 8 hours round-trip
Distance 24.5km (15.2 miles)
Difficulty moderate
Start/Finish 1913 Historic Ranger Station
Nearest Facilities St Mary Lake (p206)
Transportation Going-to-the-Sun Rd shuttle
Summary A long but undemanding ramble through forests damaged by the 2006 Red Eagle Fire to a luminous glacial lake, famous for its fishing potential.

Scene of a recent devastating forest fire – the Red Eagle Fire which blazed through 12,950 hectares (32,000 acres) in July and August 2006 – this long, but relatively straightforward, out-and-back hike (Map p200) leads to a serene alpine lake considered by anglers to be one of the best in the park for trout fishing. Meadows, forests and mountains line the route, though it is the landscape-altering effects of the fire and its aftermath that provide the most vivid distractions throughout the journey.

The trail starts out from a dirt road near the northeastern edge of St Mary Lake in a small parking lot next to the **1913 Historic Ranger Station**. After approximately 1.6km (1 mile), the shorter Beaver Pond Loop heads back to the historic ranger station but, keep right, and you'll eventually emerge into grassy meadows that are colored with wildflowers. Red Eagle Mountain, home of mountain goats, rises ahead, while Curly Bear Mountain and Kakitos Mountain look down on the trail from the southeast.

At about 6.4km (4 miles), cross a suspension bridge over Red Eagle Creek and continue to the St Mary Lake Trail junction. Keep left here and you'll soon cross another bridge over the creek from where it's a quick march to the lake.

The lovely **Red Eagle Lake** is a pleasant hidden oasis. From the lake, view the mountains that rise southeast on the Continental Divide, including the geographically important Triple Divide Peak.

Good bird-watching possibilities exist on the trail and at the lake; you may encounter thrushes, warblers and loons. Grizzlies are also known commuters near this trail. Look for scat and other signs of their presence. To head back, retrace your steps toward the trailhead.

SIYEH PASS TRAIL

Duration 6 hours one way
Distance 16.6km (10.3 miles)
Difficulty moderate–demanding
Start Siyeh Bend shuttle stop
Finish Sunrift Gorge shuttle stop
Nearest Town St Mary (p239)
Transportation Going-to-the-Sun Rd shuttle
Summary An old-timer's favorite that tracks up through expansive alpine meadows before descending to the grotto-like Sunrift Gorge.

A popular hike among Glacier old-timers, this trail (Map p200) starts and finishes on the Going-to-the-Sun Rd with a handy shuttle ready to bus you back to the start point. It also bisects colorful Preston Park, one of the region's prettiest and most jubilant alpine meadows.

At 4.3km (2.7 miles) from the Siyeh Bend starting point, stay right at the junction with the Peigan Pass Trail, heading directly for the flower-adorned oasis of **Preston Park**. In another mile or so you'll reach **Siyeh Pass**, with an elevation of 2512m (8240ft), via a series of switchbacks. Once there, brave the stiff winds for some extraordinary panoramic views. Mt Siyeh sits prominently to the northwest. Look for a **pile of rocks** to the right of the trail. It marks a spot where a bell once stood (it was removed for scrap metal during WWII) and was rung by passersby on horseback.

The second part of the hike heads down through more switchbacks toward Sunrift Gorge. In early summer, large snowfields covering the trail can make for a tricky descent. After traversing alternate scree and snow, the open terrain gives way to a firmer footing as you enter sections of alpine forest.

Up on your right, Sexton Glacier lies in the 'V' between Going-to-the-Sun Mountain and Matahpi Peak. Continue toward St Mary Lake, part of which is seen in the distance. As you descend further, lusher plant life includes huckleberry and thimbleberry patches.

The path inches closer to and then joins beautiful **Baring Creek**, with rushing streams and falls supported by red rock. You'll eventually come out at **Sunrift Gorge** on the Going-to-the-Sun Rd, a popular tourist hangout and journey's end.

ICEBERG LAKE TRAIL

Duration 5½ hours round-trip
Distance 14.5km (9 miles)
Difficulty easy–moderate
Start/Finish Swiftcurrent Motor Inn
Nearest Facilities Many Glacier Valley (p208)
Transportation East Side shuttle
Summary A well-trodden, wildlife-studded trail through relatively open terrain to the unique and otherworldly Iceberg Lake.

Famed for the bobbing bergs that float like miniature ice cubes in its still waters all summer long, the Iceberg Lake hike has long been a classic Glacier National Park pilgrimage. The popularity of the hike is understandable. Enclosed in a deep glacial cirque and surrounded on three sides by stunning 914m (3000ft) vertical walls, the

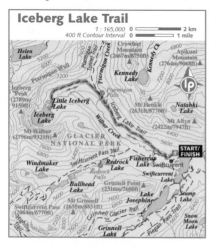

Iceberg Lake Trail

1 : 165,000
400 ft Contour Interval

lake is one of the most impressive sights anywhere in the Rockies. The 366m (1200ft) ascent to get there is gentle, and the approach is mostly at or above the tree line, affording awesome views.

Wildflowers fans will go ga-ga in the meadows near the lake. The Iceberg and Ptarmigan Trailhead is just past the Swiftcurrent Motor Inn. Bears are often sighted on this trail so check at the ranger station before setting out and take all of the usual precautions.

Starting steeply, the trail packs most of its elevation gain into the first few kilometers. But once you emerge onto the scrubby slopes above Many Glacier the gradient is barely perceptible. After 3.2km (2 miles) the path enters a small section of mature forest and arrives at Ptarmigan Creek, crossed by a footbridge, just upstream from **Ptarmigan Falls**. Here you climb gently through pine to the Ptarmigan Tunnel Trail junction, which heads right.

Continuing toward Iceberg Lake, you'll fall upon the first of several beautiful meadows under **Ptarmigan Wall**. Descend for a short distance to cross Iceberg Creek via a footbridge, and then climb up past **Little Iceberg Lake** before dropping down to the shores of your hallowed destination, the icy-blue cirque lake.

Iceberg Lake is 45.7m (150ft) deep and about 1.2km (0.75 miles) across; the granite walls average 914m (3000ft) in height, easily on a par with the big walls of Yosemite. The glacier is now inactive but, as the lake lies in the shadows on the north side of Mt Wilbur, the area remains cool all through summer.

SWIFTCURRENT PASS TRAIL

Duration 6 hours one way
Distance 12km (7.6 miles)
Difficulty moderate–demanding
Start/Finish Swiftcurrent Motor Inn
Nearest Facilities Many Glacier Valley (p208)
Transportation East Side shuttle
Summary A pleasant meander through the Many Glacier Valley, followed by a steep climb up to the Continental Divide.

This popular trail (Map p200) departs from the west side of the Swiftcurrent Motor Inn

GEORGE BIRD GRINNELL

Anthropologist, naturalist and enthusiastic student of Native American culture, George Bird Grinnell was an eco-warrior before his time and harbored influential friends in all the right places, including the White House.

Born in Brooklyn, New York in 1849, Grinnell studied zoology at Yale University and in 1874 he was chosen to accompany Lt Colonel George Custer (two years before his 'Last Stand') on an expedition to South Dakota's Black Hills as the party naturalist. Gravitating soon afterwards to the position of mineralogist at newly formed Yellowstone National Park, Grinnell became a leading conservationist in the American West, traveling extensively throughout the region and discovering, in 1885, the glacier in modern-day Glacier National Park that still bears his name. Indeed, so impressed was Grinnell by the mountains of northwest Montana that he christened them the 'Crown of the Continent,' and vexed repeatedly over how the area could best be protected from encroaching development.

Befriending a local Montanan rebel and adopted Blackfeet tribal member called James Willard Schultz, Grinnell made countless return visits to the Glacier region between 1880 and 1900, offering aid to the beleaguered Native Americans and gathering important data about the region's diverse flora and fauna. In return the Blackfeet treated him as one of their own and christened him with the honorary name, 'Fisher Cap.'

Using his influential position as editor of *Forest and Stream* magazine, and lobbying congress through powerful friends such as soon-to-be-president Teddy Roosevelt, Grinnell battled tirelessly to protect the area from commercial mining interests. In 1900 the Glacier region was declared a forest reserve, but not content with the compromise, Grinnell pushed for even greater protective measures. His efforts were rewarded 10 years later when President Taft signed the historic bill that established Glacier as America's eighth national park.

When Grinnell died in 1938, aged 89, the *New York Times* posthumously dubbed him the 'father of American conservation.' To proud Montanans, however, he will always be the granddaddy of the park he fought so hard to create.

parking lot and can be linked up with the Loop or Highline Trails (p210) to make an arduous one-day, or slightly less arduous two-day, hike.

Easing in slowly, the first 6.4km (4 miles) of the trail are relatively easy, bisecting low lodgepole forest sprinkled with aspen, the result of dynamic regrowth following the 1936 Heaven's Peak Fire. Looking around, you'll see the highest visible summit, Mt Wilbur, to the northwest, jagged Grinnell Mountain to the south, and Swiftcurrent Mountain, which this path eventually ascends, to the southwest.

Hiking through the potentially hot open terrain, you will soon find relief amid the foliage, including Englemann spruce, subalpine fir, fireweed, maple and the shade-giving quaking aspen. Wildflower spotters will enjoy colorful landscapes dotted with forget-me-nots, paintbrush, harebell, yellow columbine and Siberian chive. Watch for stinging nettle along the way and make plenty of noise to ward off Many Glacier's many bears.

Less than 2.4km (1.5 miles) into the trail, the path brushes the northern tip of **Red Rock Lake**, and the waterfalls become visible in the distance. Beavers are active along streams in this valley; look out for beaver lodges on the other side of the lake. At 5.3km (3.3 miles) you'll hit **Bullhead Lake** and from here you'll begin a 4.8km (3-mile) climb up to Swiftcurrent Pass, with an elevation of 2064m (6770ft), gaining 610m (2000ft) in the process. The switchbacks on the ascent are numerous and the path, which cuts sharply into the mountainside, becomes ever more vertiginous as you climb (if you suffer badly from vertigo, give this part a miss). The Continental Divide at **Swiftcurrent Pass** is marked by an unruly pile of rocks surrounded by dwarf trees. For a far better view, take the spur trail up a further set of switchbacks to the **Swiftcurrent Lookout** for one of the park's most tower-topping views. Returning to the pass, either retrace your steps, or head 1.5km (0.9 miles) down to the Granite Park Chalet to link up with other trails.

DAWSON-PITAMAKIN LOOP

Duration 8 hours round-trip
Distance 30km (18.8 miles)
Difficulty demanding
Start/Finish North Shore trailhead, Two Medicine Lake
Nearest Facilities Two Medicine Valley (p207)
Transportation East Side shuttle
Summary Cross the Continental Divide twice on this strenuous but spectacular hike along exposed mountain ridges that provide prime habitat for grizzly bears.

This lengthy hike can be squeezed into a one-day itinerary, if you're fit and up for it. Alternatively, it can be tackled over two or three days with sleepovers at the No Name Lake and Oldman Lake backcountry campgrounds (permit required). Blessed with two spectacular mountain passes and teeming with myriad plant and animal life, it is often touted by park rangers as being one of Glacier's hiking highlights.

As the hike is a loop, departing from the North Shore trailhead on **Two Medicine Lake**, you must first decide which direction you want to go. Progressing clockwise and tackling Dawson Pass first packs the 915m (3000ft) elevation gain into one sharp segment. Head anticlockwise and the same ascent is more drawn out. Walking clockwise, you'll be entering prime grizzly bear country (rangers have actually used it as a study

area) so be on guard and make plenty of noise. Around 8km (5 miles) in you'll reach **No Name Lake**, a prime fishing spot. The trail ascends steeply from here, gaining 366m (1200ft) in 3.2km (2 miles) during a pulse-racing climb to **Dawson Pass**, an exposed col notorious for its high winds – 160km/h (100mph) has been recorded. Follow the narrow, sheer-sided path north along the Continental Divide, taking care with your footing amid stunning high-country views. You'll cross the divide again at **Cut Bank** before descending to **Pitamakin Pass** and **Oldman Lake**, a gorgeous blue body of water encased in a cirque and framed by jagged peaks.

From the lake the hike descends into the **Dry Fork Drainage**, through fields of huckleberries interspersed with clumps of dense forest. Look out for diggings, scat and other evidence of bear activity as you make for Two Medicine Lake and your starting point.

QUARTZ LAKES LOOP

Duration 7 hours round-trip
Distance 20.5km (12.8 miles)
Difficulty moderate
Start/Finish Bowman Lake Campground
Nearest Facilities North Fork Valley (p207)
Summary Lakes, solitude and scenery are three of the North Fork Valley's primary draws, and all are on display during this multifarious hike.

Remote and hard to get to without a car, the wild North Fork Valley is a solitude seeker's utopia. The Quartz Lakes Loop is one of the area's most diverse trails, a hiking staple renowned for its wonderful scenery and close-up views of a forest still regenerating after recent (natural) fires.

From the trailhead, cross Bowman Creek before beginning a gradual ascent along the shores of **Bowman Lake**. After 1.6km (1 mile) or so you'll start a more precipitous climb up to **Cerulean Ridge**, with an elevation of 1676m (5500ft), where you'll be afforded fantastic views of a triumvirate of beautiful lakes – Quartz Lake, tiny Middle Quartz Lake and Lower Quartz Lake – shimmering like tinfoil below. The path drops down to the west side of **Quartz Lake**, passing in and out of forest and providing graphic evidence of the effects of the 1988 Red Bench Fire.

GLACIER NATIONAL PARK

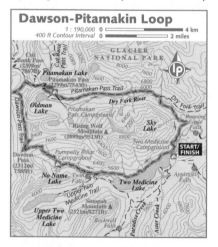

Dawson-Pitamakin Loop

1 : 190,000
400 ft Contour Interval
0 — 4 km
0 — 2 miles

Once in the valley, skirt the edges of all three lakes via a clearly marked path ending up, after 5km (3 miles), in a backcountry campground at the south end of Lower Quartz Lake. From here it's a 2.4km (1.5-mile) ascent to the crest of Cerulean Ridge – for the second time – before you drop back down to Bowman Creek.

BACKCOUNTRY HIKES
Backcountry hiking is what Glacier's all about and hitting the high trails will quickly introduce intrepid travelers to a side of the park that few other visitors see.

GUNSIGHT PASS TRAIL

Duration 2 days one way
Distance 32km (20 miles)
Difficulty moderate–demanding
Start Jackson Glacier Overlook
Finish Lake McDonald Lodge
Nearest Facilities Logan Pass (p206)
Transportation Going-to-the-Sun Rd shuttle
Summary A great introduction to Glacier's backcountry, with tremendous views and abundant wildlife, plus the opportunity to stay in the park's historic Sperry Chalet.

Truly bionic hikers knock out this spectacular trail in one day but, with copious snowfields, glaciers and lakes sprinkled along the 32km (20-mile) route that straddles the lofty Continental Divide, two days is a more appropriate time-span. The trail is doable in either direction, but most hikers kick off at the Jackson Glacier Overlook on the Going-to-the-Sun Rd (a designated free shuttle stop) and head west toward the Lake McDonald Lodge. If you are planning to spend the night at the historic Sperry Chalet (p224) en route, you'll need to book your space well in advance (a move that will save you carrying camping equipment).

Day 1
On the first day – six to nine hours, and 21.7km (13.6 miles) – follow the trail southeast through fir and spruce forest until it stumbles upon Reynolds Creek. The path follows the creek past Deadwood Falls to a junction with the Gunsight Pass Trail at 2km (1.3 miles); take the trail on the right. It crosses a bridge past Reynolds Creek Campground, and then heads alongside the St Mary River. At 6.4km (4 miles), a junction offers a 1km (0.6-mile) trail to Florence Falls.

Carry on up the valley below Citadel and Fusilade Mountains (east and west respectively), taking in views of glaciers clinging to a high ridge between Blackfoot Mountain and Mt Jackson. Soon after the Gunsight Lake Campground, 9.6km (6 miles) in, a suspension bridge traverses St Mary River and leads up numerous switchbacks through cow parsnip and alder shrub.

In all, it's a two- to three-hour hike from the campground to **Gunsight Pass**, with an elevation of 2117m (6946ft) on the Continental

GLACIER NATIONAL PARK

Gunsight Pass Trail

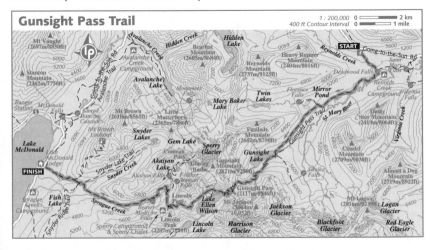

Divide. Reaching the pass involves walking over cliff ledges high above the lake, but the trail is broad. A basic emergency shelter (day-use only) stands on this narrow saddle.

Steeply descending switchbacks lead to the north shore of **Lake Ellen Wilson**, a spectacular alpine lake lying in a deep trough ringed by sheer, glaciated rock walls. The trail continues around the lake's western shore, passing above Lake Ellen Wilson Campground.

Go up the slope to a high shelf overlooking Lincoln Lake. The trail turns gradually to cross the apex of the hike, **Lincoln Pass**, with an elevation of 2149m (7050ft), just north of Lincoln Peak, then winds its way down past Sperry Campground. Four scenic sites here overlook Lake McDonald far below. Mountain goats regularly visit the camp, so always use the pit toilet.

Close by is the historic **Sperry Chalet**.

Day 2

On this day – 2½ to three hours, 10.3km (6.4 miles) – drop past Sperry Glacier Trail and across small Sprague Creek. The trail leads down into fir-spruce forest, past **Beaver Medicine Falls**. It continues 4km (2.5 miles) downvalley to cross Snyder Creek on a footbridge. You'll pass turnoffs to Fish Lake, Snyder Lakes and Mt Brown Lookout as the trail descends through a mossy forest of cedar, hemlock, grand fir, larch and yew to Going-to-the-Sun Rd. Watch out for horse droppings covering the trail; it's a favorite with riders from the Lake McDonald Corral.

CONTINENTAL DIVIDE TRAIL

Duration southern section 5–6 days, northern section 4–5 days

Distance southern section 104km (65 miles), northern section 72km (45 miles)

Difficulty demanding

Start Marias Pass

Finish Goat Haunt

Nearest Town East Glacier (p240)

Summary The northernmost leg of one of America's greatest long-distance trails hits Big Sky country as it closely tracks the imposing Continental Divide.

One of the highlights of the 5000km (3100-mile) Continental Divide Trail (CDT) that

runs from Mexico up to Canada, Glacier National Park guards the final 176km (110-mile) segment of the route, from Marias Pass in the south to the trail's northern terminus at Goat Haunt on Upper Waterton Lake. Although few people tackle the whole trail in a given season, plenty combine smaller sections of its well-marked paths to craft a decent backpacking trip.

Southern Section

From Marias Pass the route tracks the eastern side of the Continental Divide for 136km (85 miles), diverting out of the park briefly into East Glacier at 22.5km (14 miles), which offers plenty of accommodation options for a first-night stopover. Day two takes an 11.3km (7-mile) path up to aptly named **Scenic Point** for bird's-eye views of the Two Medicine Valley. Drop via copious switchbacks 4.8km (3 miles) to the Two Medicine Campground beside the lake at 38.5km (24 miles). Overnighting in one of Glacier's most pristine spots, start day three by heading up to within rock-pitching distance of the Continental Divide at **Pitamakan Pass** before swinging north toward **Morning Star Lake** and its adjoining backcountry campground at 56km (35 miles). On day four get an early start for your climb up to **Triple Divide Pass**, which has an elevation of 2255m (7397ft), just below the namesake three-sided peak that stands at the meeting point of the US's only tri-oceanic divide. End day four, 84km (53 miles), at **Red Eagle Lake**, which boasts two campgrounds and is a prized fishing spot with in-the-know anglers. On the fifth and final day follow the Red Eagle Lake Trail north before turning west and tracking the shores of windy St Mary Lake for 19km (12 miles) to **St Mary Falls**. From here it's another 2km (1.3 miles) to the trail's juncture with the Going-to-the-Sun Rd at the Gunsight Pass Trailhead shuttle stop at 104km (65 miles).

Northern Section

Starting at the Gunsight Pass Trailhead shuttle stop on the Going-to-the-Sun Rd, skirt the lower edge of Going-to-the-Sun Mountain on your way to joining up with the **Peigan Pass Trail**. Heading due north and crossing the flower-covered meadows of **Preston Park**, the climb to the pass is long but rewarding, winding around the base of **Cataract Mountain**. From your day's high-point, it's a 13.3km (8.3-mile) descent into the Many Glacier Valley at 21km (13 miles) via **Morning Eagle Falls** and the Grinnell Lake Trail. Overnight here in a hotel, motel or campground. Day two involves a 12km (7.6-mile) ascent to **Swiftcurrent Pass** and your first crossing of the Continental Divide since Marias Pass on US 2. At 33.5km (21 miles) treat yourself to a night at the **Granite Park Chalet** (p222) on the Pacific side, where spectacular sunsets are famous (reservations should be made in advance). Day three is a 19km (12-mile) ramble back over the Continental Divide to the **Fifty Mountain Campground** (Map p200), at 53km (33 miles), an area named for the 50 peaks that tower over its colorful alpine meadows. Look out for evidence of the 1998 Kootenai Fire and 2003 Trapper Fire en route. The final day is a vista-laden 19km (12-mile) hike down to Goat Haunt, at 72km (45 miles), on Upper Waterton Lake at the CDT's northern terminus, past moose-viewing opportunities at **Kootenai Lakes** and in the shadow of Glacier's highest point, glowering Mt Cleveland.

BIKING

Glacier National Park presents a dilemma to aspiring cyclists. While the region's narrow, precipitous roads and punishing 6% gradients offer a Tour de France–style challenge to hard-core biking enthusiasts, heavy traffic and a blanket ban on mountain bikes on all park trails leave many two-wheeled travelers questioning if the trip is worth it.

The answer depends on your flexibility. The blue riband for many Glacier visitors is an ascent of the 80km (50-mile) Going-to-the-Sun Rd with its spectacular vistas and copious twists and turns but, with the road officially shut to cyclists between 11am and 4pm daily (mid-June to Labor Day), you'll need to be open-minded with your schedule. If you do decide to take the plunge (and it's a memorable ride), start early, pack plenty of water and take extreme care on the long and potentially precarious descents. From a physical point of view, it is easier to start your ride in St Mary and tackle the climb east–west.

In contrast to many Canadian national parks, Glacier has only one designated bike

path, running 4km (2.5 miles) from West Glacier village to the Apgar transit center via Apgar village. The park's free Going-to-the-Sun Rd shuttles currently have limited bike-carrying potential.

The closest thing to a mountain-biking venture in the park is the Inside North Fork Rd (Glacier Rte 7) to Kintla Lake. Bikers craving trail rides should consider Waterton Lakes, which boasts four (p234).

You'll encounter plenty of colorfully clad cyclists just outside the park's eastern boundary, plying Hwys 49 and 89, on the edge of the Blackfeet Reservation. Inclines here are gentler, although the stiff winds off the adjacent prairies can be punishing.

Hiker-biker campgrounds are available at Apgar, Avalanche, Fish Creek, Many Glacier, Rising Sun, Sprague Creek, St Mary and Two Medicine Campgrounds. Rentals are available outside the park at **Glacier Cyclery** (☎ 406-862-6446; 326 2nd St, Whitefish; hybrid bike per day/week from US$25/125) – you can transport your bike from Whitefish to Glacier by train – or the **St Mary KOA Campground** (☎ 406-888-7800; per hr/day US$2.50/20).

DRIVING

Blessed with one of America's most spectacular roads, Glacier promises steely nerved motorists the drive of their life. Those less enthusiastic about crawling in second gear up gravity-defying chicanes can find solace in the park's less demanding back routes.

GOING-TO-THE-SUN ROAD

Duration 3 hours one way (with stops)
Distance 85km (53 miles)
Difficulty demanding
Start West Glacier
Finish St Mary
Nearest Town Apgar (p206)
Summary Quite literally, one of the greatest and most spectacular drives in the US.

Chiseled out of raw mountainside and punctuated by some of the sheerest and most vertiginous drop-offs in the United States, the vista-laden Going-to-the-Sun Rd is an engineering marvel without equal. In the circumstances, it is hardly surprising

Going-to-the-Sun Road Driving Tour

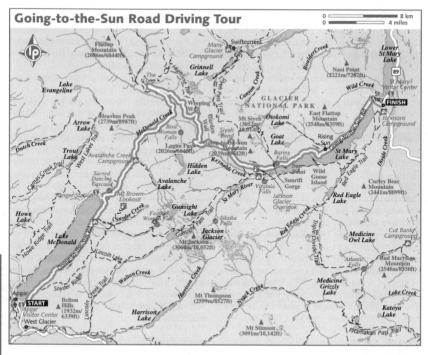

GLACIER NATIONAL PARK

that this 80km (50-mile) white-knuckle ride over some of the most hostile terrain in the Rockies is considered by many motorists to be the best drive in the country.

Giving few hints of the coming splendor, the road starts inauspiciously at the park's western entrance near Apgar village before tracking east alongside translucent **Lake McDonald**. Encased in dense rainforest and characterized by the famous Lake Mc-Donald Lodge, the valley here is lush and verdant, though a quick glance through the trees will highlight the graphic evidence of the destruction wreaked by the 2003 Robert fire on the opposite side of the water.

After tracking alongside McDonald Creek for approximately 16km (10 miles), the road begins its long, slow ascent to Logan Pass with a sharp turn to the southeast at the famous **Loop**, a hiking trailhead and the start of an increasingly precipitous climb toward the summit. Views here vary from amazing to even more amazing as the road cuts precariously into the **Garden Wall**, a 2743m (8999ft) granite arête that delineates the west and east regions of the park along the Conti-

nental Divide. Look out for **Bird Woman Falls** (p206) at 43km (27 miles) and the **Weeping Wall** (p206) at 46km (29 miles), as the gaping chasm to your right grows ever deeper.

Nearly everybody stops at 2026m (6646ft) **Logan Pass**, at 52km (32 miles), to browse the visitor center or stretch their legs amid alpine meadows on the popular Hidden Lake Overlook Trail (p209). Be forewarned: the Logan Pass parking lot can resemble a shopping-mall parking lot in July and August, particularly between 11am and 3pm.

Descending to the east the scenery almost grows in grandeur. At 58km (36 miles), you'll pass the well-positioned **Jackson Glacier Overlook** (p206), while a few clicks further on, you can sample narrow **Sunrift Gorge** near the shores of St Mary Lake. With an elevation of 2939m (9642ft), majestic **Going-to-the-Sun Mountain** – for which the road is named – is omnipresent to the north. **Wild Goose Island** is a tiny stub of land with a handful of lopsided trees that perches precariously in the middle of St Mary Lake, providing a perfect photo op for incurable camera-clickers. If you're in need of gifts or a bite to eat, **Rising Sun** has a store and the no-nonsense Two Dog Flats Mesquite Grill (p225).

The St Mary Visitor Center, at 85km (53 miles), on the lake's east end. is journey's end. The plains on this side of the park stretch east from St Mary to Minneapolis.

No vehicles over 6m (21ft) are allowed from east of Sun Point to Avalanche Creek.

THEODORE ROOSEVELT HIGHWAY

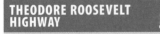

Duration 1 hour one way
Distance 92km (57 miles)
Difficulty moderate
Start East Glacier
Finish West Glacier
Nearest Town East Glacier (p240)
Summary If you enjoyed the Going-to-the-Sun Rd, this longer but quicker return spin along the park's southern border is an excellent way to get back to where you started.

This segment of US 2 between East Glacier and West Glacier doesn't get the traffic found on Going-to-the-Sun Rd. Part of the Theodore Roosevelt International Hwy, the road is well used by anglers and rafters who come for the access to Flathead River, which runs alongside much of the route.

From east to west, the highway departs the Blackfeet Indian Reservation a few miles past East Glacier, then enters Lewis & Clark National Forest. At 18km (11 miles) **Marias Pass**, with an elevation of 1590m (5213ft), once known as 'Backbone Pass' by the Blackfeet tribe, is the country's lowest pass over the Continental Divide. A memorial square here pays homage to notables, including Great Northern Railroad engineer John F Stevens and Theodore Roosevelt.

At 38km (24 miles) an access area to the Middle Fork of Flathead River is a popular jump-off for rafters, floaters and anglers. Around 800m (0.5 miles) later, the road enters Glacier National Park for just a few kilometers, taking in **Goat Lick Overlook**. Turn left into the parking lot, then walk down to a viewing platform, where you are likely to see salt-hungry mountain goats on rocks below. Bring binoculars.

GLACIER NATIONAL PARK

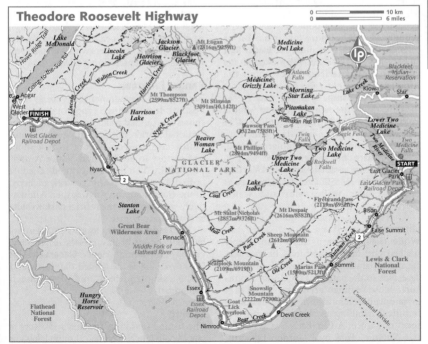

Theodore Roosevelt Highway

On the left at 45km (28 miles), a 400m (0.2-mile) road goes to the historic Izaak Walton Inn (p240). Several quiet **river access points** and **overlooks** dot the way to West Glacier, including Paola, Cascadilla and Moccasin Creeks.

OTHER ACTIVITIES

SUMMER ACTIVITIES
Canoeing & Kayaking
Glacier Park Boat Co (☎ 406-257-2426) rents out small boats (kayaks, canoes and rowboats) in the summer at Apgar, Lake McDonald, Two Medicine and Many Glacier for US$12 per hour. Motorboats, available at all but Many Glacier, go for US$22 per hour.

McDonald, Bowman, Swiftcurrent, Two Medicine and St Mary Lakes have launching ramps available for boats. Sailors might find St Mary Lake's winds to their liking. If bringing your own watercraft to Glacier, see p204.

See p205 for boat-tour information.

White-Water Rafting & Float Trips
The North and Middle Forks of the Flathead River are very popular with rafters, though all rafting tours take place on or outside the park's boundaries. **Glacier Raft Co** (☎ 406-888-5454, 800-235-6781; www.glacierraftco.com), in West Glacier village behind the Alberta Visitor Center, is arguably the most reputable raft company in the area. Prices for trips down the North Fork and Middle Fork of the Flathead River start at US$44/34 per adult/child for a half-day, and from US$76/53 for a full day. Similarly priced, **Great Northern Whitewater** (☎ 406-387-5340, 800-735-7897; www.gnwhitewater.com) and **Montana Raft Co** (☎ 406-387-5555, 800-521-7238; www.glacierguides.com) offer white-water and scenic tours.

Climbing
While Glacier's sharp ridges and steeply stacked cliff faces might look like a rock-climber's paradise, the opposite is often the case. Due to the nature of the Rocky Mountains' loose sedimentary rock – much of it metamorphosed mudstone and limestone – technical climbing in the park is not the sport of choice. *A Climber's Guide to Glacier National Park* by J Gordon Edwards,

available at visitor-center bookstores, runs through the area's basics. Climbers and adrenaline junkies can find solace in the tough, but nontechnical, ascent of the park's highest peak, Mt Cleveland, which is 3188m (10,461ft), or some more demanding high ridgeline walking or glacier traveling. Interested parties should enquire at visitor centers and ranger stations, and sign a register before setting out.

Horseback Riding
Another great way of traversing the park is to climb onto the back of a horse. You're in Montana, after all! Back in the old days, before the Going-to-the-Sun Rd was built, getting around by horse between the various tourist chalets was the primary means of transport. In fact, horses still run a regular supply line to the Sperry Chalet, a route that can be incorporated into an excellent day ride with **Swan Mountain Outfitters** (www.swanmountainoutfitters.com; ☺ early May-early Sep). The company offers a variety of other trips lasting from one hour (US$32) to all day (US$135) from its **Lake McDonald Corral** (☎ 406-888-5121), **Many Glacier Corral** (☎ 406-732-4203) and **Apgar Corral** (☎ 406-888-5010). It also staffs a small **ticket booth** (☎ 406-888-5557) in Apgar village, next to the visitor center. All trips are led by experienced wranglers who'll furnish you with plenty of entertaining tales.

Ranger Programs
Throughout the summer there are a whole host of free evening ranger talks, slide shows and guided walks available in Glacier National Park's hotels, campgrounds and visitor centers. Topics vary from culture and history to ecology and Native American Speaks. You'll find a printed schedule posted at all park visitor centers, or listed in the *Glacier Explorer* newspaper. Alternatively, you can scan the official park website at www.nps.gov/glac.

The **Glacier Institute** (☎ 406-755-1211) offers half-day or multi-day classes on history, geology and natural science. **Glacier Guides Inc** (☎ 800-521-7238) leads guided day hikes and backpacking trips from mid-May through September.

Fishing
The fishing season in streams and rivers is late May to late November, though lakes are

open for fishing year-round. While anglers explore easily accessible waters like Lake McDonald and St Mary Lake, it is some of the hike-in destinations that can prove the most tranquil getaways; try Hidden Lake, Oldman Lake or Red Eagle Lake. Glacier's store of fish includes cutthroat trout, northern pike, whitefish, burbot, kokanee salmon, brook trout, rainbow trout, mackinaw and grayling. No license is required though anglers should familiarize themselves with the general park regulations available at any visitor center (p203).

Glacier Guides Inc (☎ 406-387-5656; www.glacier guides.com) runs half-day to five-day fishing trips of the Middle and North Forks of the Flathead River. It also runs a part-classroom, part-practical fly-fishing school.

Golf

Two golf courses lie just outside the park limits. **Glacier Park Lodge Golf Course** (☎ 406-226-5642), in East Glacier, is the oldest course in Montana. **Glacier View Golf Club** (☎ 406-888-5471), in West Glacier, is another scenic gem that overlooks the Middle Fork of the Flathead River.

WINTER ACTIVITIES
Cross-Country Skiing & Snowshoeing

In winter, when the Going-to-the-Sun Rd and most services are closed, the park is left to wildlife and those who come to cross-country ski and snowshoe. Various routes fan out from the park's main hubs. A popular excursion for skiers and snowshoers is to follow the unplowed Going-to-the-Sun Rd east from the Lake McDonald Lodge toward Avalanche Creek. Some people branch off at McDonald Falls and take the 8.5km (5.3-mile) Sacred Dancing Cascades Loop on the opposite side of the river. Others continue on to Avalanche Creek and attempt the more difficult Avalanche Creek Trail up to Avalanche Lake. Other popular routes are the Red Eagle Lake Trail near St Mary and the unplowed Two Medicine Rd in Two Medicine Valley.

Guided cross-country ski tours can be organized with **Glacier Park Ski Tours** (☎ 406-892-2173; www.glacierparkskitours.com), which operates out of Whitefish. Day rates start at US$200 per person. Add on US$40 a day for longer trips where you'll be taught to build and sleep in your own igloos. Ski, boot and pole

---

> **TOP FIVE ACTIVITIES**
>
> ▨ Hiking the Highline Trail (p210)
>
> ▨ Fishing in Red Eagle Lake (p211)
>
> ▨ Horseback riding up to the Sperry Chalet (opposite)
>
> ▨ Float trip down the Flathead River (opposite)
>
> ▨ Canoeing on Lake McDonald (opposite)

---

rental starts at between US$10 and US$15 per day.

Ski lessons can be organized at the Izaak Walton Inn (p240), in Essex on US 2, for US$45 per hour; the inn also rents out skis and snowshoes (adult/child per day US$13/12).

SLEEPING

In the early 1910s James Hill's Great Northern Railroad built a series of grand hotels to lure rich tourists to Glacier National Park. Two of these so-called parkitecture structures, Many Glacier Lodge and Lake McDonald Lodge, still stand within the park boundaries, conjuring up nostalgic memories of times gone by.

In keeping with the park's back-to-nature ethos, the lodges have been kept refreshingly 'rustic', ie they are bereft of distracting modern appliances such as TVs, room phones, air-conditioning and elevators. All are also nonsmoking and offer at least one wheelchair-accessible room. Operated by **Glacier Park, Inc** (☎ 406-892-2525; www .glacierparkinc.com), the lodges can be booked through a central reservations system.

GOING-TO-THE-SUN ROAD
Camping

All of the Going-to-the-Sun Rd campgrounds act as bus stops on the free summer shuttle route, making link-ups with trailheads and visitor centers refreshingly easy.

Apgar Campground (Map p200; sites $; ☯ early May–Oct) This large wooded campground is a good choice for its proximity to Apgar village. A handy cycle path connects it to a store and restaurant, and the brand-new transit center.

GLACIER NATIONAL PARKS CAMPGROUNDS

Campground	Location	No of sites	Elevation	Open
Apgar	Apgar village	196	960m (3153ft)	May-Oct
Avalanche Creek	Lake McDonald Valley	87	1067m (3500ft)	Jun-Sep
Bowman Lake	North Fork Valley	48	1372m (4500ft)	May-Sep
Fish Creek	Apgar village	180	1067m (3500ft)	Jun-Sep
Kintla Lake	North Fork Valley	13	1372m (4500ft)	May-Sep
Logging Creek	North Fork Valley	8	1372m (4500ft)	Jul-Sep
Many Glacier	Many Glacier Valley	110	1372m (4500ft)	May-Sep
Quartz Creek	North Fork Valley	7	884m (2900ft)	Jul-Sep
Rising Sun	St Mary Valley	83	1463m (4800ft)	May-Sep
Sprague Creek	Lake McDonald Valley	25	1067m (3500ft)	May-Sep
St Mary	St Mary Valley	148	1372m (4500ft)	May-Sep
Two Medicine	Two Medicine Valley	99	1585m (5200ft)	May-Sep
Waterton Lakes National Park				
Belly River	Chief Mountain Hwy	24	1200m (3936ft)	May-Sep
Crandell Mountain	Red Rock Parkway	129	1300m (4264ft)	May-Sep
Waterton Townsite	Waterton Townsite	238	1280m (4200ft)	mid-May–Oct

Drinking Water   Restrooms   Grocery Store Nearby   Snack Shop   Fireplace   RV Dump Station

Avalanche Creek Campground (Map p200; sites $; mid-Jun–early Sep) This lush campground abutting the park's old-growth cedar forest gets more rainfall than most. Some sites are overshadowed by old stands of hemlock, cedar and Douglas fir, but you're close to both Logan Pass and Lake McDonald (off Going-to-the-Sun Rd) and right in the path of a couple of popular trailheads.

Rising Sun Campground (Map p200; sites $; late May–mid-Sep) Situated on Glacier's more un-protected eastern side, 8km (5 miles) west of St Mary entrance station, sites here vary, with a lush and diverse vegetation that provides some shade. A host of facili-ties, including the Rising Sun Motor Inn, a store, a restaurant and a boat launch, are nearby.

Reservations required?	Facilities	Description	Page
no		The park's largest campground is near to trails, a lake and Apgar village	221
no		In old growth forest and close to hikes; also has an outdoor amphitheater for evening programs	below
no		Remote and basic, but great for tent campers; pit toilets available; bring mosquito repellent	224
available		Large, wooded campground that offers plenty of privacy	225
no		The park's most remote campground; listen to the howls of wolves at night	225
no		Small and primitive with no services; there are pit toilets	225
no		One of the park's most popular campgrounds, set in a beautiful valley with facilities nearby	225
no		Smallest campground in the park, this place is primitive; RVs not recommended	225
no		Part-open, part-covered sites close to camp store, restaurant and boat launch	below
no		No RVs allowed, but tranquil lake views are hindered by proximity to Going-to-the-Sun Rd	opposite
available		Large and fairly open, with cracking views; visitor center nearby	opposite
no		Secluded campground with space for larger RVs and an evening ranger program	224
no		Primitive campground in placid parkland terrain	237
no		Tranquil place away from the urban hub of Waterton	237
available		Huge campground close to lakeside, town and trailhead; immensely popular	237

GLACIER NATIONAL PARK

Sprague Creek Campground (Map p200; sites $; mid-May–mid-Sep) Off Going-to-the-Sun Rd on the upper shores of Lake McDonald, the park's smallest campground draws mostly tents – no vehicles over 6.4m (21ft) are allowed – and feels more intimate than many of the park's other options, at least at night when the passing traffic goes to bed. Arrive early to claim a site overlooking the lake.

St Mary Campground (Map p200; sites $; late May-late Sep) Cottonwood and aspen trees predominate in the most shaded sites here: Nos 5 to 19 and 33 to 44 in the A loop. Sites in the B loop, which are bedecked with shorter and shrubbier plant life, are more open and unprotected. There is almost always space here, just west of St Mary entrance station.

Hotels

Rising Sun Motor Inn (Map p200; ☎ 406-732-5523; www.risingsunmotorinn.com; r $$; ☺ mid-Jun–early Sep) One of two classic 1940s-era motor inns in the park, the Rising Sun lies on the upper north shore of St Mary Lake, in a small complex that includes a store, campground, restaurant and boat launch. Rustic motel and cabin rooms with wooden floors offer everything an exhausted hiker could hope for, although tele-addicts and obsessive Blackberry users might find the dearth of technical gadgets a shock to the system.

Apgar Village Lodge (Map p200; ☎ 406-888-5484; r & cabins $$; ☺ May–mid-Oct) The only privately owned accommodations within the park, this lodge (one of two in Apgar village) offers well-maintained motel-style rooms and cabins. The cabins are spacious and most come with kitchenettes, while the smaller rooms are more rustic.

Lake McDonald Lodge (Map p200; ☎ 406-888-5431; www.lakemcdonaldlodge.com; r $$$; ☺ late May–mid-Sep; ♿) Built on the site of an earlier lodge commissioned by park pioneer George Snyder in the 1890s, the present building was constructed in 1913 in classic US parkitecture style. Fronting luminous Lake McDonald, the establishment originally welcomed its guests by boat, meaning that present-day visitors must enter the lodge through the back door. Once inside, a huge fireplace ignites a cozy ambience and colorfully painted paper lamps add an attractive Native American touch. Small,

old-fashioned lodge rooms (sans TV and air-con) are complemented by cottages and a 1950s motel. The location, next to boat docks and hiking trails, is perfect.

Village Inn (Map p200; ☎ 406-888-5632; www.villageinnatapgar.com; r $$$; ☺ late May–late Sep) Occupying a serene setting at the southern end of Lake McDonald in Apgar village, this well-placed accommodation option is far more spiffy than its motel billing implies. The rooms are the usual rustic, gadget-free zones, but lean out on your sunrise-facing balcony and you are, quite literally, within spitting distance of the park's largest and most tranquil lake.

SOUTH OF GOING-TO-THE-SUN ROAD
Camping

Two Medicine Campground (Map p200; sites $; ☺ mid-May–late-Sep) This campground below Rising Wolf Mountain, 4.8km (3 miles) southwest of Two Medicine entrance station, is great for families – amenities, trailheads and the lake are all close by. Good sites near the lake include Nos 34 to 38 and 83 to 95; Nos 23 to 33 and 44 to 55 are nice wooded spots.

NORTH OF GOING-TO-THE-SUN ROAD
Camping

Bowman Lake Campground (Map p200; North Fork; sites $; ☺ mid-May–mid-Sep) Rarely full, this campground, 9.7km (6 miles) up Inside North Fork Rd from Polebridge, offers spacious sites in forested grounds. There is a visitor's

---

BACKCOUNTRY ACCOMMODATIONS

Sperry Chalet (Map p200; ☎ 406-387-5654, 888-345-2649; www.sperrychalet.com; r $$) Built by the Great Northern Railroad in 1914, this 17-room historic chalet (which is a notch up from the Granite Park Chalet, above) is part of an old accommodations network that once spanned the park before the construction of the Going-to-the-Sun Rd. Still a good three-hour hike from the nearest road, guests must either walk or horseback ride here via an ascending 10.5km (6.5-mile) trail that begins at Lake McDonald Lodge. With no lights, heat or water, staying at the Sperry rates alongside a night in the African bush. But don't fret. Rooms are private and rates include three meals. There's just the small matter of the shared restrooms, which are outside. Bring a flashlight for midnight trips to the toilet!

Granite Park Chalet (Map p200; ☎ 406-387-5555, 800-521-7238; www.glacierguides.com; r $) Another historic chalet from the park's early-20th-century heyday, the Granite is even more basic than the Sperry, though its off-road setting is no less magnificent. A popular stopping point for hikers on the Swiftcurrent Pass (p212) and Highline (p210) Trails, a rustic kitchen and dining room are available for use (with propane-powered stoves), though you must bring and prepare your own meals. You can also purchase snacks, freeze-dried meals and soda drinks. Twelve guest rooms sleep two to six people each. Book in advance as it gets busy.

information tent here with reference books and local hiking information.

Fish Creek Campground (Map p200; sites $; ☼ early Jun–Sep) Cocooned inside a dense cedar-hemlock forest, 5.6km (3.5 miles) northwest of the main park entrance, this campground offers sites that are tucked among the trees; book early for one in loops C and D, which are nearest the lake.

Kintla Lake Campground (Map p200; North Fork; sites $; ☼ mid-May–mid-Sep) If you've come to Glacier to dip your nose into *Ulysses* and *War and Peace,* you'll find little to disturb you at this primitive campground, at the top of Inside North Fork Rd. No motor-boats are allowed on the gorgeous lake, so it stays wonderfully quiet.

Logging Creek Campground (Map p200; North Fork; sites $; ☼ early Jul–early Sep) It takes some determination to reach this primitive campground, on Inside North Fork Rd. 27.4km (17 miles) north of Fish Creek Campground, but it is worth it if you're looking for tranquility amid the trees. The atmosphere is very still here but for the sound of a flowing creek.

Many Glacier Campground (Map p200; Many Glacier; sites $; ☼ late May-late Sep) Its access to phenomenal trails makes this campground, next to Swiftcurrent Motor Inn, one of the park's most popular with the hiking set. You can't go wrong with any site you choose, though the even numbers among site Nos 90 to 104 feel quite tucked away.

Quartz Creek Campground (Map p200; North Fork; sites $; ☼ early Jul–early Sep) The campground here, on Inside North Fork Rd, 31.2km (19.4 miles) from Fish Creek Campground, is similar to the one at Logging Creek, though its thicker vegetation lends a more private air. The setting is ultra-quiet and, as at Logging, a creek babbles romantically nearby.

Hotels

Swiftcurrent Motor Inn (Map p200; ☎ 406-732-5531; www.swiftcurrentmotorinn.com; Many Glacier Valley; r $$; ☼ mid-Jun–early Sep; ⑁) A relic from the early days of the motor car, the Swiftcurrent, conveniently located next to numerous Many Glacier trailheads, purposefully replicates the austerity of the 1940s with basic but cozy facilities. A mixture of cabins and motel-style rooms come with or without showers and are bereft of modern luxuries such as TV and air-con. Directly outside the

front door is a handy store, a restaurant and a laundry facility. If the lack of modernity becomes too much, you can always borrow an ironing board or hair dryer from the front desk.

our pick Many Glacier Hotel (Map p200; ☎ 406-732-4411; www.manyglacierhotel.com; Many Glacier Valley; r $$$; ☼ mid-Jun–early Sep; ⑁) Enjoying the most wondrous setting in the park, this fine old parkitecture-style lodge sits pretty on the northern shore of aquamarine Swiftcurrent Lake, within binocular-viewing distance of shimmering glaciers and foraging bears. Built in the style of a huge Swiss chalet by the Great Northern Railroad in 1915, the hotel sprawls over five floors with an imposing open-plan lobby, complete with huge stone fireplace as its centerpiece. Large bar windows frame a postcard-perfect view, while upstairs rustic rooms offer comfortable beds, but no TVs or phones.

EATING

GOING-TO-THE-SUN ROAD

Jammer Joe's Grill & Pizzeria (Map p200; Lake McDonald Lodge; breakfast, lunch & dinner $) Jammer's the word in this casual, family-friendly diner, which has all-you-can-eat buffet (lunch US$7.95, dinner US$9.95) and no-frills pizza and pasta, and is invariably jammed to the rafters with Going-to-the-Sun Rd motorists or foot-sore Avalanche Lake Trail hikers. Inside, the ambience is congenial and the portions are generous.

Russells Fireside Dining Room (Map p200; Lake McDonald Lodge; lunch/dinner $/$$) Lake views and stuffed animal heads characterize the interior of this handsome restaurant at the Lake McDonald Lodge, where you can enjoy hash browns for breakfast, substantial sandwiches for lunch and crab cakes and Caesar salad for dinner.

Two Dog Flats Mesquite Grill (Map p200; Rising Sun Motor Inn; meals $$) There's definitely nothing fancy on the menu here, aside from standard Montana fare with a faintly discernable Tex-Mex twist. But, with little competition, and a clientele made up primarily of tired and famished hikers, who's complaining?

Eddie's Cafe (Map p200; ☎ 406-888-5361; Apgar village; meals $$) Luring a captive audience of energy-depleted adventurers into Apgar village, cheap and cheerful Eddie's splits

its delicious menu between a pre-hike carbo-loading breakfast (think pancakes, waffles, bacon and hash browns) and a protein-loaded après-hike replenishment burger. For those whose taste buds are still functioning after six hours of trail-blazing through the wilderness, there's vegetarian pasta and beer-battered halibut. A picnic lunch to go is US$8 and a kiosk out front sells ridiculously addictive cinnamon buns and ice-cream milkshakes.

SOUTH OF GOING-TO-THE-SUN ROAD

Two Medicine Campstore (Map p200; ☎ 406-892-2525; ⏰ 7am-9pm) While Two Medicine Valley has no standard restaurants, you can purchase coffee, ice cream and enough ingredients to make up a decent picnic at this historic building-cum-grocery store that once served as a dining hall for the erstwhile Two Medicine Chalets. It was from here that President FD Roosevelt, accompanied by John D Rockefeller Jr, chose to give one of his famous 'fireside chats' in the 1930s.

NORTH OF GOING-TO-THE-SUN ROAD

Ptarmigan Dining Room (Map p200; Many Glacier Hotel; lunch/dinner $/$$) Undoubtedly the park's most elegant eating experience, this refined restaurant inside the Many Glacier Hotel encourages slow dining, while soaking up magnificent lake views. Steak, seafood, pasta and usually one vegetarian main are among the many supper offerings.

Italian Garden Ristorante (Map p200; Swiftcurrent Motor Inn; breakfast $, lunch & dinner $) Tempt-ing famished hikers right off the trailhead, this simple restaurant churns out pizza and pasta along with a standard eggs-and-pancakes breakfast. If you're Italian, don't expect voluminous plates of veal or lovingly prepared linguine. A well-stocked camp store next door sells soda and sandwiches, or the restaurant can prepare a hiker's lunch with one day's notice.

AROUND GLACIER NATIONAL PARK

WATERTON LAKES NATIONAL PARK

While no less spectacular than Glacier, adjoining Waterton Lakes National Park is noticeably more intimate; it also boasts a wider variety of restaurants, hotels, services and multipurpose trails. Centered on the small urban hub of Waterton townsite, the park's 525-sq-km (203-sq-mile) wilderness is small compared to other protected areas in Canada, though the drama of its craggy peaks and fickle weather is no less arresting.

Embellished by majestic Upper Waterton Lake – at 146m (479ft), the deepest lake in the Rockies – Waterton is studded with plenty of energetic day hikes, along with two national historic sites, namely the Prince of Wales Hotel and western Canada's first oil well. The nation's fourth national park when it was inaugurated in 1895 (15 years before Glacier), Waterton joined with its southern neighbor in 1932 in the world's first International Peace Park.

THE APRÈS-HIKE SCENE

While Glacier's après-hike scene might lack the sophistication of Banff or the millionaire chic of Aspen, there are still a handful of cheap ways to escape the hiking hullabaloo and reignite your senses with music, dance, entertainment and – ur – beer. Inside the park, look out for the posted listings displayed in visitor centers and lodges. Evening programs include ranger talks, educational slide shows, exhibits on the park's geography and geology and colorful Native American Speaks with old sages such as Ernie Heavy Runner and Curly Bear Wagner. Summer events kick off nightly between 7:30pm to 8pm, rotating between the Lake McDonald Lodge, St Mary Visitor Center and the Apgar, Many Glacier and Two Medicine Campgrounds.

For a post-hike alcoholic beverage drop by the West Glacier Restaurant & Lounge (p242) – known locally as Frida's – just outside the west entrance, or pull up a stool at rough-and-ready **Kips Beer Garden** (US 89) in St Mary. Park rangers regularly extol the virtues of **Charlie's Place** (US 89) in nearby Babb for its music, microbrews and locally renowned pizza (the recipe's a secret). The park's three historic lodges all boast cozy bars that occasionally showcase raspy-voiced country-and-western singers.

When You Arrive

The park is open 24 hours a day, 365 days a year, although many amenities and a couple of park roads close in winter. Entry costs C$7 per adult per day and C$3.50 per child six and up. Passes, to be displayed on your vehicle's windshield, are valid until 4pm on the date of expiration. If you enter the park when the booth is shut, get a pass early the next morning at the Waterton Visitor Centre (p229) or the Parks Canada Administration office (p229). An annual Waterton pass costs C$35. For more on national park passes see p26.

Free park admission is de rigueur on Canada Day (July 1) and Parks Day (third Saturday in July).

Upon entering, you'll receive a map of Waterton Lakes and Glacier National Parks, and the quarterly information-packed newspaper *Waterton-Glacier Guide*.

Orientation

Waterton Lakes National Park lies in Alberta's southwestern corner, 130km (81 miles) from Lethbridge. From the British Columbia border to Chief Mountain Hwy, it covers 525 sq km (203 sq miles). That border is traced by the Continental Divide, which separates the provinces of Alberta and British Columbia.

Waterton townsite sits prettily on the west side of sparkling Upper Waterton Lake, which stretches south across the US border. The lake is a major centerpiece of the park, with boat tours, shuttles and limited motorboats. Waterton Ave (Main St) and its surroundings are full of lodgings, restaurants and other services such as bicycle rentals, a post office, ATMs, internet and phones.

The closest town with full services is Pincher Creek (population 3665), 55km (34 miles) north via Hwy 6. To the east, Cardston (population 3475) is 56km (36 miles) from the park on Hwy 5. En route to Cardston, the small hamlet of Mountain View, 20km (12.6 miles) from the park, has limited amenities.

ENTRANCES

The one road entrance into the park is in its northeast corner along Hwy 5. Most visitors coming from Glacier and the USA reach the junction with Hwy 5 via Hwy 6 (Chief Mountain International Hwy) from the southeast. From Calgary and Pincher Creek to the north, Hwy 6 shoots south toward Hwy 5 into the park. From the east, Hwy 5 through Cardston heads west and then south into the park.

MAJOR ROADS

Unlike vast Glacier, Waterton Lakes is not divided into distinct regions, but rather its main roadways delineate the accessible attractions for most visitors. Hwy 5 leads past the park entrance to Waterton townsite, the services hub within the park. Chief Mountain Hwy (Hwy 17 on the US side) winds its way northwest over Belly River, through the Blood Timber Reserve and into the park. Red Rock Parkway (open mid-May to mid-October) jets off from Hwy 5 and is a popular scenic stretch, particularly for Red Rock Canyon, its destination. In early May, this road is often under repair. Akamina Parkway, used mainly by cross-country skiers in winter, begins closer to the townsite, following Cameron Creek to Cameron Lake.

Information

BOOKS & MAPS

Parks Canada maps of the park and townsite are available at the visitor center, as well as at hotels and restaurants around town. **Waterton Heritage Centre** (Map p231; ☎ 403-859-2624; Waterton Ave) also sells books and maps.

MEDICAL SERVICE & EMERGENCIES

Fire (☎ 403-859-2113)
Medical emergencies (☎ 403-859-2636) For full medical help, see p266.
Royal Canadian Mounted Police (☎ 403-859-2244)

MONEY

Most businesses in Waterton townsite will accept US dollars. The following have ATMs:
Pat's (Map p231; ☎ 403-859-2266; 224 Mount View Rd)
Prince of Wales Hotel (Map p231; ☎ in season 403-859-2231, other times 406-756-2444; Prince of Wales Rd; ❧ mid-May–Sep; ♿)
Tamarack Outdoor Outfitters (Map p231; ☎ 403-859-2378; Mount View Rd; ❧ 8am-8pm) Can also exchange money.

POST & COMMUNICATION

The **post office** (Map p231; ☎ 403-859-2294; 102A Windflower Ave) is open weekdays. There are internet terminals in the Zum Eatery (p238).

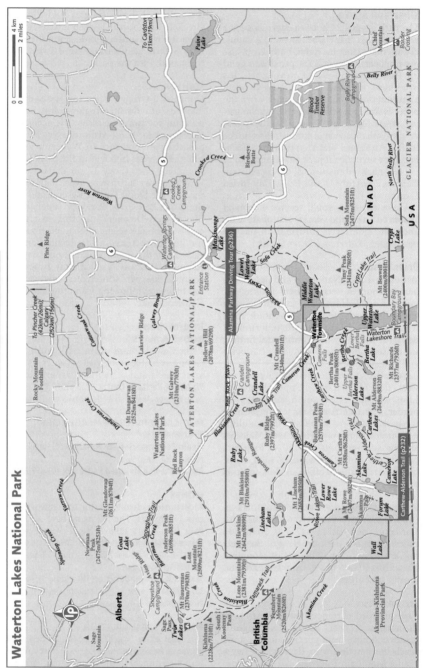

SHOWERS & LAUNDRY

The **Waterton Health Club & Recreation Centre** (Map p231; ☎ 403-859-2150; 101 Clematis Ave) has public showers (C$3) and a laundry; you can use the whole facility (pool, spa, sauna and gym) for C$6 per day.

TOURIST INFORMATION

Waterton Visitor Centre (off Map p231; ☎ 403-859-5133; www.parkscanada.gc.ca/waterton; ☒ 8am-7pm, early May-early Oct), across the road from the Prince of Wales Hotel, has a wealth of front and backcountry information. The park has no separate ranger stations, though staff at Waterton townsite and Crandell Mountain Campground can provide area information. From early October to early May, **Parks Canada Administration** (Map p231; ☎ 403-859-2224; Mount View Rd; ☒ 8am-4pm Mon-Fri) serves as the visitor center.

Park Policies & Regulations

As part of the International Peace Park, Waterton's policies are similar to Glacier's. Don't stray off trails, keep pets on a leash, and refrain from taking even the smallest rock home as a souvenir. Other prohibited activities include hunting, paragliding, snowmobiling and jet-skiing.

CAMPING

Rules for food storage at campgrounds are similar to those in Glacier. Waterton's informative *Bare Campsite Program* brochure is handed out in park campgrounds. Campgrounds hold central steel bear-proof lockers and have designated areas for wastewater.

Campfires are OK in designated areas, but be particularly cautious when it is windy, which is often.

WILDERNESS PERMITS & REGULATIONS

Permits are not required for day hikes, but overnight trips do require them. Up to 24 hours before the start of your journey, make arrangements at the visitor center. The nightly fee is C$9 per adult. Kids 16 years and under get free permits. All of the backcountry sites are reservable, and advance reservations can be made up to 90 days ahead by calling ☎ 406-859-5133; an extra fee of C$12 is charged. You can also put in your request by mail to **Parks Canada Administration** (Waterton Lakes National Park, Box 50, Alberta T0K 2M0).

EQUIPMENT & SUPPLIES

The most comprehensive equipment store is **Tamarack Outdoor Outfitters** (Map p231; ☎ 403-859-2378; Mount View Rd; ☒ 8am-8pm), which stocks everything from backpacks to bear spray. You can also pick up sundry items at **Pat's** (Map p231; ☎ 403-859-2266; 224 Mount View Rd), a hybrid gas station, bike rental, grocery and equipment store.

FISHING & BOATING

A Parks Canada permit is required to fish in Waterton. Permits cost C$9.90 for the day or C$34.65 for the season and can be purchased at the visitor center, park headquarters or at campground entry booths.

Not all lakes are open to fishing and there are some seasonal regulations; check at the visitor center. There has been a general move toward more catch-and-release fishing among anglers in recent years.

Motorboats and water skis are permissible only on Upper and Middle Waterton Lakes. Wear a wetsuit as the water is cold. **Waterton Shoreline Cruises** (☎ 403-859-2362) manages the docking facilities at the townsite's marina; phone for the latest prices.

TRASH & RECYCLING

Waterton's recycling efforts are commendable. Park brochures can be deposited in boxes in the townsite and at the visitors center for reuse. Brown bear-proof trash bins are all over the townsite and campgrounds, as are blue recycling bins for glass, plastic and aluminum containers. Green bins for cardboard can be found in the townsite.

A green trailer in the marina parking lot accepts all of the aforementioned recyclables, as well as office paper, tin cans, newspapers and magazines.

Getting Around

BICYCLE

In marked contrast to Glacier, biking in Waterton is both popular and encouraged. Indeed, you can rent out everything from mountain bikes to large two-person rickshaws from Pat's (above) in the townsite. Outside of the townsite, four designated trails are open to bicycles (p234).

CAR & MOTORCYCLE

The speed limit in the townsite is 30km/h (19mph) unless otherwise posted; campgrounds post 20km/h (12mph) limits. Akamina Parkway has a limit of 50km/h (31mph), unless otherwise posted.

The town's two gas stations are at Pat's (p229) and Tamarack Outdoor Outfitters (p229), both on Mount View Rd and open May to October; to fuel up in winter, head to Mountain View. Parking is simple around town. There are no meters or any unusual restrictions, and the town has a few free lots (no parking between 11pm and 6am).

PUBLIC TRANSPORTATION

Bus

Tamarack Outdoor Outfitters (Map p231; ☎ 403-859-2378; Mount View Rd) runs hiker shuttles that depart daily from the store in season. The Cameron Express (C$10) to Cameron Lake – handy for Carthew-Alderson Trail hikers – leaves daily at 8am and 9am; reserve your seat at least a day in advance (reservations can be made in person or by phone). Another shuttle buses hikers returning by boat from Goat Haunt back to the Canadian–US border and the Belly River parking area. The shuttle is coordinated to link up with the East Side shuttle (p204). This service must be reserved; call for current rates.

Glacier Park, Inc (☎ 406-892-2525) runs a daily shuttle leaving from the Prince of Wales Hotel at 3pm to the following points in Glacier Park: Chief Mountain (US$8), Many Glacier (US$16), St Mary (US$24) and Glacier Park Lodge (US$32). Have your documentation ready for the border crossing.

Boat

Waterton Shoreline Cruises (Map p231; ☎ 403-859-2362) operates a water shuttle service to the east shore of Upper Waterton Lake for the Crypt Lake trailhead. The boat leaves Waterton marina at 9am and 10am and picks up at the trailhead at 4pm and 5:30pm during July and August. Throughout May, June and September the service is reduced to one boat a day (10am depart and 5:30pm pickup). The round-trip fare is C$15/7.50 per adult/child.

TOURS

Waterton Shoreline Cruises (☎ 403-859-2362; adult/child/youth C$20/10/15) operates boats holding up to 200 passengers on Upper Waterton Lake. The service runs from the end of April to the beginning of October. Boat guides are knowledgeable and amusing and the laughter and chatter of the passengers often drifts across the lake to the shoreline. The 2¼-hour cruises, which are conducted on the vintage *MV International* boat, made in 1927, stop at Goat Haunt, Montana for a half-hour. Round-trip boat passengers to Goat Haunt do not have to go through customs before heading toward the Canadian sector again, though if you take the boat one way, hiking to or from Goat Haunt, you'll need a passport. The company also provides the return boat for walkers on the guided weekly International Peace Hike (p234).

Sights

With its own mini town, two national historic sites, and plenty of 21st-century services, Waterton Lakes is less daunting and a little more user-friendly than adjoining Glacier.

WATERTON TOWNSITE

Waterton's diminutive yet attractive townsite exudes the peaceful ambience of a small village, and boasts a winter-time population of around 30 permanent residents. Finding your way around the townsite is not difficult, with a number of short walking trails making the most of the lakeside vistas. A 3.2km (2-mile) **loop trail** along Upper Waterton Lake and around the townsite provides a good introduction to the area. There's also a shorter 2km (1.2-mile) **Emerald Bay Loop**.

The **Waterton Heritage Centre** (Map p231; ☎ 403-859-2624; Waterton Ave; admission free; 🕑 10am-6pm mid-May–late Sep) is a museum of sorts run by the nonprofit Waterton Natural History Association. Inside you'll find exhibits of park flora, fauna and history, a small bookstore and a large mural of homesteader and oil prospector John 'Kootenai' Brown's arrival in Waterton in the 1870s by Albertan artist Donald Frache.

Located at the west end of Cameron Falls Dr, a short hop from the central townsite, **Cameron Falls** is a dramatically poised torrent of foaming water that is notable among geologists for harboring the oldest exposed Precambrian rocks in the Canadian Rockies. Estimates suggest they are 1.5 billion years old, give or take the odd millennium. The lookout here is paved for wheelchair access and the falls are rather fetchingly lit up at night.

Visible all over town, **Upper Waterton Lake** is the deepest lake in the Canadian Rockies, sinking to a murky 120m (394ft). One of the best vantage points is from the Prince of Wales Hotel where a classic view is framed by an ethereal collection of Gothic mountains, including Mt Cleveland, Glacier National Park's highest rampart. A more placid spot is Emerald Bay, around by the marina, famous for its turquoise waters and ever popular with scuba divers.

CAMERON LAKE

Backed by the sheer-sided slopes of Mt Custer, placid Cameron Lake, with an elevation of 1660m (5445ft), is tucked tantalizingly beneath the Continental Divide at the three-way meeting point of Montana, Alberta and British Columbia.

The climax of the 16km (10-mile) Akamina Parkway, the lake is a popular des-

tination with day trippers who come here to picnic, hike and rent boats. From foamflowers to fireweed, copious wildflower species thrive here, while grizzly bears are known to frequent the lake's isolated southern shores.

There are some interesting interpretive displays outlining the area's flora and fauna under a shelter adjacent to the parking lot, along with restrooms and a hut that sells small snacks and soda. A number of trails start from here, including the short Cameron Lakeshore and the ever popular Carthew-Alderson (p232).

Hiking

There are around 200km (125 miles) of trails in Waterton, and a number of them are multipurpose routes, accommodating hikers, horseback riders, cross-country skiers and cyclists. Short, easy hikes lie in the vicinity of the townsite, while further afield, day hikes such as the much-lauded Carthew-Alderson Trail can rival anything in Glacier or Banff National Parks for variety of scenery.

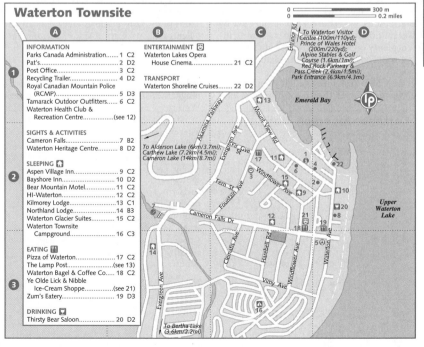

EASY HIKES

For a simple stroll, consider this trail near the townsite.

LOWER BERTHA FALLS TRAIL

Duration 1½ hours round-trip
Distance 6km (3.7 miles)
Difficulty easy–moderate
Start/Finish Waterton Townsite Campground
Nearest Town Waterton townsite (p230)
Transportation private
Summary The best short hike from Waterton townsite leads you up a quiet valley to a soothing waterfall.

An excellent post-dinner, pre-bedtime snack hike, this leafy jaunt alongside Upper Waterton Lake leads to a small waterfall and is lovely on a cool summer's evening when the trail is quiet and the sun casts long shadows over Waterton's deceptively silent mountains.

Start at the Bertha Lake trailhead next to the Waterton Townsite campground, climbing gradually on a narrow trail parallel to the lake. This is actually the start of the famous Lakeshore Trail frequented by International Peace Park hikers and it offers plenty of peek-a-boo views of shimmering water and the odd Goat Haunt–bound boat.

At 1.5km (0.9 miles) a left turn leads to a viewpoint over the lake while, 50m further on, the Lakeshore Trail branches off toward Goat Haunt and the US border.

Bear right at this junction and the path will almost immediately veer inland and begin to parallel Bertha Creek, a powerful stream that has cut a deep groove between Bertha Peak and Mt Richards. The falls are situated approximately 1.5km (0.9 miles) up this trail, at a bridge crossing the creek.

The path carries onto Bertha Lake, a further 6km (3.7 miles) up river.

DAY HIKES

Waterton's two best day hikes are also considered among the finest in the Canadian Rockies.

CARTHEW-ALDERSON TRAIL

Duration 6 hours one way
Distance 19km (11.8 miles)
Difficulty moderate
Start Cameron Lake
Finish Cameron Falls
Nearest Town Waterton townsite (p230)
Transportation Tamarack hiker shuttle
Summary A panoramic parade through myriad forests, lush meadows and rough scree, showcasing the best of Waterton Lakes National Park.

When one of America's leading outdoor magazines lists a hike as 'one of the best

GLACIER NATIONAL PARK

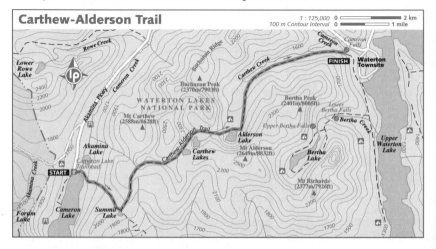

Carthew-Alderson Trail

high alpine day hikes anywhere' (as it did with this one), you know you're in for something special. It perhaps comes as no surprise to find that many seasoned visitors rate this scenic sojourn as the best in the park (and the subject of many repeat visits). As a result, the trail is well trafficked, though none of this takes away from its multifarious beauty and incredible sweeping views.

Most hikers embark from **Cameron Lake** in the west (at Akamina Parkway's end) and tramp east back to Waterton townsite (thus incorporating a gentler elevation gain). This scenario is made possible courtesy of the Tamarack hiker shuttle (p230) that runs from Waterton to Cameron Lake daily at 8am and 9am in the summer (trail conditions permitting).

The trail heads southeast from the Cameron Lake boat ramp (and tiny store) and enters a pine-encased slope alongside the lake's eastern shore, before ascending through a series of switchbacks to the smaller **Summit Lake**. This pool, surrounded by meadow and pine, incorporates the bulk of the hike's 612m (2000ft) elevation gain.

Turn left (northeast) here for the Carthew Lakes Trail, a more gradual ascent through scrub, grass and then just open mountainside, with stupendous views over Montana, British Columbia and Alberta, while the distinctive form of Mt Cleveland frames the backdrop. The ascent culminates in several switchbacks followed by a sharp scramble up loose scree to the ridgeline, where you'll get an expansive panorama: northern Glacier National Park summits to the south, Carthew Lakes to the north.

After the climbing is done, the trail descends from the ridge and weaves between the two starkly located **Carthew Lakes**, where snow can linger all summer. A steep cliff is negotiated at the exit of the Carthew basin before **Alderson Lake** becomes visible below. The trail reenters the trees shortly before the lake; a detour of 0.5km (0.3 miles) leads to the water itself.

From here the narrow path follows the Carthew Valley, descending gradually through the forest to Waterton townsite. A fitting end to the day is the impressive **Cameron Falls**.

CRYPT LAKE TRAIL

Duration 6 hours round-trip
Distance 17.2km (10.3 miles)
Difficulty moderate–demanding
Start/Finish Crypt Landing
Nearest Town Waterton townsite (p230)
Transportation water taxi
Summary A veritable obstacle course that incorporates a ride in a water taxi, a climb up a ladder and a crawl through a narrow rocky tunnel to gorgeous Crypt Lake.

Crypt Lake or Carthew-Alderson? The choice is a toss up. Indeed, both hikes have gained kudos from leading outdoor enthusiasts for their interesting nooks and delightful scenery. Throw the dice and take your pick.

Once an overnight jaunt, Crypt Lake Trail (Map p228) is now tackled in a single day thanks to a new water taxi (p230), which transports hikers to the trailhead from the townsite marina twice daily, at 9am and 10am. The return taxi is at 4pm and 5pm, allowing hikers time for a relaxed lunch break at Crypt Lake.

From the trailhead, the ascent begins quickly, forging through thick green vegetation and copious clumps of wildflowers. Make plenty of noise here as this trail has been known to attract the odd bear. Once in more open terrain, you'll take in up-close views of waterfalls, mountains and an unnamed lake below.

The hike now turns into something of an obstacle course. First, you must climb up a narrow ladder to a small tunnel that will take you – via a combination of crawling or crouching – to a glacial cirque (the tunnel, though natural, was enlarged in the 1960s). On the other side you'll encounter a sheer rock face that must be negotiated with the assistance of a cable. It is not as terrifying as it sounds, but take extra care when it's raining. The cirque encloses gorgeous **Crypt Lake**, nestled in an amphitheater-like setting close to the international boundary (which crosses the lake's southern shore). Plenty of other hikers will, no doubt, be enjoying lunch in the exquisite natural surroundings. Choose your spot and soak up the beauty.

Ensure that you allow enough time for your return trip down, as the boats to the townsite are the only easy way back!

GLACIER NATIONAL PARK

BACKCOUNTRY HIKES

Slip on the backpack for a true adventure in the wilds of Waterton.

TAMARACK TRAIL

Duration 2 days one way
Distance 31.6km (19.6 miles)
Difficulty moderate–demanding
Start Rowe Lakes trailhead
Finish Lone Lake trailhead
Nearest Town Waterton townsite (p230)
Transportation Tamarack hiker shuttle
Summary A tough meander along Waterton's northern fringes through landscapes tinged yellow by the deciduous-coniferous Tamarack tree.

Waterton's only real backcountry adventure is this moderately difficult hiking trail, which is usually tackled over two days overnighting at the Lone Lake, Upper Twin Lake or Snowshoe Campgrounds. Choose between two starting points: the Rowe Lakes Trail off Cameron Lake Rd for a clockwise loop, or the Lone Lake Trail from Red Rock Canyon for a counterclockwise alternative.

From the Rowe Lakes trailhead, the hike junctions with the main Tamarack Trail at 5.1km (3.2 miles) before ascending Lineham Ridge. Offering breathtaking panoramic views, this ridge is a true highlight of the trip. Tricky descents over scree, extreme winds at high altitude and long stretches without treatable water sources are potential difficulties that must be considered before heading out. The recompense is immersion in the scenic beauty of northwestern Waterton, with views sweeping over the mountainous grandeur of Waterton and Akamina-Kishinena Provincial Park. Glacial moraines and wildflowered meadows, lakes and larch, and perhaps even an animal or two, are viewed along the way.

Early autumn is the best time to make this journey, when the namesake Tamarack tree or alpine larch (a deciduous conifer) sheds its needles in a riot of rustic yellows. The reservation-only Tamarack hiker shuttle (p230) can deliver you to the trailhead.

Biking

In contrast to Glacier, Waterton has four trails open for cycling. On top of the two described below you'll also find the **Akamina Pass Trail**, which is 1.3km (0.8 miles) one way, and the **Wishbone Trail**, which is 21km (33.8 miles) round-trip.

Cyclists on park trails should adhere to a few basic rules. Ride single file to prevent trail damage or erosion; alert hikers ahead of you when passing; and when encountering a horse, get off your bike and stand aside until it passes. Always stay on the trail and be careful not to surprise wildlife.

INTERNATIONAL PEACE PARK HIKE

A unique opportunity to visit two parks – and two different countries – in one day, the International Peace Park Hike leads participants on a guided 13.7km (8.5-mile) walk alongside twinkling Upper Waterton Lake, from Waterton townsite in Canada to Goat Haunt in the US. Led by a duo of rangers from the US and Canada, hikers follow a gently undulating path south from the Bertha Lake trailhead, through sun-dappled forest and scenic shoreline, to the unguarded border at the 6.1km (3.8-mile) mark. Here you can enjoy a leisurely lunch while listening to interesting ranger exposés about the park's ecology, geology and ethos of peace. Arriving at Goat Haunt in late afternoon, hikers are required to show their passports to special customs rangers who have been stationed at the isolated ranger station since September 11. To commemorate the 75th anniversary of the peace park in 2007 a new interpretive exhibit was added to the site, chronicling the history of the park and exploring the meaning of the word 'peace' worldwide. When making your reservation you will have assured passage on the 6pm boat back to Waterton (US$22).

The International Peace Park Hike departs Waterton at 10am every Saturday from early June to late August. Places are available for up to 30 people, but reserve ahead as the hike is perennially popular.

Mountain bikes can be rented at **Pat's** (☎ 403-859-2266; 224 Mount View Rd; per hr/day C$8/34). Helmets are included.

CRANDELL LAKE LOOP 🚲

Duration 3 hours round-trip
Distance 20.6km (12.8 miles)
Difficulty moderate
Start/Finish Waterton townsite
Nearest Town Waterton townsite (p230)
Summary Mix road biking with single-track on a multifarious romp around Waterton's classic parkways.

Incorporating the hikeable Crandell Lake Trail with the paved Akamina and Red Rock Parkways, this popular loop (Map p228) can be tackled from one of three starting points: Waterton townsite, the Crandell Mountain Campground (off the Red Rock Parkway), or a trailhead 6.4km (4 miles) along the Akamina Parkway.

All three approaches make for a varied and pleasant half-day ride that mixes 6.4km (4 miles) of rocky off-road with 10km (6.2 miles) of smooth asphalt. The only technicalities come with the ascent to the lake (less steep if you travel anticlockwise), which involves a 100m (328ft) elevation gain from the respective Parkways. The clear **lake**, with Mt Crandell visible to its southeast, is a serene setting with sandy areas and rocks perfect for a picnic perch. Cyclists should beware of hikers on the Crandell Lake Trail and wildlife (including bears) on both parkways.

SNOWSHOE TRAIL 🚲

Duration 1½ hours round-trip
Distance 16.4km (10.2 miles)
Difficulty moderate
Start/Finish Red Rock Canyon parking lot
Nearest Town Waterton townsite (p230)
Summary Tackle part of the Tamarack Trail on this short but steep sojourn into Waterton's northwestern corner.

One in a quartet of fine Waterton cycle rides, the Snowshoe Trail (Map p228) follows Bauerman Creek on an abandoned fire road from the Red Rock Canyon parking lot. The turnaround point is a Snow-

shoe Warden Cabin, 8.2km (5.1 miles) further on.

Don't be deceived by the initial wideness of the track; the gradient gets noticeably steeper beyond the Goat Lake turnoff, and there are also a couple of rocky streams that will need to be forded in late spring and early summer.

Wedged into the park's northwestern corner, mountain views are excellent throughout this ride and vibrant wildflowers add color during the summer months. Although bikes aren't allowed on any of the connecting trails (including Castle Divide and Twin Lakes), the ride makes for a popular bike-hike excursion, with cyclists locking their bikes close to the trail junctions, before continuing along spur paths to destinations such as **Goat Lake** and **Avion Ridge**.

Driving

With only three paved roads, none of which measure more than 24km (15 miles) in length, opportunities for lengthy road trips in Waterton are limited. If you arrive by car, you'll probably end up plying at least one of the following two routes.

AKAMINA PARKWAY 🚐

Duration 20 minutes one way
Distance 16km (10 miles)
Difficulty easy–moderate
Start Waterton townsite
Finish Cameron Lake
Nearest Town Waterton townsite (p230)
Summary Winter cross-country skiing trail and summer wildlife corridor, the Akamina makes for a dreamy afternoon motoring trip.

The road begins 500m (0.3 miles) from the townsite center. After you've climbed the first 500m (0.3 miles), you'll get a sideways glance at the town and lake below. Rocky cliff faces on your right and tree-packed slopes on your left predominate during the first few kilometers, and soon you'll glimpse **Cameron Creek**.

The curious structure 7.6km (4.7 miles) from the start of your journey is the **Lineham Discovery Well National Historic Site**, the first oil well in western Canada. It was struck in 1902, along with premature optimism

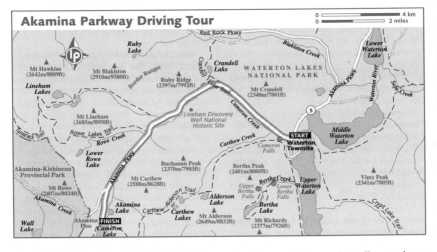

Akamina Parkway Driving Tour

GLACIER NATIONAL PARK

that led to dubbing the area 'Oil City.' After two years the flow was poor, and the well dripped her last in 1936.

The parkway ends at the stellar **Cameron Lake**.

RED ROCK PARKWAY

Duration 20 minutes one way
Distance 15km (9 miles)
Difficulty easy–moderate
Start Waterton townsite
Finish Red Rock Canyon
Nearest Town Waterton townsite (p230)
Summary A short but oh-so-sweet sojourn to Red Rock Canyon, past over 500 million years of geological history.

Red Rock Parkway (Map p228) originates at a junction with Hwy 5, about 8km (5 miles) south of the park entrance. This road, running alongside Blakiston Creek for much of its route, is full of wildflower-speckled prairie spilling onto incredible mountains. South of the parkway, the awe-inspiring Mt Blakiston is Waterton's tallest peak at 2910m (9580ft). A few picnic spots are along the way, and 4.8km (3 miles) in, a small **native history exhibit** is worth a stop.

Most visitors persevere to the end of the road, 15km (9 miles) in, where **Red Rock Canyon** sits colorfully aglow. A 700m (0.4-mile) self-guided loop trail circuits the edge of the canyon. Consisting of ancient Grinnell argillite, the canyon is a fantastic introduc-

tion to one of the geologically wondrous aspects of Waterton.

Other Activities

Waterton offers all the activities available in Glacier with a couple of hidden extras thrown in for good measure. Golf is possible inside the park perimeter, there's scuba diving to an old wreck in Emerald Bay and aficionados rave about the park's ice-climbing potential.

Visitors interested in **horseback riding** can giddyup down the trail with the help of **Alpine Stables** (off Map p231; ☎ 403-859-2462; guided rides per hr from C$30), off Hwy 5 and across the road from the golf course. It has handsome horses suited for all levels, from never-ridden-before to advanced.

Fishing is popular in Waterton Lakes National Park, with the waters swimming with 24 species of fish, including northern pike, whitefish and various types of trout. See p204 for regulations. Popular hike-in destinations for anglers include **Bertha Lake** and **Carthew Lakes**.

Rent boats for kayaking, canoeing or rowing from **Cameron Lake Boat Rentals** (☎ 403-859-2396; per hr C$25; ☑ 7:30am-7pm Jun-Aug) at the exquisite Cameron Lake.

Because its sedimentary rock is soft and crumbly, Waterton is not hugely popular for **rock climbing**, but the upper and lower bands of Bear's Hump offer 10 approaches ranging from grades 5.4 to 5.8.

Committed **scuba divers** brave the frigid waters of Upper Waterton Lake. The most popular spot to get down under is Emerald Bay, where a 1900 paddle wheeler named *Gertrude* sits 20m (66ft) below the surface. With no in-park dive specialists your closest equipment rental is **Awesome Adventures** (☎ 403-328-5040; www.awesomeadventure.com; 314 11th St S, Lethbridge).

Sterling scenery is part of the game at **Waterton Lakes Golf Course** (off Map p231; ☎ 403-859-2074); call for prices and hours.

In the winter, Akamina Parkway is the most popular access point for **cross-country skiing**, while the Cameron Lake area is a favorite for **snowshoeing**. Waterton, along with Kootenay, Jasper and Banff, is considered to be one of the world's premier waterfall **ice-climbing** destinations. Since the sport comes loaded with a number of inherent risks, aspiring climbers are encouraged to check **avalanche bulletins** (☎ 1-800-667-1105; www.avalanche.ca). *Waterfall Ice, Climbs in the Canadian Rockies* is the definitive text on the topic.

Sleeping

Compared to Glacier, Waterton – with its bustling townsite – is loaded with accommodation options, ranging from cheap, basic motels to the stately Prince of Wales Hotel. Nonetheless, visitors arriving in July and August should book ahead. Accommodations at this time are often booked well in advance, although you might get lucky.

CAMPING

In high season, Waterton Townsite Campground can fill by late morning. If staying at Crandell Mountain or Belly River Campgrounds, you can use the showers at Waterton Townsite Campground free of charge.

Waterton Townsite Campground (Map p231; sites $; ☻ mid-May–mid-Oct) The park's largest campground, on Hwy 5 at the southern end of town, has full facilities on grassy grounds. Though largely unshaded, it is near the waterfront and the townsite center. Due to gusty winds, RVs are usually placed near the lake, and tents get more shelter near the creek.

Crandell Mountain Campground (Map p228; Red Rock Parkway; sites $; ☻ mid-May–Sep) Much of this tranquil campground is wooded with lodgepole pines, but many people prefer loops K and L, which are filled with aspen

---

> ### WILD NIGHTS IN THE WILDERNESS
>
> Waterton townsite has more of a laidback buzz than Glacier, with a larger concentration of people in one place inspiring more spontaneous forms of entertainment. Hang around the lakefront of an evening and chances are somebody will be tuning up a guitar or cracking open a few beers.
>
> **Thirsty Bear Saloon** (Map p231; ☎ 403-859-2211; Waterton Ave; ☻ 7pm–2am) is the townsite's drinking nexus, a large open pub and performance space that puts on weekly live music and karaoke (not every national park visitor's cup of tea!). Expect mildly inebriated young ladies in cowboy hats cavorting with cool dudes over by the table-football machine.
>
> In **Waterton Lakes Opera House Cinema** (Map p231; ☎ 403-859-2466; cnr Cameron Falls Dr & Windflower Ave) Waterton even has its own historic cinema. Expect Hollywood movies rather than polished performances of *Madame Butterfly*.

and low-lying vegetation. Fortunately mosquitoes are not too rampant here.

Belly River Campground (Map p228; Chief Mountain Hwy; sites $; ☻ mid-May–early Sep) Outside of the pay area of the park, this primitive campground sits in placid parkland terrain with aspen trees and far-off views of the mountains.

LODGES & HOTELS

All of the lodging is based in and around the townsite. Only three lodges stay open year-round.

HI-Waterton (Map p231; ☎ 403-859-2151; Cameron Falls Dr; dm $, r $$; ☻ mid-May–Nov; ▣) This spotless hostel is Waterton's premier budget accommodations and is thus busy with travelers staying in small but comfy coed dorms and private rooms (based on triple occupancy). It has a well-equipped kitchen, lounge and laundry. Hostelers get a discount at the attached recreation center. There's an on-site café and sauna; internet access is available.

Aspen Village Inn (Map p231; ☎ 403-859-2255; www.aspenvillageinn.com; Windflower Ave; r $$$; ☻ May-Oct; ▣ ▣) Another sprawler, consisting of two main buildings and several cottage units, the Aspen is a family favorite with an on-site kids' playground and resident deer finding shade in the grounds. Barbecues and picnic tables invite a warm summer-night ambience while satellite TV can take the chill out of a damp autumn evening.

Bear Mountain Motel (Map p231; ☎ 403-859-2221; www.bearmountainmotel.com; 208 Mount View Rd; r $$; ☺ mid-May–late Oct) A bog-standard motel with none of the nostalgic value of the Swiftcurrent or Rising Sun in Glacier, the Bear Mountain, nevertheless, does a good job of offering serviceable, clean rooms at an affordable rate. The central location and friendly, knowledgeable owners are the icing on the cake.

Kilmorey Lodge (Map p231; ☎ 403-859-2334; www.kilmoreylodge.com; 117 Evergreen Ave; r $$; ☺ year-round; &) The historic lakefront Kilmorey, dating from the late 1920s, has an upscale-rustic ambience and 23 snug, charming rooms with neither TV nor phone. A red English phone box stands guard outside the front door and winter-time activities include popular murder-mystery weekends.

Northland Lodge (Map p231; ☎ 403-859-2353; www.northlandlodgecanada.com; 408 Evergreen Ave; r $$$; ☺ mid-May–mid-Oct) Can't afford the Prince of Wales? For a small drop in price and a comparable rise in privacy you can enjoy this cozy B&B, built in 1927 by none other than Louis Hill, the genius behind most of the peace park's venerable lodges. The difference with the Northland is that Hill built it for *himself*. Located on the edge of the townsite, within hearing of gushing Cameron Falls, the nine rooms in this Swiss-style establishment are suitably spiffy, all with private baths.

Waterton Glacier Suites (Map p231; ☎ 403-859-2004, 866-621-3330; www.watertonsuites.com; Windflower Ave; r $$$; ☺ year-round; &) A slightly more up-market version of the Aspen Village Inn next door, this polished year-round lodge boasts 26 rooms, all fully equipped with whirlpool baths, satellite TVs, gas fireplaces, fridges, microwaves and air-con. If it's the wilderness you're after, stick to the backcountry campgrounds. If you prefer a little frontcountry luxury this could be your bag.

our pick **Prince of Wales Hotel** (Map p231; ☎ in season 403-859-2231, other times 406-756-2444; www.princeofwaleswaterton.com; Prince of Wales Rd; r $$$; ☺ mid-May–Sep; &) With a fairytale setting on a bluff overlooking Upper Waterton Lake, this venerable establishment, built by the Great Northern Railroad as the only Canadian link in its chain of historic hotels, is a postcard photographer's dream. Mixing Swiss-style architecture with jaw-dropping views, notable royalist connections and such quaint British-isms as waitresses in kilts and high tea in the main lounge (for a hefty C$31), the place is an eye-catching example of how style and elegance can be successfully transported into the heart of an untamed wilderness.

Bayshore Inn (Map p231; ☎ 403-859-2211; www.bayshoreinn.com; 111 Waterton Ave; r $$$-$$$$) A large, sprawling place with rooms with balconies facing the lakefront, the Bayshore offers amenities that you won't find over in rustic Glacier, such as satellite TV, heart-shaped bath tubs, coffee machines and honeymoon suites. There are also four on-site eating and drinking options from the dignified Kootenai Brown dining room to the rocking-and-rolling Thirsty Bear Saloon (p237).

Eating

Ye Olde Lick & Nibble Ice-Cream Shoppe (Map p231; ☎ 403-859-2466; 309 Windflower Ave; ☺ 12:30-10pm) It's difficult to walk past this place without going inside. Go local with the Saskatoon berry ice cream or the huckleberry milkshake.

Waterton Bagel & Coffee Co (Map p231; ☎ 403-859-2466; 309 Windflower Ave; snacks $) A godsend in the middle of the wilderness, this newish caffeine stop, with its handful of window stools, does life-saving peanut butter and jam bagels and all of the essential early morning coffee treats. An iced frappuccino goes down well after a hot summer hike.

Zum's Eatery (Map p231; ☎ 403-859-2388; 116B Waterton Ave; breakfast & lunch $, dinner $$) Car license plates from all over North America decorate this friendly eatery in Waterton townsite staffed by cheery students on their summer break. While sophisticated flavors might be in short supply, the menu is peppered with good home-style cooking of the burger, pizza and fish-and-chips variety. A plethora of meat options remind you that you're in Alberta. The restaurant is family friendly and boasts a couple of internet terminals inside.

Pizza of Waterton (Map p231; ☎ 403-859-2660; 103 Fountain Ave; meals $$; ☺ noon-10pm) Competing with Glacier's Jammer Joe's for the title of best pizzeria in the peace park, this inviting townsite eatery makes a good pizza 'to go,' which you can enjoy by the lake or in the privacy of your motel room. Hunker down in the restaurant, however, and you can wash down the pepperoni slices with an ice-cold Canadian beer.

The Lamp Post (Map p231; ☎ 403-859-2334; 117 Evergreen Ave; breakfast & lunch $$, dinner $$$) About as good as it gets in the Waterton food stakes, the Lamp Post is an award-winning restaurant extraordinaire and a small slice of heaven for those who have just emerged half-starved from the backcountry and are still in possession of their credit cards. Pricey but delicious meals include Alberta beef followed by a highly recommended Saskatoon berry pie.

GATEWAY TOWNS

Glacier's gateway towns are congenial, if low-key, places that offer more accommodations options and a wider choice of eating and entertainment establishments than in the park itself. Created by the Great Northern Railroad in the late 19th century, the transport hubs of East and West Glacier have proliferated little since the halcyon days of train travel in the 1920s and '30s. Both offer classic park lodges and cheap motels, along with a smattering of gift stores, outdoor outfitters and homey, locally owned restaurants staffed by adventure-thirsty summer jobbers.

Elsewhere, diminutive St Mary sits on the Blackfeet Indian Reservation, just outside the park's eastern gate, while isolated Polebridge stands guard over the remote North Fork region. Further afield, attractive Whitefish is a little-known celebrity getaway as well as the gateway to a whole host of regional treats, while Kalispell is a larger and slightly less attractive commercial center.

St Mary

A highway junction graced by a tight cluster of shops and lodgings, St Mary makes a handy base for exploring Glacier's eastern side. The St Mary visitor and transit center, just inside the park gates, is a short stroll from the main action and easy access to East Glacier, Two Medicine, Many Glacier and Waterton is provided by the daily East Side shuttle bus. Sharp-eyed film aficionados will recognize the small bridge just inside the park gates from several key scenes in the movie *Forrest Gump*.

ORIENTATION & INFORMATION
St Mary lies less than 1km (0.6 miles) from the park's eastern entrance where the Going-to-the-Sun Rd meets US 89. Most facilities can be found at the convenience store, gift shop and gas station that adjoin the Park Café (p240). The store also offers **internet access** (per 15min US$2).

SLEEPING
Johnson's of St Mary (☎ 406-732-4207; off US 89; sites $) Set on a knoll overlooking the village, RV sites here get gorgeous views of St Mary Lake with the crenellated peaks of the Continental Divide glimmering in the background. Tents sites are shaded peacefully by some alder trees. Also on site is the Red Eagle Motel and Johnson's World Famous Historic Restaurant.

St Mary KOA Campground (☎ 406-732-4122; 106 West Shore Rd; sites/cabins $/$$; ⚹) Encased in a meadow 1.6km (1 mile) down a paved road, beside St Mary's eponymous river, this unshaded campground can accommodate tents and RVs and also offers some cottages and cabins. A plethora of other services include bike rental (per hour/day US$2.50/20), canoe rental (per hour US$10), a grocery store, coffee counter, laundry, hot tub, playground and the A-OK Grille.

Red Eagle Motel (☎ 406-732-4453; US 89; r $$; ⚹ late May-late Sep) Perched on a small hill above St Mary village, this basic motel is an agreeable crash pad for exhausted hikers. Enjoy cool tranquility and comfortable beds, without the gadgetry of TVs, microwaves or fridges. There's internet access in reception, a cold-drink machine in the corridor and various restaurants a short stroll down the hill. The views of the park from the front balcony are to die for.

St Mary Lodge & Resort (☎ 406-732-4431, 800-368-3689; www.glcpark.com; cnr Hwy 89 & Going-to-the-Sun Rd; r $$-$$$; ⚹ mid-May–early Oct; ⚹ ⚹) An extensive resort offering a whole host of different facilities, including a gift shop, coffee bar, the Snowgoose Grill (p240) and 122 rooms, from the motel-style East Lodge to the rather fancy Pinnacle Cottages. The newish (2001) three-story Great

Bear Lodge, with its hanging flower baskets and Jacuzzi suites, is about as posh as Glacier gets. Tired hikers who sink down into the soft leather sofas in the front lounge will have difficulty getting up.

EATING

Snowgoose Grill (☎ 406-732-4431; US 89; breakfast & lunch $, dinner $$) If you're craving an opportunity to break away from the hikers' breakfast/picnic lunch monotony, try this wheelchair-accessible restaurant in the St Mary Lodge & Resort, where the steaks are succulent and the footwear more heels than hiking boots.

our pick Park Café (☎ 406-732-4482; US 89; meals $$; 7am-10pm) A hiking nexus on the periphery of Glacier, the Park is one of those unsung culinary diamonds that pepper the highways and byways of rural America. Watch out for the bustling waitress who'll refill your coffee while handing out hiking recommendations, and the group of truckers exchanging macabre stories about bears. And here comes that formidable stack of maple syrup–doused pancakes furnished with a grilled-to-perfection slice of bacon and loaded with enough calories to keep you going for the next three days – at least. Only in America!

Two Sisters Cafe (Map p200; ☎ 406-732-5535; US 89; breakfast $, lunch & dinner $$; 8am-9pm) 'Aliens are welcome,' blasts the colorful sign on the roof of this Bohemian hippie joint situated halfway between Babb and St Mary. But while the building might look like a vegan-only enclave plucked straight out of San Francisco's Haight-Ashbury district, the Cajun chicken and eclectic fish dishes here are actually rather good.

GETTING THERE & AROUND

The free Going-to-the-Sun Rd shuttles terminate at the St Mary Visitor Center, a five-minute stroll from St Mary's diminutive core. They run every 30 minutes July through September. The three-times-daily East Side shuttle links St Mary with Waterton, Many Glacier, Cut Throat Creek, Two Medicine and East Glacier.

East Glacier

An important stop on Amtrak's *Empire Builder* route, East Glacier grew up around the train depot and the adjacent Glacier Park Lodge. While its eating and sleeping options offer more variety than West Glacier, its location away from the Going-to-the-Sun Rd and the free shuttle make quick forays into the park less convenient.

ORIENTATION & INFORMATION

East Glacier lies just outside the park's southeastern corner at the junction of Hwy 49 and US 2. The famous Great Northern Railroad bisects the settlement, which is dominated by the historic Glacier Park Lodge. Other facilities include a **post office** (15 Blackfoot Ave; 8:30am-noon & 1:30-5pm Mon-Fri), ATMs, internet at Brownie's (opposite) and a couple of gas stations.

SLEEPING

Firebrand Pass Campground (☎ 406-226-5573; sites $) This small campground, 4.8km (3 miles) west of East Glacier and off US 2, has 26 sites for both tent and full RV hookup. The grassy, shady grounds have an air of seclusion; the bathroom and laundry facilities are clean.

Sears Motel & Campground (☎ 406-226-4432; www.searsmotel.com; 1023 Hwy 49 N; sites & r $) Very convenient to East Glacier amenities, this pleasant place has a campground with tucked-away tent sites and 16 motel rooms. There's a free Amtrak pickup.

Brownie's (☎ 406-226-4426; www.brownieshostel.com; 1020 Hwy 49; dm & r $) Above Brownie's Grocery & Deli, this casual HI-AYH hostel is packed with travelers staying in eight-person single-sex dorms or private doubles. It has a common room and kitchen, and lockout is roughly 10am to 4pm. Sheets, blankets and pillows are provided free of charge.

Izaak Walton Inn (☎ 406-888-5700; www.izaakwaltoninn.com; 290 Izaak Walton Inn Rd; r $$; cabooses $$$; year-round) A mecca for railway enthusiasts and winter cross-country skiers, this vintage 1939 lodge was originally built to accommodate local railway personnel. Located close to the Park Creek area, the lodge became something of an incongruity after WWII, when a plan to build a new southern park entrance in the vicinity never materialized. Dubbed the 'Inn between' in the years since, the Izaak has recently enjoyed a modern renaissance with cozy rooms, a sauna and easy access to skiing trails. Caboose cottages with kitchenettes are avail-

GETTING AWAY FROM IT ALL

Seduced by its jaw-dropping vistas, the vast majority of Glacier's 1.9 million annual visitors rarely stray far from the Going-to-the-Sun Rd with its various pullouts, overlooks and interpretive hikes. But, beyond the thronging nexus points of Apgar village, Lake McDonald and St Mary, vast tracts of this splendiferous wilderness remain quiet, remote and relatively undiscovered.

Once the park's busiest hub, the **Two Medicine Valley** has transformed itself into one of the region's quietest corners since it was bypassed by the Going-to-the-Sun Rd in the 1930s. With no hotels, no restaurants and only one dead-end road, the valley is a favorite haunt for ambitious hikers intent on reaching one of a trio of high-altitude passes that guard the gusty Continental Divide. Real adventure junkies forge further west, beyond Cut Bank Pass, where faintly marked trails descend into the barely visited **Nyack Creek Wilderness**, a rough mélange of fordable rivers and primitive campsites that surround the isolated hulk of Mt Stimson, the park's second-highest peak at 3091m (10,142ft).

Served by a single unpaved road, the **North Fork Valley** is the preserve of survivalists, solitude-seekers and people in search of a therapeutic escape route. Starting from unblemished Kintla Lake, close to the Canadian border, experienced hikers can sally forth on the Boulder Pass Trail with just the birds and the bees – and perhaps a few bears – for company.

able and the inn remains a (request) stop on Amtrak's *Empire Builder* train route.

ourpick Glacier Park Lodge (☎ 406-226-5600; www.bigtreehotel.com; r $$$; mid-May–late Sep;) Set in attractive flower-filled grounds and overlooking Montana's oldest golf course, this historic 1914 lodge was built in the classic national park tradition with a splendid open-plan lobby supported by lofty 900-year-old Douglas fir timbers (imported from Washington State). Eye-catching Native American artwork adorns the communal areas and a full-sized teepee is wedged incongruously onto a 2nd-floor balcony. Other quirks include an outdoor swimming pool, rocking chairs on the porch and a singing janitor who'll bellow out erstwhile show tunes as he industriously removes yesterday's mud from the plush reception carpet. In keeping with national park tradition the rooms here are rustic with no TVs, telephones or air-con.

EATING

Great Northern Steak & Rib House (Glacier Park Lodge; lunch $, dinner mains $$) This big restaurant in the Glacier Park Lodge is a smooth operation, serving steak, seafood, chicken and more to refortify you after a day on the trail. If you're burgered-out try the salmon Niçoise or the chicken masala.

Serrano's Mexican Restaurant (☎ 406-226-9392; 29 Dawson Ave; meals $$; 5-10pm) This mouth-watering Mexican place, just across the road from the railway depot, is East Glacier's most talked about restaurant. Renowned for its excellent iced margaritas, Serrano's also serves up economical burritos, enchiladas and quesadillas in the vintage Dawson house log cabin, originally built in 1909. There's a backpackers hostel out the back.

Brownie's Grocery & Deli (☎ 406-226-4426; 1020 Hwy 49; sandwiches $; 7am-10pm) A true Montana salt-of-the-earth mercantile, Brownie's is an enterprising culinary one-man band selling pastries, strong coffee, sandwiches, internet time and – ur – even the odd brownie or three. As if that wasn't enough, it also doubles up as a popular and affordable hostel (opposite).

GETTING THERE & AROUND

The three-times-daily East Side shuttle links East Glacier with Two Medicine, Cut Throat Creek, St Mary, Many Glacier and Waterton. Amtrak's *Empire Builder* (p204) stops at the train depot once a day traveling in either direction.

West Glacier

Lying just outside the park's busiest entrance gate, West Glacier's pleasant cluster of serviceable facilities makes it an excellent base for hikers arriving either by car or train. Known as Belton until 1949, the settlement was the site of the park's oldest hotel, the Belton Chalet, built in 1910. After standing empty for nearly half a century, the chalet (p242) reopened in 1998 and has since been declared a national historic landmark.

GLACIER NATIONAL PARK

ORIENTATION & INFORMATION

West Glacier lies beside the Middle Fork of the Flathead River at the junction of US 2 and the Going-to-the-Sun Rd. It is also bisected by the Amtrak railway line. Most basic facilities can be found here including a gas station, a grocery-gift store, a post office and an ATM.

Alberta Information Centre (☎ 406-888-5743, 800-252-3782; off US 2; ☉ 8am-7pm) A potent advertisement for wilderness junkies keen on heading north to Waterton Lakes, Banff and Jasper National Parks.

Glacier National Park Headquarters (☎ 406-888-7800; www.nps.gov/glac; West Glacier, MT 59936; ☉ 8am-4:30pm Mon-Fri) Inhabits a small complex just south of the west entrance station. This location is the focus for visitor information from November to April.

Glacier Natural History Association (☎ 406-888-5756; www.glacierassociation.org; US 2; ☉ 8am-4:30pm Mon-Fri) The nonprofit association, in West Glacier's train depot, is an excellent resource for books, maps and information.

Going-to-the-Sun Road Gift Shop (per 15min US$3; ☉ 9am-5:30pm) Internet is available here.

SLEEPING

Glacier Campground (☎ 406-387-5689; camp & RV sites $) This campground, 1.6km (1 mile) west of West Glacier and off US 2, offers sites spanning 16 hectares (40 acres) of lovely wooded grounds, as well as a cute cluster of basic wooden cabins.

Glacier Highland Resort Motel (☎ 406-888-5427, 800-766-0811; US 2; r $$) This perennially popular bed-down on the park's periphery offers 33 units and an indoor hot tub; there's one wheelchair-friendly room. It sits across from the Amtrak station in West Glacier, next to a restaurant of the same name.

West Glacier Motel (☎ 406-888-5662, 888-838-2363; www.westglacier.com/motel.html; r $$, cabins $$$; ▣) The closest motel to the park entrance is located on the north side of the railroad tracks in West Glacier village and offers guests such improbable park frills as satellite TV and wi-fi. Motel-style rooms are situated in the village while cabins are perched on a bluff overlooking the Flathead River.

Vista Motel (☎ 406-888-5311; US 2; r $$; ▣) A cheap and relatively cheerful motel, the no-nonsense Vista does at least have a vista (when the weather's clear), along with comfortable beds, powerful showers and a rather spatially challenged swimming pool. Located an 800m (0.5-mile) hike from the West Glacier

train depot, it's a viable crash pad if you're arriving by train and plying the park by public transport.

Belton Chalet (☎ 406-888-5000, 888-235-8665; www.beltonchalet.com; r $$$) A parkitecture classic with notable Swiss influences, the Belton, which overlooks the railroad tracks in West Glacier, has a more spiffy, plusher feel than many of Glacier's vintage lodges – a result, perhaps, of an extensive 1998 restoration. Now in private hands, this one-time café, pizza parlor and Civilian Conservation Corps (labor groups who were involved in many public-works programs during the Depression) accommodations, sports traditional yet elegant rooms replete with art and crafts–style furnishings. A therapeutic spa offers massage and foot rubs, and the legendary on-site tap room serves a mix of local and Mediterranean snacks.

EATING

West Glacier Restaurant & Lounge (☎ 406-888-5403; 200 Going-to-the-Sun Rd; ☉ 7am-10pm May-Sep) Sitting invitingly on the cusp of the park, this place is a sure bet for filling – and calorie-packed – Montana cooking. Breakfast is classic American, with stacks of buttery pancakes and mini-mountains of hash browns, while the dessert pies are known for miles around.

GETTING THERE & AROUND

A 4km (2.5-mile) paved cycle path links West Glacier with Apgar village and transit center inside the park, from where you can catch free Going-to-the-Sun Rd shuttles. Amtrak's *Empire Builder* (p204) stops at the train depot once a day traveling in either direction.

Polebridge

Glacier's most isolated outpost spins on two hubs: the Northern Lights Saloon and the historic Polebridge Mercantile, a combination store, post office and gas station. Sandwiched between the towering Livingstone and Whitefish mountain ranges, the 'town' is a low-key place with more wildlife than people. Expect no electricity, few facilities and even fewer worries.

ORIENTATION & INFORMATION

Polebridge is located on the Outside North Fork Rd, 42km (26 miles) northwest of the park's western entrance. The Polebridge Ranger Station (p203) lies 1.6km (1 mile) to the east, next to the park entrance.

SLEEPING

North Fork Hostel & Square Peg Ranch (☎ 406-888-5241; www.nfhostel.com; 80 Beaver Dr; tents, teepees, dm & cabins $) Glacier's quirkiest hostel requires a bit of leg work to get to and lacks the basic comforts of other park lodges (there's no electricity), but in many ways that's part of the attraction. There are 13 dorm spaces and a couple of cabins, along with two vintage homesteads (sleeping six each) at the Square Peg Ranch up the road. Facilities include internet access, fax machine and a phone powered by an independent power source. There's also a fully equipped kitchen you can use, hot showers and outhouse loos. The Polebridge Mercantile is 800m (0.5 miles) away; phone ahead to arrange a lift from West Glacier Amtrak station.

EATING

Northern Lights Saloon (☎ 406-888-5669; Polebridge Loop Rd; meals $-$$; ☺ 4pm-midnight May-Sep) Most visitors to isolated Polebridge arrive with pretty low culinary expectations, meaning they walk away more than satisfied after a trip to this Old West–style park institution. Cool and casual, the Northern Lights' standard beer-and-burgers menu is supplemented by tasty vegetarian dishes and potent glasses of organic ale washed down amid tales of intrepid backcountry hikes and close encounters of the furry (read, bear) kind.

Polebridge Mercantile (☎ 406-888-5105; Polebridge Loop Rd) Next door to the saloon and dubbed 'the Merc' by those in the know, the Polebridge creates sweet and savory pastries that are talked about all over the park. The small shop also stocks some foodstuffs.

GETTING THERE & AROUND

Driving a car is the only reliable way of getting to Polebridge, although you'll need good snow tires in the winter. The North Fork Hostel (above) sometimes runs a shuttle service from West Glacier; phone for more details.

BLACKFEET INDIAN RESERVATION

The short-grass prairie east of Glacier is home to the Blackfeet Nation, which includes the Northern Peigan (Blackfeet), Southern Peigan and Blood tribes that came

south from the Alberta area in the 1700s. Originally an agrarian people, the Blackfeet took quickly to horses and guns, eventually developing a reputation as the fiercest warriors in the West. Today, approximately 7000 tribal members reside on or around the **reservation** (www.blackfeetnation.com), where the major industries are ranching, farming and pencil manufacturing. Browning, 29km (18 miles) east of Glacier National Park, is where most of the reservation's amenities lie.

The **Museum of the Plains Indians** (☎ 406-338-2230; cnr Hwys 2 & 89, Browning; adult US$4, 6-12yr US$1; ☺ 9am-5pm daily Jun-Sep, 10am-4:30pm Mon-Fri Oct-May) is one of Montana's better Native American museums. Extensive descriptions accompany fascinating exhibits of costumes, art, craftwork and more.

Rising Wolf Wilderness Adventures (☎ 406-338-3016; www.risewolf.com) runs guided hikes and fishing trips in and around Blackfeet Indian Reservation. The activities are run by Blackfeet women, and geared toward women.

Sleep in a teepee looking onto the plains at the **Lodgepole Gallery & Tipi Village** (☎ 406-338-2787; www.blackfeetculturecamp.com; US 89; teepees $), 3.2km (2 miles) west of Browning.

WHITEFISH

One of the busiest train depots on the old Great Northern Railroad route, diminutive Whitefish is Glacier National Park's largest and most attractive gateway settlement. Sitting pretty on glistening Whitefish Lake and nestled in the shadow of imposing Big Mountain, the town is embellished with a winter ski resort, copious water-based activities, a quirky downtown core, and the kind of laidback, carefree congeniality for which Montana is nationally famous.

Orientation & Information

US 93 goes through town as Spokane Ave (north–south) and 2nd St (east–west), connecting to Kalispell 20.9km (13 miles) south, and US 2; Glacier is 38.6km (24 miles) west via US 2. Wisconsin Ave goes north from downtown to Big Mountain.

Whitefish Chamber of Commerce (☎ 406-862-3501, 877-862-3548; www.whitefishchamber.org; 520 E 2nd St; ☺ 9am-5:30pm Mon-Sat summer, 9am-5pm Mon-Fri winter) has ample area information. The **Tally Lake Ranger Station** (☎ 406-862-2508; 1335 Hwy 93 N; ☺ 8am-4:30pm Mon-Fri) is 1.6km (1 mile) west of Whitefish.

Wash your clothes while you get gas at **Mike's Conoco** (☎ 406-862-6453; cnr 13th St & Spokane Ave), which has a 24-hour laundry. Use the internet for free at the **Whitefish Branch Library** (☎ 406-862-6657; 9 Spokane Ave).

Bookworks (☎ 406-862-4980; 244 Spokane Ave) has a good selection of books and maps. For gear and rentals, head to **Sportsman & Ski Haus** (☎ 406-862-3111; 6475 US 93 S), a mile or two south of the center.

Sights

Whitefish's star attraction is the **Whitefish Mountain Resort at Big Mountain** (☎ 406-862-2900, 800-858-4157; www.bigmtn.com), 11.2km (7 miles) from downtown. It has a whopping 1214 hectares (3000 acres) of skiable terrain and a snowboard-hopping terrain park. The winter season runs late November to mid-April. From June to September, 32.2km (20 miles) of trails host hiking and mountain-biking aficionados. The gondola to the mountaintop offers great views of Flathead Valley; you can ride or hike down.

The **Stumptown Historical Society Museum** (☎ 406-862-0067; 500 Depot St; admission free; ☯ 10am-4pm Mon-Sat summer, 11am-3pm Mon-Sat winter), in the old Tudor Revival Great Northern Railroad Depot, displays train memorabilia and fascinating photos of early Whitefish.

The **City Beach Park** (admission & parking free), on the southern shore of Whitefish Lake, is where the whole town comes to date and debate in the summer months. The swimming area is roped off.

Sleeping

Whitefish Lake State Park Campground (☎ 406-862-3991; State Park Rd; sites $; ☯ late May-early Oct) On the southwest edge of the lake, shady forested grounds hold 25 first-come, first-served sites, including one that is wheelchair-friendly. Day use costs US$5.

The Downtowner (☎ 406-862-2535; 224 Spokane Ave; dm & r $; ☒ ☒) Whitefish's reliable, slap-bang-in-the-middle-of-town option is a 17-room motel-style joint with an extra dorm available for groups. Comfortable rooms here are large and packed with an excellent range of amenities. All guests get free use of the motel's outdoor Jacuzzi, sauna and adjacent gym. The tasty Wrap and Roll house (open 11am to 9pm

> ### TOP FIVE LAZY-DAY ACTIVITIES
>
> ■ A leisurely breakfast at the Park Café (p240)
>
> ■ Afternoon tea at the Prince of Wales Hotel (p238)
>
> ■ Watching the sun rise from Sun Point (p206)
>
> ■ A boat trip on the mirrored waters of Lake McDonald (p205)
>
> ■ Wildlife watching from the Many Glacier Hotel (p225) bar

Monday to Saturday), selling burritos and gyros, is downstairs.

Duck Inn (☎ 406-862-3825, 800-344-2377; r $$) Under new ownership and still glowing from a spiffy refurbishment, the Duck presents a rather fetching southern Whitefish option, overlooking the town's eponymous river. Rooms are so modern you can still smell the paint, and boast TVs, internet access, phones, fireplaces and balconies.

ourpick **The Garden Wall** (☎ 406-862-3440, 888-530-1700; www.gardenwallinn.com; 504 Spokane Ave; r $$) As elegant a B&B as you'll find anywhere, the Garden Wall is a meticulously restored accommodation option nestled in a shady spot on Spokane Ave. Five guestrooms are stuffed with Art Deco artifacts, a real log fire blazes in the living room, and the welcoming owner – a qualified chef – is known to rustle up a memorable breakfast preceded by a wake-up coffee tray delivered to your room.

Eating & Drinking

Third Street Market (☎ 406-862-5054; cnr 3rd St & Spokane Ave; ☯ 9am-6pm Mon-Sat) Middle America goes organic at this alternative local grocery that wouldn't look out of place on New York's Upper East Side. Choose from a range of natural foods, bulk-bin items, vitamins, organic produce and even healthy grub for your pet.

Tupelo Grille (☎ 406-862-6136; 17 Central Ave; meals $$$; ☯ 5-11pm) Named after Elvis' Mississippi hometown, this locally famous fine-dining establishment has food with a strident Southern tinge. Delicious Cajun and Creole dishes come without the pretensions of other posh eateries and are interspersed with the odd Thai and stir-fry favorites. Viticulture aficionados will enjoy the wine list.

Wasabi Sushi Bar & the Ginger Grill (☎ 406-863-9283; 419 2nd St E; meals $$; ☺ 5-11pm Tue-Sat) A departure from the usual Montana meat staples, this Japanese-flavored place confirms Whitefish's cosmopolitan credentials with very good traditional and fusion sushi. For those who don't crave it raw, you can choose from an array of cooked pan-Asian entrées.

ourpick **Montana Coffee Traders** (☎ 406-862-4500; 845 Wisconsin Ave; ☺ 7am-6pm Mon-Sat, 9am-5pm Sun) You won't find a coffee bar this congenial – and coffee *this* good – for a good few hundred miles (try Seattle). Then there are the paninis, the cakes and the on-site equipment store; to say nothing of the free internet terminal. Situated inside the Skyles building, this buzzing place, with its distinctly West Coast ambience, invites you to 'travel the world in your coffee mug.' Don't hang around.

Bulldog Saloon (☎ 406-862-5601; 144 Central Ave; ☺ 11am-2am) In this popular place, walls are aflutter with sports flags and bulldogs, hard drinkers are playing poker, and the bathrooms boast X-rated décor.

Getting There & Around

Intermountain Transport (☎ 406-755-4011) connects the train depot in Whitefish to Kalispell once a day; its buses also mosey to Missoula, Helena, Bozeman and Seattle.

The free Shuttle Network of Whitefish (SNOW) connects Whitefish to Big Mountain during ski season. **Eagle Transit** (☎ 406-758-5728; ☺ 8am-5pm Mon-Fri) provides a bus service around Whitefish (US$1) and to and from Kalispell (US$3).

KALISPELL

Kalispell, 21km (13 miles) south of Whitefish, is Flathead Valley's commercial hub. Though not as charming as Whitefish, it's a pleasant enough place to refuel and resupply. Its concentration of budget lodging makes it a frequented gateway to Glacier, less than an hour's drive northeast. It's also used by visitors to the popular Flathead Lake, 15 to 20 minutes south by way of US 93.

Kalispell Chamber of Commerce (☎ 406-758-2800; 15 Depot Park; ☺ 8am-5pm Mon-Fri) has maps and information. Check out **Books West** (☎ 406-752-6900; 101 Main St) for its great stock of titles, including area guides.

The completely restored 1895 Norman-style **Conrad Mansion** (☎ 406-755-2166; cnr Woodland Ave & 3rd St E; adult/child US$8/3; ☺ 10am-5pm mid-May–mid-Oct), built in 1895, is worth touring. Contemporary work by Montanan artists is displayed at **Hockaday Museum of Art** (☎ 406-755-5268; 302 2nd Ave E; adult/child 6-18 yr US$5/1; ☺ 10am-6pm Tue-Fri, 10am-5pm Sat, noon-4pm Sun).

Kalispell has a good range of lodgings and eateries. **Rocky Mountain 'Hi' Campground** (☎ 406-755-9573, 800-968-5637; www.kalispell.bigsky.net/rmhc; 825 Helena Flats Rd; campsites, RV sites & cabins $), off US 2 east of Kalispell, is great for families, but kids will also appreciate the pool at **Vacationer Motel** (☎ 406-755-7144, 888-755-7144; 285 7th Ave; r $$; ☒ ☒). The best downtown pick is **Kalispell Grand Hotel** (☎ 406-755-8100, 800-858-7422; www.kalispellgrand.com; 100 Main St; r $$; ☒ ☒).

The vibrant **Knead Cafe** (☎ 406-755-7510; 25 2nd Ave; lunch & dinner $; ☺ 8am-3pm Sun & Mon, 8am-9pm Tue-Sat) has delicious Mediterranean-style fare. The menu at **Capers** (☎ 406-755-7687; 121 Main St; meals $$$; ☺ dinner Tue-Sat) has benefited from a change in ownership, with dishes such as pan-seared Alaskan scallops, bison steak and seared ahi tuna.

GLACIER NATIONAL PARK

Directory

CONTENTS

This chapter provides useful practical information that applies to all the parks covered in this book. For more specific details on each park, consult the relevant chapter.

ACCOMMODATIONS

All the national parks have a range of accommodations catering for practically every type of traveler, from backcountry enthusiasts looking to sleep out under a clear mountain sky to luxury sightseers who just can't live without a flat-screen TV and a feather pillow. Whatever type of accommodations you choose, prices are likely to be at a premium in summer, and many places are booked up months in advance – it pays to plan well ahead if you've got your heart set on somewhere specific.

In Banff and Jasper, most of the accommodations are concentrated around the main townsites, although you'll also find a few historic lodges and cabin complexes scattered around the park. In Glacier, the best (and least expensive) options tend to be located in the gateway towns of East Glacier and West Glacier, St Mary, Babb and Polebridge, while Cardston and Pincher Creek are both good options if you're visiting Waterton. Many hotels have switched to a no-smoking policy in all their rooms.

PRACTICALITIES

■ Distances in Canada are quoted in kilometers, with elevations in meters; in the US it's miles and feet. Both countries quote weights in imperial pounds.

■ In Canada, power plugs have two flat angled pins, while in the US there are two round pins. The power supply in both countries is 120V/60Hz. Adaptors to convert power plugs for use in both countries are easily available from electrical outlets and travel shops.

■ The NTSC TV system is used in both Canada and the US. DVDs are encoded in the Region 1 standard.

■ The most popular daily newspapers in Alberta are the *Calgary Herald* and *Edmonton Journal,* plus the *Calgary Sun* and *Edmonton Sun* tabloids. There are lots of small regional newspapers; look out for the historic *Crag & Canyon,* the *Canmore Leader* and the *Rocky Mountain Outlook.* In Montana look for the *Whitefish Pilot* and *Daily Inter Lake.*

■ The nationwide CBC (Canadian Broadcasting Company) is the main radio service, although reception is patchy across the parks; try 96.3FM for CBC Radio One in Banff and 98.1FM in Jasper. The volunteer-run Banff Park Radio is on 101.1FM. In Montana KJJR (880AM) has news and talk.

■ GST (Goods and Services Tax) of 6% is added to most goods in Alberta. Montana has no sales tax.

It's definitely worth making reservations as far in advance as possible whenever you visit – try the following organizations for the rundown on your various options in and around the parks.

Banff Accommodation Reservations (☎ 1-877-226-3348, 403-762-0260; www.banffreservations.com)

Banff Tourism Bureau (☎ 403-762-8421; www.banfflakelouise.com)

Canmore Bow Valley B&B Association (www.bbcanmore.com)

Glacier Park, Inc (☎ 406-892-2525; www.glacierparkinc.com)

Jasper Home Accommodation Association (www.stayinjasper.com)

National Park Hotel Guide (☎ 1-866-656-7127; www.nationalparkhotelguide.com)

B&Bs

You'll find yourself shelling out a large chunk of change while getting your forty winks in the parks. One way of cutting costs is to stay in a B&B (bed and breakfast). Generally these are private homes offering rooms to travelers, usually with breakfast thrown in for good measure. Standards vary pretty widely, from basic bedrooms to luxury suites that would give many hotels a run for their money. Not all rooms have private bathrooms, and you should check with individual places on their policies about pets, kids and credit cards. It's useful to have your own front-door key so you can come and go as you please; some B&Bs even have private entrances for guests' use. With a bit of research you'll turn up some real gems around Banff and Jasper, including several historic and heritage homes, and it can be a great way to really immerse yourself in the park and get some insiders' tips on the best things to see and do during your stay.

The B&B tradition is less common in the US than in Canada, although you might find a few places dotted around the outskirts of Glacier; motels are generally the best way to cut your accommodations bill, but they're usually a lot less fun.

Camping
BACKCOUNTRY CAMPING
To cater for people on multi-day backpacking trips, there are lots of designated backcountry campgrounds dotted along the main trails where you can break your

---

SOLO WOMEN TRAVELERS

The national parks don't present many unusual dangers for women traveling alone. Both the parks and the main townsites are generally friendly and safe places to visit, although obviously it pays to take the usual precautions – keep your wits about you if you're traveling through unlit or unpopulated areas after dark and join up with other people if you're walking home late at night.

If you're camping alone, especially in the backcountry, you might feel safer pitching your tent near to other campers, or hooking up with people while on the trail; it's also worth bringing along emergency items such as a whistle, cell phone and possibly bear spray and/or bear bangers as an extra precaution.

If you can, it's also worth avoiding traveling in the backcountry during your period, as bears and other wild animals do seem to be more attracted to menstruating women, although as yet there's been no concrete scientific link.

---

walk overnight. These are usually very simple, mostly just a cleared camping area with leveled tent pads and sometimes a pit privy for that extra touch of luxury. Food storage cables are usually provided where you should suspend toiletries, garbage and food items to avoid attracting bears to your tent.

You'll need to specify your chosen campgrounds when you purchase your wilderness pass (Banff, Jasper and Waterton Lakes, C$8.90 per night) or backcountry permit (Glacier, free in winter, US$5/3 per adult/child per night in summer plus a US$30 processing fee if ordering the permit in advance). The maximum stay at one campsite is generally three nights.

In some very remote areas of the parks, wild camping is allowed – choose a site 50m from the trail, 70m from water sources and 5km (3 miles) or more from the trailhead.

See p42 for further advice on backpacking trips and backcountry regulations, or visit www.leavenotrace.ca. Specific backcountry rules for each park are detailed in the individual chapters.

FRONTCOUNTRY CAMPING

Unsurprisingly, camping is a massively popular way of experiencing the natural beauty of the national parks. All of the Canadian and US parks offer a selection of frontcountry campgrounds that are easily accessible from the main roads, but it's worth doing a bit of research to make sure your chosen campground is going to meet your needs, as the standards and settings can be pretty varied. In general, the more popular campgrounds (especially those near to tourist hot spots and sights) are better equipped than those further afield; flush toilets, drinking water, public phones, fire pits and RV hookups are all offered at the large campgrounds at Tunnel Mountain, Johnston Canyon and Lake Louise in Banff, and Whistlers and Wapiti in Jasper. Some also have paved pull-throughs designed for RVs, sometimes with dumping stations for waste, but not every campground is set up to cater for trailers – consult the relevant campground entry in this guide or contact parks staff for further information.

Move out into the countryside and things become altogether more rudimentary. At many isolated campgrounds you'll find just the bare minimum of facilities – pit toilets, drinking water and basic, cleared sites are pretty much all you can expect, although some grounds also have recycling bins and bear-proof storage lockers. Many remote campgrounds also operate on a self-registration basis, where you find an available site, fill in your details (name, site number, length of stay, registration number of your vehicle) on the payment envelope and then deposit it in the box near the entrance. Rules and regulations vary between sites, but the maximum stay is usually 14 days, fires are allowed in designated fire pits (provided no fire restrictions are currently in force) with the additional purchase of a fire permit and campers are encouraged to keep a clean and tidy site to avoid attracting wildlife.

A reservation service has been introduced for the main campgrounds, including Tunnel Mountain and Lake Louise (Banff), Pocahontas, Whistlers, Wapiti and Wabasso (Jasper), Redstreak (Kootenay) and the townsite campground in Waterton. Contact the **Parks Canada Reservation Service** (☎ 1-877-737-3783; www.pccamping.ca); reservations can be made up to three months in advance. All others operate on a first-come, first-served basis – arrive before the standard checkout time of 11am for the best chance of securing a site, and listen out for bulletins on park radio and at visitor centers.

Reservations in Glacier National Park are available at Fish Creek and St Mary campgrounds through the **National Park Reservation Service** (☎ 1-800-365-2267; www.reservations.nps.gov).

Hostels & Lodges

Another cost-cutting way of visiting the parks is to stay in a hostel. Long a staple for backpacking travelers looking to squeeze the most time out of their shoestring budgets, hostelling is rapidly gaining favor with travelers of a more senior persuasion, especially among hikers, cyclists and skiers who prefer to spend their money on outdoor activities rather than boring old overnight accommodations.

The best hostels in Banff and Jasper are run by **Hostelling International** (HI; www.hihostels .ca), which has great establishments in Banff town, Lake Louise and Jasper town, but there are also several smaller independent hostels scattered around the parks. Accommodations are usually in dorms with four to 10 beds, with a communal kitchen and lounge. Some also have extra facilities such as cafés, games rooms and TV rooms as well as organized activities. Bathrooms and showers are usually shared, and dorms are sometimes organized along gender lines. If you're traveling in a group or as a family, booking out a four- or six-bed dorm as a private room works out a lot cheaper than staying in a motel or hotel, and while the facilities are obviously a little less luxurious, it can often be a lot more interesting than staying in a bland old roadside motel. If you're a HI member, you'll qualify for discounts on nightly rates in the hostels and organized activities; annual membership costs C$35 and is free for people under the age of 17.

In addition to the townsite hostels, you'll also find a few rustic lodges (such as those at Mosquito Creek and Rampart Creek) where you'll really get a taste for the backcountry lifestyle. These places are mostly just wood cabins with a basic kitchen, dining area and communal lounge (often with a cozy wood-burning stove), with gender-sorted dorms in separate cabins; they're very basic, but you're guaranteed to make some friends. The **Alpine Club of Canada** (☎ 403-678-3200; www.alpineclubofcanada .ca) also operates simple hut hostels in the backcountry, all of which are several hours hike away from the nearest main road. Reservations are essential – the last thing you want is to turn up at one of the huts to find every available berth is occupied by a slumbering climber.

Hotels

For more traditional travelers there's no shortage of hotels in Banff, Jasper and Glacier, especially in and around the main townsites – including a couple of landmark, chateau-style hotels at Banff and Lake Louise that are among the most famous hotels in Canada. Room rates, especially in Banff, are notoriously expensive, and always shoot upward in the peak season between May and September. Things are a bit more affordable in Jasper, as well as in the neighboring provincial parks and gateway towns. Except at the top end of the price ladder, the standard of accommodations is often pretty mediocre for the price – decor and facilities can feel rather dated, and service often leaves a lot to be desired at the larger and busier hotels.

There's usually a string of cheap, standard motels on the edges of the larger towns. Practically all hotel rooms come with en suite bathroom, telephone and cable TV, and wi-fi is becoming increasingly widespread, although some of the more remote places (such as Num-Ti-Jah Lodge on Peyto Lake) make a deliberate point of not providing the distractions of TVs and telephones to encourage guests to adapt to the more laid-back wilderness lifestyle. Room rates are nearly always quoted without sales tax, so remember to add 6% GST (Goods and Services Tax) in Canada.

ACTIVITIES

While many people visit the parks just to drink in the scenery, for other people it's the fantastic range of outdoor activities on offer that is the major attraction. There's something to suit everyone here, whether it's a leisurely nature walk or a hard-core alpine climb that you're after. Hiking, cycling,

horseback riding, scrambling and canoeing are probably the most popular activities, but there are also lots of more esoteric pastimes. See the Activities chapter (p37) for the full lowdown.

BUSINESS HOURS

Business hours are fairly flexible in the US and Canada. Standard opening hours for banks, retailers and services are generally from 9am to 5:30pm, although grocery and convenience stores, tourist services, gift shops, cafés and large chain stores often open later. Banks are usually only open Monday to Friday and post offices Monday to Saturday. Restaurants vary widely in opening hours; breakfast usually runs from around 7am to 10:30am, lunch from 11am to 2:30pm or 3pm and dinner from 5pm to 10pm. Bars open any time from 4pm onwards to around midnight or later. Unless we've specified otherwise in the guide, you can assume the place in question has opening hours that are pretty close to these ranges.

CHILDREN

Children are welcome pretty much everywhere and there are enough activities and things of interest to keep their minds off the TV and the Nintendo (well, for a few days at least). Kids are welcome on most activities and tours, but bear in mind that journey times between sights can be pretty long, so it's worth having a few back-up plans to keep them from getting bored. Not all hotels, B&Bs and restaurants are geared up to cater for kids, so it's worth asking at the time of booking about the specific facilities on offer, especially if you're bringing very young children. For more ideas on bringing kids to the parks, see the Kids & Pets chapter, p54.

CLIMATE CHARTS

The weather in the mountains is notoriously unpredictable. Clear blue skies can turn into rolling thunderheads in the space of a few minutes, so it's always worth bringing wet-weather gear and checking the forecast carefully before setting out. Temperatures drop quickly at night, and the wind can be biting at higher elevations. The climate is generally colder the further north you go, and snow can linger in many locations as

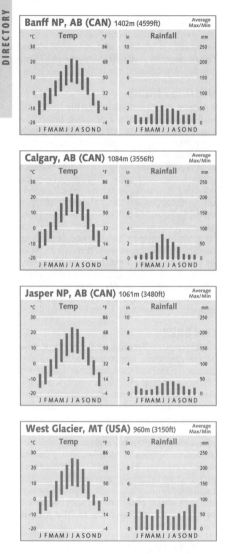

late as June. For more information on the seasons, see p23.

CUSTOMS

Visitors entering either Canada or the US can bring 200 cigarettes (one carton), 50 cigars and 14 ounces of tobacco; 1.1L or 40 imperial ounces (one bottle) of liquor or wine, or 24 cans of beer; and gifts up to the value of C$60 (US$100) per item. Small amounts of food are allowed, but there are strict restrictions on the import of plants, seeds and animal products to prevent the spread of pests and diseases. Importing firearms, weapons, explosives and other dangerous goods is generally illegal, so it's best to leave the pump-action at home unless you fancy a short spell in the clink.

FESTIVALS & EVENTS

There are lots of annual celebrations that you could choose to base your trip around. Highlights include the Banff Winter Festival in January (with an accompanying ice sculpture competition at Lake Louise), the lively Banff Arts Festival from May to August, the Jasper Folk Festival in August and Banff's Winterstart festival, a huge two-day street party in November with parades, an outdoor bonfire, snowboard party and a light-filled parade through the town. Accommodations are often harder to come by during major events, so book well ahead. For a full list of events, check out the boxed text, p28.

FOOD

For ease of use, we've arranged our restaurant reviews in this book by budget, ranging from the cheapest up to the most expensive. Restaurants, diners and cafés are easy to find around the park townsites, and some of them are real culinary wonders. Meat (especially Albertan steak), game, fish and chicken tend to feature pretty heavily, but there are usually a few vegetarian options on offer – veggie-friendly dishes are usually marked on menus, although you'll probably need to inquire specifically about nut and wheat allergies. There's even a place where you can tuck into rattlesnake and shark fondue (p141). Main meals are usually in the C$15 to C$25 range; expect to splash out at least C$60 to C$70 on a meal for two with wine and starters. If you're eating out, remember that service is usually not added to your bill – a tip of 15% to 20% is the expected norm.

Self-caterers will find large Safeway supermarkets in Banff and Jasper, with a smaller mini-mart in Lake Louise and basic grocery stores dotted around the rest of the park, often handily situated near the main campgrounds.

HOLIDAYS

Both Canada and the USA observe a number of national holidays, when most shops, visitor attractions and services shut or operate on limited hours, and banks, schools and post offices are all closed. Accommodations, transportation and main highways are usually very busy around major holidays, especially Easter, Labor Day, Thanksgiving and Christmas, so try to avoid traveling at these times if you possibly can.

Canada

New Year's Day January 1
Good Friday March/April
Easter Monday First Monday after Good Friday
Victoria Day Monday preceding May 25
Canada Day July 1
Labour Day First Monday of September
Thanksgiving Day Second Monday of October
Remembrance Day November 11
Christmas Day December 25
Boxing Day December 26

USA

New Year's Day January 1
Martin Luther King Day Third Monday in January
President's Day Third Monday in February
Memorial Day Last Monday in May
Independence Day July 4
Labor Day First Monday in September
Columbus Day Second Monday in October
Veterans' Day November 11
Thanksgiving Day Fourth Thursday in November
Christmas Day December 25

INSURANCE

Travel insurance is always a worthwhile investment if you're visiting another country. Choose your policy carefully, especially for coverage against flight delays, 'acts of God' or *force majeure* events and baggage loss. If you're undertaking lots of outdoor activities such as hiking, biking, climbing or water sports, and especially if you're planning to do any skiing or snowboarding, make sure your travel insurance policy covers you against medical treatment and also for emergency repatriation (many off-the-shelf policies don't). Also check the excess you'll have to pay in the event of a claim – what can seem a really cheap policy often becomes very expensive if you have to pay a heavy excess charge before you get any money back. Travelers arriving from outside the US or Canada should make extra sure the policy has good coverage against medical costs – you'll be charged for any medical or dental treatment you receive and hospital bills are usually cripplingly expensive.

Auto insurance purchased in Canada and the US is usually applicable to either country – in other words if you're an American who's planning on driving your car into Canada, your auto-insurance policy should provide the same level of coverage across the border. As always, though, this tends to vary from policy to policy and it's worth checking coverage carefully with your insurer before you set out rather than leaving the important questions until it's too late. It's also worth noting that many auto insurance policies extend to rental cars, and some credit-card providers also provide additional coverage if you pay for the car with your card.

Most standard US health plans aren't valid for treatment in Canada, so you'll need to ensure you're covered under a separate travel-insurance policy. Since most basic Canadian health care is free at the point of delivery for Canadian residents (excluding most prescriptions, dentistry and eye care), many Canadians don't have private health cover and so won't be covered for treatment in the US.

INTERNATIONAL VISITORS
Entering the US & Canada

Visitors from many countries, including the US, most European Union nations, the UK and British Overseas Territories, Australia and New Zealand, do not require a visa to enter Canada. You are usually permitted to remain in the country for six months, after which you will have to apply for an extension to your visa. If you're arriving in the US from one of these countries, you should qualify for entry under the Visa Waiver Program; you'll have to fill in an application form as well as a customs declaration on the plane, which you'll present to immigration officials. This will qualify you to remain in the US for a stay of up to 90 days. Under new rules you will need a valid machine-readable passport and your photo (and possibly your fingerprints) will be digitally scanned on entry.

Citizens of other countries will need to apply for a visitor's visa from either the **Citizenship and Immigration Service Canada** (☎ 1-888-576-8502; www.cic.gc.ca) or the **US Citizenship and Immigration Services** (☎ 1-800-375-5283; www.uscis.gov.uk), or apply directly to the embassy or consulate in their own country. There's a comprehensive list of Canadian consular offices at www.cic.gc.ca/english/information/offices/apply-where.asp and of US embassies at www.usembassy.state.gov.

ENTERING CANADA VIA THE LAND BORDER

Most US-based visitors heading for Canada will want to cross via the land border, either by train, bus or more likely by car. With thousands of people crossing the border on a daily basis it's one of the busiest land borders in the world and, unsurprisingly, the wait-times can be horrendously long (you can get the heads-up on delays at specific checkpoints at www.cbsa-asfc.gc.ca/general/times/menu-e.html). Most crossings are pretty smooth; you'll need to present your passport, plus driver's license, insurance and registration if you're arriving by car. Note that if you're bringing a rental car across the border, you will have to have cleared this with the rental company beforehand, and you might have to present your rental agreement to border officials for inspection. If you're on public transportation, you may have to disembark and carry your own luggage across the border. Be prepared to answer standard questions from border guards about the purpose of your visit, length of stay and any items you're intending to bring across the border. Unless you fancy prolonging the experience, answer sensibly and politely; this is definitely not a time for wisecracking. It's also probably best if you leave those CND and Che Guevara T-shirts at home.

For rules on items that are legally allowed to cross the US border, see the Customs section (p250).

INTERNET ACCESS

Net access is widespread around the main gateway towns in both of the Canadian parks; in Glacier National Park it's almost nonexistent. A few years ago it was still fairly uncommon for hotel rooms in the Canadian parks to offer anything other than an expensive dial-up connection, but these days most hotels offer free wireless access to customers with their own laptops, and wi-fi hot spots are becoming increasingly common in cafés and restaurants. Where we've used this icon (▢), it denotes wireless access. If you're traveling without your own computer, the best idea is to dig out an internet café – most of the main towns have at least one place where you can sip a cappuccino while surfing the web, and we've listed these in the Information sections of individual town entries. Failing that, public libraries also offer internet access, usually for a small fee. If you're using public computers, remember to log off after each session and be alert for dangers such as keystroke capturing software – avoid accessing sensitive information (such as online banking or credit cards) on a public computer.

Outside the main towns, net access starts to get pretty patchy. The deeper you travel into the countryside the more uncommon it is for hotels, restaurants and cafés to offer any form of internet service (many of the more remote places don't even offer in-room phones). And that's not such a bad thing – after all, you didn't decide to visit a national park to spend half your time online, did you?

Check out p27 for some useful websites while you're planning your trip, and also visit some of the other sites we've recommended in the sidebars.

LAUNDRY

If you've messed up your togs out on the trail, getting them clean again can be a bit of a challenge. A handful of the larger campgrounds have laundry facilities; otherwise you'll have to head for town. Try **Cascade Coin Laundry** (Map p94; basement, Cascade Plaza) in Banff and the **Coin-Op Laundry** (Map p170; 607 Patricia St) in Jasper. HI hostels usually have on-site laundry facilities as well.

MONEY
Canada

If you're a US or Canadian visitor, you should be able to get your hands on cash fairly easily within the parks, although as ever services are more limited outside the townsites. Banks and ATMs are fairly widespread, and you'll find branches of at least one major bank (CIBC, ATB, Scotiabank or Bank of Montreal) in Jasper, Banff and Canmore as well as in several other gateway towns. Many gas stations, supermarkets and malls also have ATMs, and there are handy ATMs at Samson Mall in Lake Louise village and at The Crossing on the Icefields Parkway.

If you're an overseas visitor, there are *bureaus de changes* in Banff at the **Foreign Currency Exchange** (Map p94; ☎ 403-762-4698; Clock Tower Mall, 110 Banff Ave) and **Custom House Currency Exchange** (Map p94; ☎ 403-660-6630; Park Ave Mall, 211 Banff Ave). If your bank is a member of the Cirrus or Maestro networks, you should also be able to withdraw cash from ATMs for a small charge.

Visa, MasterCard and American Express are accepted practically everywhere that takes credit cards. Prices for almost everything in Canada are quoted without GST, so you'll need to factor in an extra 6% at the till.

USA

In Glacier, the nearest banks are in Columbia Falls and Browning. The lodges at Lake McDonald, Glacier Park and Many Glacier have ATMs, as does Eddie's Camp Store in Apgar and the St Mary supermarket.

For exchange services in Waterton, head for Waterton Visitor Services at **Tamarack Outdoor Outfitters** (Map p231; ☎ 403-859-2378; Mount View Rd; ☺ 8am-8pm). The closest banks are in Cardston and Pincher Creek.

Credit cards and traveler's checks are widely accepted, and there's no sales tax in Montana.

POST

Mail services are much the same in the national parks as in the rest of the US and Canada, although it can take longer for letters to arrive in winter, when heavy snow cover sometimes causes delays. Banff, Jasper and Glacier all have large, efficient post offices, while you'll find smaller branches in most gateway towns.

Banff Post Office (Map p94; ☎ 403-762-2586; 204 Buffalo St)

East Glacier Post Office (☎ 406-226-5534; 15 Blackfoot Ave)

Jasper Post Office (Map p170; 502 Patricia St)

Waterton Post Office (Map p231; ☎ 403-859-2294; 102A Windflower Ave)

TELEPHONE

You'll find plenty of payphones in the main towns, as well as at park lodges, the better-equipped campgrounds and some visitor attractions. In Canada, it costs 50¢ to make a call from a payphone, or 35¢ in the US. The international prefix for both countries is ☎ 1. Toll-free numbers are prefixed by ☎ 1-800 or ☎ 1-888, while area codes are denoted by the first three digits of phone numbers (eg ☎ 403 or ☎ 780 in Alberta, ☎ 406 in Montana).

Cell-phone coverage outside the main towns can be extremely patchy, especially in the backcountry. While it's always worth taking a cell with you if you're on a wilderness trip, don't automatically assume it'll have reception if you need to contact the emergency services. Canadian and US cell-phone networks are generally compatible, so if you've already got a US or Canadian cell, you should be fine. If you're bringing a phone from abroad, check that it works with the cell-phone systems in the US and Canada – while most of the world uses the GSM standard, many American and Canadian operators use alternative systems such as CDMA and often operate on different frequencies. In general, if you've got a newer tri-band or quadband GSM handset, you should be able to pick up a network somewhere, although it might be worth investing in a temporary pay-as-you-go SIM card from one of the local cell-phone retailers to avoid expensive roaming call charges.

For emergency numbers in the park, see the inside back cover of this book.

TIME

Alberta and Montana are both in the 'Mountain Timezone,' one hour ahead of Pacific Time (Los Angeles, San Francisco, the US west coast and most of British Columbia), one hour behind Central Time, two hours behind Eastern Time (New York and the US east coast) and seven hours behind Greenwich Mean Time (London).

Like most Canadian provinces, Alberta observes daylight saving time between the second Sunday in March and the first Sunday in November. The clocks are put forward one hour during this period so mornings are shorter and evenings are longer.

TOURIST INFORMATION

For general information on the national parks, your first port of call should be the comprehensive websites for either **Parks Canada** (www.pc.gc.ca) or the **US National Park Service** (www.nps.gov). For more specific information, the staff at the main park visitor centers are hugely knowledgeable and very helpful, and can provide leaflets, brochures and guide booklets on practically every imaginable activity in the park. All the other provincial parks have their own visitor centers – see the relevant chapters for details. For advice on hotels, restaurants and other tourism services, contact the tourism bureaus, which are usually located inside the same building.

Banff

Banff Information Center (☎ 403-762-1550; www .parkscanada.gc.ca/pn-np/ab/Banff)
Banff Tourism Bureau (☎ 403-762-8421; www .bafflakelouise.com)
Lake Louise Visitor Center (☎ 403-522-3833; ll.info@pc.gc.ca)

Glacier

Apgar Visitor Center (☎ 406-888-7939)
Glacier National Park (☎ 406-888-7800/6; www .nps.gov/glac)
St Mary Visitor Center (☎ 406-732-7750)

Jasper

Icefields Center Parks Information (☎ 780-852-6288)
Jasper Information Centre (☎ 780-852-6176; www .pc.gc.ca/pn-np/ab/Jasper)
Jasper Tourism & Commerce (☎ 780-852-3858; www.jaspercanadianrockies.com)

Waterton Lakes

Waterton Lakes National Park (☎ 403-859-2224; www.parkscanada.gc.ca/waterton)
Waterton Visitor Centre (☎ 403-859-5133)

TOURS

If you've got limited time to spend in the parks, or you just prefer letting someone else do the planning, taking an organized tour can be a great way of cramming in lots of must-see sights into a short space of time. Most sightseeing tours are conducted in minibuses or coaches, usually with a guided commentary on the sights provided by a well-informed guide. Others are multi-day adventures that explore several national parks. They pack a lot in, so there won't be much time for dawdling, but you'll certainly be able to tick off the essentials.

We've suggested operators for specific guides or activities (eg hiking, horseback riding and rock climbing) under the relevant entry in the Activities chapter (p37). General tour operators include the following:

Brewster (☎ 403-762-6750, 877-791-5500; www .brewster.ca) Long-standing Banff-based tour company with a selection of routes around Banff and Jasper in purpose-built minibuses and coaches, ranging from easy three-hour Banff trips (C$70) to a marathon seven-hour epic taking in Banff, Johnston Canyon, the Icefields Parkway and Jasper (C$104).
Discover Banff Tours (☎ 403-760-5007; www .banff tours.com) Another popular and reliable bus-tour company, with tours of the Banff area (C$49), Lake Louise and Moraine Lake (C$59) and the Icefields Parkway (C$145), including a trip on a Snocoach. It also organizes a whole host of different activity trips – contact the company for full details.
Jasper Adventure Tours (☎ 780-852-5595; www.jas peradventurecentre.com) Sporty adventure tour company that offers several round-trips in Banff and Jasper, including a Maligne Valley Tour (C$60), a 'Watchable Wildlife' Trip (C$68), a Jasper–Banff route (C$325) and lots of guided day hikes, nature walks and adventure expeditions.
Rocky Mountain Tour Center (☎ 877-852-7682; www.tourrockies.com) Ten-seater Dodge Sprinter buses zip around the park from Jasper on wildlife tours (C$65) and a multi-sight Jasper Super Tour (C$99).
Snocoach (☎ 877-423-7433; www.columbiaicefield .com) Brewster also operates the all-terrain buses that crawl up onto the Athabasca Glacier from the Icefields Center, which can be taken either as part of one of Brewster's longer tours or as a stand-alone 1½-hour trip (C$34).
Sundog Tours (☎ 780-852-4056; www.sundogtours .com) Based in Jasper, Sundog offers a huge selection of half- and full-day tours, ranging from a Maligne Valley wildlife tour (C$49) to an all-in-one Jasper–Banff route via Athabasca Falls, the Weeping Wall, Bow Lake, Crowfoot Glacier and Lake Louise (C$134). It also offers multi-day vacation packages, guided hikes and tailored sightseeing trips and can organize other activities with local companies.
True North Tours (☎ 403-934-5972; www.backpacker -tour.com) Well-organized, friendly tour company specializing in multi-day trips for budget travelers, including a four-day trip around Waterton Lakes and a 10-day journey through Banff, Jasper, Calgary and Waterton (C$950), with accommodations in hostels.

TRAVELERS WITH DISABILITIES

While in theory the national parks are intended for the use and enjoyment of everybody, in practice visiting Banff, Jasper and Glacier still presents quite a challenge for people with auditory, visual or physical disabilities and people with restricted mobility. Having said that, parks authorities have made serious efforts to address accessibility problems and things have improved in leaps and bounds in recent years. Your best bet is to contact parks visitor centers directly with questions and queries on specific activities. In the US, the National Parks Service publishes the *Accessibility Guide*, with lots of helpful information and details for Glacier.

Most hotels have at least some wheelchair-accessible rooms (although often that simply means you can access rooms by elevator). If you're planning on camping, the larger and more modern campgrounds at Tunnel Mountain, Johnston Canyon and Lake Louise (plus Waterfowl Lakes) in Banff, as well as Whistlers, Wabasso and Wapiti in Jasper, have the best facilities for disabled users, including wheelchair-friendly campsites and washrooms. We've used the wheelchair icon (&) to indicate access for people with mobility problems, but you should always check ahead to confirm the exact facilities available.

Many of the more popular sights in Banff and Jasper have interpretive listening posts designed for visitors with auditory problems.

Banff

Most of the main sights in Banff, including Lake Louise, Banff's museums, Upper Hot Springs Pool and Peyto Lake along the Icefields Parkway are all wheelchair-accessible, as is the main visitor center. Other paved trails that are good for wheelchair users include the lower section of Johnston Canyon, the paved section of the Lake Minnewanka Shoreline Trail, the Lake Louise Shoreline Trail and the mixed-use Sundance Trail in Banff. In Kananaskis Country, William Watson Lodge has been designed specifically to give people with disabilities access to the area, with 22 fully accessible cottages and over 18km of accessible trails. Ask for the free guide in Kananaskis visitor centers.

Glacier & Waterton Lakes

In Glacier, two short, scenic trails are paved for wheelchair use: Trail of the Cedars, off Going-to-the-Sun Rd, and the Running Eagle Falls Trail in Two Medicine. Hearing-impaired visitors can get information at ☎ 406-888-7806. Park visitors centers have audio tapes for visually impaired visitors. At least one or two ground-floor, wheelchair-friendly rooms are available at all in-park lodges. Several campgrounds have wheelchair-accessible bathrooms.

The Waterton townsite campground has wheelchair-accessible bathroom facilities. The hostel can accommodate travelers using a wheelchair, as can a few of the lodges in the townsite.

Jasper

Jasper's museum, Miette Hot Springs, Maligne Lake, Medicine Lake, Jasper Tramway and the visitor center are all wheelchair-accessible, as is Athabasca Falls and the Icefields Center along the Icefields Parkway. Several trails are good for wheelchair users, including the initial paved section of the Mary Schäffer Loop, Maligne Lake, the Clifford E Lee Trail at Lake Annette and Pyramid Isle in Pyramid Lake.

Few accommodations in Jasper have dedicated rooms for wheelchair users, although most have elevators, and there are usually ground-floor rooms that can accommodate disabled visitors. Many of Jasper's restaurants are on ground floors and have accessible toilets.

VOLUNTEERING

There's no end of organizations that volunteer their efforts for free to ensure the continuing welfare of the parks. Top of the heap are the Friends organizations (Friends of Banff, Friends of Jasper, Friends of Kootenay), which undertake everything from administrative work and fundraising to on-the-ground trail maintenance; they're often looking for volunteers to help with current programs. Check out www.friendsofbanff.com for more information and links to the other Friends websites. For more suggestions on giving up your time for a good cause in the park, check out the boxed text, p52.

Transportation

GETTING THERE & AWAY

AIR
Airports
BANFF & JASPER NATIONAL PARKS

Calgary (YYC; ☎ toll-free 1-877-254-7427, 403-735-1200; www.calgaryairport.com) and **Edmonton** (YEG; ☎ 780-890-8900; www.edmontonairports.com) are the closest international airports to Banff and Jasper respectively, but it's worth checking flight prices to both for deals. It's just about feasible to fly into **Vancouver** (YVR; ☎ 604-207-7077; www.yvr.ca), but you'll be faced with a long drive – it's 847km (525 miles) to Banff and 794km (492 miles) to Jasper, so you'll face at least 10 hours behind the wheel.

The national airline, Air Canada, and its subsidiary Jazz, plus Westjet, cover the majority of Canadian routes, and connect through Montreal and Toronto en route to many European destinations. There are also direct flights to LA, New York, Seattle and Heathrow. US-based airlines, including Continental and United, connect with larger American cities, while smaller carriers such as Northwest, Delta and US Airways serve several minor cities.

GLACIER & WATERTON LAKES NATIONAL PARKS

Glacier's nearest airport is **Glacier Park International Airport** (FCA; ☎ 406-257-5994; www.glacier airport.com), halfway between Whitefish and Kalispell, and serviced by Delta, Horizon Air, Northwest Airlines and United. Destinations include Salt Lake City, Minneapolis, Denver and Seattle.

You could also choose to fly into **Great Falls International Airport** (GTF; ☎ 406-727-3404; www.gtfairport.com), 249km (155 miles) from Glacier, or **Missoula International Airport** (MSO; ☎ 406-728-4381; www.msoairport.org), 241km (150 miles) from the park, but you'll face a long drive once you've landed, so any flight savings will probably be eaten up by the cost of a rental car.

Lethbridge County Airport (YQL; ☎ 403-329-4466) is the closest to Waterton Lakes, 129km (80 miles) to the northeast. It's served by Air Canada and Integra Air, but the limited flight schedule usually means it's more convenient (and cheaper) to fly into Calgary, 266km (165 miles) north of Waterton.

Airlines
FLIGHTS FROM USA & CANADA

Air Canada/Jazz (☎ 888-247-2262, 514-393-3333; www.aircanada.com) International flights connecting through Canadian hubs including Toronto, Ottawa and Montreal, plus Canadian destinations including Saskatoon, Edmonton, Grande Prairie, Lethbridge, Medicine Hat, Kamloops and Fort McMurray. Also direct routes to London Heathrow, Seattle, New York and LA.

American Airlines (☎ 800-433-7300; www.aa.com) Current routes include Calgary to Dallas.

Continental Airlines (☎ 800-231-0856; www.continental.com) Calgary to Houston.

Delta Airlines (☎ 800-241-4141; www.delta-air.com) Current routes include Salt Lake City to Edmonton.

Horizon Air (www.horizonair.com) Regional airline in Alaska, with connections to Glacier via Seattle.

Northwest Airlines (☎ 800-225-2525; www.nwa.com) Connects Edmonton, Calgary and Glacier with Minneapolis.

United Airlines (☎ 800-241-6522; www.united.com) Major US cities, including San Francisco, Denver and Chicago, to both Edmonton and Calgary, plus daily flights from Denver to Glacier.

US Airways (☎ 800-428-4322; www.usairways.com) Calgary to Phoenix.

Westjet (☎ 800-538-5696; www.westjet.com) Canadian destinations, including Regina, Toronto, Montreal, Winnipeg, London Ontario, Halifax, Abbotsford, Comox and St Johns.

CLIMATE CHANGE & TRAVEL

You'd have to have been living in a cave for the last few years not to be aware of the issues surrounding international travel and climate change. The threat of global warming looming on everyone's collective horizon is based on serious science and hard evidence – we're already starting to see the first effects of climate change, and the problem is likely to get worse as the century wears on. Here at Lonely Planet we think it's worth remembering the positive benefits we can have as global travelers, but we also believe it's everyone's duty to do their bit to help the planet.

Transport & Climate Change

Unfortunately nearly every form of modern human transport spews out carbon dioxide (the main cause of human-induced climate change) but planes are far and away the worst offenders, not just because of the sheer distances they allow us to travel, but because they release greenhouse gases high into the atmosphere. The statistics are frightening: two people taking a return flight between Europe and the US will contribute as much to climate change as an average household's gas and electricity consumption over a whole year.

Carbon Offset Schemes

Climatecare.org and other websites use 'carbon calculators' that allow travelers to offset the level of greenhouse gases they are responsible for with financial contributions to sustainable travel schemes that reduce global warming – including projects in India, Honduras, Kazakhstan and Uganda.

Lonely Planet, together with Rough Guides and other concerned partners in the travel industry, support the carbon offset scheme run by climatecare.org. Lonely Planet offsets all of its staff and author travel.

For more information check out www.lonelyplanet.com.

FLIGHTS FROM UK & IRELAND

Air Canada and British Airways are the established carriers to the UK, but there are a number of low-cost airlines that have entered the market and are carrying an increasing number of passengers to the gateway airports. There are currently no direct flights from Ireland, and almost none from Europe, so non-UK travelers will generally have to connect through London first.

Air Transat (☎ 020-7616-9187; www.airtransat.com) Good quality cut-price carrier with scheduled services from UK airports to Calgary, and Frankfurt to Edmonton.

British Airways (☎ 0870-850-9850; www.ba.com) London Heathrow to Calgary.

Flyglobespan (☎ 0871-271-0415; www.flyglobespan .com) No-frills operator with weekly flights from Calgary to London Gatwick, Glasgow and Manchester.

Thomas Cook (☎ 0870-750-5711; www.thomascook .com) Flights to Calgary from London Gatwick.

Zoom (☎ 0870-240-0055; www.flyzoom.com) Budget carrier with flights from London Gatwick to both Edmonton and Calgary. Also offers flights from Calgary to Paris Charles de Gaulle.

FLIGHTS FROM AUSTRALIA & NEW ZEALAND

There are currently no operators offering direct services to either Calgary or Edmonton from Australasia. The only option is to connect through one of the other major Canadian cities – most obviously Vancouver – and either drive or catch a flight on to the mountain airports with one of the Canadian regional carriers.

BUS
Banff & Jasper National Parks
AIRPORT SHUTTLES

There are a number of shuttle services from Calgary to Jasper and Banff.

Airporter Shuttle Express (☎ 403-509-1570; www .airportshuttleexpress.com) Charter minibuses costing C$225/263/323 for five/10/15 people between Calgary airport and any Banff hotel. Buses can also be chartered to Jasper.

Banff Airport Taxi (☎ 403-678-2776; www.banffairport taxi.com) Offers a similar service and also travels on to Lake Louise on request. It monitors incoming flights, so if you're delayed it'll automatically adjust its arrival time to

TRANSPORTATION

make sure there's still someone there to meet you at the airport. The price for one to four passengers is $200 one way, $400 return.

Banff Airporter (☎ 888-449-2901, 403-762-3330; www.banffairporter.com) Ten daily scheduled shuttles from Calgary airport to Canmore and Banff (adult/child one-way C$50/25).

Brewster (☎ 800-760-6934; www.brewster.ca) Connects Calgary airport with Banff and Lake Louise twice daily, with an early morning bus that continues on to Jasper.

Rocky Mountain Sky Shuttle (www.rockymountain skyshuttle.com) Thirteen daily year-round buses from Calgary airport to Banff (adult/child one way C$53/29), plus nine that stop at Canmore (C$53/29) and Lake Louise (C$62/36).

Sundog Tours (☎ 780-852-4056; www.sundogtours .com; ✷ Oct-Apr) Operates a winter-only service called the Mountain Connector, which travels from Calgary airport to Banff, Lake Louise and Jasper. You'll be met by a representative at the airport who'll transfer you to Banff within an hour of your flight's arrival, from where you can catch a connecting bus to Lake Louise. If you're traveling on to Jasper, you'll need to arrive before 11:30am to guarantee a connecting service, otherwise you'll need to overnight in Banff and catch the connecting bus the following day. Private charters are also available.

PUBLIC BUSES

Greyhound (☎ 800-661-8747; www.greyhound.ca) has four daily departures to Jasper from Edmonton (five hours, C$57.35) and two daily from Vancouver (11 hours, C$115.90). Neither bus route travels via the Icefields Parkway.

Buses also travel to Banff from Calgary (C$23.85, one hour 40 minutes, five daily) and Vancouver (C$115.90, 14 hours, four daily); some routes also stop in Golden, Field and Canmore.

Purchase tickets from the airports, Jasper's **Via Rail train station** (☎ 888-842-7245; 607 Connaught Dr; ✷ ticket counters 9am-4:45pm Mon-Sat, 9am-12:45pm Sun) and Banff's **Greyhound bus depot** (☎ 403-762-1091; 327 Railway Ave; ✷ 7am-6pm Mon-Sat, 8am-6pm Sun).

Glacier & Waterton Lakes National Parks

AIRPORT SHUTTLES

There are two shuttle services from Glacier airport on to Whitefish and Kalispell; book a seat on an **airport shuttle service** (☎ 406-752-2842), or charter a minibus from the **Flathead-Glacier Transportation Co** (☎ 406-892-3390).

> ### THINGS CHANGE...
>
> The information in this chapter is intended as a guide to help you plan your trip and give you a general idea of getting to and from the national parks, but do be aware that this kind of practical info is particularly vulnerable to change. Air fares, train tickets and transport routes often change very quickly, so do your research, use the internet to cross-check prices and shop around. Make sure you're familiar with the rules and restrictions of any ticket you buy – particularly the policy on route changes and refunds – and bone up on the latest information on visas, airport security restrictions and travel warnings before you leave home. We've done our bit to get you started, but nothing beats your own careful up-to-date research.

PUBLIC BUSES

Greyhound Canada (☎ 403-627-2716, 800-661-8747; 840 Main St) in Pincher Creek, 53km (33 miles) from the Waterton townsite, connects with other locations in Alberta and Canada. To reach Banff from Pincher Creek, head for Fort Macleod, go on to Calgary and then on to Banff.

Intermountain Transport (☎ 406-755-4011) connects the **Kalispell bus station** (☎ 406-755-4011; 1301 S Main St; ✷ 9am-5pm Mon-Fri, 9am-noon Sat & Sun) to the Whitefish railroad depot and various other local towns.

CAR & MOTORCYCLE
Major Routes
BANFF & JASPER NATIONAL PARKS

From Calgary, follow Trans-Canada Hwy (Hwy 1) west to Banff via Canmore. To reach Jasper from Edmonton, take Hwy 16 west. Between Edmonton and Calgary, Hwy 11 heads west of Red Deer, entering Banff along the Icefields Parkway, just south of the border with Jasper.

Coming from Vancouver, head east to Hope and follow the Coquihalla Hwy (Hwy 5) north to Kamloops; there is a C$10 toll to use this road. From Kamloops you can travel north to Jasper by following Hwy 5 via Mt Robson Provincial Park, or east to Banff along Hwy 1 through Mt Revelstoke National Park, Golden and Yoho National Park.

GLACIER & WATERTON LAKES NATIONAL PARKS

The west side of Glacier is most easily reached from Whitefish, Kalispell and Flathead Lake; the east side is closer to Great Falls and Helena. West Glacier and East Glacier are connected by US 2, below the southern boundary of the park.

If you're traveling north across the border into Waterton Lakes, you'll have to pass through customs en route. On US 17, you'll pass through via the **Port of Chief Mountain** (☎ in Canada 403-653-3535, in US 406-732-5572; ⏰ 7am-10pm Jun-Aug, 9am-6pm Sep), but this gate is closed in winter, so you'll have to use the **Port of Peigan/Carway** (☎ in Canada 403-653-3009, in US 406-732-5572; ⏰ 7am-11pm), along Trans-Canada Hwy 2 (US Hwy 89), instead. You'll need to show two forms of ID; driver's license and passport are the standard items. For more details on customs, see p250.

From Calgary and Pincher Creek to the north, Hwy 6 shoots south toward Hwy 5, into Waterton Lakes. From Banff National Park, visit via Calgary and Cardston or, in the summer, Kananaskis Country.

Automobile Associations

Alberta Motor Association (☎ in Calgary 403-240-5300; www.ama.ab.ca) is the province's main motoring organization and is affiliated with the Canadian Automobile Association (CAA). It can help with queries on driving in Alberta, as well as arrange breakdown cover and insurance for members; you'll also sometimes qualify for special rates on hotels and other services.

The **American Automobile Association** (☎ 406-758-6980; www.aaa.com; 135 Hutton Ranch Rd, Ste 106, Kalispell) is the US equivalent, and offers a similar range of services. There are other branches in Missoula, Great Falls and Bozeman.

The **Better World Club** (☎ 866-238-1137; www.betterworldclub.com) is an ecologically minded automobile club that offers roadside assistance to its members in the USA.

Driver's License

Foreign driver's licenses can be used in Alberta for up to three months. International driver's licenses can be used for up to 12 months or the duration of the license (whichever ends sooner). It's required that you carry your license and vehicle registration at all times.

Rental

CAR

Most people visiting the parks rent a car. It's the most convenient way to travel, allowing you to explore at your own pace and visit even the most remote sights, though you have to be prepared to deal with the usual issues including fuel costs, traffic and (perish the thought) breakdown. All the international car-rental agencies have branches at the main airports and towns, which usually stay open from 6am to midnight; town branches generally stick to normal business hours.

Booking online before you leave home will usually secure the best rates, but check carefully for hidden premiums such as high insurance excess, mileage caps, limits on interstate travel and GST. One-way rentals will also usually incur a surcharge. If you're doing a lot of driving, it's best to get an all-inclusive mileage deal. Check the insurance cover carefully: rental deals will include standard liability insurance and breakdown cover with the CAA, but US and Canadian visitors (and some international drivers) may be covered under their own existing insurance policy. Check before you leave home. You'll also be offered Collision Damage Waiver (CDW), which covers you for any damage to the vehicle itself. It adds a hefty whack to the daily rate (C$15 to C$30), but if you put a dent in the fender it'll definitely work out cheaper in the long run. Also watch out for any excess charge in the event of a claim. You can often have this waived in exchange for an extra fee.

Banff & Jasper National Parks

All of these rental agencies have branches at the three main airports (Calgary, Edmonton and Vancouver), and most have offices in Banff and Jasper.

Avis (☎ 800-879-2847; www.avis.com)
Budget (☎ 800-268-8900; www.budget.com)
Discount (☎ 800-263-2355; www.discountcar.com)
Enterprise (☎ 800-261-7331; www.enterprise.com)
Hertz (☎ 800-263-0600; www.hertz.com)
National (☎ 800-227-7368; www.nationalcar.com)
Thrifty (☎ 800-847-4389; www.thrifty.com)

Glacier National Park

There are branches for the following agencies at Glacier Park International Airport.
Avis (☎ 800-527-0700; www.avis.com)

TRANSPORTATION

Budget (☎ 406-755-7500, 800-527-0700; www.budget
.com)
Hertz (☎ 406-758-2220, 800-654-3131; www.hertz.com)
National (☎ 406-257-7144; www.nationalcar.com)

You'll find several other companies based
in Kalispell:
Dollar (☎ 800-800-3665; www.dollar.com; 5506 Hwy 2
W; ◷ 6am-1am)
Enterprise (☎ 800-261-7331; www.enterprise.com;
2177 Hwy 2 E; ◷ 8am-6pm Mon-Fri, 9am-2pm Sat)
Thrifty (☎ 800-847-4389; www.thrifty.com; 4785 Hwy
2 W; ◷ 8am-6pm Mon-Sat)

There are also a few local rental firms dotted
around the park – try the **Glacier Highland Resort** (☎ 406-888-5427, 800-766-0811; ◷ 8am-10pm)
in West Glacier, or the Avis office based
at the **Glacier Park Trading Co** (☎ 406-226-9227,
800-331-1212; ◷ 9am-9pm mid-Apr–mid-Oct) in East
Glacier.

Waterton Lakes National Park
Rental agencies at Lethbridge County Airport include the following:
Budget (☎ 403-328-6555, 877-213-6555; www.budget
.com; ◷ 7:30am-11pm Mon-Fri, 9am-5pm Sat, noon-
11pm Sun)
Hertz (☎ 403-382-3470, 800-654-3131; www.hertz
.com; ◷ 9am-5pm Mon-Sat)
National (☎ 403-394-7235, 800-227-7368; www
.national.com; ◷ 8am-8pm)

RECREATIONAL VEHICLES & CAMPERVAN RENTALS
Like the motor-powered equivalent of a
pioneer setting out on the trail, renting a
recreational vehicle (RV) is many people's
dream way of touring the parks. Driving an
RV certainly has many advantages: you'll be
able to cut back on hotel bills; cook your
own meals; tour the parks at your leisure;
and experience a taste of the outdoors life
without having to rough it too much. However, it's not without its problems. These
road-ruling beasts are big, unwieldy, heavy
on fuel and excruciatingly slow, and it's really important that you familiarize yourself
with RV driving, preferably before you pick
up your holiday automobile. Controlling
such a large chunk of automobile takes
some getting used to, especially if you're
trying to coax them around awkward
parking lots, campgrounds and twisty park
roads. Ask for a thorough rundown on all

the intricate workings of the RV before you
leave the rental agency. Also check that the
campground you're planning on staying at
has spaces for RVs. Kitchen kits, furniture,
bike racks and child seats are available at
extra cost.
CanaDream (☎ 800-461-7368; www.canadream
.com) Offers various types of truck campers, campervans
and motor homes from locations in Calgary, Edmonton
and Vancouver. Prices start from between C$115 and
C$125 (plus mileage) for a mid-sized motor home, or
C$130 to C$150 per night for a slightly sportier all-in-one
campervan.
Cruise Canada (☎ 800-671-8042; www.cruisecanada
.com) Rents three sizes of RV from locations in Calgary and
Vancouver for between C$500 and C$700 per week plus
mileage (around C$350 per 1000km). There's a three-night
minimum rental.
Cruise America (☎ 480-464-7300; www.cruiseamerica
.com) The same company rents RVs in the US, although
there are no dealerships in Montana.

Road Rules
In Canada and the US, driving is on the
left. Speed limits in Alberta are 100km/h
(62mph) on major highways, 90km/h
(56mph) on main routes within the park
limits and 70km/h (43.5mph) or sometimes
less on minor roads, dropping to 50km/h
(31mph) or even less in townsites and built-
up areas (watch for speed signs). You are legally required to wear a seatbelt at all times,
and headlights must be turned on when visibility is restricted to 150m (500ft) or less.
Motorcyclists are required to wear helmets
and drive with headlights on. In Canada and
the US, it's legal to turn right on a stop-light
as long as there is no traffic coming from
the left. At four-way stop junctions, driver's
should pause and allow the first vehicle that
stopped to pull away first.

Penalties are severe for 'driving under the
influence,' so there's a simple rule to follow:
don't drink and drive, and you'll be doing
everyone a favor.

TRAIN
Banff & Jasper National Parks
VIA Rail (☎ 888-842-7245; www.viarail.com) stops in
Jasper on its route between Vancouver and
Edmonton at least three times per week;
you can connect onto this route from most
other US and Canadian cities.

The only trains to Banff are offered by
Rocky Mountaineer Rail Tours (☎ 800-665-7245;

www.rockymountaineer.com), which operates several multi-day rail tours between Vancouver and Calgary, with stops possible at Kamloops, Jasper, Banff, Yoho and the Icefields Parkway, depending on the route you choose. There are two travel classes available (Red and Gold Leaf), and most of the travel is done during daylight hours so you can appreciate the views. Hotels and meals are included in the package; prices start at around C$1129 for the basic three-day trip in standard class, and skyrockets to over C$8149 for the luxury 10-day 'Canadian Rockies at Leisure' excursion.

For a bit of out-and-out luxury, **Royal Canadian Pacific** (☎ 403-508-1400; www.royalcanadian pacific.com; s/d C$6600/7100) offers the ultimate train trip through the Rockies: a 10-day loop in a heritage train carriage that takes in Calgary, Banff, Lake Louise and Golden before traveling on to other classic sights such as Cranbrook, Okotoks, Eltham, Head-Smashed-In Buffalo Jump and Lethbridge.

Glacier & Waterton Lakes National Parks

Amtrak (☎ 1-800-872-7245; www.amtrak.com) operates the cross-country *Empire Builder* line from Seattle all the way to Chicago, serving stations in **East Glacier** (☎ 406-226-4452; ☽ 8:45-11:15am & 5-7:30pm), **West Glacier** (☽ 7:30am-4:30pm & 7:30-8:30pm Mon-Fri, 7:30-8:30am & 7:30-8:30pm Sat & Sun) and **Whitefish** (☽ 6am-2pm & 4-11:30pm) en route. Eastbound trains stop in the early morning before continuing to West Glacier (1¾ hours) and Whitefish (2¼ hours). Westbound trains travel through in the early evening. There are ticket offices at East Glacier and Whitefish, but you'll have to pre-book or buy on board from West Glacier. Sample one-way fares are US$5 from Whitefish to West Glacier, and US$13 from West Glacier to East Glacier.

GETTING AROUND

Practically all the main sights in the national parks are accessible by road, but you'll nearly always need your own wheels to reach them. With the exception of Glacier, public transport around the parks leaves a lot to be desired; hopefully the other mountain parks will follow Glacier's lead and intro-duce shuttle buses in the near future, but for the time being most people will have to bring along their own automobile.

BICYCLE

Cycling is a popular – and very green – way of getting around the parks, but it's definitely not for weekend pedallers. The distances between sights are pretty hefty, so bikes are mainly useful for commuting around the main townsites, unless you fancy taking on a serious point-to-point bike trek.

Bikes are available for rent in Banff, Jasper, Glacier and Waterton – see the individual park chapters for details. Note that bikes are banned on all trails in Glacier, but are allowed on most trails in the other parks. Most places rent full-suspension, front-suspension and road bikes, as well as children's bikes and chariots – expect to pay C$5 to C$15 per hour or C$35 to C$45 per day for an adult bike.

BUS

Traveling around by bus in Banff and Jasper is tough going unless you're on an organized tour. The only scheduled buses around the park are operated by **Brewster** (☎ 1-800-760-6934; www.brewster.ca), which has at least two daily buses from Calgary to Lake Louise, and one through-service to Jasper, and **Sundog Tours** (☎ 780-852-4056; www .sundogtours.com), which has a daily connector bus from Banff to Jasper stopping in Lake Louise. Both operate year-round, but only stop in the main townsites. If you want to get to most other sights or trailheads, your only option is to cycle, drive or go on an organized tour.

There are a few notable exceptions. Maligne Lake in Jasper, Sunshine Meadows in Banff, and Lake O'Hara in Yoho are all served by private shuttle services – see the individual chapters for details on fares and reservations.

The **Banff Transit Service** (☎ 403-762-1215) has three local bus routes around Banff town, stopping at points including the Banff Gondola, the Upper Hot Springs and Tunnel Mountain. Tickets (C$2/1 per adult/child) are available from the driver.

Public transport in Glacier is far superior thanks to the introduction of free biodiesel shuttle buses along the

---

DRIVING IN WINTER

Driving around in winter in any of the parks can be dangerous, but especially so in the two Canadian parks, which are blanketed by snow and ice for well over six months of the year. Whiteouts are not uncommon and several roads are closed during mid-winter or sudden periods of heavy snow – check ahead with the parks offices and keep abreast of local news and traffic bulletins.

In Banff and Jasper, it's legally required that you carry snow tires or chains on all roads in winter except the main Trans-Canada Hwy 1 (obviously it's also worth knowing how to fit them). Car-rental agencies should provide these if you're renting from them in winter, although you might be charged extra. It's also worth carrying a small emergency supply kit, including antifreeze, blankets, water, flashlight, snow shovel, matches and emergency food supplies – a cell (mobile) phone will also come in handy in case you need to phone for an emergency tow. Top up antifreeze, transmission, brake and windshield-washer fluids.

Be especially careful of invisible patches of ice on the road, especially once the temperature drops at night. Slow down, take extra care and use your gears rather than your brakes to slow down (look for the 'L' or 'Low' gear if you're driving an automatic). Slamming on your brakes will only increase your chances of skidding.

Going-to-the-Sun Rd. There are three color-coded routes: blue along the western section of the Going-to-the-Sun Rd from Apgar to Logan Pass, red from Logan Pass down to St Mary Visitor Center at the park's eastern gate, and green from Apgar Village to the Fish Creek Campground. Buses run every 15 to 30 minutes between 7am and 11:30pm, from July 1 to Labor Day, and stop at major trailheads, campgrounds and other points of interest.

There's also a shuttle bus run by **Glacier Park, Inc** (☎ 406-892-2525; per segment C$8; ☼ Jun–early Sep) between East Glacier and Waterton (Canada), stopping at Two Medicine, Cut Throat Creek, St Mary, Many Glacier and Chief Mountain. The same company also operates Glacier's famous vintage 'jammer' buses, which visit various points around the park and trundle over to Waterton; see p205 for details.

CAR & MOTORCYCLE
Fuel & Spare Parts
Gas is generally only available in and around the main townsites around Jasper, Banff and Lake Louise, so if you're setting out on a driving tour, make sure you fill your tank before you start. There are also gas stations at Castle Mountain and Saskatchewan Crossing in Banff – remember, prices are likely to be more expensive here. The same goes for spare parts, including bulbs, fan belts, fuel caps and fuses, and for major repair shops – you'll find these only in the main townsites. Most car-rental com-

panies provide breakdown cover as part of the rental package, but if you're driving your own vehicle, it might be worth joining one of the major breakdown agencies (see p259) to avoid getting stranded somewhere in the event of a breakdown.

Road Conditions
Most of the main roads through the parks are of a high quality and are well-maintained, although minor roads to trailheads and mountains are often steep, narrow and winding, making them far from ideal territory for RVs. Some roads (such as the Smith-Dorrien Hwy from Canmore into Kananaskis) are unsealed dirt tracks, so take special care when you're driving on them. Ice and snow are frequent hazards in winter, so be prepared if you're driving during the colder months.

Jasper and Banff National Parks are also notorious for animal collisions, especially along the quieter roads away from Hwy 1 – accidents involving trains and automobiles are one of the major causes of animal fatalities in the mountain parks. Wildlife (especially skittish creatures such as elk and bighorn sheep) can often appear suddenly, and tend to bolt across the roads when scared, so slow down and be alert.

HITCHHIKING
Hitching is never entirely safe in any country, and we don't recommend it. Travelers who decide to hitch should understand that they are taking a small but potentially seri-

ous risk. That said, thumbing a lift is an option in the mountain parks, although you might find you're waiting out on the highway for quite a while before anyone stops. As always, take the usual precautions: hitch in groups (especially if you're a solo female traveler), avoid hitching in remote areas and after dark, and make sure you keep an eye on your pack at all times. On the trail you can often hook up with hikers who have their own transport, or bum a lift by hanging around at the trailhead; most people will give you a lift if you smile sweetly and they've got space in the car.

TRANSPORTATION

Health & Safety

Keeping healthy while on vacation in the national parks depends on your pre-departure preparations, your daily health care while traveling and how you handle any medical problems that develop. While the potential problems can seem quite daunting, in reality few travelers experience anything more than an upset stomach.

If you have an emergency while staying in the national parks dial ☎ 911. Major centers like Banff, Jasper and Waterton have medical facilities; see opposite. If you're traveling out of your home country, be sure to purchase medical insurance before you leave. It is also important to read the policy's small print and ascertain exactly what you are being covered for. Medical services in Canada and the US are not reciprocal.

BEFORE YOU GO

Since most vaccines don't produce immunity until at least two weeks after they're given, visit a physician four to eight weeks before departure. Ask your doctor for an International Certificate of Vaccination (otherwise known as 'the yellow booklet'), which will list all the vaccinations you've received. It's a good idea to carry a record of all your vaccinations wherever you travel.

Bring medications in their original, labelled, containers. A signed and dated letter from your physician describing your medical conditions and medications, including generic names, is a good idea. If carrying syringes or needles, be sure to have a physician's letter documenting their necessity.

Some of the walks in this book are physically demanding and most require a reasonable level of fitness. Even if you're tackling the easy or easy–moderate walks, it pays to be relatively fit, rather than launch straight into them after months of fairly sedentary living. If you're aiming for the demanding walks, fitness is essential.

Unless you're a regular walker, start your get-fit campaign at least a month before your visit. Take a vigorous walk of about an hour, two or three times per week, and gradually extend the duration of your outings as the departure date nears. If you plan to carry a full backpack on any walk, carry a loaded pack on some of your training jaunts.

If you have any medical problems, or are concerned about your health in any way, it's a good idea to have a full check up before you start walking – better to have problems recognised and treated at home than to find out about them halfway up a mountain.

MEDICAL CHECKLIST

- acetaminophen (paracetamol) or aspirin
- adhesive or paper tape
- antibacterial ointment for cuts and abrasions
- antibiotics
- antidiarrheal drugs (eg loperamide)
- antihistamines (for hay fever and allergic reactions)
- anti-inflammatory drugs (eg ibuprofen)
- bandages, gauze swabs, gauze rolls
- DEET-containing insect repellent for the skin
- elasticized support bandage
- iodine tablets or water filter (for water purification)
- nonadhesive dressing
- oral rehydration salts
- paper stitches
- permethrin-containing insect spray for clothing, tents and bed nets

- pocket knife
- scissors, safety pins, tweezers
- sterile alcohol wipes
- steroid cream or cortisone (for allergic rashes)
- sticking plasters (Band-Aids, blister plasters)
- sun block
- sutures
- syringes & needles – ask your doctor for a note explaining why you have them
- thermometer

INTERNET RESOURCES

There is a wealth of travel-health advice to be found on the internet. For further information, **lonelyplanet.com** (www.lonelyplanet .com) is a good place to start. The **WHO** (www .who.int/ith) publishes a superb book called *International Travel and Health,* which is revised annually and is available online at no cost. Another website of general interest is **MD Travel Health** (www.mdtravelhealth.com), which provides complete travel-health recommendations for every country and is updated daily.

It's usually a good idea to consult your government's travel-health website before departure, if one is available:

Canada (www.travelhealth.gc.ca)
USA (www.cdc.gov/travel)

FURTHER READING

International Travel Health Guide by Stuart R Rose MD (Travel Medicine Inc) is the only traveler's health book that is updated annually.

Medicine for Mountaineering & Other Wilderness Activities by James A Wilkerson is an outstanding reference book for the layperson. It describes many of the medical problems typically encountered while trekking.

Hypothermia, Frostbite and Other Cold Injuries by James A Wilkerson is good background reading on the subject of cold and high-altitude problems.

Backcountry Bear Basics: The Definitive Guide to Avoiding Unpleasant Encounters by Dave Smith is good on the basics of bear behavior and biology.

Mountaineering: The Freedom of the Hills, edited by Don Graydon and Kurt Hanson, discusses outdoor fundamentals from beginners to advanced.

IN THE PARKS

National parks are pristine wilderness areas that are enjoyed annually by millions of people. But, due to the natural hostilities present in regions replete with mountains, glaciers, wild animals and fickle weather, visiting city dwellers will need to keep their wits about them in order to minimize the chances of suffering an avoidable accident or tragedy. Dress appropriately; tell people where you are going; don't bite off more than you can chew; and, above all, *respect* the wilderness and the inherent dangers that it conceals.

Crime is far more common in big cities than in sparsely populated national parks. Nevertheless, use your common sense: lock valuables in the trunk of your vehicle, especially if you're parking it at a trailhead overnight, and never leave anything worth stealing in your tent.

MEDICAL ASSISTANCE
Banff National Park

For medical emergencies, head to the modern **Mineral Springs Hospital** (Map p94; ☎ 403-762-2222; Bow Ave). For all other emergencies, dial ☎ 911.

Jasper National Park

The two local hospitals are **Seaton General Hospital** (☎ 780-852-3344; 518 Robson St) and **Cottage Medical Clinic** (☎ 780-852-4885; 505 Turret St).

Glacier National Park

Basic first aid is available at visitor centers and ranger stations in the park. The closest hospitals to the west side are **Kalispell Regional Medical Center** (☎ 406-752-5111; 310 Sunnyview Lane) and **North Valley Hospital** (☎ 406-863-3500; 6575 Hwy 93 S) in Whitefish. If you're in the northeast, you may find that **Cardston Municipal Hospital** (☎ 403-653-4411; 144 2nd St W, Cardston), in Alberta, Canada, is the closest

HEALTH & SAFETY

EMERGENCY NUMBERS

The following are the emergency 24-hour park warden numbers for each park:

Banff (☎ 403-762-4506)
Glacier (☎ 406-888-7800)
Jasper (☎ 780-852-6155)
Waterton Lakes (☎ 403-859-2224)

bet, though customs could consume time en route.

Waterton Lakes National Park

The summer-only number for ambulance service and other medical emergencies in Waterton is ☎ 403-859-2636. Full medical help is available at **Cardston Municipal Hospital** (☎ 403-653-4411; 144 2nd St W) and **Pincher Creek Municipal Hospital** (☎ 403-627-1234).

INFECTIOUS DISEASES
Giardiasis

While water running through the mountains may look crystal-clear, much of it carries *Giardia lamblia,* a microscopic parasite that causes intestinal disorders. To avoid getting sick, boil all water for at least 10 minutes, treat it with water tablets or filter at 0.5 microns or smaller. Iodine doesn't destroy giardiasis.

Symptoms include stomach cramps, nausea, a bloated stomach, watery, foul-smelling diarrhea and frequent gas. Giardiasis can appear several weeks after you have been exposed to the parasite. The symptoms may disappear for a few days and then return; this can go on for several weeks.

Seek medical advice if you think you have giardiasis, but where this is not possible, tinidazole or metronidazole are the recommended drugs. Treatment is a 2g single dose of tinidazole or 250mg of metronidazole three times daily for five to 10 days.

West Nile Virus

Little is known about this virus, but it's believed to be carried by mosquitoes that have fed on the blood of an infected bird. Many people who become infected with the virus have no symptoms and don't get sick; others develop flu-like symptoms within two to 15 days, including headache, fever and body aches and occasionally mild rashes and swollen lymph glands.

People with weaker immune systems, such as the elderly, are at greater risk of developing serious neurological effects; symptoms in these cases include the rapid onset of severe headache, high fever, stiff neck, vomiting, drowsiness, confusion, loss of consciousness, muscle weakness and paralysis. Severe cases can be fatal, and immediate medical attention should be sought. There is no vaccine for the virus and no specific treatment. Watch for any warnings

that the virus has been detected in the area, and try to avoid mosquito bites.

ENVIRONMENTAL HAZARDS
Altitude

Altitude sickness can strike anyone heading up into the mountains, whether it's your first visit or your 100th. Thinner air means less oxygen is reaching your muscles and brain, requiring the heart and lungs to work harder. Many trailheads begin at high elevations (particularly along the Icefields Parkway), meaning that you don't have to go very far before feeling the effects.

Symptoms of Acute Mountain Sickness (AMS) usually develop during the first 24 hours at altitude but may be delayed up to three weeks. Mild symptoms include headache, lethargy, dizziness, difficulty sleeping and loss of appetite. AMS may become more severe without warning and can be fatal. Severe symptoms include breathlessness, a dry, irritative cough (which may progress to the production of pink, frothy sputum), severe headache, lack of coordination and balance, confusion, irrational behavior, vomiting, drowsiness and unconsciousness. There is no hard-and-fast rule as to what is too high – AMS has been fatal at 3000m – although 3500m to 4500m is the usual range.

Treat mild symptoms by resting at the same altitude until recovery, usually a day or two. Paracetamol or aspirin can be taken for headaches. If symptoms persist or become worse, however, *immediate descent is necessary;* even 500m can help. Drug treatments should never be used to avoid descent or to enable further ascent.

The drugs acetazolamide and dexamethasone are recommended by some doctors for the prevention of AMS; however, their use is controversial. They can reduce the symptoms, but they may also mask warning signs; severe and fatal AMS has occurred in people taking these drugs. In general we do not recommend them for travelers.

To prevent acute mountain sickness:

- Ascend slowly – have frequent rest days, spending two to three nights at each rise of 1000m. If you reach a high altitude by trekking, acclimatization takes place gradually and you are less likely to be affected than if you fly directly to high altitude.
- It is always wise to sleep at a lower altitude than the greatest height reached during the

day if possible. Also, once above 3000m, care should be taken not to increase the sleeping altitude by more than 300m per day.

- Drink extra fluids. The mountain air is dry and cold and moisture is lost as you breathe; evaporation of sweat may occur unnoticed and result in dehydration.
- Eat light, high-carbohydrate meals for more energy.
- Avoid alcohol as it may increase the risk of dehydration.
- Avoid sedatives.

Bites & Stings
MOSQUITOES
Mosquitoes can be rampant in all parks, particularly on summer evenings. In Banff and Jasper, you'll notice them around lakes and on wooded hikes, although many areas along the Icefields Parkway are mosquito-free due to the high elevation. In Glacier and Waterton Lakes, mosquitoes tend to be more annoying on the west side of the park than in the windier east. Use repellent, wear light-colored clothing and cover yourself in the evening.

TICKS
Always check all over your body if you've been walking through a potentially tick-infested area as ticks can cause skin infections and serious diseases. Ticks are most active from spring to autumn, especially where there are plenty of sheep or deer. They usually lurk in overhanging vegetation, so avoid pushing through tall bushes.

If a tick is found attached to the skin, press down around its head with tweezers, grab the head and gently pull upward. Avoid pulling the rear of the body as this may squeeze the tick's gut contents through its mouth into your skin, increasing the risk of infection and disease. Smearing chemicals on the tick will not make it let go and is not recommended.

Cold
HYPOTHERMIA
This occurs when the body loses heat faster than it can produce it and the core temperature of the body falls.

It is frighteningly easy to progress from very cold to dangerously cold due to a combination of wind, wet clothing, fatigue and hunger, even if the air temperature is above freezing. If the weather deteriorates, put on extra layers of warm clothing: a wind and/or waterproof jacket, plus wool or fleece hat and gloves are all essential. Have something energy-giving to eat and ensure that everyone in your group is fit, feeling well and alert.

Symptoms of hypothermia are exhaustion, numb skin (particularly toes and fingers), shivering, slurred speech, irrational or violent behavior, lethargy, stumbling, dizzy spells, muscle cramps and violent bursts of energy. Irrationality may take the form of sufferers claiming they are warm and trying to take off their clothes.

To treat mild hypothermia, first get the person out of the wind and/or rain, remove their clothing if it's wet and replace it with dry, warm clothing. Give them hot liquids – not alcohol – and some high-energy, easily digestible food. Do not rub victims: instead, allow them to slowly warm themselves. This should be enough to treat the early stages of hypothermia. The early recognition and treatment of mild hypothermia is the only way to prevent severe hypothermia, which is a critical condition.

FROSTBITE
This refers to the freezing of extremities, including fingers, toes and nose. Signs and symptoms of frostbite include a whitish or waxy cast to the skin, or even crystals on the surface, plus itching, numbness and pain. Warm the affected areas by immersion in warm (not hot) water, or with blankets or clothes, only until the skin becomes flushed. Frostbitten parts should not be rubbed. Pain and swelling are inevitable. Blisters should not be broken. Get medical attention right away.

Heat
DEHYDRATION & HEAT EXHAUSTION
Dehydration is a potentially dangerous and generally preventable condition caused by excessive fluid loss. Sweating combined with inadequate fluid intake are one of the common causes in trekkers, but other causes are diarrhea, vomiting and high fever.

The first symptoms are weakness, thirst and passing small amounts of very concentrated urine. This may lead to drowsiness, dizziness or fainting on standing up, and finally, coma.

It's easy to forget how much fluid you are losing via perspiration while you are trekking, particularly if a strong breeze is drying your skin quickly. You should always maintain a good fluid intake – a minimum of 3L a day is recommended.

Dehydration and salt deficiency can cause heat exhaustion. Salt deficiency is characterized by fatigue, lethargy, headaches, giddiness and muscle cramps. Salt tablets are overkill; just adding extra salt to your food is probably sufficient.

HEATSTROKE

This is a serious, occasionally fatal, condition that occurs if the body's heat-regulating mechanism breaks down and the body temperature rises to dangerous levels. Long, continuous periods of exposure to high temperatures and insufficient fluids can leave you vulnerable to heatstroke.

The symptoms are feeling unwell, not sweating very much (or at all) and a high body temperature of around 39°C to 41°C (102°F to 106°F). Where sweating has ceased, the skin becomes flushed and red. Severe, throbbing headaches and lack of co-ordination will also occur, and the sufferer may be confused or aggressive. Eventually the victim will become delirious or convulse. Hospitalization is essential but, in the interim, get victims out of the sun, remove their clothing, cover them with a wet sheet or towel, and then fan continually. Give fluids if they are conscious.

Snow Blindness

This is a temporary painful condition resulting from sunburn of the surface of the eye (cornea). It usually occurs when someone walks on snow or in bright sunshine without sunglasses. Treatment is to relieve the pain – cold cloths on closed eyelids may help. Antibiotic and anesthetic eye drops are not necessary. The condition usually resolves itself within a few days and there are no long-term consequences.

Sun

Protection against the sun should always be taken seriously. Particularly in the rarified air and deceptive coolness of the mountains, sunburn occurs rapidly. Slap on the sun-screen and a barrier cream for your nose and lips, wear a broad-brimmed hat and protect your eyes with good-quality sunglasses with UV lenses, particularly when walking near water, sand or snow. If, despite these precautions, you get yourself burnt, calamine lotion, aloe vera or other commercial sunburn-relief preparations will soothe.

SAFE HIKING

AVALANCHES

Avalanches are a threat during and following storms, in high winds and during temperature changes, particularly when it warms in spring. Educate yourself about the dangers of avalanches before setting out into the backcountry. Signs of avalanche activity include felled trees and slides. Bears love avalanche shoots because of the fresh-frozen food they produce (casualties such as goats and sheep) – another good reason to steer clear. For up-to-date information on avalanche hazards, contact ☎ 403-762-1460 in Banff, Kootenay and Yoho, ☎ 780-852-6176 in Jasper and ☎ 250-837-6867 at Roger's Pass. For other areas, contact the **Canadian Avalanche Association** (☎ 800-667-1105) or local park information centers.

Before adventuring in Waterton, check with the **park warden** (☎ 403-859-5140) for avalanche updates, as winter trails are not maintained. In Glacier, call ☎ 406-257-8402 or ☎ 800-526-5329 for information. Local radio stations broadcast reports on area avalanche conditions studied by the Northwest Montana Avalanche Warning System.

If you are caught in an avalanche, your chance of survival depends on your ability to keep yourself above the flowing snow and your companions' ability to rescue you. The probability of survival decreases rapidly after half an hour, so the party must be self-equipped, with each member carrying an avalanche beacon, a sectional probe and a collapsible shovel.

CROSSING STREAMS

Sudden downpours are common in the mountains and can speedily turn a gentle stream into a raging torrent. If you're in any doubt about the safety of a crossing, look for a safer passage upstream or wait. If the rain is short-lived, it should subside quickly.

BEAR ISSUES

Although people have an inordinate fear of being hurt by bears, the Canadian Rockies are a far more dangerous place for the bears themselves. In Banff National Park alone, 90% of known grizzly bear deaths have occurred within 400m (0.25 miles) of roads and buildings, with most bears either being killed by cars or by wardens when bears and people got mixed up.

Bears are intelligent opportunists that quickly learn that humans come with food and tasty garbage. Unfortunately, once this association is learned, a bear nearly always has to be shot. Remember: 'A fed bear is a dead bear,' so never feed a bear, never improperly store food or garbage, and always clean up after yourself.

Bears are also dangerous creatures that can sprint the length of a football field in six seconds. Although such encounters are rare, bears will readily attack if their cubs are around, if they're defending food or if they feel surprised and threatened. Your best defenses against surprising a bear are to remain alert, avoid hiking at night (when bears feed) and be careful when traveling upwind near streams or where visibility is obscured.

If you do encounter a bear, there are several defensive strategies to employ, but no guarantees. If the bear doesn't see you, move a safe distance downwind and make noise to alert it to your presence. If the bear sees you, slowly back out of its path, avoid eye contact, speak softly and wave your hands above your head slowly. Never turn your back to the bear and never kneel down.

Sows with cubs are particularly dangerous, and you should make every effort to avoid coming between a sow and her cubs. A sow may clack her jaws, lower her head and shake it as a warning before she charges.

If a bear does charge, do not run and do not scream (which may frighten the bear and make it more aggressive), because the bear may only be charging as a bluff. Drop to the ground, crouch face down in a ball and play dead, covering the back of your neck with your hands and your chest and stomach with your knees. Do not resist the bear's inquisitive pawing – it may get bored and go away. Climbing a tree is one option, but only if you have time to climb at least 4.5m (15ft).

If a bear attacks you in your tent at night, you're likely dealing with a predatory bear that perceives you as a food source. In this extremely rare scenario, you should fight back aggressively with anything you can find; don't play dead.

While it has not been proven that bears show an affinity for menstruating women, more than one woman has been attacked by a bear during her period. If you have your period while hiking in bear country, be sure to carry plenty of tampons (pads are not recommended) and sealable plastic bags in which to dispose of them. If you accidentally bleed on clothing or gear, wash it out immediately. Women who have a heavy menstrual flow may want to schedule their trip for before or after their period.

If you decide it's essential to cross (late in the day, for example), look for a wide, relatively shallow stretch of the stream rather than a bend. Take off your trousers and socks, but keep your boots on to prevent injury. Put dry, warm clothes and a towel in a plastic bag near the top of your pack. Before stepping out from the bank, unclip your chest strap and belt buckle. This makes it easier to slip out of your backpack and swim to safety if you lose your balance and are swept downstream. Use a walking pole, grasped in both hands, on the upstream side as a third leg, or go arm in arm with a companion, clasping at the wrist, and cross side-on to the flow, taking short steps.

LIGHTNING

If a storm brews, avoid exposed areas. Lightning has a penchant for crests, lone trees, small depressions, gullies, caves and cabin entrances, as well as wet ground. If you are caught out in the open, try to curl up as tightly as possible with your feet together and keep a layer of insulation between you and the ground. Place metal objects such as metal-frame backpacks and walking poles away from you.

RESCUE & EVACUATION

If someone in your group is injured or falls ill and can't move, leave somebody with them while another one or more goes for

---

WALK SAFETY – BASIC RULES

▪ Allow plenty of time to accomplish a walk before dark, particularly when daylight hours are shorter.

▪ Study the route carefully before setting out, noting the possible escape routes and the point of no return (where it's quicker to continue than to turn back). Monitor your progress during the day against the time estimated for the walk, and keep an eye on the weather.

▪ It's wise not to walk alone. Always leave details of your intended route, number of people in your group and expected return time with someone responsible before you set off; let that person know when you return.

▪ Before setting off, make sure you have a relevant map, compass and whistle, and that you know the weather forecast for the area for the next 24 hours.

---

help. They should take clear written details of the location and condition of the victim, and of helicopter landing conditions. If there are only two of you, leave the injured person with as much warm clothing, food and water as it's sensible to spare, plus the whistle and torch. Mark the position with something conspicuous – an orange bivvy bag, or perhaps a large stone cross on the ground. Remember, the rescue effort might be slow, perhaps taking days to remove the injured person.

Travelers should also note that rescue operations are expensive. Try to avoid risky situations that could land you in trouble in the first place.

SAFE BIKING

Cycling is perennially popular in the Rocky Mountain national parks, be it straightforward road biking or more technically challenging single-track. One of the most common problems riders will encounter is unobservant motorists busy gawping at the (admittedly stunning) scenery, when they really ought to be concentrating on the obstacles up ahead. This issue is particularly prevalent in areas frequented by wildlife, such as the Bow Valley Parkway in Banff and the Maligne Lake Rd in Jasper. While most of Banff and Jasper's roads are wide and spacious, the arterial Going-to-the-Sun Rd in Glacier, built in the early days of the motor car, is notoriously precipitous and narrow, with no shoulders for cyclists. Jammed with dawdling people-carriers and oversized SUVs, the highway is a cycling obstacle course and, as a result, bikers are prevented from using it between 11am and 4pm (June to September), largely for their own safety.

Wildlife is another problem, particularly for off-roaders who run the risk of surprising large animals such as moose or bears when progressing rapidly along twisting forested trails. To avoid potentially dangerous encounters with foraging megafauna, bikers are encouraged to take heed of posted trail warnings and make plenty of noise on concealed corners and rises (remember, a bear can easily outsprint a cyclist).

Helmets are mandatory in all North American national parks. Off-roaders may also want to invest in elbow and knee pads. Many of Banff and Jasper's off-road trails are riddled with roots, stones and seasonal mud, and plenty of aspiring bike fiends have been tossed unceremoniously into the dirt.

Clothing & Equipment

Just as you can judge a man by his shoes, you can usually judge a hiker by his or her boots. But successful hiking is about more than just footwear. Take the time to get kitted out correctly and you're near guaranteed to have a safer, surer and more comfortable trip.

Visitors to the Rocky Mountains should prepare themselves for fickle weather, whatever the season. Jasper can be chilly in July while in Glacier, in 1992, 30cm (1ft) of snow fell in August, flushing hundreds of hikers out of the backcountry. On top of all the equipment listed here, you may want to consider carrying pepper spray to use as a last resort against aggressive wild animals, especially bears.

CLOTHING
Layering

A secret of comfortable walking is to wear several layers of light clothing, which you can easily take off or put on as you warm up or cool down. Most walkers use three main layers: a base layer next to the skin; an insulating layer; and an outer, shell layer for protection from wind, rain and snow.

For the upper body, the base layer is typically a shirt of synthetic material that wicks moisture away from the body and reduces chilling. The insulating layer retains heat next to your body, and is usually a (windproof) fleece jacket or sweater. The outer shell consists of a waterproof jacket that also protects against cold wind.

For the lower body, the layers generally consist of either shorts or loose-fitting trousers, thermal underwear ('long johns') and waterproof overtrousers.

Waterproof Shells

Jackets should be made of a breathable, waterproof fabric, with a hood that is roomy enough to cover headwear but still allow peripheral vision. Other handy accessories include a capacious map pocket and a heavy-gauge zip protected by a storm flap.

Overtrousers are best with slits for pocket access and long leg zips so that you can pull them on and off over your boots.

Footwear, Socks & Gaiters

Running shoes are OK for walks that are graded easy or moderate in this book. However, you'll probably appreciate, if not need, the support and protection provided by boots for the more demanding walks. Nonslip soles (such as Vibram) provide the best grip.

CLOTHING & EQUIPMENT

ROUTE FINDING

While accurate, our maps are not perfect. Inaccuracies in altitudes are commonly caused by air-temperature anomalies. Natural features such as river confluences and mountain peaks are in their true position, but sometimes the location of villages and trails is not always so. This may be because a village is spread over a hillside, or the size of the map does not allow for detail of the trail's twists and turns. However, by using several basic route-finding techniques, you will have few problems following our descriptions:

1. Be aware of whether the trail should be climbing or descending.
2. Check the north-point arrow on the map and determine the general direction of the trail.
3. Time your progress over a known distance and calculate the speed at which you travel in the given terrain. From then on, you can determine with reasonable accuracy how far you have traveled.
4. Watch the path – look for boot prints and other signs of previous passage.

NAVIGATION EQUIPMENT

Maps & Compass

You should always carry a good map of the area in which you are walking (see p27), and know how to read it. Before setting off on your walk, ensure that you are aware of the contour interval, the map symbols, the magnetic declination (difference between true and grid north), plus the main ridge and river systems in the area and the general direction in which you are heading. On the trail, try to identify major landforms such as mountain ranges and valleys, and locate them on your map to familiarise yourself with the geography.

Buy a compass and learn how to use it. The attraction of magnetic north varies in different parts of the world, so compasses need to be balanced accordingly. Compass manufacturers have divided the world into five zones. Make sure your compass is balanced for your destination zone. There are also 'universal' compasses on the market that can be used anywhere in the world.

1	Base plate
2	Direction of travel arrow
3	Dash
4	Bezel
5	Meridian lines
6	Needle
7	Red end
8	N (north point)

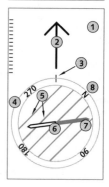

How to Use a Compass

This is a very basic introduction to using a compass and will only be of assistance if you are proficient in map reading. For simplicity, it doesn't take magnetic variation into account. Before using a compass we recommend you obtain further instruction.

Reading a Compass

Hold the compass flat in the palm of your hand. Rotate the bezel (4) so the red end (7) of the needle (6) points to the N (north point; 8) on the bezel. The bearing is read from the dash (3) under the bezel.

Orienting the Map

To orient the map so that it aligns with the ground, place the compass flat on the map. Rotate the map until the needle is parallel with the map's north–south grid lines and the red end is pointing to north on the map.
You can now identify features around you by aligning them with labelled features on the map.

Buy boots in warm conditions or go for a walk before trying them on, so that your feet can expand slightly, as they would on a hike. Most walkers carry a pair of sandals to wear at night or at rest stops. Sandals are also useful when fording waterways.

Gaiters help to keep your feet dry in wet weather and on boggy ground; they can also deflect small stones or sand and maintain leg warmth. The best are made of strong fabric, with a robust zip protected by a flap, and secure easily around the foot.

Walking socks should be free of ridged seams in the toes and heels.

EQUIPMENT
Backpack & Daypacks

For day walks, a day pack (30L to 40L) will usually suffice, but for multi-day walks you will need a backpack of between 45L and 90L capacity. Even if the manufacturer claims your pack is waterproof, use heavy-duty liners.

Tent

A three-season tent will fulfil most walkers' requirements. The floor and the outer shell, or fly, should have taped or sealed seams and covered zips to stop leaks. The weight can be as low as 1kg for a stripped-down, low-profile tent, and up to 3kg for a roomy, luxury, four-season model. Dome- and tunnel-shaped tents handle windy conditions better than flat-sided tents.

Sleeping Bag & Mat

Down fillings are warmer than synthetic for the same weight and bulk but, unlike synthetic fillings, do not retain warmth when wet. Mummy-shaped bags are best

Taking a Bearing from the Map

Draw a line on the map between your starting point and your destination. Place the edge of the compass on this line with the direction of travel arrow (2) pointing toward your destination. Rotate the bezel until the meridian lines (5) are parallel with the north–south grid lines on the map and the N points to north on the map. Read the bearing from the dash.

Following a Bearing

Rotate the bezel so that the intended bearing is in line with the dash. Place the compass flat in the palm of your hand and rotate the base plate (1) until the red end points to N on the bezel. The direction of travel arrow will now point in the direction you need to walk.

Determining Your Bearing

Rotate the bezel so the red end points to the N. Place the compass flat in the palm of your hand and rotate the base plate until the direction of travel arrow points in the direction in which you have been walking. Read your bearing from the dash.

Global Positioning System

Originally developed by the US Department of Defense, the Global Positioning System (GPS) is a network of more than 20 earth-orbiting satellites that continually beam encoded signals back to earth. Small, computer-driven devices (GPS receivers) can decode these signals to give users an extremely accurate reading of their location – to within 30m, anywhere on the planet, at any time of day, in almost any weather. The cheapest hand-held GPS receivers now cost less than US$100 (although these may not have a built-in averaging system that minimises signal errors). Other important factors to consider when buying a GPS receiver are its weight and battery life.

Remember that a GPS receiver is of little use unless used with an accurate topographical map. The receiver simply gives your position, which you must then locate on the local map. GPS receivers will only work properly in the open. The signals from a crucial satellite may be blocked (or bounce off rock or water) directly below high cliffs, near large bodies of water or in dense tree cover and give inaccurate readings. GPS receivers are more vulnerable to breakdowns (including dead batteries) than the humble magnetic compass – a low-tech device that has served navigators faithfully for centuries – so don't rely on them entirely.

for weight and warmth. The given figure (-5ºC, for instance) is the coldest temperature at which a person should feel comfortable in the bag (although the ratings are notoriously unreliable).

An inner sheet helps keep your sleeping bag clean, as well as adding an insulating layer; silk 'inners' are lightest but they also come in cotton or synthetic fabric.

Self-inflating sleeping mats work like a thin air cushion between you and the ground; they also insulate from the cold. Foam mats are a low-cost, but less comfortable, alternative.

Stoves & Fuel

The easiest type of fuel to use is butane gas in disposable containers; true, it doesn't win many environmental points but it's much easier to come by than liquid fuels.

The most widely used brands are Coleman and Camping Gaz, available from outdoor gear shops and, in some remote areas, from small supermarkets.

Liquid fuel includes Coleman fuel, methylated spirits and paraffin. Again, outdoor gear shops, possibly hardware stores or even small supermarkets are the best places to look for it. You may be able to obtain small quantities of unleaded petrol from service stations.

Airlines prohibit the carriage of any flammable materials and may well reject empty liquid-fuel bottles or even the stoves themselves.

BUYING & RENTING LOCALLY

Specializing in the great outdoors, the national park towns offer some stellar options for buying and renting gear. Check out the

EQUIPMENT CHECKLIST

This list is a general guide to the things you might take on a walk. Your list will vary depending on the kind of walking you want to do, whether you're camping or planning to stay in hostels or B&Bs, and on the terrain, weather conditions and time of year.

Clothing

- ☐ boots and spare laces
- ☐ gaiters
- ☐ hat (warm), scarf and gloves
- ☐ overtrousers (waterproof)
- ☐ rain jacket
- ☐ runners (training shoes) or sandals
- ☐ shorts and trousers
- ☐ socks and underwear
- ☐ sunhat
- ☐ sweater or fleece jacket
- ☐ thermal underwear
- ☐ T-shirt and long-sleeved shirt with collar

Equipment

- ☐ backpack with waterproof liner
- ☐ first-aid kit*
- ☐ food and snacks (high energy) and one day's emergency supplies
- ☐ insect repellent
- ☐ map, compass and guidebook
- ☐ map case or clip-seal plastic bags
- ☐ plastic bags (for carrying rubbish)
- ☐ pocket knife
- ☐ sunglasses
- ☐ sunscreen and lip balm
- ☐ survival bag or blanket
- ☐ toilet paper and trowel
- ☐ flashlight (torch) or headlamp, spare batteries and bulb (globe)
- ☐ water container
- ☐ whistle

Overnight Walks

- ☐ cooking, eating and drinking utensils
- ☐ dishwashing items
- ☐ matches and lighter
- ☐ sewing/repair kit
- ☐ sleeping bag and bag liner/inner sheet
- ☐ sleeping mat
- ☐ spare cord
- ☐ stove and fuel
- ☐ tent, pegs, poles and guy ropes
- ☐ toiletries
- ☐ towel
- ☐ water purification tablets, iodine or filter

Optional Items

- ☐ backpack cover (waterproof, slip-on)
- ☐ binoculars
- ☐ camera, film and batteries
- ☐ candle
- ☐ emergency distress beacon
- ☐ GPS receiver
- ☐ groundsheet
- ☐ cell (mobile) phone
- ☐ mosquito net
- ☐ notebook and pen
- ☐ swimming costume
- ☐ walking poles
- ☐ watch

* see the Medical Checklist (p264)

individual park chapters for stores in Banff (p93), Jasper (p166), Waterton (p229) and Glacier (p202). More specialized gear such as bikes (rental per day C$30), snowshoes (C$15), hiking poles (C$5) and climbing harnesses (C$5) can usually be rented.

Glossary

ACC – Alpine Club of Canada
ACMG – Association of Canadian Mountain Guides

backcountry – anywhere away from roads or other major infrastructure
bear spray – pepper-based deterrent used to ward off bears during attacks
bivouac (bivvy) – rudimentary shelter under a rock ledge; tent-like bag for one person
bruin – Canadian word for bear
buffaloberry – small red berry that ripens in July and August and is a favorite delicacy for grizzly and black bears

cairn – pile or stack of rocks used to indicate the route or junction of a trail
capilene – synthetic material that wicks moisture away from the skin, used in long underwear
cirque – rounded, high ridge or bowl formed by past glacial action
Continental Divide – the ridge of mountains that separates the eastern (Atlantic) and western (Pacific) watersheds of North America; sometimes called the Great Divide
cornice – an overhanging edge of snow along the *crest* of a mountain
CPR – Canadian Pacific Railway
creek – small stream, pronounced 'crick' in the Rocky Mountains
crest – a minor ridge or rise
crevasse – dangerous, often concealed, canyon common on glaciers and ice fields

doubletrack – a mountain-biking trail that's wide enough for bikers to pass each other
downhill – form of mountain biking in which riders compete down prescribed courses against the clock
drumlins – hills of glacial rubble (or 'till') with a streamlined or teardrop profile, shaped by the effect of advancing glacial ice
dubbin – wax product used to soften and condition leather

fenland – area of natural wetland and marsh, often frequented by wildlife
foot – base of a mountain; lower end of a valley or lake
ford – to cross a river by wading
fork – a branch or tributary of a stream or river
freeride – type of mountain biking in which cyclists travel down obstacle courses, crossing jumps and technical

sections while performing tricks; similar to *downhill* but without the time-trial element
frontcountry – the easily accessible areas of a park, usually near main roads and services

gondola – mechanical cable car designed to carry people up mountainsides
gorge – large, steep-sided valley, usually surrounded by rocks or high cliffs
GPS – global positioning system; an electronic, satellite-based network that allows for the calculation of position and elevation using a hand-held receiver/decoder

HI – Hostelling International
hoodoo – fantastically shaped rock formation produced by weathering
hookup – facility at a campground for giving an RV water and/or electricity

krummholz – wind-twisted, stunted trees found near treeline

lean-to – simple shelter, usually without walls, windows or doors, with a steeply slanting roof that touches the ground on one side
limestone – sedimentary rock composed mainly of calcium carbonate
loonie – $1 coin in Canada

MPHIA – Mountain Parks Heritage Interpretation Association
moraine – ridge, mound or irregular mass (mostly boulders, gravel, sand and clay) deposited at the face or along the flanks of a glacier
MTB – abbreviation for mountain bike

NPS – National Park Service

out-and-back – of a hike, a route that backtracks to its starting point from its destination
outfitter – business supplying guides and equipment for fishing, canoeing, hiking, rafting or horseback trips
overlook – a lookout (above a scenic feature)

prescribed burn – a forest fire deliberately set by park rangers to help regenerate overgrown or diseased areas of woodland

ridgeline – *crest* of a ridge, often used for travel through alpine areas

saddle – low place in a ridge

sandstone – sedimentary rock composed of sand grains

scramble – to climb a steep slope with the help of your hands

scree – weathered rock fragments found at the foot of a cliff or on a hillside, often difficult to walk across; also called talus

scrub – thick, low vegetation that's difficult to walk through

serac – column or slab of ice formed by conjoining crevasses

singletrack – a mountain-biking trail that's only wide enough for one bike

switchback – route that follows a zigzag course up or down a steep grade

tarn – a small mountain lake

timberline – upper limit of forest; also tree line

toonie – $2 coin in Canada (sometimes known as twonie)

watershed – drainage basin from which water flows towards a specific body of water

wicking – the act of removing moisture away from the skin; usually describes clothing

wilderness – an (officially designated) primitive area

wildfire – an out-of-control forest fire

Behind the Scenes

THIS BOOK

This 2nd edition of *Banff, Jasper & Glacier National Parks* was researched and written by Oliver Berry and Brendan Sainsbury. The 1st edition was written by Korina Miller, Susan Derby and David Lukas. This guidebook was commissioned in Lonely Planet's Oakland office, and produced by the following:

Commissioning Editor Heather Dickson
Coordinating Editors Victoria Harrison, Andrew Bain
Coordinating Cartographers Ross Butler, Corey Hutchison
Coordinating Layout Designer Yvonne Bischofberger
Senior Editor Helen Christinis
Managing Cartographer Alison Lyall
Managing Layout Designer Celia Wood
Assisting Editor Anne Mulvaney
Assisting Cartographer Fatima Basic
Assisting Layout Designer David Kemp
Cover Designer Amy Stephens
Project Managers Glenn van der Knijff, Bronwyn Hicks

Thanks to David Connolly, Melanie Dankel, Ryan Evans, Jennifer Garrett, Erin Corrigan, Suki Gear, Michelle Glynn, Brice Gosnell, James Hardy, Laura Jane, Lisa Knights, Adriana Mammarella, Adam McCrow, Jessica Rose, Helen Rowley, Wibowo Rusli, Cara Smith, Louisa Syme

THANKS
OLIVER BERRY

As always, there's a mountain of people to say a huge thank you to, and without whom this book wouldn't have been possible. Thanks firstly to all the Canadian friends I made along the way, and the many park rangers, tourist offices, residents and business people who gave up their time to spare me some. Special thanks to Jill Moellering at Warner Stables and Tom Boyd at the Plain of Six Glaciers Teahouse for answering all my odd questions, and to Christoph and Christina Doehner who gave me a bolt-hole in Canada. Back at the Planet, massive thanks to our man in Jasper and Glacier, Brendan Sainsbury, for his hard work and ever-helpful suggestions, and to Heather Dickson for keeping us on course and giving us the chance to work on the book. In the UK, thanks to Susie Berry, who kept me refueled throughout and was always ready to lend an ear; to Mark Jenkin, my fellow shipmate on the Ark; to Adam Laity for fishing trips and grilled mackerel; to TSP for making me smile; to the old man Hobo who's always there; and to everyone else I haven't mentioned by name but deserve my heartfelt thanks.

BRENDAN SAINSBURY

A hearty thanks to all the untold park rangers, bus drivers, tourist-info reps, cycle-shop owners and

---

THE LONELY PLANET STORY

Fresh from an epic journey across Europe, Asia and Australia in 1972, Tony and Maureen Wheeler sat at their kitchen table stapling together notes. The first Lonely Planet guidebook, *Across Asia on the Cheap,* was born.

Travelers snapped up the guides. Inspired by their success, the Wheelers began publishing books to Southeast Asia, India and beyond. Demand was prodigious, and the Wheelers expanded the business rapidly to keep up. Over the years, Lonely Planet extended its coverage to every country and into the virtual world via lonelyplanet.com and the Thorn Tree message board.

As Lonely Planet became a globally loved brand, Tony and Maureen received several offers for the company. But it wasn't until 2007 that they found a partner whom they trusted to remain true to the company's principles of traveling widely, treading lightly and giving sustainably. In October of that year, BBC Worldwide acquired a 75% share in the company, pledging to uphold Lonely Planet's commitment to independent travel, trustworthy advice and editorial independence.

Today, Lonely Planet has offices in Melbourne, London and Oakland, with over 500 staff members and 300 authors. Tony and Maureen are still actively involved with Lonely Planet. They're traveling more often than ever, and they're devoting their spare time to charitable projects. And the company is still driven by the philosophy of *Across Asia on the Cheap*: 'All you've got to do is decide to go and the hardest part is over. So go!'

innocent bystanders who helped me during my research, particularly to Heather Dickson, my commissioning editor, and coordinating author Oliver Berry. Special thanks also to Manabu Saito and Ted Dolan for their thoughts and insights on life in Jasper, and to my wife, Elizabeth, and son, Kieran, for accompanying me for most of the research.

OUR READERS

Many thanks to the travelers who used the last edition and wrote to us with helpful hints, useful advice and interesting anecdotes:

Mike Bateman, Alison Course, Hugh Dowd, Lynne Gonzales, P Grainger, Natalie Horsfield, E van Hunter, Kum Mak, Mary Otto, Marianne Robinson, Liz Schumann, Barbara Spender, Veerle Stoffelen, Darla Tishman, Hilary Walker, Neil Wedin, Rich Wrigley

ACKNOWLEDGMENTS

Many thanks to the following for the use of their content:

Regional-based map data ©Department of Natural Resources Canada. All rights reserved.

Internal photographs by Danita Delimont/Alamy p4 (#2); Eye Ubiquitous/Alamy/Photolibrary p5 (#4); Woodfall Wild Images/Alamy p5 (#5); Jasper Tramway p9 (#4); Matt Zieminski/Flickr p9 (#6); Tom Uhlman/Alamy p10 (#3); Robert McGouey/Alamy/Photolibrary p11 (#1). All other photographs by Lonely Planet Images: Gareth McCormack (p3); Adina Tovy Amsel p4 (#1); Andrew Bain p6 (#2), p8 (#1); Witold Skrypczak p6 (#6), p7 (#5), p12 (#4); Philip & Karen Smith p7 (#1), p15 (#5), p16; Frank Carter p8 (#3); Carol Polich p10 (#6); Mark Newman p11 (#4), p14; Christer Fredriksson p11 (#5); Lawrence Worcester p12 (#3), p13 (#2); David Tomlinson p13 (#6); Rick Rudnicki p15 (#2).

All images are the copyright of the photographers unless otherwise indicated. Many of the images in this guide are available for licensing from Lonely Planet Images: www.lonelyplanetimages.com.

SEND US YOUR FEEDBACK

We love to hear from travelers – your comments keep us on our toes and help make our books better. Our well-traveled team reads every word on what you loved or loathed about this book. Although we cannot reply individually to postal submissions, we always guarantee that your feedback goes straight to the appropriate authors, in time for the next edition. Each person who sends us information is thanked in the next edition – and the most useful submissions are rewarded with a free book.

To send us your updates – and find out about Lonely Planet events, newsletters and travel news – visit our award-winning website: **www.lonelyplanet.com/feedback**.

Note: we may edit, reproduce and incorporate your comments in Lonely Planet products such as guidebooks, websites and digital products, so let us know if you don't want your comments reproduced or your name acknowledged. For a copy of our privacy policy visit www.lonelyplanet.com/privacy.

Index

See also separate subindex for Hikes (p293).

000 Map pages
000 Photograph pages

INDEX

000 Map pages
000 Photograph pages

HIKES

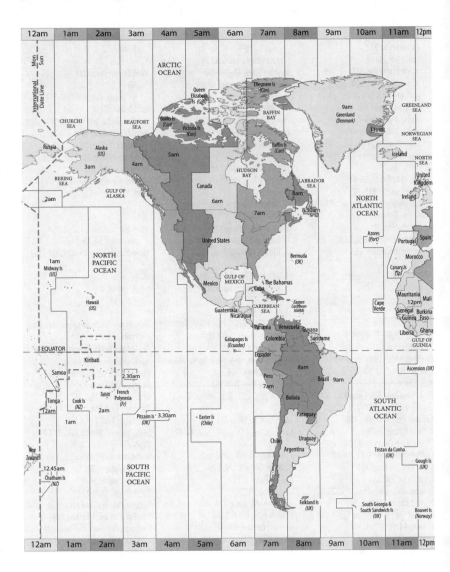